To Pauline and John Weber

our friends and neighbors

with best wishes

Mal Gross

NINE LIVES

ADVENTURES OF A
LUCKY PILOT

January 1955 to November 2008
6,850 Total Flying Hours

MALVERN J. GROSS

Foreword by Paul Poberezny, Founder,
Experimental Aircraft Association

ISLAND IN THE SKY PUBLISHING CO.
60 Meadow Lks, East Windsor
New Jersey 08520
www.NineLivesLuckyPilot.com

ABOUT THE PHOTOGRAPHS, MAPS ILLUSTRATIONS AND COVER
Except as indicated in the text, all of the photographs, maps and illustrations were taken or prepared by the author or his family. The December 24, 1986 editorial, *Voyagers*, in the Washington Post was reprinted with their permission. This aerial view of Mt. Baker on the cover was taken by the author from 12,000 feet while en route to his home on Orcas Island, WA, barely 50 miles away. The bottom of the right wing tip can be seen at the top of the picture.

Published by Island In The Sky Publishing Co.
60 Meadow Lakes, East Windsor, NJ 08520
www.NineLivesLuckyPilot.com

Publisher's Cataloging-in-Publication data

Gross, Malvern J.
    Nine lives : adventures of a lucky pilot / Malvern J. Gross ; foreword by Paul Poberezny.
    p. cm.
    ISBN 978-0-9760328-4-7 (Hardcover)
    ISBN 978-0-9760328-0-9 (pbk)

1. Gross, Malvern J. 2. Air pilots —United States —Biography. 3. Radio beacons—History. 4. Aeronautics—History. 5. Airplanes—Piloting—Anecdotes. 6. Air pilots—United States—Anecdotes. I. Poberezny, Paul H. (Paul Howard), 1921- 2. Title.

TL540 .G76 2010
629.13/092-dc22   2009909833

Jacket design by Lia Griffith, Portland, Oregon
Printed in the United States of America by Patterson Printing Co.

Table of Contents

Part IV—The Long Descent
1996 to 2008

Part V—Reflections
2009

Folio of color photographs, following page 394

Foreword
By Paul Poberezny, Founder, EAA

Nine Lives was not what I expected when Mal Gross asked me to review his manuscript. I can honestly say that I was not prepared for this book taking my total interest for almost two weeks.

The Most Educational
Aviation Story I've Read

I have read many aviation stories but they are usually based on a short period of time—a year, or a little more—and they are soon forgotten. *Nine Lives* is about a general aviation pilot and covers more than fifty years, with many and varied aeronautical experiences. His life as a pilot is the most documented and interesting account of any aviator I have read about. I was impressed with the detail given to each segment which made me feel that I was right with him, not only in the cockpit, but in that part of his life.

In many situations his experience was similar to my own, from his first interest in aviation, his first solo, the many friends made and challenges that were met.

His love affair with aviation started out like so many "young eagles" with his first flight in 1940, but with a difference. He waved goodbye to his parents and boarded a United DC-3 at Chicago Midway Airport for the 12-hour flight to Portland, Oregon where he would spend the summer with his grandparents. He was six years old, but he never forgot that flight.

Like most budding pilots he had to wait until after college graduation before learning to fly. He was then a ground officer in the Air Force, and stationed at Presque Isle AFB in northern Maine. There was a local flying club at a nearby grass strip airport, and he soloed in January, 1955, in an Aeronca Champ on skis. By the time he closed the hangar door for the last time he had accumulated almost seven thousand hours over 54 years, and was still as enthusiastic about flight as he was in 1940. I was amazed how he was able to document his adventures and love of flight in such overwhelming detail.

Luck Plays A Major Role

The author goes beyond just relating his adventures. He has woven into the book a lifetime of aviation experience, and lessons learned, many times the hard way. One recurring theme is the part that luck played in his flying. He defines luck as being a situation that would have ended in tragedy except that he happened to be in the right place at the right time. Ernie Gann first introduced this theme in his classic 1961 book, *Fate Is The Hunter*. That certainly resonated with me, and I suspect will do so with many other pilots. Too many pilots are not with us today because their luck ran out. The title of the book, *Nine Lives*, derives from this theme. You can judge for yourself as you read this book.

This theme leads directly into Mal's emphasis on the importance of managing risk, and learning from every flight what he could have done to have made the flight safer. One paragraph in particular jumped out at me:

No matter how many hours you have, or how few, your airplane can kill you on your very next flight. The laws of physics and gravity never take a vacation, and every flight is a contest between you and your airplane, with the airplane playing for keeps.

He describes in detail how he managed risk, and all who fly will benefit from his experience.

Adventures

This is a book describing in great detail his aviation adventures, from his early days of learning to fly to his love of cross-country flying, and high altitude flight. I found myself riveted to his well-written adventures.

For example, Mal describes in detail his first flight home just a few days after he got his private license. He had a total flying time of just 44 hours when he started out on the 550-mile flight from northern Maine to Rochester, New York. That route took him over uninhabited, wooded and mountainous terrain, navigating solely by using sectional charts. He made his first night landing on that flight, with the Rochester tower reporting wind gusts to 60 miles per hour. He was short on fuel with the engine sputtering when he entered the landing pattern at Rochester. Before his first year was over, he had made four additional flights to Rochester.

There is a detailed account of an official FAI altitude record (32,420 feet), and the risks he unknowingly was taking. I felt like I was in the cockpit with him flying IFR across Greenland en route to Reykjavik, Iceland, when one-too-many gremlins popped up. He wisely turned around and returned home. The author and his then 12-year-old son set a speed record from San Francisco to Washington, D.C. on New Years Day, 1970 (11 hours, 7 minutes). He shares with the reader the flight as it unfolded.

Instrument Flight Rating

By the end of his first year of flying Mal recognized that his life expectancy would likely be short if he continued scud-running. Few private pilots had an instrument rating in 1956. Mal, with the help of his Air Force friends, obtained his rating in August, 1956 in his Cessna 140 with only a low-frequency radio receiver for navigation, and a ten-channel transmitter. The only navigation system in northern Maine at that time were the low-frequency radio range stations. He has included a chapter on these range stations, describing how they worked, and the skills needed to use them. This provides insight into the early days of IFR navigation.

When to Stop Flying

I agonized with the author when he made the decision at age 69 to sell his Cessna T210 because he concluded he was not always "connecting the dots" and should no longer be flying IFR. All pilots are faced with this issue, and most pilots can relate to this. Perhaps his frank discussion of his decision may be helpful to others.

He continued flying for another six years, first his Mooney Mite, and later a Tecnam Bravo Light Sport Aircraft. In 2008 he closed the hangar door for the last time because he was not flying enough to stay current.

Educational Book

This book is far more than just a story of the adventures of a lucky pilot. Virtually every chapter provides insight into lessons this pilot learned, mostly from hard experience. Every pilot, or would-be pilot, can benefit from the frank analysis of his experiences. He also provides his views on a number of aviation issues in a chapter titled: Observations of an Old Timer, and he is not hesitant to offer his views. His theme of managing risk is apparent throughout the book.

Mal is a CPA by profession, and he has provided financial data of his cost over this fifty year period, by aircraft owned, with key figures indexed to provide data in 2008 dollars. Many readers should find his data helpful as they contemplate the purchase of an aircraft.

Who should read this book? I would say this book should be read by every pilot, including airline pilots. It will be of particular value to new student pilots, or one of the millions of non-pilots who would also like to fly. They can join Mal in the cockpit on some of his adventures, as I did in reading the book. Perhaps his enthusiasm for flight will rub off on the reader, and he or she will want to join the airmen's world.

Paul Poberezny
Founder
Experimental Aircraft Association

Preface

There are old pilots,
and there are bold pilots,
but there are no old, bold pilots.

That is what I was told on January 8, 1955, when I had my first familiarization flight in a ski-equipped Aeronca Champ on a cold winter day in Northern Maine. For most of my 54 years of private flying I believed that axiom. I no longer do.

I now believe there is a third category of pilots—pilots who have been lucky. I also believe that there are no old pilots who have not also been lucky pilots. This book is about the adventures of a very lucky pilot who is now an old pilot.

When I started writing this book I had intended to title it *The Flight Log*. Then as I started reviewing my nine log books, flight by flight, and reliving them, I was struck by the number of times it had been just plain dumb luck that I had survived a particular situation. Often I happened to be in the right place at the right time. 15 minutes earlier or later and I would not have made it.

I have defined "luck" as a situation where by hindsight I have concluded that I had more than an even chance of not surviving that event. I detail more than nine such incidents in these pages although in the final chapter I list the nine I feel were the ones where I was at the greatest risk. I leave it to you, the reader, to judge for yourself my conclusions on each.

I have deliberately used the word "luck." Some might prefer "guardian angel," or their "God," or "it just wasn't my time, yet." I am reminded of Ernest K. Gann's 1961 book, *Fate Is The Hunter,* which also had much the same theme. He used the word "fate," and in his single line dedication of the book to some 400 mostly airline pilots who had died, he stated: *"Their fortune was not so good as mine."*

I do not believe my experience has been unique. I have known many private pilots over the years who had more experience and skill than I had. Some survived, but some—whose luck ran out—didn't. Many of the lucky ones recognized that luck had been with them, and stopped flying. Others, like myself, flew on, and continued to be lucky.

I have also been lucky in another respect. I have been privileged to have been involved in the leadership of a number of aviation organizations: the National Aviation Club, the National Aeronautic Association, the Fédération Aéronautique Internationale and, most important, the Experimental Aircraft Association. Several of the chapters in the book relate to these nonflying experiences I had in connection with these organizations, and I hope the reader also finds them interesting.

Book Organization

This book is divided into five parts:

Part I—The Carefree Years (1955 and 1956)
Part II—The Struggling Years (1957–1971
Part III—The Mature Years (1972–1995)
Part IV—The Long Descent (1996– 2008)
Part V—Reflections (2009)

The first chapter following the start of each part provides an overview of my aviation experience during the years covered. The second and subsequent chapters in each part look in depth at some of my adventures. The final part, Reflections, covers a number of subjects in which I offer my own observations from the perspective of 54 years of flying. The final chapter sums up why I feel I was a very lucky pilot.

Statute Miles, Nautical Miles, and Flight Levels

My aviation friends will note that I have converted all distances and speeds into statute miles rather than nautical miles which today is the aviation and maritime unit of measurement. Statute miles are used in the United States for measuring distances. Throughout this book I have used statute miles to make it easier for the non-pilot to relate to, both distances and speeds. Also in 1975, the air speed instrument in Cessna aircraft (and probably other makes of airplane, too) was based on statute miles. To convert statute miles to nautical miles, divide by 1.1507; thus 100 statute miles would be 86.9 nautical miles.

The reader should also be aware that at or above 18,000 feet, clearances and reference to altitudes are expressed as "flight levels." For example 25,000 feet would normally be referred to as "flight level two–five–zero." To make it easier for the reader not used to this terminology I will use the altitude itself, and not the "flight level" terminology.

Acknowledgments

I am indebted to many friends who have read all or parts of this manuscript. Ellie Whitney has spent many hours editing the manuscript, particularly in helping simplify the sentence structure and offering observations on superfluous detail that did not add to the telling of the story. She also offered comments from the vantage point of someone interested in aviation, but not as a pilot. She felt this book would interest some of the millions of people who have always wanted to learn to fly, but never did. She suggested the Glossary of Aviation Terms.

My long-time pilot friend from British Columbia, Dave Rutherford, was especially helpful. A retired English teacher, he not only brought his own aviation experience to his review, but also ensured that the manuscript was grammatically correct. I don't think I failed English in grammar school, but I suspect there were times when Dave had his doubts. I am grateful to him for his efforts to ensure the manuscript justified a passing grade.

Don Dick in Rochester, New York, took his first flying lesson as a result of a 70th birthday gift from his family, and subsequently earned his private license. He stopped flying five years later as a result of a combination of age and cost, but has not lost his love of flying. He reviewed the manuscript throughout the writing process and brought a top-level overview to what he was reading. On a number of occasions he offered pointed comments, resulting in my going back to the drawing board on more than one occasion and totally rewriting a particular chapter. His candor was refreshing and greatly appreciated.

Linda Sinrod, my sister, also read the manuscript and was particularly effective in pointing out inconsistencies either in verbiage, or in factual data. The book was written a chapter at a time, and not in the sequence appearing in the book. I was not always consistent between chapters. Her eagle eyes, and memory of what I said in an earlier chapter, was extremely helpful. While not a pilot herself, her encouragement on this five-year project was very important.

My thanks also go to many others who read all or part of the manuscript. Among those are Jim Newland, Orcas Island, Washington, and Henry Cox of East Windsor, New Jersey.

Without Her Support..

One Saturday night in October of 1957, I gave Inge Stanneck a flight over New York City at midnight. We were on our first date, having attended a dance earlier in the evening. Afterwards, before taking her home, I mentioned that I had a small airplane, and asked if she would like to see it. She said, "yes."

A full moon reflected off the still waters of Long Island Sound that evening. It could not have been a more romantic setting. She loved that midnight flight and I knew then that I had found the person I wanted to share my life with.

We were married the following June. A few years later she got her own private pilot license. Over the ensuing years right up to today, she has been supportive of my love of aviation, and understanding of the disproportionate amount of our income that we have spent on this love. Without her total support my aviation activities would likely never have taken the path they did.

M. J.Gross
October, 2009

Glossary of Aeronautical Terms

Some readers may not be familiar with some of the aeronautical terms I use. This glossary does not pretend to include all aeronautical terms, only the ones used in this book.

Aero Club of America Aero Club of America, incorporated in 1905, and the predecessor of the National Aeronautic Association.

ADF Automatic Direction Finder. An aircraft navigation system which senses and indicates the direction to a nondirectional ground radio beacon. This system has been obsoleted by more modern navigation systems.

AGL Above ground level, as distinct from above sea level.

Altitude Encoder An electronic device that encodes the plane's barometric altitude and transmits this information when interrogated by ground radar or airborne collision avoidance equipment (see TCAS).

Approach Control Air traffic control for incoming aircraft as they approach their destination airport. Approach Control provides vectoring instructions to position the aircraft on the final approach to the runway. At that point the control tower provides the clearance to land.

ATC Air Traffic Control, the name of the FAA organization that controls IFR traffic, and VFR traffic in certain classes of airspace where such control is required.

ATIS Automatic Terminal Information Service, which provides pilots with recorded information of current aviation weather conditions, landing and takeoff information. Updated hourly or sooner if conditions change.

Avionics Refers to all of the communication, navigation, and electronic instrumentation including the autopilot in an aircraft.

AWOS An automatic weather collection and reporting system that continually broadcasts current airport conditions at a non towered airport which a pilot can monitor.

Borescope An optical device that can be inserted into an engine cylinder through the sparkplug opening to examine the interior condition of the cylinder walls without having to remove the cylinders from the engine.

BFR Biennial Flight Review. Required of all private pilots by an instructor every two years.

Broken Clouds   Clouds which cover between 6/10 and 9/10 of the sky

CAA   Civil Aeronautical Authority, the predecessor of the FAA.

CAVU   Ceiling and Visibility Unlimited. A term used by pilots to describe exceptionally good visual flying conditions.

Ceiling   The height of the lowest layer of clouds, when the sky is broken or overcast.

Cell   Usually refers to a thunderstorm cell in which there are violent up and downdrafts.

Class A Airspace   Airspace above 18,000 feet in which all aircraft must be on an IFR flight plan.

Class B Airspace   Generally the airspace from the surface to 10,000 feet surrounding the nation's busiest airports.

Class C Airspace   Generally the airspace from the surface to 4,000 feet above an airport that has a control tower and Approach Control.

Class D Airspace   Generally the airspace from the surface to 2,500 feet above an airport that has only a control tower and no radar control.

Dead Reckoning   A term used to refer to navigating without reference to electronic aids, usually by flying a compass course corrected for expected winds.

Dead-Stick-Landing   A landing after an engine failure.

Departure Control   Air traffic control for departing aircraft. The reverse of Approach Control.

DME   Distance Measuring Equipment which measures the slant range distance in nautical miles of the aircraft from a ground-based DME transmitter. Introduced in the 1970s, DME is largely obsoleted by GPS navigation.

EAA   Experimental Aircraft Association, located in Oshkosh, Wisconsin. Founded under the leadership of Paul Poberezny in 1953 initially by a group of aircraft homebuilders. Today EAA embraces virtually all categories of sport aircraft, including warbirds, vintage aircraft, ultralights and manufactured airplanes. See chapter 31.

EFIS   Electronic Flight Information System. An electronic system displaying multiple flight data information on a flat screen cockpit display. Historically, such data has been displayed on multiple analog instruments.

ELT   Emergency Locator Transmitter. A self-contained transmitter that is designed to activate and transmit an emergency signal in the event of an airplane crash to allow rescue crews to locate the scene of the accident.

FAA Federal Aviation Administration, the name of the federal government agency regulating aviation in the United States.

FAI Fédération Aéronautique Internationale, the world organization of aero clubs from about 100 countries that governs air sport competition. It is also the body that certifies all world aviation and space records.

FBO Fixed Base Operator, the name given to a business on an airport providing services to pilots and aircraft owners. Usually this includes flight training, aircraft maintenance, and refueling services. Some FBO's also handle new and used aircraft sales, and charter operations. Often they have an aircraft lounge for pilots, but all have a hot coffee pot—a must for pilots.

Final Approach The flight path leading directly to the beginning of the landing runway.

Fixed Landing Gear An aircraft landing gear that is permanently attached to the aircraft in the "down position" and cannot be retracted.

Flight Level Altitude expressed in hundreds of feet above sea level used above 18,000 feet based on a standard barometric pressure of 29.92. The pilot adjusts his altimeter barometric pressure to 29.92 inches of mercury upon reaching 18,000. For example, FL 250 would be 25,000 feet.

Flight Service Station An FAA communication facility that provides pilots with weather and flight plan information by radio or telephone. At one time there were hundreds of such facilities which were located at individual airports, but they have now been consolidated into a handful of locations for economic reasons.

Freezing Level The altitude where the temperature is 32 degrees F.

G-Load An engineering term describing the structural loading which an airplane can sustain before the structure will fail. "G" being the weight of gravity. A five G-load would be five times the weight of gravity.

Get-Home-Itis A slang expression describing a pilot who is so anxious to get to his destination that he fails to use good judgement and takes chances that put him at increased risk.

Glass Cockpit A term used to refer to a cockpit largely consisting of digital electronic equipment in an EFIS format (see above).

Glide Slope The part of the Instrument Landing System (ILS) that provides vertical guidance for the aircraft during approach and landing.

GMT   Greenwich Mean Time. The time at the prime (zero) degree longitude. This prime degree extends north and south from Greenwich, England. Used in aviation to avoid time zone confusion.

Go Around   The expression that means the pilot who is trying to land is unable to do for what ever the reason and is climbing back to traffic pattern altitude and will then make another attempt. Most often it is because of not being lined up with the runway, going too fast, or conflicting traffic.

GPS   Global Positioning System. A satellite-based, accurate navigation system that provides three dimensional position information.

Great Circle Route   The shortest distance between two points over the surface of the earth.

Ground Control   Ground Control handles aircraft movement on the airport.

Ground Looper   An airplane with a tail wheel that has a tendency to ground-loop, where the tail section of the plane starts to turn to one side or the other, causing the pilot to lose directional control if not quickly corrected.

GS   Usually refers to the glide slope portion on the ILS system. See Glide Slope above.

Hangar Flying   A term referring to a group of pilots informally discussing their flying experiences, often exaggerating them.

IAS   The speed of the aircraft as shown on the aircraft's airspeed indicator, and is used by pilot-to-controller communications.

IFR   Instrument Flight Rules, the rules governing the procedures for conducting instrument flight.

ILS   Instrument Landing System, a precision approach system which normally consists of a localizer, glide slope, outer and middle markers and approach lights.

Instrument Rating   The FAA pilot rating held by those who have met the requirements to fly under IFR conditions.

Iron Compass   A slang expression used by a pilot who is navigating by following railroad tracks.

Kilometer   A unit of distance measurement which is 0.621 statute miles.

Knots   A unit of speed based on nautical miles.

KTS   Abbreviation often used for "knots" (see above).

LAMA Light Aircraft Manufacturers Association, the association of light sport aircraft manufacturers that establish and enforce the standards for the manufacture of Light Sport Aircraft.

Landing Pattern The normal VFR landing pattern is a left-hand pattern, consisting of a downwind leg parallel to the landing runway but in the opposite direction, followed by a 90 degree left turn onto the base leg, followed by a further 90 left turn onto the final approach leg with the runway then straight ahead, all the while descending from the pattern altitude. A right-hand pattern would be a pattern where the pilot would make a 90 degree right hand turn onto base leg, followed by a further right turn onto the final approach leg.

Light Sport Aircraft A one or two-seat aircraft, weighing not more than 1,320 pounds on takeoff, a maximum speed of 135 mph, a stall speed of not more than 51 mph, fixed landing gear, fixed or ground-adjustable propeller, and a single engine.

Localizer The component of an instrument landing system (ILS) which provides directional course guidance to the runway.

Localizer Approach An instrument approach using only the localizer component with no vertical or glide slope guidance.

LORAN A maritime navigation system that became available for aviation use in the 1980s, but has now been obsoleted by GPS.

Low-Frequency Radio Range An early radio navigation aid using frequencies in the 150 to 400kc band width. First introduced in the late 1920s. It was replaced by the VOR omni range navigation system after World War II. See Chapter 6 for further description.

MDA Minimum Descent Altitude, the altitude below which an aircraft may not descend during an ILS landing unless certain minimum visual references are in sight and a normal visual landing can be made.

MEA Minimum En route Altitude between navigation fixes that ensures the pilot on an IFR flight plan of adequate navigation signal reception, and obstacle clearance.

Meter A unit of distance measurement which is equal to 3.281 feet.

Missed Approach The term used to describe an aircraft on final approach to landing when the pilot aborts the landing for any reason.

NAA National Aeronautic Association, the national aero club of the United States. See Chapter 26.

National Aviation Club Not to be confused with NAA (above). A Washington, D.C. aviation club that at one time had its own club building and restaurant, and everyone involved in aviation was a member. By the 1970s it was principally a luncheon club.

Nautical mile   A unit of measurement used in aviation and nautical charts. A nautical mile is 6,076 feet, or 1.1507 statute miles.

NDB   Nondirectional beacon, a ground station which can be "homed in on" by an aircraft with ADF equipment.

Normally aspirated engine   An engine that does not use a turbocharger to compress air for use in engine combustion.

Oil Galley   A series of very small holes and passageways that connect the oil pump to the main bearings, crankshaft bearings, cam bearings and other oil-critical parts of the engine.

Pilot's Discretion   A term used by Air Traffic Control to authorize the pilot to climb or descend to a specified altitude whenever he wishes. Under this authorization the pilot can temporally stop the climb or descent at any point but then may not return to a vacated altitude.

Pilot Reports   A report usually made in flight by a pilot of unusual or unexpected weather or other conditions encountered.

Pitot Tube   The tube extending into the airstream which is used to measure the indicated airspeed. See IAS above.

PLB   A personal locator beacon is an ELT intended for personal use not only by pilots but hunters, skiers, hikers or anyone traveling in remote locations. It contains a 406 MHz transmitter and usually a GPS receiver, which transmits both location and identification to a worldwide satellite network.

Pressure Altitude   The altitude based on standard baseline pressure settings and temperature.

Private License   The FAA license held by those who have met the requirements to fly and carry passengers for non commercial flights under VFR conditions, subject to limitations of the license itself. This is the license most pilots have.

Radar Contact   Used by AirTraffic Control to inform an aircraft that it is identified on the radar display and the pilot can discontinue reporting at compulsory reporting points.

Radar Vectors   Navigation guidance by a ground controller to an aircraft providing specific headings based on the ground controller's radar.

ROTC   Reserve Officer Training Corps. A military program offered at some colleges to train students for the reserve officer program. Students who successfully complete this program receive officer commissions as 2nd lieutenants upon graduation from college.

Runway Designations   Every runway has a one or two numerical designation painted in large numbers at each end of the runway, based on the magnetic heading that the aircraft would have in landing or taking off. For example, runway 16 would be on a 160 degree heading., and the other end would be runway 34, the reciprical of 16.

Scattered Clouds   A sky coverage of 1/8 through 4/8.

Scud-running   The term used to refer to VFR flying below a cloud layer where the ceiling is less than 1,000 feet and/or the visibility is less than 3 miles.

Sectional Lines   North-south and east-west lines every one mile, formed by roads which are perfectly straight and aligned with the cardinal compass headings.

Sectional Map   An aeronautical contour map showing airports, airways, navigation, communication, obstructions, airspace restrictions, and other VFR-oriented information. The scale is 8.5 statute miles and 7 nautical miles to the inch.

Service Ceiling   The highest altitude an aircraft can fly and still have the ability to climb 100 feet a minute.

Statute mile   A unit of measurement commonly used in the United States, and equal to 5,280 feet, or 1.609 kilometers.

Stormscope   An avionics device that displays lightning strikes on a radar-like scope by detecting the electromagnetic pulse emitted by a lightning strike.

TAS True Airspeed, the airspeed of an aircraft relative to undisturbed air.

TBO   Time Between Overhaul. Usually refers to the time between overhaul of the engine as recommended by the engine manufacturer.

Tie-Down   A rope or chain firmly secured in the ground to which an airplane can be attached to keep from moving in a strong wind.

Tail Dragger   An aircraft with a tail wheel.

T-Hangar A unit in a row of airplane hangars designed to provide an individual space for an `aircraft in the shape of a "T" rather than a rectangle. The hangars are alternated, with individual hangar doors on opposite sides, and individual hangars have walls between adjacent hangars.

TCAS   Traffic Alert and Collision Avoidance System, an airborne collision avoidance system based on radar beacon signals which operates independently of ground-based equipment.

Transponder An airborne radar beacon receiver and transmitter, which automatically responds to interrogations from the ground or other aircraft.

Tricycle Gear Aircraft An aircraft that has a nose wheel but no tail wheel. The center of gravity of the plane is forward of the main landing gear.

Turbocharger A device that compresses outside air for use in the engine combustion process. See chapter 25.

Turn and Bank Indicator A an airplane instrument that coordinates the rate of turn with the degree of bank to help the pilot avoid a slip or skid.

Undercast A cloud layer which is below the aircraft.

Ultalight Aircraft An airplane that has only one seat, weighs less than 254 pounds empty, a maximum fuel capacity of 5 gallons, a top speed of 63 mph and a power-off stall speed of 28 mph.

Unicom A non-government communication facility which may provide airport information at certain airports.

VFR Visual Flight Rules govern the procedures for conducting flight under visual flying conditions. The minimum visibility and distance from clouds varies depending on the airspace the aircraft is flying in.

VHF Frequency A radio frequency between 30 and 300 MHz. 108 to 118 MHz is used for certain navaids, and 118 to 136 MHz is used for voice communications.

VOR Very High Frequency Omni Range Station is a ground-based navigation aid transmitting navigation signals 360 degrees in azimuth. It has been used since the late 1940s for navigation in the National Airspace System. In recent years GPS is becoming the prime navigation system.

This book is dedicated to the memory of
my good friend and mentor

A. Scott Crossfield

X-15 Rocket Pilot
First man to fly twice the speed of sound
One of the greatest test pilots of our time

His luck ran out in 2006

Scott Crossfield and the author, 2005

1

The Beginning
June 24, 1940

I can pinpoint with absolute precision when my lifelong aviation "adventure" started:

June 24, 1940 at 2:40 a.m.

It was scheduled to start 35 minutes earlier but, not unlike today's times, the inbound United Airlines Flight #5 from New York City was late. We left Chicago 35 minutes late, en route to Omaha, Nebraska; Denver, Colorado; Salt Lake City, Utah; Boise, Idaho; Pendleton, Oregon and my destination, Portland, Oregon. By the time I arrived in Portland we had lost an additional 25 minutes, arriving an hour late at 4:20 in the afternoon. I was met by my Grandmother and Grandfather Gross, and by a reporter and photographer from the *Portland Oregonian*. My arrival did not merit front page attention, but it did result in a picture and short article commenting on my "first" flight.

You see, I was then only six years old, and my parents had sent me to spend the summer with my grandparents in Oregon. Those were the days when the airlines were desperately trying to convince a skeptical public that flying was the only way to travel. And that it was safe. Few apparently believed this because aviation was truly in its infancy. So a six-year-old traveling 2,000 miles across the country without his parents was news that the airlines wanted to publicize. "If a six-year-old boy can fly across the country, why can't you?" United Airlines for their part were willing to assign an off-duty stewardess to make sure I didn't get off at Pendleton or Boise or some other intermediate stop. That would not have been the kind of publicity they wanted.

6-Year-Old Boy Flies Overland

A boy who likes to get both feet off the ground is 6-year-old Malvern J. Gross Jr. of Chicago.

Master Gross, who "dropped in" on his grandparents in Portland, said Wednesday that he had thoroughly enjoyed his 1765-mile airplane debut even though he was accompanied only by a United Airlines special stewardess during the almost 12-hour flight.

Malvern will remain in Portland through the summer, visiting two sets of grandparents, Mr. and Mrs. C. H. Gross, 2932 NE Jarrett street, and Mr. and Mrs. Clyde Henderson, 3438 SE Caruthers street.

While stretching it a little bit, I look upon this first flight as my "solo" flight. I was, after all, leaving home and traveling half a continent away from the security of my parents. I do not recall any trepidation on my part but I can imagine that it must have taken courage on my parents' part to see their six-year-old, and only child, disappearing into the dark night skies of Midway Airport.

Portland Oregonian, 1940

United was then flying Douglas DC-3s, the latest in transport aircraft. Flying at 190 mph, the scheduled flight time was 11 hours, plus an average ground time of perhaps 20 minutes

My grandmother took this picture as I was walking from the DC-3 to the passenger terminal using an old fashioned box camera. The flight took about 12 hours and made a number of stops. I credit this flight with igniting my lifelong love of flying.

at each stop. The DC-3s carried 21 passengers. The round trip fare in 1940 was $160 ($2,300 in 2008 dollars). I suspect my parents paid only half fare for me; even so, that was a lot of money in those days.

Back then, the Captain would let the passengers know the progress of the flight by passing back to the cabin a hand-written "flight log" on which he would indicate key information. There was no public address system. Here is the Flight Log approaching Denver.

I do not remember any details of that flight other than "throwing up" when landing at Salt Lake City. For those of you who are not familiar with the Salt Lake City airport, it is located in a valley at an elevation of 4,200 feet. But only 15

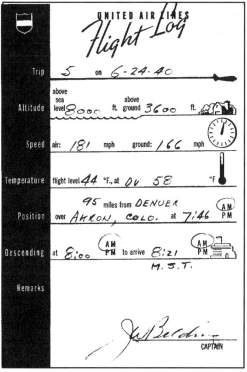

I kept this flight log all these years as a treasured memento of my first flight, and it provides written evidence of that flight. Note that we are flying almost 3,600 feet above the ground, have a 15 mph headwind, and are expecting to land in Denver at 8:21 a.m. The flight had been scheduled to land at 7:21 (see the airline schedule on the next page). The flight left Chicago 40 minutes late, so it lost only a few minutes on the 925 miles to Denver. That is fairly impressive for that era.

miles to the east of the airport are the Wasatch Mountains. Flying from Denver to Salt Lake City the pilot would need to fly at thirteen or fourteen thousand feet to stay safely above these mountains. Once past the Wasatch Mountains the pilot then had to descend steeply to the airport. A descent of close to ten thousand feet would require some steep turns in an effort to lose altitude, and this precipitated my "moment of stomach unrest." As far as I can recall, it was the only time I have ever become airsick while flying.

The Return Flight

At the end of the summer I returned to Chicago, again via United Air Lines—most of the way, that is. Apparently the weather was not good, and the flight "terminated" in Omaha with United putting everyone on an overnight train to Chicago. An off-duty stewardess was with me just to handle such unforeseen circumstances.

MALVERN J. GROSS JR.
Chicago boy visits here.

Fast-Forward to 1950

My next flight was not until 1950, my senior year in high school, when I traveled from Washington, D.C. to Albany, NY on Capital Airlines. The next flight after that was not until January 8, 1955, when I took my first flying lesson.

Clearly, my flight at age six was the defining moment in what has become a lifelong aviation adventure. The realities of World War II and tight finances prevented me from nurturing a growing desire to fly while growing up. But these "solo" flights across the United States were the dormant seeds that truly germinated on January 8, 1955.

The pages that follow trace the influence that aviation has played in my life. But every story has a beginning.

Mine began at 2:40 a.m. on that dark night of June 24, 1940.

UNITED [UNITED AIR LINES] AIR

FASTEST, SHORTEST BETWEEN THE ⌄ EAST AND MOST

UNITED AIR LINES TRANSPORT CORPORATIO
GENERAL OFFICES: 5959 So. CICERO AVE., CHICAGO, ILLINOIS   CABLE ADDRESS—"UALTRA

W. A. PATTERSON	R. W. SCHROEDER	HAROLD CRARY	JACK HERL
President	Vice President	Vice Pres. Traffic	Vice Pres. Charge o

WESTBOUND—Read Down   **Complete COAST-TO-COAST Sche**

31 Daily	15 Daily	Over-land Flyer 5 Daily	Con-tinen-tal 9 Daily	Con-tinen-tal 3 Daily	7-17 Daily	25-11 Daily	41 (b)	Cali-fornian 1 Daily	Mls.	**17**		O la Fl D
PM	PM	PM	PM	PM	PM	PM	PM	AM				A
.....	10 45	9 45	5 45	5 15	4 00	3 15	.....	8 30	0	Lv....NEW YORK (Newark),(ET) Ar		9
.....	–	–	–	–	4 00	–	.....	–	72	Lv....Philadelphia (Camden)..... Ar	
.....	–	–	–	–	4 40	–	.....	–	71	Lv....Allentown-Bethlehem..... Lv	
.....	–	–	–	–	6 57	–	.....	–	393	Lv...........Akron.......... Ar	
.....	1 40	12 40	8 35	–	7 30	–	.....	11 30	406	Lv.....CLEVELAND.......... Ar		6
.....	–	–	–	–	–	–	.....	–	492	Lv.........(a) Toledo...... (ET) Ar	
.....	2 45	1 45	9 40	8 50	8 35	6 50	1 15	12 35	723	Ar........CHICAGO.. (CT) Lv		4
.....	3 05	2 05	9 55	9 25	↙	7 10	1 15	12 50		Lv........CHICAGO........ Ar		3
.....	–	–	–	–	.....	8 24	2 29	.....	867	Lv..Moline-Rock Island-Davenport.. Lv	
.....	–	–	–	–	.....	8 57	3 02	.....	923	Lv......Iowa City........ Lv	
2 35	–	–	–	–	.....	9 50	3 55	.....	1032	Ar.......Des Moines........ Ar	
3 31	–	4 59	–	12 19	.....	10 56	.....	3 44	1149	Ar........OMAHA......... Lv		1
.....	–	5 14	–	12 34	.....	11 11	.....	3 59		Lv........OMAHA......... Ar		1
.....	–	–	–	–	.....	11 43	.....	–	1202	Lv.......Lincoln........ Lv	
.....	–	–	–	–	.....	12 25	.....	–	1241	Lv.....Grand Island....... Lv	
.....	–	–	2 27	–	.....	1 22	.....	–	1380	Lv.......North Platte.... (CT) Lv	
.....	7 35	–	–	2 35	.....	.....	.....	–	1618	Ar.......CHEYENNE.... (MT) Lv	
.....	7 50	–	–	2 50	.....	.....	.....	–		Lv.......CHEYENNE........ Ar	
.....	–	7 21	–	x 3 50	.....	.....	.....	6 06	1635	Ar........DENVER......... Lv		9
.....	–	7 36	–	x 1 25	.....	.....	.....	6 21		Lv........DENVER......... Ar		9
.....	10 33	10 45	5 22	5 33	.....	.....	.....	9 30	2009	Ar.....SALT LAKE CITY.. (MT) Lv		6
.....	↘	11 10	.....	5 50	.....	.....	.....	9 50	2009	Lv.....SALT LAKE CITY....... Ar		6
.....	.....	–	.....	–	.....	.....	.....	10 14	2229	Ar...........Elko....... (PT) Lv	
.....	.....	12 56	.....	–	.....	.....	.....	11 51	2439	Ar...........Reno........ Lv		2
.....	.....	2 02	.....	–	.....	.....	.....	12 57	2562	Lv.......Sacramento........ Lv		1
.....	.....	2 41	.....	8 41	.....	.....	.....	1 36	2639	Ar.....SAN FRANCISCO..... Lv		12
.....	.....	3 09	.....	9 09	.....	.....	.....	2 04	2651	Ar.........Oakland ...(PT) Lv		12
.....	.....	11 05	5 52	.....	.....	.....	.....	9 45	2009	Lv..SALT LAKE CITY (WAE)(MT) Ar		8
.....	.....	f12 20	7 12	.....	.....	.....	.....	11 05	2375	Lv Boulder Dam (Las Vegas).. (PT) Lv		2
.....	.....	1 55	8 37	.....	.....	.....	.....	12 40	2613	Ar LOS ANGELES (Un. Air Term.). Lv	
.....	.....	4 25	9 10	.....	.....	.....	.....	.....		Lv LOS ANGELES (Un. Air Term.) Ar		12
.....	.....	–	9 25	.....	.....	.....	.....	.....	2642	Ar.......Long Beach........ Lv		12
.....	.....	5 20	10 10	.....	.....	.....	.....	.....	2736	Ar......San Diego...... (PT) Lv		11
.....	.....	11 15	7 5 55	.....	.....	.....	.....	.....	2009	Lv.....SALT LAKE CITY.. (MT) Ar		...
.....	.....	1 20	7 52	.....	.....	.....	.....	.....	2307	Ar........Boise....... (MT) Lv		...
.....	.....	1 50	8 20	.....	.....	.....	.....	.....	2500	Ar........Pendleton.... (PT) Lv		...
.....	.....	3 20	9 45	.....	.....	.....	.....	.....	2694	Ar.......PORTLAND, Ore...... Lv		...
.....	No. 5	4 15	10 00	.....	.....	.....	.....	.....		Lv.......PORTLAND, Ore...... Ar		...
.....	.....	5 15	11 00	.....	.....	.....	.....	.....	2835	Lv........SEATTLE (n)...... Lv		...
.....	.....	.....	11 30	.....	.....	.....	.....	.....		Lv........SEATTLE (n)...... Ar		...
.....	.....	.....	12 26	.....	.....	.....	.....	.....	2969	Ar.....Vancouver, B. C.... (PT) Lv		...

17

The westbound flight schedule above is really quite impressive, given the era. I was on Flight 5, daily service from New York to the West Coast. It looks as if Salt Lake City was a "hub." I believe Flight 5 continued on to Portland, but that is not entirely clear from this schedule. Note the number of daily departures from New York City.

PART I

THE EARLY, CAREFREE YEARS
1955 and 1956

2

The Early, Carefree Years
An Overview
1955 and 1956

The years immediately following my graduation from Lehigh University in June, 1954, and particularly the two years in the Air Force beginning in late December, 1954, were carefree years— the transition years between youth and adulthood. They were also the years when I learned to fly and was able to spend all of my free time, energy and income on aviation. Being in the military, my housing and food were taken care of by the government and although my monthly income was only $221 ($1,700 in 2008 dollars) it was all available for spending on whatever I wanted. And flying was what I wanted.

Learning to Fly

I had joined the Air Force Reserve Officers Training Corps (ROTC) in college, both because of my interest in aviation and because the Korean War was on. This kept me from being drafted but required a two-year service commitment after graduation. I was an accounting major and joined the public accounting firm of Price Waterhouse right after graduation, knowing, of course, that I would be called up shortly thereafter. I was, in mid-December. I was assigned to the Air Force Auditor General's office which had responsibility for auditing all Air Force bases. I was sent to Presque Isle AFB in northern Maine to be a resident auditor. I stayed at Presque Isle for my entire two-year commitment.

I arrived at Presque Isle AFB on December 27, 1954. Presque Isle is two hundred thirty air miles north of Portland, Maine. The Northeast Airlines flight I was on was grounded at Portland because of weather, and the passengers were sent by bus on the long drive to Presque Isle. When I arrived the temperature was minus twenty-five degrees Fahrenheit. Somehow when being told I was going to Presque Isle I had visions of being on an island off the Maine coast. That first evening the temperature firmly removed my ignorant expectation—the closest ocean was more than two hundred miles south of Presque Isle.

I quickly learned that there was a civilian flying club at Presque Isle. I say "civilian" but all the club members were from the base, and they had formed a non-military club. The club then contracted with a local instructor who had a grass strip in Fort Fairfield, Maine, about ten miles to the northeast. John Philbrick, the instructor, was in his late twenties. He rented club members his two Aeronca Champs for only three dollars an hour, but with the understanding that the club would put up eight hundred dollars to be forfeited if we damaged or destroyed one of his planes. I don't recall what he charged for instruction.

I immediately joined the club. My first flying lesson was on January 8, less than two weeks after getting to Presque Isle. I soloed two weekends later on January 23 with 6.8 hours. What is truly unusual about this is that I was flying a plane on skis, not wheels. With the cold temperatures and deep snow it would have been impossible to keep a

This was one of John Philbrick's two Champs. Notice the skis and snow. I learned to fly in this plane in January, 1955.

runway clear of ice and snow. Being on skis had real advantages because that part of the country had lots of snow-covered frozen lakes. A lake could become a landing strip. We would go out to practice landings and take offs on a ten-mile-long lake. We would climb to, say, five hundred feet, cut the power, and glide to a landing on the lake. Then we would give the plane power, take off, climb back up to five hundred feet, and repeat the process. I am sure this was why I soloed in so few hours. There was no wasted time lining up with a fixed runway.

Virtually all winter, private flying in northern Maine was on ski-equipped planes. The first time I landed an airplane with wheels was after I had received my private pilot's license on March 30, and by that time I had forty-four hours total time.

My First Plane

I bought my first airplane on March 12, 1955, a used two-seat 1946 Cessna 140. I then had 27 hours. It was also equipped with skis. The plane cost $1,500 ($12,000 in 2008 dollars), which I didn't have. I had no savings. I turned to my parents and sort of blackmailed them

My first plane, a 1946 Cessna 140, 2-seat, 85-horsepower, 105 mph, 5 hours fuel.

into lending me the money. The thrust of my request was, "wouldn't you prefer that I had a solid, well-maintained plane rather than some wreck that would not be as safe?" I am sure they were apprehensive about their little boy learning to fly but they were wise enough not to say so, and they did lend me the money.

The Cessna 140 had an 85-horsepower engine and a speed of about 105 miles per hour. It carried five hours of fuel, which gave it a theoretical range of about five hundred miles. Realistically, however, I would always plan on a maximum of three hours. Too often, headwinds reduced the 105 miles per hour to 80 or even less.

I had no automobile while I was at Presque Isle; I couldn't afford both an automobile and an airplane. Before I bought my Cessna, when I wanted to rent an airplane at Fort Fairfield, I had to depend on someone else for a ride. One of the attractions of having my own plane was that I could petition the base commander at Presque Isle to let me keep it on the base. He gave permission and my plane became the only civilian plane on the base. That solved the transportation problem, because I could walk from the Bachelor Officers Quarters to the plane and then fly to Fort Fairfield.

Presque Isle Air Force Base from my Cessna 140. Located 230 air miles north of Portland, it was a fighter base to intercept Russian bombers during the cold war. This was my home for two years. Temperatures of minus 25 were common in winter.

Cross-Country Flights

By the end of my first year of flying I had 269 hours of flying, much of it in long, cross-country trips from Presque Isle to Rochester, New York, where my parents lived. Rochester is approximately 550 miles from Presque Isle, and the first half of the trip is over desolate, mountainous terrain, largely uninhabited.

I made five round trips to Rochester that year. I describe two of these flights in detail in Chapters 3 and 5. The first flight started before the ink on my private license had dried, and I had only 44 total hours. I barely made it to Rochester, and it was only luck that I did. In fact, all five of these long cross-country flights were notable in two respects: first, I pushed the envelope, and second, I was a quick learner. I learned from each of these flights and by the end of 1955 I was a reasonably seasoned, cross-country pilot. Not necessarily a safe pilot, but certainly a seasoned one.

The only navigational equipment I had was a compass and an aviation sectional map. This was truly "dead reckoning." I would calculate the compass heading to fly, and then follow my progress on the map. Sounds easy, but any pilot who has tried to follow his progress solely by reference to a map over desolate areas with few distinctive landmarks knows it is not.

It was 300 miles between Presque Isle and my fuel stop, usually Burlington, Vermont, or Plattsburgh, New York. That route took me a few miles across a section of Quebec, Canada, where the Canadian border juts into the direct route. The only small airport on my direct route to Burlington is just over the Canadian border, Megantic, Quebec. En route weather information was nonexistent. The only weather reporting station between Presque Isle and Burlington was at Megantic.

I said I made five trips that year. Actually there was a sixth trip where I had to turn around and return because the weather beyond Megantic, Quebec, started turning sour. I needed fuel to get back to Presque Isle, and although I had no permission to stop in Canada, I decided it was prudent to do so. The airport authorities sold me the ten or so gallons I needed and never raised any question about my entry into Canada. I mention this because my experience over the years is that if you use good judgement the government authorities ignore technical violations.

High Altitude Flights

Most pilots do not think of a Cessna 140 as being an aircraft that can fly very high. But on October 16, 1955, I flew to an indicated altitude of 14,300 feet! It took me 55 minutes to reach this altitude. Then a week later on October 24, I climbed to an indicated altitude of 16,150 feet, in 70 minutes! See the picture below.

These are approximate altitudes. To get true altitude you would need to correct the indicated altitude either up or down based on air temperature.

Let me put this into perspective. The higher you fly, the less air, and thus less oxygen, there is. This affects both engines and people. Pilots flying above 12,500 feet for more than 30 minutes are required to use supplemental oxygen. I had no oxygen. At about 7,500 feet the engine can produce only about 75 percent of the horsepower it can at sea level, and this 75 percent is the normal power setting on a trip. An altitude of 7,500 feet is pretty much the optimum altitude for most aircraft. By the time the plane gets to 16,000 feet, the power is probably down to 25 percent or less. My Cessna 140 barely managed to fly at that altitude.

Right from the beginning, I have always been fascinated with high altitude flight and, as you will read in chapter 18, I set an altitude record of 32,420 feet in my turbocharged Cessna T210 in 1978.

This blurred picture was taken on Oct. 24, 1955 showing that I was at an indicated altitude of 16,150 feet. The air speed was barely above the plane's stalling speed.

1956

The year 1956 was another year of constant flying in my free time, and by the end of that year I had flown an additional 350 hours, bringing my total at the time of discharge from the Air Force in December to slightly more than 600. By then I had earned both my commercial license, and, more importantly, my instrument rating.

Instrument Rating

As I accumulated hours and experience, I had a number of close calls, and I started paying attention to aviation risks. I read every accident report of others because it was obvious to me that if I continued flying the way I was, it was only a matter of time before I would run out of luck. I was essentially playing Russian roulette. Fortunately, I was, and am, a very pragmatic person, and I correctly concluded that weather was my greatest risk. I had limited control over the weather, but with an instrument rating, and an airplane qualified to handle at least some weather, I could reduce my risk.

Several of my friends at Presque Isle were Air Force pilots and they encouraged me to get an instrument rating. One of these friends, Arnie Greene, became my instructor. It took two steps to qualify. The first step was to take the three-hour written exam, which, while difficult, was easy for me. The second step was to demonstrate to a Civil Aeronautics Authority (CAA) flight examiner that I was competent to fly under instrument conditions.

I have long since forgotten how many hours of instrument flight time were required, but it was a lot, and involved far more than learning to fly itself. After all, one has to learn to fly the airplane by interpreting flight instruments while ignoring extraneous senses like the "seat of your pants" feelings that would likely be giving false information. I was fortunate in that I was able to use the base's T–33 jet flight simulator. While a T-33 has totally different speeds and performance, the flight instruments were essentially the same and the skills I learned in this simulator could easily be transferred to my Cessna. In total I spent twenty-nine hours in this simulator.

My Cessna 140 was used in both the training and the CAA flight check. The only gyro instrument I was allowed to use was a "turn and bank." The only navigation radio was a low-frequency receiver that could receive the radio range signals, a primitive navigation system by any standards. Few pilots alive today can say they flew the "low-frequency airways" that used this system. I describe this in detail in Chapter 6. By the time I took my check ride I had a ten-channel transmitter and I thought I was at the leading edge of technology.

Arnie Greene was a tough taskmaster and it took six months before he was willing to sign me off to take the check ride. The check ride was on July 24, 1956. My log book entry states:

> *First CAA check ride for instrument ticket. Passed partial panel but failed low-frequency range approach because I did not descend to MDA [minimum descent altitude] fast enough. Examiner wants more practice and then retake check ride.*

I was a fast learner and ten days later, on August 3, I retook the check ride and received my instrument rating. At the time very few private pilots had an instrument rating. It was probably the most important thing I did in my early flying. At the time I had a respectable 425 hours. But given the way I had been almost recklessly scud running I doubt that I could have flown another 425 hours and lived to tell about it.

Purchase of a Cessna 170A

By mid-1956, I had repaid my parents for the loan to pay for the Cessna 140. The Cessna 140 was clearly a marginal airplane to be flying in clouds and I concluded that I needed a bigger, faster airplane. More importantly, I needed a plane with far more electronic equipment.

In late September, I sold my Cessna 140 and bought a used 1951 Cessna 170A. In the eighteen months I had owned the Cessna 140, I put 432 hours on it. I sold it for $2,100, which was $600 more than I paid for it. I am a CPA and have always kept good records. They show that my net total cost of flying the airplane was only $655. Based on 432 hours, that works out to a net cost per hour of only $1.52. This was, of course, the mid-nineteen fifties and fuel was only thirty-five

This picture of my new plane was taken in November, 1956 at Fort Fairfield. There had already been a light snow, and it must have been cold. Note the parka. I spent a great deal of time at Fort Fairfield during my 2 years at Presque Isle.

cents a gallon. Buying the plane at a low price and selling high was the key to these low costs.

I used the $2,100 toward the $3,800 purchase price, and easily obtained an airplane loan for the difference. I vividly recall that monthly payments were $131.07.

The Cessna 170A was a four-place aircraft, the forerunner of the Cessna 172, the most popular general aviation airplane of the last fifty years. It cruised at 120 mph, and had a new navigation radio called an "omnigator," one of the first VOR/omni range receivers. There were no omni stations in northern Maine, but by 1956 the CAA had replaced the totally outdated radio range stations in most parts of the United States. I realized I would need more modern equipment once I returned to civilian life.

On November 22, I took my commercial flight check ride, and received my commercial license. This license allows me—even today—to fly an aircraft for hire, provided I have a 2nd class medical certificate. I have never exercised commercial privileges, but it is a badge attesting to my one-time skills.

Discharge from the Air Force

Only two weeks later, on December 8, my two-year ROTC active duty commitment ended and I was discharged and returned to civilian life. December 8 was clearly the end of an era of my life that I fondly recall as my "carefree years." Even more than graduation from college, December 8, 1956 was the day when my youth clearly ended. I now faced the realities of adulthood, the need to establish my professional life, and hopefully to marry and start a family.

3

The First Flight Home
April 9, 1955

My first flight home is one that my parents never forgot. I have never forgotten it either.

Rochester, New York, is about 550 miles from Presque Isle Air Force Base in Maine where I was on active duty with the Air Force, strictly as a ground officer. I purchased my first plane, a Cessna 140, on March 12, and on March 30 I received my private license. Two days later I took the skis off the plane and installed wheels so that I could fly to Rochester where my parents lived, not only to show them the plane, but also to show them what a fearless pilot I was.

I was a very "green" pilot, and that is the biggest understatement in this book. I had had my first flying lesson on January 8, barely three months before. I had only 44 total flying hours, all of it on ski-equipped aircraft. I had never made a flight at night, much less landed at night. I had made only one or two very short flights with wheels instead of skis. And yet I was about to make a flight across some of the most forbidding wilderness east of the Mississippi, with only a map for navigation.

Door Hinge Breaks

Here is the broad outline of the flight to Rochester as it actually transpired. I started out from Caribou, Maine. About 20 minutes into the flight, en route to my first intended landing at Plattsburgh, New

York, the top hinge of the door on the pilot side broke. That left only the hinge on the bottom of the door and a door latch basically keeping the door from being torn off into space. I don't recall how or why the hinge broke. I do remember that I was able to use my left hand to grip the door handle and keep the door in place. At the time of this incident I was fairly close to the airport at Houlton, Maine, about 50 miles south of Caribou. I was able to make an uneventful landing, using one hand to hold the door and the other hand to land the plane.

It was a Saturday morning but I was able to find someone who could fabricate a new hinge and install it. My recollection is that this took several hours and I probably got back in the air at about 11 a.m. From Houlton I flew directly to Plattsburgh, with a little jog to stay south of the Canadian border. My log shows that this 302 mile leg took three hours fifty minutes, which meant an average ground speed of 79 miles an hour. My log book entry, "Headwind quite strong,"

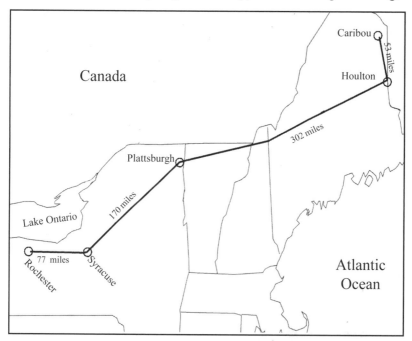

The route of my first flight home on April 9, 1955. This flight was full of "firsts:" my first long-distance flight, my first night landing, my first trip after removing the skis, the first time I had a serious in-flight mechanical problem, my first time in confronting 50+ mile headwinds, and the first time where luck was truly with me.

confirms this. In Plattsburgh, I refueled and called home to say I had been delayed. My Mother in the account below indicates that she received this call about 3:30 p.m. I refueled and started on the 247-mile leg to Rochester.

Syracuse to Rochester

I have little recollection of the first two-thirds of the flight from Plattsburgh to Rochester. Plattsburgh is at the north end of the Adirondack Mountains. I flew southwest, and after the first 30 minutes the mountains were behind and to the east of my flight path. I was then over the St. Lawrence valley and able to fly at a fairly low altitude without being concerned about mountains. I flew to the Syracuse area before turning west, and then proceeded directly to Rochester. That routing meant that I would intercept the airway at Syracuse, and then could follow it to Rochester. This would provide me with some radio navigation guidance after dark. It was early April, and I suspect it got dark at about 6 p.m., which after a 3:30 departure meant it would have been getting dark when I was between Syracuse and Rochester.

It was on this final third of the flight (Syracuse to Rochester) that I realized I was fighting stronger headwinds than I had ever experienced. I started to worry about my fuel situation because my ground speed seemed so slow. I had not worried about fuel in Plattsburgh because it was only 247 miles to Rochester, and if there were no headwinds I should be able to fly 500 miles. But when I finally landed at Rochester, four hours and 20 minutes had elapsed, which meant I had had a ground speed of 57 mph. Evidently I had been fighting an average headwind of close to 50 mph! The headwind between Syracuse and Rochester was probably even stronger, and it was bumpy most of the way.

The view from my parents' standpoint was harrowing. They fully recognized how inexperienced I was, and as you might expect, were very concerned, particularly when hour after hour passed and they did not hear from me. My mother recorded their side of this drama in a letter she wrote at the time to several relatives, and I have taken the liberty of reproducing it exactly as she wrote it on April 25, 1955:

A Flight I Will Never Forget

Well, we really had a week—week before last. Malvern flew home the day before Easter and was here all that week. He had not intended to be here all week, but the weather was lousy, so he was! But his arrival—never to my dying day will I forget that experience. Are you interested —do you want to hear the blow by blow description?

First of all, he had not had his little plane very long, and of course had never made any such trip. It is about 550 miles as the crow flies, and over mountainous and wild terrain the entire way. He would have to make one stop for his gas tanks hold enough for only 5 hours and he figures on about 100 miles per hour. He had written that he would leave that Saturday if the weather was good. We checked the night before with the weather bureau and they said it would be good the entire way.

He had expected to leave at about 6 a.m. So around noon we went to the airport to meet him. Mal [my father] had fussed about going out—said it would be better to wait until he got in and phoned us. We offered to leave him home, but you know how that would be—he wasn't going to let us be there without him, so he brought along some work, I took my knitting, and Mother [my grandmother] her crocheting. Linda [my 15-year-old sister] didn't think we would be doing any waiting, so she took nothing. We got out there about at 12:15 and sat, and then we sat, and we sat. We finally compromised with Mal that we would go home at 3 if he was not there by then. He wasn't, so we wearily went home, a little concerned, but not much.

At 3:30 we had a phone call from him—he was at Plattsburgh, N.Y.—a little over halfway here—and was about ready to take off. Seems that morning as he got in the air, the hinge on his door had cracked and he had to land and have it fixed, so he had not gotten away until late in the morning. Had to have a new hinge made. He allows as how he would be in Rochester between 5:30 and 6:30.

So at 5:30 we went back to our favorite spot and took up our waiting again. Now it had been a gloriously clear sunny day, but there had been increasing windiness, and by that time it was beginning to blow very hard indeed—very gusty. And, unfortunately, he was heading into it. So we knew he would not be making his 100 miles per hour. Well, we sat and we sat, and it became dusk and I began to get more and more nervous.

Finally a man came by and stopped, and asked if we were waiting for someone, that he had seen us there all day (true enough) and we said as how we were, etc. Then it comes out that he is a CAA (Civil Aeronautics Administration) official and he said he would phone the control tower and that we could go up and see what they had on him. So we drove over to the tower and Mal refused to let us all go up, so I stayed down with Mother and Linda went up with him.

Well, we waited and we waited and nothing happened. We could see them walking around up in the tower, but no one came down so I was sure they had no word or Linda would have come down to report it. It got darker and darker, and then finally pitch dark. By that time I had enough butterflies in my stomach to start a collection, for I knew he had never made a night landing in his life, and knew also that he hadn't made many landings on wheels. (It transpired that he had made 4, and 3 of them were that day!) He had learned on skis. Well, anyway at 8 o'clock I was beside myself. Mother was nervous and she was chattering because she was nervous, and I was nervous and clamming up because I was nervous, so we were quite a pair!

By that time I was certain he could not still be in the air, and was anxious to get along home so we could hear from him. About the time I was going to go up there after them, Linda came down in great excitement and said they had just heard from him, that he was about 20 miles out and would soon be here. She let me go up this time, and I didn't stop to argue but flew up those stairs as fast as my girth would permit.

It seems that he had filed a flight plan (as is usual) in Plattsburgh, and that he expected to be here not later than 6:30, and he was overdue, so even before Mal got up there they were beginning to make inquiries and had just learned that he had contacted Syracuse some time before. He should have gone into Syracuse, but he did not realize the extent of the headwinds—he was cruising at his 105 miles per hour all right, but the gusts were 40 miles an hour and occasionally more, so he wasn't making 105 miles in relation to the ground. And by the time he realized it, he decided to come on, which wasn't sensible.

At the time I got up there they heard him faintly, and had to use ear phones, but within a few minutes as he got closer he got stronger and they put it on the loud speaker so Mal and I could hear, too. You have both been to movies where "you" were in the control tower and they were "bringing-in" the hero in his crippled plane—well, that was what it was like—only a thousand times more so. But I couldn't help but be reminded of that. Mal and I kept still and listened, of course, and this is about the way it went.

| N76527: | Cessna 76527 to Tower, can you help me locate the airport, over. |

| Tower: | Tower to aircraft 527, we are outlining the field in blue, the runway in white—use Runway 25. *(Runway "25" told Malvern the direction to land.)* |

A little time elapsed then

| N76527: | 76527 to Tower, I still can't tell which is the field—I can see three searchlights from here, over. |

| Tower: | Tower to 527, we will blink the lights on the runway *(which they did, and then)* |

| N76527: | Cessna 527 to tower, I see it now. |

At this point they told us that they could see him, but it was minutes before Mal or I could see his red wing tip. They said he was only making about 40 miles an hour against the wind. It took a long time! At about this time they learned from us that this was his first night landing, and that we were worried about his gas supply.

| Tower: | Tower to Cessna 527, use Runway 25, over. |

| N76527: | Cessna 527 to tower, Roger. |

| Tower: | Tower to 527 do you want to come right in or circle the field, over. |

| N76527: | 527 to tower, I will circle the field once to get bearings and lose altitude. |

About that time Mal and I saw him, just a tiny red dot, then about 5 miles away. He came so slowly against the headwinds. In the meantime there was no activity on the field, I don't think that he actually held up any other aircraft or we would have heard the directions, but I do know that for at least 15 minutes the Monroe County Airport was entirely at the disposal of young Malvern. They were so nice to us— there were 3 of them—the one in charge kept telling us what they were doing, and giving the other two instructions. Then as Malvern approached the field and started down the outside, he just seemed to crawl - I thought he would never get down—about that time they ordered out crash equipment, a fire truck, and an ambulance. Maybe you don't think that made me feel good! They had turned out the blue field lights and just the lighted runway showed up. As Malvern said later, from the air, at the start, it had looked like another lighted street until they blinked the whole set of lights!

Now he had finally reached the end of the field. Said the tower man to us, watch him now, when he gets going with the wind he will scoot - and sure enough, he raced around the end and up towards the side.

This picture of my Cessna 140 was taken the day after the flight to Rochester. I took both my parents, my sister and my grandmother up for rides. I suspect they had some uneasiness. My flight hours at that time added up to just barely 50.

Tower: *Tower to 527, wind in gusts to 60 miles an hour.*

N76527   *527 to tower, Roger.*

When he got to about the 2 o'clock position (with 12 the start of his landing), all of a sudden his voice came sharp:

N76527:   *Cessna 527 to tower, request immediate permis-*
                sion to land, engine sputtering for lack of gas,
                over!

Tower: *Tower to 527, cleared to land.*

And then, the most agonizing part of all for Mal and me, watching that little red light, which was all we could see in the darkness, slowly (for he was now back in the headwinds) wobbling (as he was hit by a gust of wind), gently like a drifting feather, settle down, and down to a perfect landing.

Tower: *Tower to 527, good landing, follow the truck.*

And the little truck scurried out, took its position in front of the now faintly visible plane below us, and the two of them taxied off the field. The lights on runway 25 were shut off, and it was over. I felt like a limp rag doll. The ambulance and fire truck drove off, Mal and I shook hands all around and thanked them sincerely. The leader only said of it: "Tell that young man not to push it quite so close next time!" To which Mal and I added our amen!

That he was frightened, too, there is no doubt, and admitted that he should have landed at Syracuse. The darkness came on him too quickly and he just had not realized how much his progress was being delayed because of the winds. The winds were so strong by the time he landed that it was most uncomfortable to be outside at all.

The next day he moved the plane to a small private airport, and I had my first ride with him. It was fun, and I was not afraid.

* * * * *

My Mother was right. I was mighty glad to be back on the ground—
that is, yes, I was "frightened," too. And, I should have stopped at
Syracuse for fuel.

While I was low on fuel, it was not quite as critical as my "request
immediate permission to land" radio message had indicated. What had
happened was that as I was circling the airport, in very gusty, bumpy
conditions, the fuel in the tank —which was low—sloshed away from
the fuel line leading down to the engine. The fuel flows by gravity
feed. Once I had completed my turn to final—with the sputtering engine—the fuel again re-entered the fuel line and the engine resumed.
If the engine had stopped I would have merely glided to the runway.
Once I was over the airport the real risk was behind me. My log book
shows total flight time for that flight was 4:20, so in theory I had forty
minutes of fuel left. Still too close.

I learned a valuable lesson. Running out of fuel is unforgivable,
and often fatal. If you start having questions about your fuel supply,
then land, before it becomes a crisis. Every flight is a learning experience, and certainly this one was a pivotal one.

*I was fascinated with high altitude flight from the beginning. I was probably at
about 5,000 feet here in N76527. At one time I went to 16,000 feet in this plane,
which was unwise because of the lack of oxygen at that altitude.*

Return Flight to Caribou

By contrast, the return flight to Caribou on April 17-18 was less well documented, but also significant to my "crash" course in flying.

Let me quote directly from the log book entries for that day:

Rochester to Plattsburgh, via St. Lawrence Valley
2 hours 10 minutes. High level storm, occasionally light rain.

Plattsburgh to Burlington, VT
30 minutes. Tried to get over mountains. Turned back and landed at Burlington because of low visibility, etc.

Burlington to l00 miles north of Burlington and return
1 hour, 45 minutes. Tried to go up St. Lawrence Valley. Low visibility and ceilings forced return and 180 degree turn about 100 miles north of Burlington, VT.

Apparently I then spent the night in Burlington. The next day's entry:

Burlington to Caribou
3 hours, 20 minutes. Straight flight over clouds for 150 miles at about 7,000 to 8,000 feet.

Looking back from the vantage point of fifty-plus years of flying, it is obvious that I was getting another lesson on the problems of flying under visual flight rules (VFR), particularly in mountainous areas. But this time I twice used good judgement. First, when I deviated south from the direct Plattsburgh to Caribou route, and stopped for fuel at Burlington. Second, when I made a 180 degree turn and returned to Burlington after I tried a northern route but found low ceilings and visibilities.

Flying Above the Clouds

Notable, too, was my decision to fly above the clouds the next day. The log book entry does not indicate this, but I suspect the layer I was flying over consisted of scattered to broken clouds, because there were no navigation aids in that part of the country and I was still dependent on a map. With only scattered or broken clouds I should have been able to see the ground part of the time and been able to pick out landmarks from my map. I assume the weather forecast gave me reason to believe that the farther northeast I went the more the clouds would dissipate. Certainly neither I nor my Cessna were equipped at that time for instrument flight.

All in all, in nine days I had increased my total flying time by almost 50 percent and learned more about the real world of long-distance cross-country flying than I could possibly have imagined before making this trip.

I was still very green when I got back to Caribou, but I had learned many valuable lessons, which were reinforced by my being in some tense situations where I had to make judgements, some of which were better than others. That is the hard knock way of learning.

I was also very lucky. This flight could have been my last one. I didn't really appreciate that fact at the time; I was young and believed I was immortal.

Despite whatever risks I had taken, this flight ignited my love of the challenge of long-distance flight, which has stayed with me for more than fifty years.

4

Sixty Seconds I Will Never Forget
June 4, 1955

The following is an account I wrote in June, 1955, telling of another lesson I learned the hard way, and luckily, without tragic consequences. At the time I had just 89 hours total flying time.

My recollections are hazy as to why I wrote up this account at the time. I may have submitted it to *Flying Magazine* for possible publication. I kept a carbon copy of the account, which is reproduced below as I wrote it fifty years ago:

Presque Isle Air Force Base, located at the northern tip of Maine, where I am stationed, is the home field for my Cessna 140. Presque Isle is an F-89 jet interceptor base, and my Cessna is the only civilian aircraft allowed on the field. I am a ground officer with duties not involving flying, so most of my flying takes place on Saturdays and Sundays. The pilots in the F-89s don't appreciate my presence when they're making practice instrument landings, so every Saturday and Sunday I take my Cessna to Fort Fairfield, some twelve miles from Presque Isle. Fort Fairfield is a small grass strip where most local flying in northern Maine takes place. It was on one of these short, eight-minute flights that I learned about flying.

That particular Saturday was reasonably uneventful. I spent most of the day at Fort Fairfield doing miscellaneous maintenance, shoot-

31

ing a few landings, and in general passing the day by accomplishing very little, but having a great time hangar flying, discussing a little of everything.

Late in the afternoon, we started getting local thundershowers, and I debated whether I should try to sit them out or go back by car with some of the other fellows from the base who had driven. The weather forecaster at Presque Isle indicated that the thundershowers were only local and that I could probably get back to the field if I wanted to wait until later in the evening. I didn't want to have to leave the plane at Fort Fairfield because I knew I would have difficulty getting back the next day to retrieve it. I often returned to the base after dark, so I decided to sit it out. One of the men from Loring Air Force Base, a nearby Strategic Air Command base, stayed around to keep me company.

At about 10 p.m., it looked as if I could easily make it. There had been no thunderstorm activity or rain for about two hours. I could see the lights of the Canadian customs house about three miles to the east and the glow of the lights from Loring AFB about twenty miles to the north. Several stars were visible. I was sure the weather was well above visual flight rule minimums, but just to be sure, I invested fifteen cents and called the Presque Isle tower to check field conditions. The weather was not as good there, although the field was only twelve miles to the west—there was no rain or thunderstorm activity, but there were scattered clouds at two thousand feet and visibility was down to five miles. That should have been a warning, but I was anxious to get back, and I told the tower I would be over the field in about ten minutes.

My radio equipment at that time was only a low-frequency receiver and a single frequency transmitter, 3023.5 kilocycles. Presque Isle does not monitor that frequency, although they could call me over the radio range station at Presque Isle. After a good preflight of the plane to be certain it was ready for flight, I lined the plane up at one end of the 1,000 foot grass runway. The runway had no lights, so my friend lined his car up at the other end of the runway with its lights on. The procedure was for me to aim for his lights, then make my takeoff run. I did so, taking off to the east. It was only then—after I had gotten into the air—that I sensed that all was not well with the weather. By then it was too late. You can take off but not land at Fort Fairfield after dark.

At six hundred feet I started my turn to the left and it was then that I saw the solid wall of fog and clouds between Fort Fairfield and Presque Isle. It was clear with good visibility and ceilings to the north and east, but not to the west, toward Presque Isle. I flew along the edge of this wall of fog and clouds for about five minutes. I could not get over or under it.

The only other lighted field in the area was at Loring Air Force Base, for which I had no clearance to land. Fortunately Loring does monitor 3023.5 kc. I switched to their range frequency. Although I knew I would at best be an unwelcome guest, I saw little choice but to call them and then land. At least I knew they could quickly establish my identity.

I was just about to turn toward Loring when suddenly I saw the Presque Isle beacon through a break in the clouds. I had no desire to land at Loring, and I quickly turned toward the beacon, increasing power at the same time. I thought that I must have come to the edge of the wall of fog and clouds. In my haste to avoid having to land at Loring, it never occurred

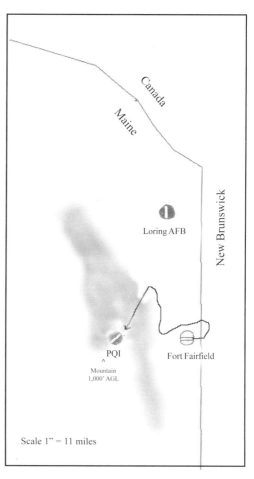

Fort Fairfield is a grass strip with no runway lights so once you take off at night you cannot return. The fog/cloud layer was not apparent until I was in the air. A "sucker" hole in the clouds enticed me to try to sneak through, but then closed up once I had started through. I was very lucky to have survived. Many don't.

to me that perhaps I was trying to sneak back to Presque Isle through a narrow break in the clouds—a break that might close up behind me.

Presque Isle was only ten miles away when I turned toward the beacon, and with an airspeed in excess of 100 mph I covered ground rapidly. I was just a couple of miles from Presque Isle and beginning to relax when all of a sudden I was in the middle of a cloud that had closed up the opening I was trying to sneak through. I was flying blind.

The next sixty seconds I will never forget—I had read articles in *Flying Magazine* about instrument flying, and I had several hours in the link trainer, but this was the first time I had ever been in the midst of instrument conditions, and at night, and only 800 feet above the ground. The first thirty seconds were the worst—I lost 300 feet of altitude and swung off to the right before I got the plane, and myself, under some semblance of control. The next thirty seconds I sweated out not knowing where I was—whether in a single cloud or a whole wall of them. Six miles to the west of Presque Isle and directly in my path if I went on beyond the field was a mountain more than a thousand feet high. I didn't know whether I would break into a clear area before then or not. I also knew that if I didn't come out of the clouds in a hurry I would have to start climbing and then make a 180 degree turn to get out into the clear area behind me.

Fortunately, as it turned out, I did come into the open, just over the edge of the field. There was a blanket of fog starting to envelope the far edge of the field. It didn't take me long to get on the ground.

* * *

From this experience I learned at least a couple of lessons. Never assume that because the weather is good at your point of departure and at your destination, that it is good in between, no matter how short the distance may be. In this case it was only twelve miles!

The other lesson, probably just as important, is not to be afraid to swallow your pride once you find out you are wrong. In this case, once I determined that I could not safely get to Presque Isle under visual flight rules I should have landed at the only other field available, even if I would have been an unwanted guest at a Strategic Air Command base. It would have been far better to have been an unwanted guest there than to have entered a graveyard spiral, foolishly attempting to get to Presque Isle. As I look back over those first thirty seconds when I lost three hundred feet of altitude and veered off to the right, I can't help thinking how close I must have come to being another statistic.

Some Observations—Fifty Years Later

Luck was truly with me that night, although I am not sure I fully appreciated this at the time. I was scared, however, and I started to realize that I was not invincible.

This started my lifelong practice after every flight of consciously asking myself "what aspect of this flight could I have done better?" and "how would I rate my performance on this flight?" Even today when reviewing my log book I can often focus my mind back to a given flight and remember not only the thrill of that flight but also what I could have done better.

The Other "Me"

Another thing I got into the habit of doing when flying was to have an ongoing dialogue with myself strictly about the flight. Some part of me acts as my subconscious flight instructor who is continually watching my performance, and when he notices something he doesn't like, he will interrupt whatever I am doing to tell me so. This dialogue is often sarcastic: "Who is flying this airplane? Are you going to leave the flaps down for the entire flight? Get with it, Gross!"

In turn, I am expected to respond to this "other me." But the key is that this dialogue is out loud and takes place whether I have a passenger with me or not. In fact, I could be having a conversation with a passenger, and this "other me" will interrupt with no apology for doing so.

One of his favorite commands—and that is what it was—"Fly the airplane!!!"

This "out loud" voice comes whenever my internal pilot thinks I need advice. He is not timid about providing it, and loudly. I usually acknowledge with something straightforward and honest, like: "thank you!" Pilots who survive fifty years of flying have learned that alibis and excuses have no place in the cockpit.

After such an exchange I usually turn to my passenger and make the excuse that "I talk to myself when I am flying." I do not attempt to explain further. My passenger will not understand that there really are two of us flying.

I suspect that to most people this sounds corny. You may think I am either a little off my rocker, or in my own world. I plead guilty: I am in my own world, a world that exists when the wheels of my plane leave the ground.

At that point I am on my own "Island In The Sky."

5

A Few Seconds of Stark Terror
September 9, 1955

There is an old saying in aviation:

Flying is hours and hours of sheer boredom,
punctuated by a few seconds of stark terror!

The problem is that you never know when those few seconds of stark terror will occur. And they don't necessarily wait until the pilot has had lots of experience.

September 9, 1955

I had with me another second lieutenant who was bumming a ride to Rochester, New York. Normally I would have left early enough in the day to complete the flight in daylight, but for some long-forgotten reason, we got away from Presque Isle in early afternoon. This was my fourth trip to Rochester, and, in fact, I had made the same trip just the previous weekend. With just 190 hours of flying time, I was then in that dangerous stage in my flying where I was overconfident. I also had fewer than nine hours of night flying experience.

The weather en route to Burlington, Vermont—our fuel stop— was adequate but there were strong headwinds. This normally three-hour flight took four hours, and we landed in Burlington about 30 minutes after dark. Our average ground speed was 73 mph.

Oil Level Not Checked

Under the arrangement at the time, passengers bumming rides paid for the fuel and oil costs. Once on the ground, I left my passenger to supervise and pay for the refueling while I went into the flight service station to check on weather. When I came back, the plane was fueled. I asked my passenger about the oil, and apparently it had not been checked. The engine has a four quart capacity, and when I checked, it only had 2 ½ quarts left. I went to find the gas attendant but found that he had just left for the evening, and that no oil was available. I had yet to learn the hard way to always carry an extra quart with me.

Then my almost-fatal rationalization took place. I had used 1½ quarts on the four hour flight to Burlington. I reasoned that if it took another four hours to Rochester and used another 1½ quarts, that would still leave a full quart in the system. It would be close, but certainly that seemed like an adequate margin. Or so I rationalized. The alternative was to stay overnight in Burlington and wait until the gas attendant came back in the morning. I decided to fly on.

There was a weather front between us and Rochester, and I realized from my weather briefing that I could not get over the Adirondack Mountains in the dark which I would have to do if I went direct. The alternate route was to take the low-frequency airway south to Glens Falls and Albany, and then the low-frequency airway—identified as Green 2—that goes west to Utica, Syracuse and Rochester. That way, if we needed fuel, we could always stop at Syracuse. The forecast was for ceilings to remain at about 3,000 feet overcast over the entire route, and headwinds the whole way. We really had no choice, so we started out about 7 p.m.

Headwinds at Night

As forecast, we had headwinds, and we were bounced around a great deal. The visibility was probably 5 miles. The ceiling was pretty much the forecast 3,000 feet, which was adequate, but certainly not good. We had no real trouble staying on the Green 2 airway, using the radio range "beams," but we could not easily determine where along the beam we were at any given moment. Every 40 or 50 miles, we would pass over one of the low-frequency range stations, and only then would we know with precision where we were. Such was the navigation system of that era. The headwinds we had had on the flight into Burlington were still with us and we were making poor time. I concluded we would probably have to stop in Syracuse for fuel.

Punctuated By Stark Terror

Three-and-a-half hours after leaving Burlington, we ran out of the "boredom" and into the "seconds of stark terror" stage of the flight. Our oil pressure gauge showed that the oil pressure was rapidly falling toward zero!

Zero oil pressure? How long will an air-cooled engine run without oil? Probably only a few minutes. And without an engine—what then?

Where were we? How far ahead was Syracuse? We didn't know exactly, but we knew it was too far. We had to get to an airport quickly. Visibility below the clouds remained about five miles, but we were bouncing around like a drunken sailor in the night sky.

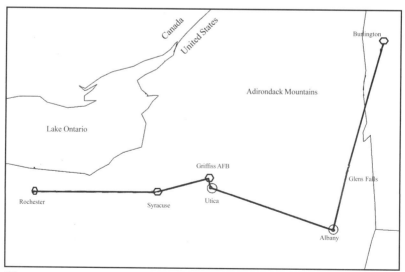

The route was not a straight line, but fortunately the low-frequency airway followed the major cities and towns, including Utica, which was close to Griffiss Air Force Base. If we could have gone directly from Albany to Syracuse or Rochester, we would have been too far from Griffiss AFB to see their split beacon.

Airport Split Beacon

Then, out in the distance, just becoming visible, was the split white light of a rotating airport beacon about 45 degrees off to our right. An airport beacon rotates approximately once every second or two, with a green beam and a white beam, 180 degrees apart. A split beam where the white beam is actually two distinct beams very close together was what we were seeing, and a split white beam was used to designate military airports. Then we both knew where we were!

There was only one military airport along our route—Griffiss Air Force Base. We immediately turned toward the rotating beacon, now only three or four minutes away if the engine kept running. It was about 11 p.m. Could we raise the tower by radio?

"You can't land here"

As I explained earlier, in those days the radio we had was rudimentary by any standard, particularly for small civilian aircraft. The standard transmitting frequency was 3023.5 kilocycles, and we listened for a reply on 278 kilocycles. The range of the transmitter was about 30 miles, but that depended largely on atmospheric conditions. We were lucky; we made contact on the first try.

A very sleepy airman's voice responded to our distress call. In a very authoritative tone he told us that we could not land at Griffiss since it was a military field. I am not sure exactly what words we used in response but the long and the short was that we were going to land, and the only question was whether he was going to help us land on the correct runway or not. Then I added: "There are two Air Force officers on board."

"Did you say, Sir, there were two Air Force officers on board?"

"Affirmative!" I responded and, of course, this young airman had no idea whether we were a four-engine aircraft with two generals on board, or, as in fact, we were only two very anxious second lieutenants. We didn't enlighten him.

Full Cooperation

We had his full cooperation at that point and landed without incident—our engine was still running. A follow-me jeep led us to base operations where the Officer of the Day had been roused out of bed to welcome the two Air Force generals or whoever might be on board.

The rest was anti-climactic. We were down to about a quart and-a-half of oil. The oil pressure had dropped to zero because the oil pump was not picking up any oil from the oil pan, only air. I suspect our being bounced by the heavy winds aggravated the problem. I also suspect that the engine was not intended to run on less than two quarts. Oil is, of course, the lifeblood of an engine, so starve the engine of oil and it won't run for very long.

The Air Force gave us some oil to get us back to the four-quart level, but did not have low-octane aviation fuel so we could not get fuel. After about an hour on the ground we took off to make the short hop over to Syracuse for fuel, 35 miles west of Griffiss.

Continue On To Syracuse and Rochester

Once we got to Syracuse you would have thought we would have collapsed onto a couch in the pilots lounge—a motel would have required money. But such is the energy of youth that once refueled we got right back into the Cessna and once again fought headwinds for two hours into Rochester. And, when I say "fought" consider this: it is 77 miles between Syracuse and Rochester. My flight log says it took 2 full hours (at 38 mph!). The understatement of the evening: my pilot log notation says: "very heavy headwinds."

And so, about 3 or 4 in the morning, a flight that just the previous week had taken 6 hours 25 minutes ended up taking 10 hours 15 minutes, plus ground time at three airports, instead of just one.

Quick Turnaround

My log book shows that on September 12—barely two days after we arrived—I turned around and flew back to Presque Isle, this time in 5 hours and 40 minutes, flying directly across the Adirondacks to

Burlington. Neither my recollection nor my log book shows whether my passenger returned with me or not.

A final note. I had learned an obvious lesson: oil consumption is not proportional to flight time; it is also dependent on the amount of oil in use. As oil is consumed, the remaining oil has to do the work of a larger quantity. It gets hotter and is consumed at an increasing rate. How much longer would the engine have continued? I will never know. But I do know that if the engine had "seized," I would not likely be around to relate this experience.

We were lucky. If we had not been on the Green 2 airway we would not have seen the Griffiss AFB beacon. Five miles visibility may sound like a long distance to the uninitiated, but at midnight in turbulent skies, and in a crisis, it is not very much. And if the oil pressure had dropped five minutes earlier, or five minutes later, we would not have had an airport immediately at hand.

6

Low-Frequency
Radio Range Stations

I started flying at the tail end of an era often referred to as the "Bonfires to Beacons" era. This was the transition period between the pioneers of flying and the start of the era where pilots were able to fly under instrument conditions. I feel very privileged to have experienced that long-forgotten time.

Air Commerce Act

The "Bonfire to Beacons" era started in 1926 with the passage of the Air Commerce Act. This Act established the Aeronautics Branch under the Department of Commerce, and was the first involvement of the federal government in the regulation of aviation. Until about that time almost all flying was in daylight and in visual flight conditions. Early on, the Aeronautics Branch concluded that the most important step it could take initially was to develop a lighted airway system that would permit pilots to fly visually from beacon to beacon at night. The first airway light beacon was put in operation in December, 1926, and by the following July the Aeronautics Branch had 2,000 miles of lighted airways. By 1929 this number had increased to 10,000 miles, and by 1933 to 18,000 miles. At first these beacons were placed at 10-mile intervals, but with higher candlepower they eventually were placed

43

every 15 miles. Given the distances involved, installing this beacon system was a massive undertaking.

While lighted airways permitted flying at night, they did so only under visual flight conditions in which pilots could see where they were going. Two things were needed: a way for pilots to fly in bad weather without visual reference to the ground, and the ability to communicate with ground stations. By that time, the Army had developed heavy direction-finding equipment that could be put in an aircraft to identify the bearing to a ground station, but the weight of such equipment, including large, direction-finding antennas, made this equipment impractical. What was needed was a system in which most of the equipment was on the ground, and the equipment in the aircraft was very light weight.

This is one of the early beacon lights located 10 miles apart, along the entire 18,000 mile airway system. This allowed pilots to fly under visual flight conditions at night. Note the identifying number on the roof.

Development of A New System

By late 1928 a new system was being developed which met these requirements. It involved extensive equipment in a series of ground stations along the airways, but required only a light-weight receiver in the aircraft itself.

Three elements were involved in this system:

(1)   Ground to air voice communication;
(2)   A radio navigation system; and
(3)   A series of radio markers at key locations

The first was a series of ground radio communication stations that could communicate with aircraft using the human voice. These ground stations were connected with each other over telephone lines and permitted pilots to get weather information while en route, as well as to obtain landing instructions at key airports. This was a "duplex" system, with the pilot transmitting on one frequency and listening on the other. In 1955, when I started flying, the pilot transmitted on 3023.5 kilocycles and listened on 278 kilocycles, or on the Low-Frequency Range Station frequency (see below).

The second of the three elements was a navigation system referred to as Radio Range Stations, or Low-Frequency Radio Range Stations. These radio range stations had an effective range of about 100 miles in every direction and were located typically every 200 miles except in congested areas. Each radio range station involved a complex outdoor antenna system, an 18 by 21 foot building, and a great deal of on-going maintenance. The initial cost of each installation was $270,000 in 2008 inflated dollars, and annual maintenance amounted to an additional $125,000. That was a huge sum when you consider how many installations were required with an 18,000-mile system of airways.

The signals transmitted by these radio range stations were received by pilots on the same receivers on which they received voice communications but on different low frequencies. The antennas were set up to create "beams" which allowed the pilot to stay on a known course, although he could not know where along the beam he was actually at. However, when a plane passed directly over a range station he would know his exact position because he would pass through a "cone of silence." With range stations up to two hundred miles apart, and the slow speeds of the aircraft, the pilot would know where he was and his actual ground speed only once or twice an hour.

The third element was a series of "fan" markers at key points along the

The antenna system for a radio range station. It was a high maintenance system but permitted instrument flight in bad weather.

airway, and in the landing approach. They transmitted low-power signals that were received only as the aircraft passed directly over the beacon transmitters. This provided positive identification of exactly where an aircraft was, which was particularly important on the landing approach.

All three of these elements were essential to allow flight in bad weather. It was not enough that the pilot was able to travel from one radio range station to another along an airway; he also had to know what the weather would be at his destination. Without voice communications, even a rudimentary air traffic control system was not possible. The fan markers provided the final element—certainty as to exact position when passing over a specific point along the airway or the final approach fix to the runway in landing.

The first installation of a series of radio range stations along an airway of any distance was in late 1928. Initially, expansion was slow. The Aeronautics Branch was concentrating their limited funds on expanding the airway light beacons. But progress accelerated in the early 1930s, and by late 1933, had expanded to include all 18,000 miles of airways. For the first time, scheduled air service was possible both in good weather and in bad.

How the Radio Range Stations Worked

The heart of the radio range system was the station itself, and, to appreciate fully this era in aviation, it is important to understand how the station actually functioned.

The antenna system of each ground station created two simultaneous transmissions on the same frequency. These two transmissions were directional, and each transmission sent out a radio signal in a pattern that, when looked at from above, looked like two sets of figure "8." As can be seen from the diagram on the next page, the two figure 8 patterns were created at approximately right angles to each other.

The radio signal sent out by one of the two transmission patterns was the Morse code letter "A," which in code sounds like "dit-dah." The radio signal sent out by the second of the two transmission patterns was the Morse code letter "N" which in code sounds like "dah-dit."

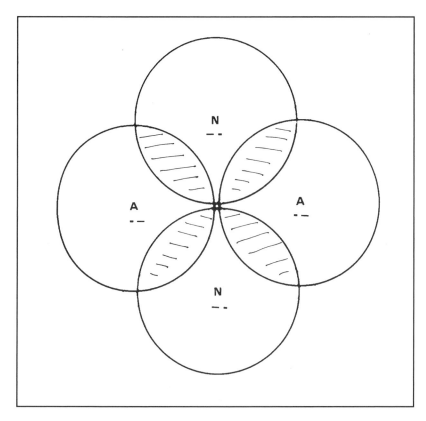

These two transmissions were simultaneous: that is, at the exact instance that the Morse code letter "A" was transmitted by the first transmitter the second transmitter was sending the Morse code letter "N." If you were in one of the two circles labeled "A" on this diagram, you would hear only the Morse code letter "A" or "dit-dah dit-dah."

Likewise, if you were in one of the two circles labeled "N" you would hear only the Morse code letter "N" or "dah-dit dah-dit."

But if you were in an area where the "A" and "N" circles overlapped (the shaded area) you would hear both the "A" and the "N" and close to the center of the shaded area you would hear a solid tone. It is this solid tone (or the beam) that tells the pilot that he is either on, or crossing, an area where the two patterns overlap.

If you were receiving this solid tone, and were flying outbound or inbound on the precise magnetic inbound or outbound course to or from the station, you would continue to hear the solid tone. But if crosswinds started pushing your aircraft from this precise course and the plane wandered off of this overlapping signal, the solid tone would start to change to either the letter "A" or "N" depending on where you were. The pilot would then adjust his heading slightly to correct for the wind drift to get back "on the beam."

Pilot Orientation

With a little bit of patience a pilot could easily locate which of the four sectors he was in. Looking at the illustration (with north being to the top), assume the pilot picks up the letter "N" distinctly. He knows he is in either the north or the south sector, and that he is not crossing an area where the two patterns overlap. He probably already thinks he knows which "N" sector he is in, but to make certain, he would turn the airplane so that he would be going generally toward the station (the center point in the illustration). Assuming the pilot believed he was in the top, or northern sector, he would turn the airplane so it was flying "south." At the same time he would turn the volume on his headset down so that he could just barely hear the signal. In a few minutes the volume in his headset would either increase or decrease, and this would tell the pilot whether he was north or south of the station. If the pilot wanted to fly to the station, and knew he was north of the station, he would fly a 180 degree heading, knowing that he would eventually intercept the overlap of one of the "A" and "N" sectors. He would then turn to the inbound heading.

The pilot then had to be quite alert to the slightest change in signal strength or variation in the solidness of the "A"+ "N" tone. It was very easy to wander off this narrow beam. The beam would get narrower the closer the plane got to the station, requiring constant correction and enabling the pilot to precisely home in on his chosen route.

Directly over the station there was a "cone of silence" and when he encountered this "silence" he knew exactly where he was. Often this cone of silence was the final approach fix to the runway. At low altitudes the cone of silence might last only one or two brief seconds.

Now take a look at the second illustration on the next page which is different only in that it depicts the "beam" itself. This is what it would look like on the Sectional or Approach chart, although the "beam" designation would also show the inbound or outbound magnetic heading.

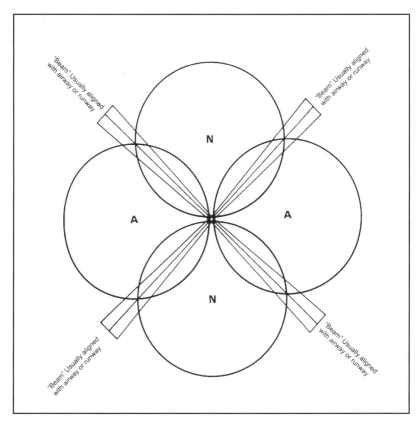

Beams Aligned With Runway

The two figure "8" patterns were not always at 90 degrees to each other, but could be varied based on the requirements of a particular location. For example, an east-west airway might have one of the two transmission patterns aligned precisely to the direction the airway was from the station. But the second transmission pattern might be aligned with the instrument runway, which was unlikely to be precisely 90 degrees from the first transmission pattern. Obviously, placement of the ground antenna was critical when the station was being used in connection with instrument landings.

Since this radio range station was also used to align the plane with the instrument runway, there could be more than one radio range station but on different frequencies to provide landing input for more than one runway.

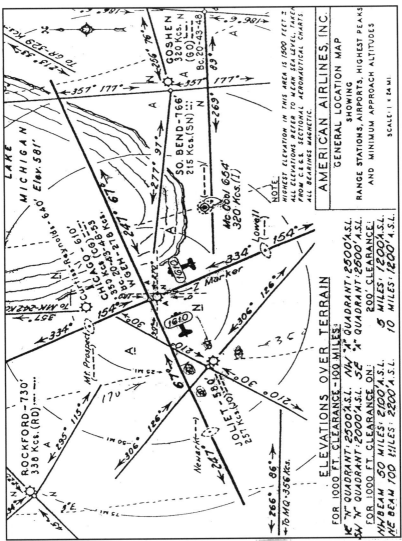

The two low-frequency range charts on this and the next page are copies of plates provided to American Airline pilots in 1940. The plate on this page is a "general location map" of the Chicago area, centering on Midway Airport in Chicago. Note that there are radio range stations shown at Rockford, Joliet, South Bend, and Goshen, as well as the Chicago station. Looking at the Chicago station you will see the four legs outbound clearly shown along with both the outbound and inbound courses. The frequency of the range station (350 kilocycles) and the minimum crossing altitude at the station (1610 feet) are both shown. The incoming pilot would use this chart to fly to the Chicago range station, and would then go to the approach plate shown on the next page to make his actual approach.

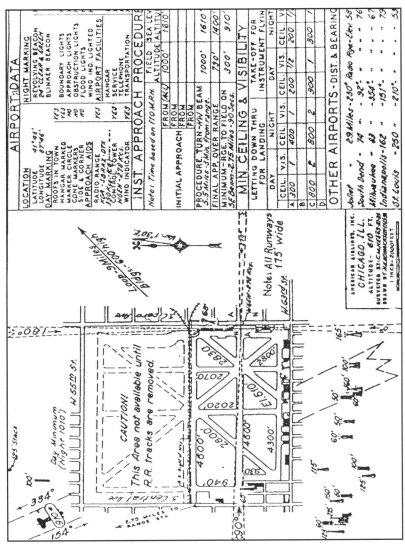

This is the approach plate to the Midway Airport. At the lower left hand corner is an airplane symbol and the number "910." This indicated that 910 feet above sea level (300 feet about the ground) was the minimum descent altitude to which the pilot was allowed to go on his final approach until he saw the runway. Also note the inbound heading of 154 degrees. This is heading to the runway from the Chicago range station shown on the previous page. The incoming pilot in bad weather would have flown to the Chicago range station, flown outbound on the NW beam (334 degrees), made a procedure turn reversing direction, flown back to the range station to cross the range station at 1,400 feet, then would descend to 910 feet for the 2.75-mile leg from the range station to the landing runway.

Nonprecision Approaches

I am sure your first impression in today's era of global positioning satellite navigation (GPS), instrument landing system (ILS), and auto-pilot coupled approaches, is that this system was very crude, and truly it was. Today a pilot primarily has to know which buttons to push. But in this earlier era, the pilot had to have constant situational awareness and pay continual attention to what he was hearing. When flying to a station, even when fully "on the beam," winds constantly changed causing the aircraft to drift to one side or another. The pilot had to be sensitive to the slightest change in tone in his headset because at 50 or 75 miles from the station the beam, or overlap of signals, was quite wide. Close to the station, the beam became quite narrow and if the pilot was not on top of it, he could easily fly over the station slightly to one side and entirely miss the cone of silence.

Pilots using this system became very skilled. This can best be illustrated by the landing minimums. Look at the minimums shown on the approach plate (page 51) and the Minimum Ceiling and Visibility table on the lower right hand corner:

Landing: day–300 feet; night–400 feet; one mile visibility.
Takeoff: day or night–200 feet; one-half mile visibility.

There is not much difference between these minimums and the minimum of a nonprecision GPS approach today. The skill level required, however, was several magnitudes greater.

Static Interference

Probably one of the most difficult problems encountered with the radio range navigation system was that the low frequencies used (190-565 kilocycles) were also subject to static interference, particularly from thunderstorms, even storms that were hundreds of miles away. Snow and rain also created static that could wipe out reception. Thus, when a pilot needed the navigation system the most—in a storm, or an instrument landing down to minimums—he always had the risk that he would lose all reception completely, and would truly be blind. If en route, he could proceed on a dead reckoning course, hoping that by the time he got close to his destination airport the static would clear up and he would regain a usable signal, or possibly reach visual flight conditions. Static was a constant problem until the VOR system of navigation was introduced, which uses very high-frequency radio signals that are not subject to static.

Low-Frequency Airways Continued Into the 1950s

The radio range stations were the standard until well after World War II when the first VOR navigation systems were installed. However, the switchover to the VOR system took many years. In mid-1952, there were 45,000 miles of new VOR airways, but still 70,000 miles of the low-frequency radio range airways. Some were still in operation in remote areas of the United States into the late 1950s. I learned to fly in northern Maine, and because of its relative remoteness, this was one of the last areas to install a VOR navigation system. Most pilots getting their instrument ratings in the 1950s were in more populated areas and never had the unique opportunity that I had to fly with the older system. I did find several radio ranges still in operation in central Alaska in the mid-1970s, but they have all been decommissioned by now.

Lucky To Have Experienced

I said at the beginning that I learned to fly at the end of the radio range era. If you flew only under VFR conditions, radio range stations were not a factor, but if you wanted to fly under instrument conditions you had to be able to demonstrate that you could fly solely by reference to radio range stations.

I had relatively little occasion to use my instrument rating with the radio range system. I got my instrument ticket on August 3, 1956, but sold my Cessna 140 the following month, buying a more sophisticated aircraft, a Cessna 170A, which was equipped for VOR navigation. My military service ended in December and I moved to the New York City area where only the VOR system existed.

I never again spent any significant time in an area where the radio range stations were still operational. But I relish my memories of using the radio range system. Even today, whenever I hear the Morse code letters "A" or "N," my heart speeds up and my mind jumps back to that era. I think I can appreciate more than most the dramatic changes that have taken place in the last fifty years. I was truly lucky to have experienced the tail end of that era.

7

Survival On Squapan Lake
January 18–22, 1956

The northern two-thirds of Maine from about Bangor north was largely unpopulated, with forests, low mountains and many lakes. There was a narrow population belt running up the east side of the state along the New Brunswick-Canadian border. At Presque Isle, about 40 miles south of the Canadian border, this narrow population belt was perhaps only 15 miles wide. It was quite desolate from that point westward to the Province of Quebec

If an aircraft were to go down in this area, rescue would be difficult, not only because of the terrain and lack of roads, but also because of the weather. It gets very cold in northern Maine, and temperatures of minus 25 degrees in January and February were not uncommon. For this reason the Air Force had developed a winter survival course for aircrews, and this course was taught at Presque Isle Air Force Base. Pilots from all over the northern part of the United States were brought in to attend this week-long program.

Winter Survival Course

The program consisted of classroom discussions on Monday and Tuesday. Then on Wednesday morning the crews were trucked out to Squapan Lake, about 15 miles to the west of Presque Isle, with only the equipment and clothing they would have if they had to bail out of their aircraft. They were then left to "survive" until Saturday morning when they were trucked back to Presque Isle. Each class consisted of 15 to 20 students, but once on Squapan Lake they paired off since two was the number of crew members in an F-89. Each pair then fended for themselves, independent of the rest of the class.

Fifteen miles from Presque Isle may not seem very far, but it was. Squapan Lake was remote and, particularly in winter, difficult to get to. There was no one then living within miles, so this remoteness served well to enforce the classroom lessons. Crew members had to be resourceful to survive in this harsh environment. An instructor of the program had a cabin on Squapan Lake and generally kept his eye on things but offered no help to the participants.

But fifteen miles is not very far away if you have a ski-equipped airplane, and therein lies this story.

Conspiracy

I was a ground officer and therefore not required to attend the survival course. I had a roommate in our bachelor officer quarters, and as the radar observer, he was the second crew member of the two-man F-89. And I was only 21. Perhaps you can see where this story is going.

He suggested that it would be very nice if I would fly in and provide "nourishment" for him and several of our friends. After all, he pointed out, the two legs of Squapan Lake were each seven or eight miles long and half a mile wide. I could land after dark and no one would be the wiser. Certainly not the instructor, whose cabin was back a quarter of a mile from the northern end of one of the legs. Once I dropped off my "logistical support," I could then take off to the south and return to Presque Isle AFB where I had special permission to keep my Cessna 140.

It would be easy to make the ten minute flight and land on Squapan Lake on skis. If I did not turn on the plane's "position lights," there would be little likelihood that anyone on the ground, and particularly the instructor, would ever suspect I had been there. How could I not accept that challenge?

I was a little uneasy, but agreed, on the condition that I make the flight on Friday evening. I rationalized that since the camp broke up the following morning, my "deed," or should I say "misdeed," would be somewhat less serious than if it were at the beginning of the encampment. (Wednesday). We agreed on where I would land between 5 p.m. and 6 p.m. It gets dark around 3 p.m. in January.

Weather and Ice Conditions

Now let me digress a moment and say something about the normal weather conditions one finds when landing on lakes in northern Maine in January. Temperatures well below zero Fahrenheit are the rule at that time of the year. Typically a lake freezes solidly by the beginning of December and snow that falls thereafter on the ice makes a good runway for landing an aircraft. You need some snow to provide friction to slow the plane. Ski-equipped aircraft have no brakes and friction with the snow is what stops them.

Airplanes on wheels use differential braking to turn, but ski-equipped airplanes have no brakes. The only way to turn a ski-equipped

Squapan Lake as seen from my Cessna 140 looking toward the north. The lake is shaped like a "U." The survival camp was on the leg on the right, at the very end. I approached the lake from the south and landed three quarters of the way up the right leg, to the north (arrow). No one could have heard the engine noise at the survival camp.

airplane is to have enough speed so that air passing over the rudder has a turning effect. That requires a speed close to the takeoff speed.

January, 1956, was not a normal January. For about a week, the outside air temperatures had become unseasonably warm, and, in fact, had risen above 32 degrees. That, plus the warming action of the sun, caused the snow on top of the ice of the lake to melt. Then, each night, the temperature dropped below freezing and this top level of snow became ice again. The result after a week of this melting and freezing was a surface on Squapan Lake that can best be described as "glare ice." There was no snow layer—only ice. Glare ice provides virtually no friction.

The Landing

Friday, January 18 was the date. I landed my plane without incident about two miles from the northern end of the eastern leg of Squapan Lake. I slowly taxied toward the northern end of the lake. I say slowly, but what I really mean is I went as slowly as I could with the engine barely idling. I was still moving between ten and fifteen miles an hour which was much too fast under the circumstances.

I stopped the engine about half a mile from the northern shoreline. The engine stopped; the plane did not. The glare ice was providing too little friction. After coasting perhaps two hundred feet, I finally came to a standstill.

I waited. After about five minutes I saw several people with flashlights coming out from shore toward me, obviously my roommate and our friends. But they seemed to be coming very slowly, obviously affected by the glare ice as well. That was when I made my mistake.

I got impatient, and started the engine to close the distance between us. With the absolute minimum power setting, the plane quickly accelerated back to ten to fifteen miles an hour with little control or ability to turn or stop quickly.

Unfortunately, the northern end of Squapan Lake was very shallow and contained a number of tree stumps sticking up out of the ice—not tall ones but mostly stumps sticking two to four feet above the ice. While there was a full moon that night, it was partly cloudy and I did not see that I was headed directly toward two or three of these stumps.

By the time I did, it was too late to stop or turn. About all I could do was turn off the engine, and hope for the best.

I avoided hitting one of the stumps head on, but the top of that stump grazed my left wing strut as I went by. The leading edge of the horizontal stabilizer in the tail section then took a bigger hit, impacting the stump with enough force to cause the plane to lurch to a stop.

I got out and looked at the horizontal stabilizer damage. Initially I did not realize in the dark how much damage had been done. The tail section of the airplane had been twisted and was no longer lined up with the fuselage. The plane was clearly no longer airworthy. I was grounded!

Joined by the Co-Conspirators

Shortly thereafter my roommate and our friends reached me. There was nothing we could do. The airplane could not fly.

You can see the damage in two places in this picture. The point of impact was the horizontal stabilizer on the pilot side. Note the dented metal. When the horizontal stabilizer hit the tree stump, the momentum of the plane then twisted the tail section. Note the bends in the vertical stabilizer close to the fuselage. The whole tail section had to be taken apart, and the bulkheads replaced as well as part of the metal skin. It was just luck that I happened to have my camera with me.

I had been taught from my very first flying lesson that flying an airplane in northern Maine imposed unique survival requirements on the pilot, particularly in the winter. The snow is usually so deep by mid-December that if you go down in an airplane you have no chance of walking anywhere unless you have large, web-type snow shoes. With ordinary boots, you would sink up to your thighs with each step and quickly become exhausted. Even if you think there is a house only a mile or two away, you are taught to stay with the plane. A downed airplane can be seen; a person cannot.

I was prepared, or at least I thought I was. I was carrying a sleeping bag and had rudimentary equipment (knife, first aid kit, signal mirror, etc.). I was young and healthy and felt confident. And I was now faced with my first "for real" survival experience.

The first thing we did was unload the plane of its liquid refreshments. We carried them and my sleeping bag back to shore, and sat down to enjoy the "nourishment." At first it was fun, and sort of like

This picture was taken the next morning. It is interesting because you can see all three skis (see arrows), and how little loose snow there is on the lake. If there had been more snow I would have had more control both in turning and stopping. That night a blizzard came and by the time it stopped there were 8 to 12 inches of fresh snow. This picture also vividly shows how the entire tail section had been twisted. Airplanes are really very fragile.

"beer call" at the Officers' Club. There were about five or six in our little conspiracy including, fortunately, the deputy base commander for Presque Isle. That probably saved me from any official reprimand for this little adventure.

After a couple of hours I learned the first of the episode's many lessons. Lesson #1: Alcohol, while it creates immediate warmth and glow, is terribly wasteful of body energy and heat. By that time the temperature was down to 15 to 20 degrees, and I started feeling cold, and hungry. I had no real food with me; I had expected to be back in time for dinner and thought I would not need food.

Lesson #2: You should assume that every flight, no matter how close to home, can end in tragedy. Having no food with me violated the Boy Scout rule: be prepared.

Lesson #3: I also found out that even with my heavy Air Force arctic parka, my body regulatory system was not able to keep me warm. I had wasted too much heat on the alcohol. I decided it was time to get into my sleeping bag and warm up to keep from freezing. That was when I learned that the sleeping bag I was carrying was also inadequate. I don't recall what it was rated for in terms of low temperature, but whatever it was, it was not enough. I had a long, cold night and swore that the first thing I would do when I got back to the base was buy a warmer bag.

Survival, and A New Day

Dawn came, and the moment of reckoning. With only the six or so friends aware of what had happened the night before, it was somewhat hard to hide the presence of an aircraft a quarter of a mile from shore, or the bedraggled stranger who was now among those on Squapan Lake. I took the initiative and found the instructor, a lieutenant from another base who did not know me. I am not sure exactly how I explained my presence but told him I needed to stay with my plane when the group broke camp that morning. He was gracious enough to say I could use his cabin—and the food supplies in it.

I made arrangements with my roommate to contact Bill, the mechanic at the Fort Fairfield Airport, to tell him of my problem and ask him to fly in to see what needed to be done. The reason I could not leave the plane is that if an airplane is abandoned—or appears to be—

someone else can come along and claim it, or at least take the radio and other equipment. Since virtually everyone flying in this area is doing so on skis, there was a strong possibility that someone would see the plane sitting on the lake unattended, and help themselves.

The survival group left Squapan Lake at about 9 a.m. At about 2 p.m. Bill flew in to assess the damage. He quickly concluded that repairs on the spot were out of the question, and that it would be necessary to remove the wings and haul the plane out. He agreed to return the next day, Sunday, with a truck and several other people to help. With that he flew away.

That night a blizzard hit northern Maine. I was comfortable because I was in the instructor's cabin with an adequate sleeping bag and plenty of food. The next morning there was no question I would not be seeing Bill that day—or anyone else for that matter. The storm continued all day Sunday and all day Monday and finally abated Tuesday morning. By afternoon the sun was out. It looked as if we had gotten eight to twelve inches of snow.

Rescued

Wednesday morning was bright and sunny, and by mid-morning Bill showed up with friends in several vehicles, including a four-wheel-drive flatbed truck complete with chains. I don't recall the details of how the plane was disassembled, but before the day was out, it had been moved to Fort Fairfield, 10 miles east of Presque Isle.

It turned out that although Bill was an excellent mechanic he did not have his CAA Aircraft and Power Plant repair license. He had just never gotten around to getting it, and had technically been working under the supervision of John Philbrick, the owner of the fixed base operation, who was licensed. John, however, was in Florida.

It is almost impossible to make a living in aviation in the winter in northern Maine. John and his wife had therefore gone to Florida where there was plenty of work available. Without him being there to sign off on the work, Bill could make the repairs but could not legally sign off on the work. The plane had to sit until John returned toward the end of March. The plane did not fly again until April 8, 1956.

Airplanes can be insured for ground and in-flight risks, or just for ground risks. I had only ground coverage. Since I had stopped the airplane after landing, and turned off the engine, the accident clearly took place while I was taxiing, and accordingly I was covered by insurance. My recollection is that the total cost of repairs was around $300 in 1956 dollars—$2,000 in 2008 dollars.

Postscript

Of course my presence at Squapan Lake became well known, although not officially. One evening a month or so later at a Friday night "beer call" the Base Commander came up to me and casually said: "Gross, I haven't seen your plane outside of Base Operations recently. Where is it?"

He knew full well where the plane was but I guess he'd decided to needle me. One of my close friends standing nearby responded for me: "Colonel, it was like this. Gross was out flying one night and he flew too low and hit a tree stump." The Colonel smiled, said nothing, and walked away. I never heard anything more about the incident.

8

My Short Career
In Off-Field Landings
1955 and 1956

When you are 22 you know no fear and believe you are immortal. You also think you are a "hotshot" pilot and can do anything. This chapter is a testament to the folly of youth.

I had a short career in landing my Cessna 140 off-field. I made a total of five such landings. Two were at Long Lake in Northern Maine, one was at Bridgewater, Maine, one was at Squapan Lake as described in the last chapter, and the final landing was at Madawka, Maine, on the Canadian border.

Long Lake

Long Lake is about 25 miles north of Presque Isle, and just 15 miles south of the Canadian border. It is a narrow lake, ten miles long. Unlike many lakes in northern Maine, it is accessible by road, and was a favorite place for campers. The terrain is generally hilly, and a hill on the west side of the lake rises to perhaps 300 feet above the water, with about a 15 percent slope. There was a primitive campground at the water's edge, and I saw only a handful of campers when I was there.

I am not sure what prompted several of us to wonder if it would be possible to land an airplane on the up-hill slope. Certainly the slope would greatly shorten the distance the plane would roll, and likewise the takeoff downhill. The idea was to approach the hill at an altitude of fifty or seventy-five feet above the lake, and essentially fly nose high into the hill.

We weren't totally foolhardy; in late July we drove to Long Lake and walked the slope of the hill that we proposed to land on. We needed to be sure that there were no large rocks hidden in the grass, or crevices the wheels could fall into. The hill was not as smooth as a hard-surfaced runway but appeared to be smooth enough. We concluded that our proposed "adventure" was doable.

August 6, 1955: Off-field landing #1. The Saturday following our reconnoitering trip, two of us—a friend in an Aeronca Champ, and I in my Cessna 140—successfully accomplished our objective, landing uphill. The only problem we had, which we had not fully anticipated, was the need to carefully position our planes to keep them from wanting to roll downhill once we had shut down the engines and disembarked from the planes. We turned the planes perpendicular to the slope using engine power, and chocked the wheels with some rocks. When the time came, we removed the chocks, jumped into the planes, started the engines, and after the run-up, turned the planes and took off downhill. It was a rough takeoff but both planes were quickly airborne. That evening we celebrated our successful first attempt at being "barnstormers."

October 8, 1955: Off-field landing #2. We repeated the landing, again without difficulty. Our egos were boosted considerably when one of the campers walked up the hill and introduced himself as a B-36 bomber pilot at nearby Loring AFB. He indicated that he was impressed with our landing technique, and offered his congratulations. The takeoff was uneventful but that was probably because our egos had been inflated by the Air Force pilot's compliments. We were hotshots!

Bridgewater, Maine

October 23, 1955: Off-field landing #3. Since there is no airport at Bridgewater, I landed on a road in a farmer's potato field near the town. Our office secretary lived in a house adjacent to the farm, and I just "dropped in" on her. I am not sure why, other than to impress her with my pilot prowess. She was forty years old, and I suspect the only person impressed with the landing was me. I had no problems with either the landing or the takeoff and I was getting cocky.

Squapan Lake

January 21, 1956: Off-field landing #4. The landing (on skis) was fine. The taxi to shore was a disaster, as described in the last chapter. Maybe I wasn't quite the hotshot I thought I was.

Madawka, Maine

May 13, 1956: Off-field landing #5. My final off-field landing, and

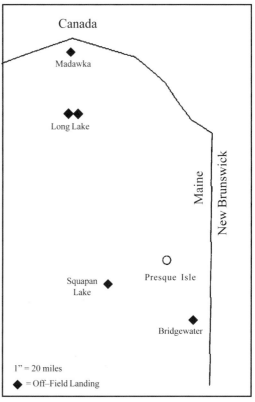

This map shows where each of my five off-field landings took place. I made two successful landings at Long Lake.

the one that convinced me that I was not a budding bush pilot, was at Madawka, Maine, located at the northern tip of Maine on the Canadian border. At the time, it was a small village, with potato fields extending from the border south, east, and west. The Saint John River is the border between the countries. At that time there was no airport at Madawka; I decided to create one, on an impromptu basis. I had a friend with me, and this would give me a chance to demonstrate my flying skills.

Potato fields in northern Maine typically have narrow dirt roads running through them, allowing farmers to move farm tractors or trucks to various parts of the field. The fields themselves were often very muddy, and this was the case on May 13. I selected a field that had a road running approximately north and south not far from the village.

The narrow truck road had two minor curves in it, but I foresaw no problem in being able to keep the plane on it. I touched down headed north at the point marked "A" (see diagram on page 69). I was able to keep the plane on the road at the first, slight bend, and was still rolling out when I reached point "B."

That was when my series of off-field landings came to an abrupt end. My eyes had not been as sharp as I thought. There was a rock on the right side of the road. It was not a big rock, probably only six or eight inches across, and probably about the same height. But the landing gear wheel is not very big either. The right wheel hit this obstacle while the plane was still traveling at perhaps fifteen or twenty miles an hour in the landing roll.

The rock abruptly stopped the right wheel; the left wheel kept going. This caused the plane to swerve to the right, off the narrow road and into the muddy potato field. Both tires then sank into several inches of mud, and the plane's forward inertia caused the tail to rise. The next thing I knew, I was looking straight down into the mud.

It was fortunate that we were not going faster. The tail rose to about 75 degrees from the horizontal, then shuddered a little, and slowly fell back onto the road. The wooden prop had stopped.

Silence.

My passenger and I looked at each other, then slowly opened our respective doors and climbed out into the mud.

Brake and Prop Damage

The propeller obviously needed repair. It was probably out-of-balance, as the leading edge was badly nicked. There was mud on the end that contacted the ground first and stopped the engine.

The right landing gear looked all right but it appeared that we had brake damage. And we certainly needed a new tire and tube.

What to do? It was a Sunday morning, so there were no farmers in the field to come over and help us. Even if there had been someone in the field, they could do little in terms of repair. We were probably a mile or so from the village, so we left the plane and walked into town to a gas station. I called John Philbrick at the Fort Fairfield Airport.

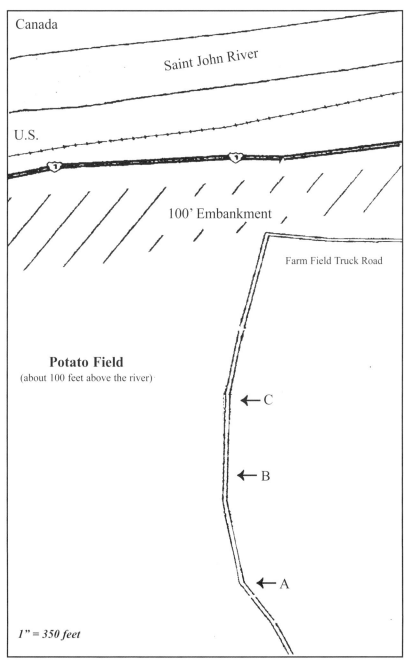

This is the landing area at Madawka, Maine. See text for explanation.

This is how the plane ended up. You can see a lot of large stones behind the tail alongside the road. It was a similar-sized stone on the road which the right wheel hit in landing.

John was my instructor and owner of the Fort Fairfield Airport and he said he would bring a replacement wheel and prop and would drive up and see if he could help us get back into the air.

It was perhaps two hours before John showed up with several others. They quickly and easily replaced my damaged prop with a used one they had brought. Likewise they had a replacement wheel which they installed.

The brake system was another matter. John confirmed that the right brake was broken. I would have to fly the plane back to Fort Fairfield and land, without having a right brake. But could I?

Normally you steer a tail dragger (an airplane without a nose wheel) by using differential braking to control direction on the takeoff roll until the plane gets up enough speed so that rudder becomes effective. This is somewhere around twenty-five or thirty miles per hour. If there is no crosswind, and the plane is lined up directly down the runway, or in this instance, the farmer's tractor road, it should go pretty much in a straight line. There was little or no wind, so a crosswind was not an issue.

Here is another view. The road actually looks pretty solid, albeit rough. You can see why, once the plane went into the field, it stopped so suddenly. There is nothing smooth about the potato field.

With the left brake working, I could keep the plane from turning to the right, but if the plane started to turn slightly to the left, there would be no right brake to help keep it from running off the road on the left side.

But the problem was even more serious. Look at the diagram on page 69 and note that there are two places where the road actually turns ten or fifteen degrees to the right—just to the south of point B where the plane hit the rock, and at point C. Clearly I could not start my takeoff run south of point C since I could not turn. But was the straight road north of point C long enough to get into the air before the road made a ninety degree turn to the right? If not, the plane would go over the embankment.

I paced out the distance. It was about seven hundred feet. The aircraft pilot manual said at gross weight and with no wind I needed 594 feet, but this road was far from a smooth runway, and I probably needed to add an additional fifty or maybe even a hundred feet. Too close for comfort considering the consequences of not being off the ground before the turn in the road. My life would be on the line.

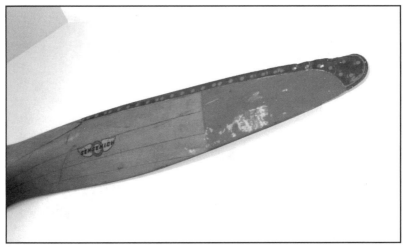

This is the prop that was on the plane. You can see the mud from the potato field, on the center right side of the propeller, untouched since then. The propeller hung on the wall in my library for fifty years. This picture was taken in 2004.

John Philbrick suggested I drain most of my fuel, let him take my passenger, and remove all excess equipment from the plane. I believe he even suggested removing the copilot seat. I did all of this, reducing my weight by probably two hundred fifty or maybe even three hundred pounds. I figured that this should reduce my takeoff run by at least a hundred feet, and perhaps more.

A Dicey Takeoff

As I said at the start of this chapter, I was 22 and immortal. Here I was, on a stretch of narrow dirt road, without a right brake to help in steering, and with a road barely long enough to get off the ground before the road made a right hand turn. I was also assuming that there had been no internal damage to the engine by the sudden engine stoppage. I shudder today at the risks I was taking.

Obviously I made it, or I would not be writing about this incident. I don't recall any of the particulars of how much of the road I actually used, and if I had any trouble keeping the plane lined up on the road. I do recall landing back at Fort Fairfield and being nervous about keeping the plane going straight down the thousand-foot grass runway.

The End

That ended my short career in off-field landings. Looking back, I gambled five times and lost twice; not a very good track record. The two failures were expensive, and discouraged me from continuing with an off-field career. I could ill afford a new prop, brake, or other repairs, or even the down time while the plane was being repaired— three months, in the case of the Squapan Lake incident.

I am not sure that I ended my off-field landing career for the right reason. But end it, I did. My next landing off-field was fifty years later, and that landing was not by choice.

PART II

THE STRUGGLING YEARS
1957 to 1971

9

The Struggling Years
An Overview
1957 to 1971

My two years in the Air Force ended just before Christmas, 1956. This also ended my carefree years in which I could concentrate on what had become my passion—living on an "island in the sky" where I saw the world in three dimensions. Returning to civilian life was like parachuting from a plane over an unknown and desolate wilderness. I was not prepared for the realities of adulthood.

Yes, I had a job with the prestigious accounting firm, Price Water-house in New York City and the prospect of a fine career ahead of me. But I was still a junior accountant, unproven and wet behind the ears, in an extremely demanding, professional world. To have career success I faced the prospect of long years of proving myself. Somehow the fact that I could fly a plane didn't cut much mustard with those with whom I worked at Price Waterhouse. My two years of intense aviation experiences had no place on a junior accountant's resume.

Another reality hit me almost immediately. I now had to support myself, find a place to live, buy professional clothes, find a place to keep my plane, commute to New York City, and make payments of $130.07 a month on my airplane, all on a gross income of a little over $300 a month. All of my military pay had been used for flying; now my starting salary was not much bigger, and virtually all of it had to cover the necessities of life (which included the airplane).

So, when I was discharged in mid-December, I faced the formidable task of adjusting to the realities of adulthood. I reported to Price Waterhouse on January 2, 1957.

Morristown Airport

One of my first tasks was to find an airport where I could keep the plane, one that I could get to without a car because there was no way I could afford both a car and an airplane. I was lucky. One of the partners at Price Waterhouse suggested that I consider living in Morristown, New Jersey, located about twenty miles west of New York City. Morristown had good commuter train service into New York. More importantly, it had an airport with two runways, each 4,000 feet long. It was just three miles from the center of town.

Just before Christmas, I borrowed a car from my parents who were then living in Boston, and explored both the airport and the town. The airport was exactly what I wanted, and the three miles took me less

My Cessna 170A (arrow) on the tiedown line at the Morristown Airport. The rectangular building behind my plane is the Cessna Aircraft parts warehouse built when I was chairman of the Morristown Airport Commission.

than an hour to walk. I found a furnished room in a boarding house in a not-so-desirable part of town, but the rent was only $12 a week. Later, another Price Waterhouse junior accountant joined me and, by pooling our resources, we became able to afford an attractive two-bedroom unit in a garden apartment complex near the commuter railroad station in town. I lived in this apartment until my marriage in 1958.

Flying was a struggle, primarily because there was little money left over from my living expenses. Looking back, I am not sure how I managed to fly as much as I did. My flight log shows that by the end of 1957 I had managed to fly 171 hours, a respectable number, particularly considering my financial struggle. I remember that my Mother was always very good in paying for the fuel whenever I visited my parents in Boston.

I was very frugal in my everyday life. I had to be. Not having a car helped and the exercise in walking to the airport yielded a double benefit. In addition to saving money, it usually meant that once I had walked to the airport I tended to stay there for most of the day, participating in a lot of hangar talk. As a 23-year-old with an impressive airplane, I made friends easily and often traded rides in my plane for fuel. I seldom had to walk back to my apartment since everyone was willing to give me a ride. I largely lived at the airport on weekends that first year.

In fact I made so many friends it was suggested in the summer of 1957 that I try to convince the local town authorities to appoint me to the Morristown Airport Commission. This is exactly what happened, as more fully described in *Chapter 12, Morristown Airport Commission.*

IFR Flying

As described earlier, I had obtained my instrument rating in August, 1956 while in Presque Isle, utilizing the Low-Frequency Radio Range Stations which were then on their way out. Shortly thereafter I purchased my Cessna 170A which was equipped with the new Very high-frequency Omni-directional Radio Range (VOR). I never really learned all of the ins and outs of this new navigation system before I returned to civilian life in the New York area just a few months later. I was ill prepared to fly using this new navigation system, and I certainly wasn't used to the high traffic volume of the New York area, nor the intensity and rapidity of air traffic controllers' instructions. I recall that on one IFR flight from Boston to Morristown I was overwhelmed by the controllers' instructions and the complexity of the system. Fortunately I broke out of the clouds into clear air near Hartford and could cancel my IFR flight plan. I realized at that point how little I knew. It wasn't until 1972 that I really became proficient and comfortable flying IFR.

Romance, and Sale of the Plane

As fully described in the next chapter, I met Inge Stanneck in the fall of 1957, and we were married the following June. While she shared my love of flying—our honeymoon was in our Cessna 170A—our priorities changed. In early 1959 we sold the plane for a down payment on a small house. We couldn't afford both.

From 1959 to 1963 I did not fly, but that did not mean I was out of aviation. In the spring of 1960 Inge and I decided to make a pioneering automobile trip, driving our car behind the Iron Curtain. We visited the Soviet Union, Poland, and Czechoslovakia for a total of four weeks. I call this trip "pioneering" because this was the first year the Soviet Union allowed tourists to drive in their country. Very few took advantage, probably fewer than 25 cars the whole summer.

The reason I mention this non-aviation trip is that there were two Russian aviation aspects—a visit to the Central Aero Club of the U.S.S.R., and the public display of the wreckage of the U-2 spy plane that had been shot down just two months before

Central Aero Club of the U.S.S.R.

One of the things we had been most interested in doing while in Moscow was learning something about the sport flying clubs in the Soviet Union. I had written in advance requesting an interview with the president of the local flying club.

It turned out that there were, in fact, a number of government-sponsored flying clubs in the Soviet Union. At the top of the flying club organization was the Central Aero Club of the U.S.S.R., located in Moscow. The primary purpose of these Aero Clubs appeared to be to train men and women for international competition.

The president of the Central Aero Club was a government employee, and, judging from his office, a well paid and important official. He had two assistants with him, as well as an interpreter. One of the assistants seemed to be making notes and was probably bilingual.

It was an interesting experience and thirty years later when I represented United States sport aviation at the Fédération Aéronautique International meetings, my Russian counterpart, General Karmaloff, who held the title "Hero of the Soviet Union," was impressed that I had taken an interest in Russian sport flying at such a young age.

The U-2

On May 1, 1960, the U-2 spy plane flown by Gary Powers was shot down. We were in Moscow just two months after this incident and the

The wreckage of the U.S. U-2 spy plane which had been shot down only two months before. You are looking at the wings here. A Russian SAM missile exploded below the U-2 in a near miss. The concussion caused the plane to violently flip over, at which point the wings broke off. Gary Powers, the pilot, then bailed out and landed in the outskirts of Sverdlovsk. The wings "fluttered" down to the ground. I learned these details 44 years later from his son, Gary Powers, Jr.

Soviets were exploiting the downing of the U-2. The wreckage was on display, and the line of people waiting to get into the exhibit was a couple of blocks long. We did not have to stand in this line, but were taken directly to the exhibit. They wanted to be sure that we saw what our government had done. Interestingly, the Russians made a distinction between the U.S. government and the American people. They didn't hold us responsible for our government's policies, and we were clearly welcomed in their country.

The Wife Should Fly

From an aviation standpoint, 1961 and 1962 were quiet years. We still wanted another plane, but the time for it had not yet come. Little by little our finances were becoming less strained. There never was any doubt that we would get another plane. The only question was when.

By 1963 our finances had improved enough to permit us to start thinking about another aircraft. Our focus, however, was on having Inge learn to fly. "If a family has a car, the wife should be able to drive it." It seemed to us that this should apply to an airplane, too. Inge was enthusiastic.

I had learned to fly in an Aeronca Champ (7AC) back in 1955, and I figured that would be a good training airplane for Inge. In addition, it would get us back in the air with a minimum cost.

On May 15, 1963, we purchased a 1946 Aeronca Champ and decided we would keep it at the Lincoln Park Airport in northern New Jersey. It had a grass runway and was owned by Ed Gorsky, an eccentric aviation pioneer. We could not keep the plane at the Morristown Airport because it had no radio to communicate with the control tower.

We paid $800 for the plane. Then we had to install an overhauled 65-horsepower engine which added another $500 to our investment. The plane had no electrical system or lights, and the propeller had to be hand-propped to start the engine. Maintenance was virtually nil because the engine had just been overhauled.

As expected, Inge quickly learned to fly the Champ and started to experience the thrill of flying. She soloed just a month later on June 28. Once her instructor said she was ready, she flew to Rochester, New York where my parents had moved from Boston. Inge repeatedly said "Flying was a feeling of freedom for me and I love it."

Both Inge and I had our initial flight training in an Aeronca 7AC "Champ," which had two-seats, one behind the other, and a 65-horsepower engine which was hand-propped.

We kept this plane for only five months. During this period I also flew the plane, accumulating 79 hours. On July 21 my logbook shows I flew my 1,000th flight hour—a milestone for any pilot.

Luscombe 8A

In October, 1963, we had a chance to buy a Luscombe 8A which had been lovingly reconditioned. It, too, had two-seats but with side-by-side seating. It used the same 65-horsepower engine but was faster than the Champ. My logbook entry for my first flight in this aircraft on October 2 consisted of two words: "What performance!"

Inge had to transition to the Luscombe which had a bad reputation of being a "ground looper." The main landing gear were close together and the pilot had to stay on top of the landing roll to keep the plane going straight down the runway until it slowed to taxi speed. She had a good instructor and never had any problem with the plane. When she flew to a neighboring airport to take her private pilot flight test the inspector was impressed when he saw that she had flown the Luscombe. He said he should just sign her off without the flight check but he did

Our Luscombe 8A, a two-seat side-by-side, and a 65-hp engine. Inge got her private license in this plane and looked upon it as her airplane.

give her a check ride, which she easily passed. Inge considered the Luscombe to be "her" aircraft.

As with the Aeronca, the Luscombe had no electric system and no radio. Shortly after we purchased the plane, a portable 90-channel transceiver came on the market. It was a big unit, about the size of a fat briefcase. It weighed about ten pounds and contained rechargeable batteries. It was ideal to use in an aircraft without an electrical system such as the Champ or Luscombe. I purchased one so that we could move the aircraft to the Morristown Airport.

Emergency Landing at LaGuardia Airport

While this book is about my aviation experiences, obviously Inge's experiences and enthusiasm contributed to mine. Here is her account of landing at LaGuardia Airport in New York City one Saturday evening:

One of my memories is landing at LaGuardia Airport in New York one Saturday evening, something that few private pilots ever do. I had flown from Morristown to a private airport on Shelter Island, near the eastern end of Long Island, to attend a fly-in of women pilots, the

Ninety-Nines. It was about one hundred and twenty miles from Morristown, and with a tailwind I made the trip in just an hour.

By late afternoon when it came time to return to Morristown, the winds had increased, and I now had a headwind of close to forty miles per hour. Instead of returning home as quickly as I had come, I found that I was just crawling along. The Luscombe held only thirteen gallons of fuel, and as I got near New York City, I became concerned that I would not have enough fuel to get back to Morristown. To compound my anxiety, it was getting dark and I had never flown or landed at night.

Well, I did the only sensible thing I could do. I was getting fairly close to LaGuardia Airport, and I called them. The conversation went something like this:

N71497:	LaGuardia Tower this is 71497 (my plane number).
Tower:	71497 Go ahead.
N71497:	LaGuardia tower I am a sixty-five horsepower Luscombe airplane about five miles east of you—I am getting low on fuel and need to land—I don't think I can make Morristown because of headwinds.
Tower:	Roger 497—Winds are two-nine-zero at twenty-five knots—Plan straight-in for Runway 31.
N71497:	Tower, I am a new pilot and have never landed at night—I would like to overfly the airport to get oriented.
Tower:	497, Understand this is your first night landing—what is your altitude?—Turn on your landing light.
N71497:	I am at 2,000 feet but I do not have a landing light.
Tower:	Roger 497 proceed directly to the Airport and enter downwind for Runway 31

A few minutes pass.

Tower:	497 we see you over the field—you can turn downwind now—remember you will have a tailwind and will be going much faster—Do you see the runway?
N71497:	Affirmative—do you want me to land on the first part of the runway?
Tower:	497 you can land anywhere on the runway—the Airport is all yours.

Needless to say I was nervous, but I made a perfect landing in that I gently rolled onto the big numbers at the beginning of the runway. The wind was so strong that I came to a complete stop almost immediately. My airplane was still on the big numbers.

Tower:	That was a good landing, 497—Now just taxi straight ahead and turn left at taxiway Joliet.

I had to taxi slowly in this strong wind, and it seemed to take a long time before I came to the first taxiway to get off the runway. The tower then directed me to an area where I could park the plane. All of this probably took about fifteen minutes, and I learned later that the tower officials effectively closed the airport to everyone else while I landed. I am sure I was one of the most inexperienced pilots to have ever landed at LaGuardia, but the tower personnel could not have been more considerate and helpful. They were obviously concerned about my safety and recognized that my decision to land was exactly the right decision on my part.

Once I got parked, I called Mal who drove to LaGuardia. He then had the plane refueled, and flew it back to Morristown while I drove home. That was my one and only landing at LaGuardia Airport, and Mal's first and only takeoff from LaGuardia as pilot.

* * * * * *

I was also flying Inge's airplane, and in 1964 I flew N71497 on a circle tour of the United States, which is described in detail in *Chapter 13, A Solo Flight Around the United States.*

Now We Were Four

Thanksgiving, 1964, was a momentous time for us. Our adopted son, Randolph Eric, joined the family. Three years later our daughter, Michele Andrea joined us. There were now four of us. It was obvious that we needed to sell the Luscombe because a two-place airplane was impractical. The only real decision we had to make was whether to get another, bigger plane, or wait a few years until our children were a few years older when it might be easier to travel.

I felt we could afford a bigger airplane and really wanted to continue flying. Obviously a new airplane had to have seats for four people. I concluded that we should buy a used Cessna 172, a tricycle-geared version of the Cessna 170A that we had owned. A tricycle-geared airplane is one where there is a nose wheel and two main landing gears. There is no tail wheel, and it is much easier to both taxi and land.

The 172 is a popular airplane and more of these planes have been made than any other aircraft. They are still being made as I write this book in 2009. Flying at 124 mph, and carrying about five hours fuel,

This was a fine airplane but it had several maintenance surprises in store for us. It did provide us with a glimpse of the kind of long-distance flying we would be doing once we purchased our Cessna 182 and then our Cessna T210.

the 172 could cover a good deal of distance in a day. It was big enough to carry our family.

On July 25, 1967, we purchased N2549Y for $7,900. In the ensuing 21 months we flew the plane 161 hours, flying several times to El Paso, Texas and Daytona Beach, Florida. From a flying standpoint it certainly served us well during this period. It not only had the seats we needed for the children but it also had enough equipment to allow us to fly long distances and to again fly under IFR conditions.

Unfortunately, this plane had a lot of maintenance issues, and every time we turned around it seemed we had another big bill. We sold the plane in March, 1969, in large part because we saw no end to the unbudgeted and surprise maintenance costs. We sold it for $5,500, about two-thirds of what we had paid.

We did not buy another plane until September, 1972. Finances were certainly a major reason but it was also a very busy time in our lives. I had advanced steadily in Price Waterhouse and was made a partner in 1969. This added further responsibilities involving long hours. Then in 1972, between January and September, I wrote a 540-page book, *Financial and Accounting Guide for Nonprofit Organizations,* which is now in its seventh edition, thirty-seven years later.

I had not lost interest in aviation; to the contrary, I just did not have the time nor money.

10

Romance In The Air
1957

In September of 1957, I briefly met Inge Stanneck in the laundry room of the garden apartment complex we were both living in. She was charming, but our conversation was very brief. I assumed she was already married but asked the wife of one of my airport friends to inquire for me. She was the "Welcome Wagon Hostess" for Morristown and the ideal person to find out. She did and I learned that Inge was a recent immigrant from Germany and was living with her brother and mother. I then got up my courage and asked her for a date. Inge has since written her own autobiography, so let me quote from her book what happened on our first date, on October 19, 1957:

Our first date was a Square and Round Dance at the Morristown Area Newcomers' Club. Mal had borrowed his roommate's car for this date because he did not own a car. On the way back from the dance, he told me that he owned an airplane and asked if I would like to ride out to the airport to see it. Of course, I wanted to. I had never seen a small airplane up close. The Morristown Airport was less than three miles down the road from where we lived.

After we got to his plane, Mal showed me the inside and pointed out that it was not much different in size from the inside of a car. "Would you like to sit in it?" was the next question. Why, yes, I wanted to sit in it. He helped me into the right front seat.

He must have untied the plane when he walked around to the other side, and then got in. He told me that since he did not own a car, he did not get out to the airport very often, and that he would like to take this opportunity to start the engine and run it for a few minutes. At the same time, I could hear what the engine of a small plane sounded like. I told him I had flown in an airplane only once before, from Berlin to Hamburg, at the time I immigrated to the United States.

Mal started the engine, and then began to taxi, pointing out that the plane "drives" just like a car. I was intrigued, of course. I cannot remember whether or not he mentioned that he would take off, but before I really became aware of what was happening, we were in the air!

It was a beautiful, clear night. Not long after we were off the ground we could see the lights of Manhattan, about twenty miles away. Above Manhattan was a full moon. What a beautiful night to go flying, and I have loved night flights ever since.

Those were the days before there were traffic restrictions over large cities, and it was permissible to fly right over Manhattan and sightsee. I was enormously impressed. Next we flew out over the water from Long Island towards Connecticut, and with the moonlight reflecting on the water, it was a picture-perfect sight and a most memorable experience. We landed back at the Morristown Airport about forty-five minutes later. I could not believe that this had happened to me.

My log book shows this entry:

> 10/19/57   First flight with Inge—from Morristown over Long Island Sound at night!

I have always been shy with girls, yet with Inge I felt comfortable enough to take her flying on our first date. Inge had never even been near a small plane, much less flown in one, and yet she was comfortable enough to trust me, and relaxed enough to enjoy it.

Pilots learn to make decisions quickly, and while it may sound trite, I knew that night we would be married. This was the start of our life together. Love at first sight—at the airport!

Several days later I was sent to the Dominican Republic on Price Waterhouse business, and returned just before Christmas. Our second date was on New Year's Eve.

Honeymoon By Air

A little over a month later, on Valentine's Day, and at the Morristown Airport, I asked Inge what her future plans were. She said she wanted to travel. I told her I did, too, and why didn't we travel together. I then asked her to marry me. She said "yes." We were married five months later on June 28, 1958. We have now been married for more than fifty years. My pilot's instincts on our first date were correct.

We took a month for our honeymoon, flying west across the northern part of the United States to Billings, Montana, then north to Calgary, Alberta, Portland, and Corvallis, Oregon. We returned via San Francisco, California, the Grand Canyon, and Kansas City, Missouri. We met all my relatives. For an immigrant who only four years before had been living in Berlin under constant Russian threats, these 68 flying hours on our honeymoon opened up a whole new world for her. Her enthusiasm for travel was, and still is, contagious. She is a gypsy at heart.

Here we are at the airport with our Cessna 170A, just after our marriage ceremony.

Landing at Billings

We had one experience that Inge also recorded in her autobiography more vividly than I could write now, fifty years later. Here are her own words:

Mal had told me that an airplane would always be a part of our lives, so our honeymoon was a trip around the United States and southwestern Canada in his plane. We flew northwest via the Chicago area, Fargo, Bismarck, and Billings, heading for Yellowstone National Park. Billings, Montana, was to be our overnight stop on that particular day. We were glad, because as we approached Billings there were huge storm clouds in the vicinity. They looked menacing with streaks of green in them. We wondered about the brilliant green streaks in those clouds and were to find out very shortly what they meant.

The Billings Airport is located on a plateau overlooking the city. Mal's airplane was a Cessna 170A, a tail dragger, and upon landing the tail spring broke, disabling the plane. Mal informed the tower, and they sent a truck out to meet us on the runway. Just as the truck arrived, the tower informed us that a tornado had been sighted heading for the airport and that we had to immediately get to a protected area. The truck driver had me go with him to a small executive terminal. Mal, in the meantime, was told by the tower where to taxi, and with sparks flying from the broken tail spring as it was dragged along the pavement, went as fast as he could to find protection for the plane in-between rows of T–hangars. The storm hit the airport scant minutes later.

Three men and I stood in the little terminal building and watched from behind a huge plate glass window as the storm unleashed its fury. Cherry-sized hailstones started to fall and were accumulating fast. The wind was ferocious and broke one of the tie-down chains which had been attached to a twin-engine plane just outside the terminal window on the ramp. This plane was then rocking like crazy, tugging on the remaining chain. One of the men said that we had better get away from the window and behind a sturdy wall before that plane came crashing through the floor-to-ceiling plate glass window. The terminal was small, and the only solid wall we could get behind was the one dividing the restrooms. I was semi-hysterical. The crashing, howling noises of the storm brought back memories of air raids. Where was Mal? Nobody knew, but one of the guys assured me he would be OK. But would he be? He was out there somewhere in that turmoil. All I could think of was that I did not want to be a widow at age twenty-three, and after only four days of marriage. As we were heading for the restroom area, the men told me to come with them. Mindlessly I did, not caring that they were going into the men's room. I certainly was not going to be taking shelter in the ladies room all by myself.

We waited until the storm calmed down considerably before we emerged from the men's room. Outside it looked like winter wonderland, except that it was hail instead of snow. Two inches of cherry-sized hail had fallen in only twenty-five minutes. We also found out that we had just survived the only tornado ever recorded in Billings. The wind velocity instrument had been knocked out when the winds hit one hundred fifteen miles an hour!

In the meantime, Mal had taken refuge between two rows of T-hangars, where he was able to partially shelter his plane by moving it as close as possible to one of the hangar doors. However, the plane was not tied down and if a good gust of wind had hit it, the plane would have been badly damaged or destroyed. He was very lucky. Nothing happened to him or the plane, which was a miracle. The tornado had ripped right across the airport and turned

This T-hangar was struck by the tornado, taking off part of the roof and then turning the aircraft upside down. It was just luck that Mal selected a space between the rows of T-hangars that escaped the brunt of the storm.

some hangars and many airplanes upside down. Numerous other planes were badly damaged from the hail. We were awed by the damage. The area where Mal had been had escaped direct contact with the tornado. But, oh, so close it came!

July 2, 1958, went down in history as a day to remember, not only by the Billings Airport, which was partially destroyed, but also in our minds. Every time we fly into Billings, which we do on most of our coast-to-coast flights, we remember that day. I will never forget the only time in my life when I've been in a men's room, with a bunch of men!

* * * * *

We had originally intended to fly from Billings to Livingston, Montana, about 100 miles further west, one of the gateways to Yellowstone Park. We had reservations for a three-day bus tour of the Park. With a broken tail spring the plane was grounded. It would take several days before a replacement could be obtained and installed.

Billings is on a major passenger railroad and we were able to get a train to Livingston and keep our sight-seeing schedule. At the end of this side trip we returned to Billings, picked up our plane, and proceeded on our trip.

11

Mr. Witty's Last Flight
May, 1958

The following is a true story.

As I indicated in a previous chapter, when I was discharged from my Air Force active duty in December, 1956, I moved to Morristown, New Jersey. I rented a room on a weekly basis in a house in a not-too-nice section of Morristown but close enough to the train station for commuting into the City. That was all I could afford. Young staff accountants were not paid very much in those days.

By spring, 1957, another Price Waterhouse friend also had returned from his military service and we decided to rent a garden apartment together in Morristown in the Jacob Ford Village complex of about 150 apartments.

In those days the rental agents for most nice garden apartments were reluctant to rent to bachelors, but when I went looking I put on my business suit and hat, and tried to appear as professional and substantial as I could. I even mentioned I owned an airplane, conveniently neglecting to mention I could not afford a car. So, in May of 1957, we were told by the superintendent's wife, a Mrs. Witty, that an apartment was ours. Nothing was said about a lease, and we did not raise the question.

A Phone Call

Around the end of September, I got a phone call one Friday evening from Mrs. Witty asking me to come to the office the next morning. She did not say why, but I assumed that she now wanted us to sign a lease. The next morning when I went to the office, to my surprise, she cordially invited me into the Witty's private quarters. The office was attached to their apartment.

Mrs. Witty then started beating around the bush, not knowing how to discuss the reason for asking me to the office. After a lot of hemming and hawing it became apparent that Mrs. Witty was more interested in my having an airplane than in getting me to sign a lease. It seems she wanted me to take her and Mr. Witty for a ride over the Delaware River in Pennsylvania. She then made perfectly clear that it was her intention that Mr. Witty would not return from that nonstop flight.

She implied that Mr. Witty would be leaving the airplane—in-flight! Now many people take airplane rides and do not return with the airplane: They jump out of them. But good practice dictates that if you are going to do so, you wear a parachute. Mrs. Witty indicated that Mr. Witty did not have a parachute, would not return, and obviously would be quite dead by the time this was over!

Wow! How does a staid conservative 24-year-old Price Waterhouse accountant respond to a request like that? I certainly did not want to antagonize Mrs. Witty. We had no lease and could be asked to vacate our apartment. We would have no legal recourse. And, of course, she would deny that she had made this request.

Saved By The Firm

Fortunately, just the day before, I had been told I was going to be sent to the Dominican Republic for two months on Price Waterhouse business. I respectfully told Mrs. Witty that I would have to think about her request, but that in any case I would be gone for two months. She reluctantly accepted my excuse, and I got out as quickly as I could.

Now just so there is no misunderstanding, Mr. Witty was about 50 years old, and like the superintendents of many apartment complexes, was a grouch and always complaining to the residents about what they had done to make his job more difficult. No one would be unhappy to see Mr. Witty gone. Mrs. Witty had not suggested or implied that I had to do anything other than just "provide the transportation." I didn't know whether Mr. Witty's departure would be his doing, or, as seemed more likely, Mrs. Witty's. All I was supposed to do was to fly them to a remote area over the Delaware River.

As I said, I got off the hook fairly easily and I hoped that by the time I got back from my trip she would have changed her mind. After all she was obviously troubled by making the request and could not be sure I wouldn't go to the authorities. Maybe with the passage of time she would have second thoughts.

I got back from the Dominican Republic just before Christmas. I didn't call Mrs. Witty.

She Called Me

Alas, just after Christmas she called me. "Mrs. Witty," I said, "don't you think that the Christmas holidays are the wrong time to be making this kind of a flight?" And before she had much of a chance to answer I suggested we wait until after the holidays.

January 15th came around, and guess who called? Now Mrs. Witty had been fairly specific where she wanted me to fly, and using that, I pointed out that there would likely be ice on the Delaware River in January. I noted that the Delaware River flows past Philadelphia and eventually when the ice broke up Mr. Witty might end up floating on an ice patch past the entire city. I wondered if she really thought that was so smart. She got my point.

February came. The weather was terrible. I told her I could not fly in snow and blizzards, and we had to wait until March.

March winds were ferocious. I asked Mrs. Witty whether she would get air sick in all these winds. She had not thought of that.

I am not sure what excuse I gave in April, probably rain.

Ran Out of Excuses

I ran out of excuses in May, and realized she was not going to give up. Reluctantly I agreed to a date toward the end of the month. I was sort of boxed in because my wedding was scheduled for June and I knew that if I didn't get this over with I might have real troubles with my bride ("Sorry, dear. I have to go and drop off Mr. Witty today.") What a way to start a marriage!

So, the flight went pretty much as she wanted. Mr. Witty went for that flight; he did not return. There was never any official inquiry. Mrs. Witty obviously didn't report him missing. His remains never showed up.

The irony of all this was that Mrs. Witty lost her job about six months after her husband "disappeared." She had apparently expected that she would be kept on by the owners. There were one or two maintenance men so she had no trouble keeping the maintenance up. I never did hear what happened, but I suspect she was fired. Perhaps that is justice of sorts.

Now you may ask why am I telling you this. Well, it is part of my "aviation" history, and you will have to admit it is a unique experience.

Statute of Limitations

Yes, I know, there is no statute of limitations for certain crimes. But I was only the taxi driver. I was aware of a draft of air at one point during the flight, but I can't be responsible for what may have happened in the back seat. My eyes were focused straight ahead.

I would point out that it has been more than fifty years since this incident. There was never any record made of his disappearance, and there is no "body" left that can even prove that he had died. By this time Mrs. Witty is probably gone, too. My guess, also, is that it would be difficult from what I have related here to even prove Mr. Witty ever existed.

But I can assure you that he did. I can also assure you there is no way someone leaving an airplane 1,000 feet above the Delaware River without a parachute can possibly survive.

As they say, truth is sometimes stranger than fiction. And that is the truth

12

Morristown Airport Commission
1958 to 1962

At the time I moved to Morristown, the Morristown Airport probably had a hundred small, single-engine airplanes based on the airport, with two large companies keeping business airplanes. In those days large business planes were usually World War II aircraft that had been modified for executive use. I recall that one company had a large hangar at Morristown and operated a modified B-26 and a B-24.

The airport itself was not located in Morristown but was acquired by the town in the 1930s. I do not recall if it was then a small airport but the present airport was built in 1943, presumably as part of the war effort.

In 1957 it had two intersecting, hard-surface runways, each four thousand feet long, and 150 feet wide. It also had an ADF instrument approach to runway 5, utilizing the Chatham low-frequency beacon (still in existence in 2009). There was a control tower, but it was operational only on weekends. The airport was far enough from both the Newark and Teterboro airports so that traffic at these airports did not conflict with our traffic. Clearly the airport had the potential to handle far more traffic. It was a fairly laid-back airport and its activities revolved mostly around small planes and private pilots.

I moved to Morristown in January, 1957, and the airport became the center of my recreational activities. I was then 23 years old and easily fit into the pilot community. My four-seat Cessna 170A was impressive, but more impressive was the fact that I had an instrument rating, something that few private pilots had at the time.

During college I had been quite active in student government and other extracurricular leadership positions, and I became quite accustomed to assuming responsibility. I mention this because in June of that first year, some of my friends at the airport urged me to see if I could get myself appointed to the Morristown Airport Commission. Like most government-run airports, the pilot community felt the members of the Commission did not understand the needs of the airport or of the pilot community. Since the airport was owned by the Town of Morristown, the only people appointed were those living in Morristown, which, of course, I was.

Morristown Airport, circa 1958, located just 20 miles west of Manhattan was an underdeveloped airport at the time. There were two 4,000 foot runways, each 150 feet wide, ideal for the WW II surplus planes that were converted into executive business aircraft. The big hangar was where the B-26 and four-engine B-24 were kept. There were five rows of T-hangars at the lower right side of the picture (2 arrows), plus the tiedown area in the upper right side (arrow) where I kept my plane.

Getting Appointed

I accepted the challenge. The Commission was composed of five commissioners appointed by the mayor of Morristown upon the recommendation of individual aldermen. The key to getting appointed was to convince the alderman in my district that I should be appointed.

The obvious and time-proven method of endearing yourself to an alderman was to work in his election campaign. This I proceeded to do starting in July, and I worked harder than any of his other non-family volunteers.

Unfortunately, towards the end of September I was sent by Price Waterhouse to the Dominican Republic for ten weeks. The month of October and first week in November were critical in an election campaign and, obviously, I could do little to help from the Dominican Republic.

I thought my chances of getting the appointment had fallen through the cracks. I had my roommate keep me informed of the election process, and I kept in touch with my alderman. On election night I sent him an "overseas" telegram to him within hours of his election. It worked, and he recommended me to the Mayor, who then appointed me to a five-year term. I had to be one of the youngest persons appointed. All of the other commissioners had been appointed for political reasons but as I recall, none had any aviation experience. I am sure that having an airplane helped to qualify me.

Authority of the Commission

The ordinance which established the Airport Commission explicitly gave the Commission the authority and responsibility of running the Airport. We were not micro managed by the town's Board of Aldermen. We had to get their approval of our budget, but as long as it was balanced, they had little authority to dictate details to us. We did have to get their approval if we needed to make capital expenditures that involved the credit of the town.

The Commission had two or three employees, and a manager. They were involved primarily in airport maintenance, including grass mowing which was a major function. They also handled all fuel sales, T-hangar rentals, leases of land for large hangars, and tie-down fees.

Since public monies had been involved in building the runways, we also worked with the Federal Aviation Agency, which later became the Federal Aviation Administration (FAA). They rightly wanted to see the airport developed.

Like many government-run airports, the staff were the biggest obstacle to making changes. It was a typical municipal operation—-inefficient, not open to new ideas, and certainly not particularly friendly to the pilot community.

Period of Change and Growth

The late 1950s were a time of great advances in both personal and business aircraft. The use of World War II planes for business travel was largely over. Beech, Cessna, and Piper started

MALVERN GROSS JR.
Airport Commission

The above picture was published in the Daily Record, the local newspaper in Morristown, on Jan. 2, 1958.

to produce comfortable twin-engine aircraft. Single-engine aircraft also made their appearance—the Bonanza, Cessna 172 and 182, and the Piper Tri-Pacer. All these aircraft opened up opportunities for rapid growth in not only personal flying, but also the potential for business aircraft. The first Boeing 707 had been introduced to commercial service in 1954, and it was obvious that at some point executive jets would be available. Ten years later the first Learjet would be delivered. Today there are more than eleven thousand executive or personal jets flying in the world, the majority of them in the United States.

The Airport Master Plan had to keep pace with these changes. Morristown Airport was in a strategic location being only twenty miles from New York City. If carefully developed, the Airport could become a hub for business aviation in the metropolitan area. But we had to change our orientation from one of selling fuel and tie-down space to attracting business from nearby Teterboro and Newark, particularly for business and utility aircraft.

When I joined the Commission in 1958, the local FBO was a two or three person operation, primarily involved in flight instruction. Their office was a two-room shack, and they barely eked out a living. Its character was more akin to barnstorming than to modern business operations. My recollection is that they had limited maintenance facilities. They hired instructors on an hourly basis, usually only on weekends. The few business aircraft based on the airport were owned by several large companies which had their own hangars, mechanics, and professional pilots. Private owners had to get their maintenance done elsewhere. I ended up having most of my work done in Providence, Rhode Island.

In short, Morristown was a very underdeveloped airport. I think this was primarily because the commissioners did not have enough aviation background to recognize either the need for, or the potential of development. That was to change.

New Full-Service FBO

We made significant progress during my five-year term as a commissioner. Probably our most important accomplishment was the formation of a new fixed-base operation, embracing major maintenance facilities for aircraft owners, flight training, charter operations, and eventually fuel service for their customers.

One of the pilots on the field was George Mennen, then vice president of The Mennen Company, the personal products company. He was an avid pilot and aircraft owner, and he fully recognized the need to establish a modern FBO at Morristown. He and others put together an investor group and formed Chatham Aviation, which then built a large maintenance hangar. That attracted many aircraft owners, including businesses, to base their aircraft at Morristown.

As both a knowledgeable pilot and a CPA with Price Waterhouse, I played a major part in the negotiations that led to Chatham Aviation being established at the Morristown Airport. In my opinion the establishment of Chatham Aviation was a turning point for the airport. We were starting to enter the big leagues.

Cessna Aircraft Hangar

During this period, the Cessna Aircraft Company, which is located in Wichita, Kansas, decided to build a hangar to be used as a parts distribution warehouse at the Morristown Airport. Their objective was to be able to deliver parts overnight to their dealers on the East Coast. This was before the establishment of Federal Express. Cessna also recognized that Morristown Airport would develop into a major general aviation airport in the future.

I recall vividly the public dedication of the Cessna hangar. Dwayne Wallace, long-time President and Chairman of Cessna and the nephew of Clyde Cessna, was there. At one point when I mentioned that I had a Cessna 170, he tried to give me the key to the brand new Cessna 172 in which he had flown to Morristown. He told me to take it up for a flight. The 172, a tricycle version of the Cessna 170, had only recently been introduced. I was very impressed that he trusted me with his plane, but I declined his offer. I felt that while he meant well, it was inappropriate, since I was a public official. Besides, I was mature enough not to want the responsibility of flying a brand new airplane without a proper checkout. Nevertheless, the fact that I still remember that incident fifty years later shows that my ego was inflated by his offer.

Chairman of the Commission

During the fourth year of my five-year term, the chairman of the Commission abruptly resigned. I never found out why, but I suspect he had used his position as chairman to benefit the company he worked for. The remaining commissioners elected me as their chairman, and I served in that capacity for the remaining fifteen months of my term.

One of the contentious issues that I was never able to resolve was the Airport's role as the sole retail aviation fuel provider, and the refusal to share this role with Chatham. My concern was both financial and political. Financial, because I felt we were losing money, and political because the airport's employees were not actively interested in aviation and conveyed this lack of interest in dealing with the public. Pilots wanting fuel often had to wait 10 or 15 minutes for an employee to stop whatever maintenance job he was working on, and then go to the fuel pump. The obvious solution would have been to turn this function over to Chatham Aviation and have them pay a usage fee on every gallon sold. Eventually the airport agreed to let Chatham sell to its own customers.

I also felt that we should get out of both the T-hangar and tie-down business and allow Chatham Aviation to handle such services, again paying us a commission.

There was another reason for these views. The FBO business is very competitive, and all but the largest operations eventually go bankrupt. To survive, they need the revenue that sales and services provide, particularly in the slow winter months.

Fifty years later, I still believe government-owned airports should not be in the fuel business. This view has been tempered only slightly in the last ten years by the trend to self-service fuel operations.

One Term as Commissioner

In the summer of 1959, Inge and I moved from Morristown to Denville, seven miles away. Since the town of Morristown owned the airport, I could have been asked to resign once I moved out of Morristown, but I was not, and continued to serve out the balance of my five-year term.

Morristown Airport fifty years later. About the only thing I recognize from this picture are the two intersecting runways. While it is hard to see in this small picture, most of the planes on the ramps in front of these hangars are business jets. The general aviation tie-downs and hangars are on the left side of the picture. Most of the buildings shown on the 1958 picture no longer exist. The vision I had fifty years ago was the foundation upon which the airport has been developed.

As my last act as chairman on December 31, 1962, I issued a detailed report titled: *A Report...Containing Comments and Recommendations to Help Guide the Progress and Development of the Airport.* In re-reading that report almost fifty years later, I can't help feeling it was a professional report that contained sound advice, and was worthy of being associated with Price Waterhouse.

I served my five years with distinction and brought professionalism to the Morristown Airport Commission. It was a great experience for a young man, and I am sure it did not hurt my professional career with Price Waterhouse.

13

A Solo Flight Around
the United States
1964

The following is an account of a flight I made around the United States in 1964. While it was not the first transcontinental flight I had made—our honeymoon trip in 1958 was the first—it was the only time I flew completely around the country in a small aircraft, our Luscombe. It was quite different from our first trip and from the many subsequent trips in the following forty-five years. My numerous other trips were in aircraft with highly sophisticated radio and navigation equipment, capable of flying under instrument flight conditions.

I wrote this account shortly after the flight, and have included it here because my impressions on the flight were vivid. I was still young and impressionable, and I was struck with awe, crossing the country at such a low altitude. After this trip I lost my innocence and in many ways started to take for granted the beauty and surprises that came with flying pretty much by the seat-of-your-pants, without fancy equipment. Hopefully this account will also give the reader a glimpse of what early flying in small unsophisticated airplanes was like for the general aviation pilot. Here, unedited, are my words of that account.

Saturday, May 23, 1964

Shortly before six a.m., as the sun was emerging from the gray Atlantic, a tan and brown monoplane rolled down Runway 22 at Caldwell Wright Airport and lifted gracefully into the westward sky. Climbing rapidly, this lone aircraft made a wide circle of the field, dipped its wings to the single well-wisher on the ground, and then turned away from the sun toward the Pacific Ocean, twenty-eight hundred miles away. Twenty days, many mountain ranges, and hundreds of miles of desert later, this small plane returned to Runway 22, this time landing toward the setting sun. In the intervening days, sixty-four hundred miles of this great country passed beneath the plane's small wings. Summarized below is a chronicle of those flight hours and my impressions on spanning this mighty country.

Flight 1—Caldwell, NJ to Selinsgrove, PA
135 miles in 1 hour 55 minutes

This was the first leg, and the one that was to set the pattern for the next three days. The first clue as to the ground speed I could expect on the trip came as I passed over the Delaware River at Phillipsburg. My average ground speed was just 65 miles an hour! At that rate it would take a month to cross the continent—one-way!

N71497 is a two-seat, all metal, high-wing monoplane manufactured in 1946 by the Luscombe Company. It is powered by a Volkswagen-sized, four-cylinder engine producing only 65 horsepower on takeoff. At cruising power this engine develops less than 50 horsepower. Because the engine is so small, there is no electrical system in this plane and therefore no lights for night flying, and no radio. You start the engine the old-fashioned way—by hand-propping. This is strictly a good weather, daytime flying airplane. It carried 14 gallons of fuel.

At cruising speed the plane flies at an airspeed of 90 miles per hour, consuming about 4 gallons of fuel an hour. But this 90 miles turned out to be a fiction; the plane only achieves that ground speed when there are no headwinds and when flying near the ground. Al-

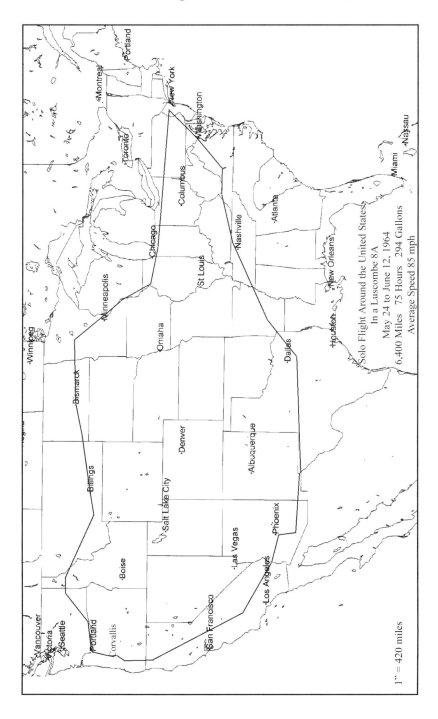

Solo Flight Around the United States
In a Luscombe 8A
May 24 to June 12, 1964
6,400 Miles 75 Hours 294 Gallons
Average Speed 85 mph

1" = 420 miles

ready, at the start of this long trip, the prospect of crossing the country with headwinds of 30 or 35 miles an hour seemed not only a possibility but a probability. On this first portion of the first flight, there were headwinds of that velocity, reducing my gallant plane's speed from a respectable 90 miles an hour to a turnpike 65. Things looked dim.

But I couldn't turn back. Months of preparation had gone into the planning of this trip, including arrangements to visit relatives and friends, and vacation time taken from work. All I could do was to drop the nose of the plane to get close to the ground where, hopefully, the winds would be somewhat reduced, and keep the nose of the plane headed westward toward the Rockies.

As I crossed over Allentown, Pennsylvania, it became apparent that I would not get as far on the first leg as I had hoped. Unfortunately, I had to leave Caldwell Wright Airport in New Jersey with only 12 gallons on board. This was only enough fuel for about two hours of flight, plus a 30 minute margin. At 65 miles per hour, this would mean a flight distance of about 130 miles.

I looked at the sectional chart for an airport about 130 miles from Caldwell, and one that would likely be open early. That was important. One of the problems of flying so early in the day is that many airport fueling facilities don't open until nine a.m. It would be frustrating to have gotten up at four in the morning for a dawn start only to end up sitting on the ground waiting for someone to sell us gasoline.

It looked like the best bet was an airport near the Susquehanna River at Selinsgrove, Pennsylvania. It was about the right distance away, and my Airport Directory showed that someone arrived at the airport at eight. So, taking up a heading that was slightly north of the original flight plan, I pierced the early morning silence—at the ego deflating speed of 65 miles per hour. Right on course, an hour and 55 minutes later, there appeared the airport. It was 7:50 a.m. and not a soul was there.

Flight 2—Selinsgrove to Sharon, PA
188 miles in 2 hours 45 minutes

To my relief, a few minutes after eight o'clock, an elderly attendant showed up. He pumped 9.4 gallons into my tank, and in minutes

I was climbing back into the early morning sky, resuming the westerly course that had been interrupted a half hour before.

I say "westerly course," for this was not a flight navigated by radio or by the stars. This flight, from start to finish, depended on the pilot and on the maps he carried in his small craft. The procedure was a simple one—just fly an exact compass course, which, in the absence of winds from either side, should take the plane exactly along the selected course. But, of course, there usually are winds, and therein is the need for maps and the pilot's ability to use them. For it was my job not only to keep the plane on the desired compass heading, but also to watch the valleys and roads and rivers and towns below or off to one side, and to check them against the aeronautical charts. When I found the plane drifting off course, I made a correction to the compass heading in order to bring the plane back to the desired route.

So, this was the routine that I followed for seventy-five hours. First I would take off and take up the preplotted heading. Then every ten minutes or so, I would compare what was passing under my wing to the map. More often than not, I made a small course correction. Also, I would check my instruments: oil pressure 50, normal; oil temperature 160 degrees, normal; airspeed 90 mph; rate of climb, zero; fuel three quarters full; directional gyro, 280° and in agreement with the compass; tachometer, 2175 rpm; altitude fourteen hundred feet—all "OK."

And so the flight across the Appalachian Mountains continued. Up and down I went, following the contour of the land to keep below the strong headwinds as much as possible. Mostly the flight was only four or five hundred feet above the mountainous terrain and it took constant attention to stay on course. While I was disappointed that I had a ground speed of only 65 miles an hour, I covered a lot of ground in a few minutes and I had to pay attention. The mountains were not tall by western standards, but they would sure spoil the whole day if I became distracted and ran into one.

At about ten a.m., the mountains gradually disappeared and rolling hills took their place. Then half an hour or so later the hills also disappeared and the countryside became mostly flat. And as the mountains started fading behind us, the frequency of towns increased, until by the time Sharon, Pennsylvania, appeared, the signs of civilization were all about us. When I landed at Sharon, the vast Midwest lay before me.

Flight 3—Sharon, PA to Sandusky, OH
132 miles in 1 hour 40 minutes

After taking off from Sharon, it was necessary to fly somewhat south of a direct course to Sandusky because of the large airports and their related activity at Youngstown, Ohio. Generally, it is necessary to avoid such areas unless you are flying at an altitude of at least 3,000 feet above ground. Since I was still encountering strong headwinds, my flight was at only 1,000 feet, hence the deviation.

I also had to watch more carefully than before for other planes and high towers (more about this later). Because it was a Saturday, and mid-morning, many other pilots were out exercising their planes, so vigilance was essential. This leg was fairly short and uneventful. My ground speed jumped up to 75 mph on this leg. Hurray! It was also getting warmer, with the temperatures in the low 90s.

Flight 4—Sandusky, OH to Goshen, IN
163 miles in 2 hours 25 minutes

Sandusky is right on Lake Erie, somewhat west of Cleveland. I was able to find a mechanic at Sandusky to change the engine oil, and

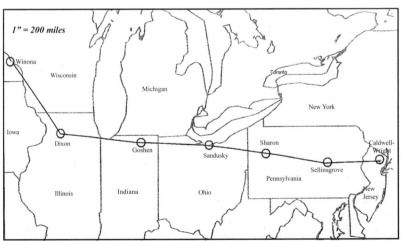

The first day's flight, 1,002 miles, took almost 14 flying hours. It was a long day, and with thunderstorms and darkness approaching Winona, MN, I could not have gone further.

while that was being done, I got a short bite to eat. I had a long distance to fly before I hit the Mississippi River later in the day.

The terrain approaching Goshen was fairly flat with only an occasional hill to tease the countryside. The navigational aspects, while not serious, did require constant attention. If I had been flying at 5,000 feet I would have been able to see far enough on all sides to minimize these difficulties, but I was flying at only four or five hundred feet above the ground. You just can't see as far or get as good a perspective of where you are from a low altitude. To a large extent the navigational aspects of this leg were a preview of the work that lay ahead. Of course, there was little chance of getting completely lost or, as pilots prefer to say, disoriented, for the Ohio and Indiana Turnpikes also go along this route, except about 50 miles to the south.

So, if I really got disoriented, it would only be necessary to fly due south to the turnpike. Then, from the limited access roads, it would be fairly easy to determine exactly where over the turnpike I was.

But this was never necessary, and I landed at Goshen pretty much on time. The winds on the ground, however, were beginning to pick up to 20 miles an hour, making landing somewhat more difficult.

Flight 5—Goshen, IN to Dixon, IL
188 miles in 2 hours 55 minutes

Then on towards Chicago. My route took me along the tip of Lake Michigan and Chicago, and then west toward the Mississippi River. A short distance shy of Goshen my route and the Indiana Turnpike converged enough that I could use the turnpike for navigation. This can be a pleasure since it takes the work out of navigating, but in high headwinds and low ground speeds it can be somewhat humbling. Who likes to be flying along and finding that the cars on the turnpike below are keeping up or even passing you? I certainly found it disconcerting. The speed limit on the Indiana Turnpike is either 65 or 70. My ground speed on this leg was just 65!

Part of the reason for this decrease from my earlier 70 to 75 miles an hour speeds was that it was necessary to climb somewhat as I approached the Chicago area. The regulations provide that I could fly at any altitude under 3,000 above the ground I wanted away from towns so long as I didn't unduly present a hazard to property or people on the ground.

The rules with regard to flying over cities were different. First, I had to be at least 1,000 feet above the highest building within 2,000 feet horizontally of me. Second, I had to be at an altitude where, in the event of an engine failure, I could glide outside the city limits or make a landing without presenting an undue hazard to persons or property on the ground. The Luscombe glides about seven or eight feet for every foot of altitude that it loses. Therefore, if I were at 3,000 feet, the plane could glide about twenty to twenty-five thousand feet, or four to five miles before touching down.

Obviously, it is almost impossible to fly high enough over a large city like Chicago to be able to glide outside the city limits, so it is prudent to stay in areas that offer some sort of landing facility in an emergency. Turnpikes can offer such emergency help, but I am quite sure the State Police would be unhappy to find that a plane had used a turnpike to land on. Still, it is better than landing on someone's house or in a school playground. While most of the turnpikes have a lot of traffic, I am quite confident that if a plane started to land in front of traffic going the same direction, the drivers would slow down mighty fast, leaving ample area to land in. But, of course, I have never had to try it and I hope that I never will.

Another problem with flying over or near cities and towns at low altitude is the proliferation of radio and TV towers that can extend as high as two thousand feet above the ground. Anyone flying this low had better be watching for these obstacles.

Dixon, Illinois, is a long way west of Chicago, and the airport was hard to find. It blended in with farm fields, and it took me some fancy map shuffling to find the Dixon Airport without undue delay.

Flight 6—Dixon, IL to Winona, MN
196 miles in 2 hours 3 minutes

I had been flying pretty much on a westerly heading all day, but after refueling at Dixon I turned to the northwest, heading towards

Minnesota. At the same time the winds started to shift, coming more from the south than from the west. This meant that I lost my headwind. Ground speed increased, and on this two-hour leg I averaged 98 miles an hour—a big improvement over the earlier 65.

It was getting late in the day and the visibility started dropping, eventually to only eight or nine miles. It would have been easier to fly due west to the Mississippi River and then follow the river to Winona, but this would have taken 15 to 20 minutes longer. I was fighting the sunset-deadline since I had no lights for flying at night. Official sunset must have been about 8:10; I landed at 8:20, with a little light still visible from the sun. The landing was extremely difficult, however, because all of a sudden the winds near the ground turned gusty and picked up speed. Because of these winds I could not get the plane lined up with the runway on my first attempt, and I had to go around for a second try. The second time I made it down.

I quickly found the tie-down area where there were ropes in the ground for tying the plane down. Almost immediately after that, the sky broke loose with thunder, lightning, rain, and very high, gusty winds. Apparently, this was a squall line associated with a cold front. It was a good thing that I arrived when I did, and not five minutes later.

On leaving the plane, I got soaked in the rain. Some other pilots at the airport took me to a nearby motel for the night where I put on some dry, warm clothes. Unfortunately, the storm knocked out the lights in the area and the restaurants couldn't cook anything. I ended up going to bed without trying to find anything to eat. I was more tired than hungry.

Sunday, May 24, 1964

I set the alarm for six a.m., but one look at the sky at that hour convinced me that I was not going to be flying until the storm passed over, so I went back to bed until about eight. By that time the storm had indeed passed, and it was a beautiful Sunday morning. The manager of the motel lent me his Cadillac to go for breakfast and afterwards drove me out to the airport for my late, nine a.m. departure.

Flight 7—Winona to St. Cloud, MN
161 miles in 2 hours 25 minutes

Winona is right on the Mississippi River and my flight for the next hundred miles took me northwest up into the Twin-City (Minneapolis-St. Paul) area and then towards St. Cloud, where the river seemed to fade away. Between Winona and Minneapolis, however, the Mississippi is a wide and winding river; so wide that I didn't dare cross it in places at low altitude. Had my engine failed, I would not have been able to glide to land. I was amazed, for I had assumed that the river would narrow down as I went north. Only at Minneapolis did the river suddenly do just that, becoming only a small stream with no real vitality.

Speaking of the Twin-Cities, I had really expected Minneapolis and St. Paul to have a common downtown business area, with only the river separating them. But no, each city had its own personality and it seemed just a coincidence that they were neighbors across the river. In any case, the business areas appeared to be eight or ten miles apart.

I again encountered winds which increased the further northwest I flew. My average speed for the 161 miles from Winona to St. Cloud was less than 70 mph.

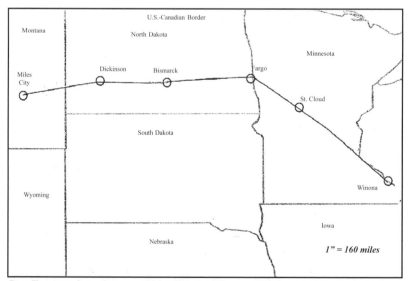

Day Two was less rigorous–751 miles in little over ten hours. The biggest uncertainty in planning a trip like this is what the weather will be. So far so good.

Flight 8—St. Cloud, MN to Fargo, ND
150 miles in 2 hours 10 minutes

This was an unremarkable leg of my flight until I got near Fargo. Then the countryside started flattening out and sectional lines started marking the landscape. For those who have never seen sectional lines, they are north-south and east-west lines every mile, formed by dirt roads. They must date back to the time of our westward expansion and the homesteading of the area. They make navigation easy because these roads are perfectly straight and perfectly aligned with the cardinal compass headings (north, east, south and west). It is impressive to see from the air how accurately they divide up the land.

The airport at Fargo was a small grass airport southeast of town. I could not land at the main Fargo airport because it had a control tower that required two-way radio. Fortunately, many towns have more than one airport, and generally only the main one used by commercial airlines will have control towers. There are probably fewer than 300 airports where I cannot land, and about 6,000 where I can. This restriction, while annoying at times, is not too serious a limitation. Nevertheless, I would have liked to have used the main Fargo airport because the one I used had short runways which made it necessary to be very careful in landing and taking off.

Flight 9—Fargo to Bismarck, ND
200 miles in 2 hours 40 minutes

Hey! My speed jumped up to all of 75 mph on this leg of the flight. Progress. Other than that, it was just a question of following the main highway west to Bismarck, or, to be more accurate, to Mandan and its small airport. Mandan is on the west side of the Missouri River and Bismarck is on the east side. The Missouri River meanders north from Bismarck, eventually turning westward in northern North Dakota before eventually petering out.

I refueled, and, after some small talk with the personnel at the airport about my good looking Luscombe, off I went.

Flight 10—Bismarck to Dickinson, ND
92 miles in 1 hour 10 minutes

The flight to Dickinson again followed the highway on strictly an east-west line. This, too, was an uneventful flight. It was short because I wanted to refuel just before the 150 miles I would have to fly across the badlands between Dickinson and Miles City.

Flight 11—Dickinson, ND to Miles City, MT
148 miles in 1 hour 57 minutes

This flight was one of the most beautiful of the trip, and also one of the most difficult from a navigational standpoint. I had no highway, and no really good checkpoint for about a hundred miles, and the countryside, while extremely beautiful, was unsuitable for landing. I had to hold a precise compass heading, then, after an hour or so, check to see where I was by locating the river and roads which converge on Miles City. Obviously I made it without incident.

The countryside warrants description. For the first thirty or forty miles west of Dickinson, the countryside was much as it had been since Fargo, with lots of farms, some sectional lines and a few cars and houses. Suddenly the landscape changed into small barren mountains with craters and rocks, looking much as I envision the moon's surface. The suddenness of it all was impressive. One minute you are over small farms and the next minute the land drops down about 300 feet and the badlands start and continue like this for 100 miles or so. I would see many other barren, mountainous areas on this trip, but none quite like this one. It is one vista you can see only from a low, slow flying airplane.

Monday, May 25, 1964

Flight 12—to Billings, MT
137 miles in 1 hour 25 minutes

When I arrived in Miles City my flying day was done, although, because of the late start, I had traveled only a relatively short distance—751 miles. I wanted to get an early start the next day, and when I went in to close my flight plan with the FAA, I asked how early in the morning the sun came up; I wanted to get started early because I would be approaching the Rockies on this next leg. I was both pleased and dismayed to learn that I could be in the air at 4 in the morning. After two days of flying the thought of arising at 3 a.m. and being in the air at 4 a.m. left me with mixed emotions.

Still, I had the whole of the Rockies ahead of me. I was anxious to cross them as early as possible during the day, since updrafts, and, more importantly, downdrafts take place in the afternoon. Thinking up an excuse to start later, I pointed out to the FAA gentleman who gave me the cheerful 4 a.m. information that it would do me little good

Here I am with our Luscombe 8A at the Caldwell Wright Airport.With only a 65-horsepower engine, there was no electrical system and you started the engine by using an Arm-Strong starter.

to fly at 4 a.m. only to have to land at 6 a.m. for fuel and then find myself sitting at the airport waiting for someone to pump gas. He suggested that I fly into Billings where I could get fuel earlier, maybe on a 24 hour basis. I pointed out that Billings was one of the "controlled" airports requiring two-way radio, but he assured me that if I would phone the Billings tower before leaving Miles City, permission to land would be granted. That left only the nagging doubt that perhaps no fuel would be available early, but when I phoned Billings I found that they started selling fuel at 6 a.m. With no excuse left, I took a cab into Miles City for a short seven hour sleep and a hot dinner.

Bright and early at 3:30 the next morning, the cab drove through the predawn stillness to take me the three miles out to the airport. Once there, I filed my flight plan and called the Billings tower to get permission to land there. Before the first ray of sun shone above the horizon, I was in the air barreling toward the Rockies. The uncertainties of what I would find and the unknowns that I would face had been on my mind almost from the start of planning for the trip. Now, in the stillness of the morning, I was about to find out.

During the night a frontal system had passed eastward through the area, with heavy rain and high winds. As on the previous night in Winona, I had been lucky enough to be on the ground and sleeping during the storm, which meant that I had not been delayed at all. Now, flying toward Billings, I realized that I had lost my unwelcome companion—the headwind. I found I was traveling at a respectable 90 miles per hour. This was a good sign, with so many uncertain miles ahead of me.

It wasn't until I was within 25 miles of Billings that I made a sudden and exhilarating discovery—the tall clouds I'd been seeing on the distant horizon weren't clouds at all, but were snow-capped mountains. Oh, how beautiful they were. They seemed to start like a wall at the ground level, and then rose until they blended right into the clouds. The valley I was flying over was at an elevation of about 3,000 feet, and the tops of the mountains approached 10,000 feet in places. You can't imagine the majesty of nature until you have seen your first snow-covered mountain from an airplane flying at an altitude well below their tops. Certainly you don't see this from an airliner.

Almost as soon as I made this discovery, Billings was within sight. The procedure for an airplane without radio is to circle the airport until the tower gives you a light signal—green for "ok" to land, and red to continue circling. The signal is a high-powered light aimed directly at the airplane. It is quite easy to see. You acknowledge receipt of the message by rocking your wings and then proceeding to follow the instructions provided by the light. Needless to say, at 5:30 a.m. there was no other traffic; I received a green light and was cleared to land.

I was a little early for the 6 a.m. refueling time, I found a nice airport restaurant open and had breakfast. By the time I finished, the gas boy was there and I was refueled. A phone call was made to the tower to advise them I was about to take off and would need light signals again.

Flight 13—Billings to Butte, MT
200 miles in 2 hours 15 minutes

My route through the Rockies was not a random selection. Instead, I very carefully chose my route from a number of possibilities. I could have flown as far south as Salt Lake City or as far north as the Canadian border. The route I chose had three things in its favor: First, it was well traveled, with enough airports to accommodate my limited fuel capacity. Second, it was a fairly low-altitude route, with only two

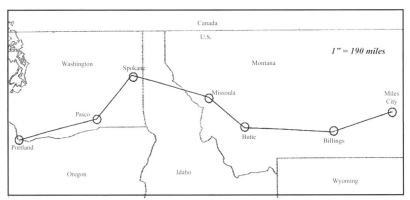

Day Three, 952 miles in ten hours and thirty minutes. I arrived in Portland at 4:30, but I had been in the air since 4 a.m. I had started early in order to get over the Rockies before afternoon thunderstorms or turbulence made it more difficult. As it turned out, I had enjoyed good weather all the way from the east coast.

or three mountain passes at around 6,000 feet, although I would be flying through valleys surrounded by much higher mountains the whole way. Third, I faced no likelihood of getting lost, because the Northern Pacific Railroad, the main highway, and an occasional river took much the same route.

So, taking off from Billings, I had little to do but to gain altitude, sit back, and enjoy the spectacle. On both sides of me unfolded a winter scene of ice and snow. I flew along at 90 miles an hour at 10,000 feet without a care in the world. No updrafts. No downdrafts. Just pleasant flight conditions and the Rockies' high mountains at my window.

After two hours of flying, I suddenly realized that I was getting close to Butte and should be seeing it, but all I could see were mountains. Where was Butte? I knew from my maps that I was within 15 to 20 miles of Butte, but in spite of excellent visibility, I couldn't see what I knew to be a good size town.

Then it dawned on me that the mountain I was approaching was part of the range that surrounded Butte. Sure enough, as soon as I had crossed this 7,500-foot mountain, there was Butte nestled right next to it, out of sight only moments before. The airport was at 5,600 feet, which is high for an airport, but it still took me a few minutes to lose enough altitude to land after crossing the mountain. On the western side of the town was a wide valley; the mountains close to the town were only on the eastern side. What a surprise for the unwary flyer who is seeing the world as few see it.

Flight 14—Butte to Missoula, MT
121 miles in 1 hour 27 minutes

It was cold in Butte! I'd had the foresight to get out a sweater and suede jacket from my baggage area, and I needed both. The temperature generally drops three degrees for every 1,000 feet of elevation, which means that at 10,000 feet it is typically 30 degrees colder than at sea level. Well, Butte is at almost 6,000 feet and a long ways north to boot. The temperature seemed right about freezing but actually it was around 40. Still, the long hours at 10,000 feet, where the temperature was almost 15 degrees colder, were beginning to tell. There was a small heater in the airplane, but it was so cold I couldn't even laugh at that joke. So, the hot pot of coffee at the airport was almost more welcomed than the fuel for the plane.

The refueling of plane and pilot took only a few minutes and then I was on the way again. I was pleasantly surprised at the plane's performance on takeoff. Normally at high altitude the performance of an airplane deteriorates noticeably because the air is thinner. This has two effects. First, the plane has to go faster to get the same amount of lift. Second, there is less oxygen for the engine, reducing its power output. Offsetting this somewhat was the cold temperature. Cold air is denser than warm air. So the plane was off the ground in only a slightly greater distance than normal. Once airborne I turned northwestward toward Missoula.

The flight was routine by this time, with the Anaconda Range—10,000 to 11,000 feet—on my left, and a lesser, unnamed range on my right. I followed the highway and railroad through valleys all the way to Missoula. Missoula, like Billings, required two-way radio, and I had phoned ahead from Butte for landing permission. Compared to the 5,600 foot airport elevation at Butte, Missoula's 3,200 foot elevation seemed like sea level. Actually there are few airports in the U.S. that are even that high.

Flight 15—Missoula to Spokane, WA
174 miles in 2 hours

Upon taking off from Missoula, I was to encounter only one more high mountain pass before my "crossing" was over. It was then about 11 a.m. and the winds were beginning to pick up somewhat, resulting in some updrafts and downdrafts, although none of them were strong. Updrafts occur when wind hits the side of a mountain and is forced up over the top. An updraft, upon reaching the top of a mountain, tends to rush down the other side, creating a corresponding down-draft.

In theory, if you are flying parallel to a mountain range and you know which way the wind is blowing, you should be able to stay on the windward side of the mountains and enjoy continual updrafts, which, far from being dangerous, gives you a "free" ride. In reality, though, the winds in mountains are not always steady, either in velocity or in direction. You can be flying along in an updraft one minute only to find yourself in a downdraft the next. You can avoid most updrafts and downdrafts if you fly well above the mountains, but this strategy is of limited usefulness when the mountains are ten or eleven thousand feet high. Once the plane gets to ten thousand feet, it struggles to climb higher.

My route from Missoula to Spokane took me mostly west along narrow but continuous valleys with high mountains on both sides. Most of the peaks were under 8,000 feet and the valley was probably an average of 3,000 feet above sea level. So it would have been possible to fly at, say, five thousand feet with comparative safety. The only place where I would have to fly higher was the 5,300 foot Mullen Pass at the Idaho-Montana border. But since the visibility and weather were excellent, it seemed to make more sense to fly high to avoid up and downdrafts as much as possible. Accordingly, I flew this leg of the flight mostly at 10,000 feet. Even at that altitude, I hit an occasional up or downdraft, but nothing that affected my altitude by more than 500 to 1,000 feet before I flew out of it. So this flight had presented relatively few difficulties.

Incidentally, before I'd set out, I had carefully and thoughtfully packed a 35 pound survival kit. In one respect, I goofed. I had forgotten about the snow in the mountains, and there was a lot of it. It seemed like the snow line was at about 4,000 feet, although it may have been as high as 5,000 to 6,000 feet in many places. I say I "goofed" in that I forgot all about the problems of mountain snow. I would have been in tough shape if I had gone down in the snow-covered mountains, for I had no heavy boots, parka, gloves, or the like. Of course, since I was flying along a valley I would probably have landed there if I'd had engine difficulty, but you never can tell what might happen in bad weather. Let there be no doubt: it is easy to get lost in an airplane.

Preparing to meet survival needs deserves careful thought. Since this flight covered every extreme of climate and terrain, it was necessary to include many things that you might not think of. For example, I carried two gallons of water as well as chap stick and suntan lotion for my flight over the desert. I carried splints in case I broke a leg or arm—very likely in an aircraft forced landing—and I took a couple of sheets to use as bandages or for protection against the desert sun. I carried a spray can of fluorescent orange paint to spray one of the sheets to attract attention. I carried special signal mirrors to flash the sun into the eyes of pilots flying overhead. I took along a few small flares and some miracle drugs (good against anything) in case I got sick. I had a six-pound tin, a six-day supply of special survival crackers, along with matches that were guaranteed to ignite even after being under water for 30 minutes. I had an odd looking machete-like hatchet-knife to cut my way out of the plane, the woods, or the jungle. In short, I tried to anticipate everything I might need in the event of a forced landing—a form of insurance which I hoped I would never need.

Oh yes, there was one other unusual item in the kit—100 feet of nylon rope. If a plane goes down in the woods, it may lodge in a tree and the pilot, of course, needs to get down. This last point may raise doubts, but remember a small airplane does not weigh very much and can easily get caught in the canopy of a forest. One reason why it is so hard to locate an aircraft, even when the searchers know fairly accurately where it went down, is that the plane may never have reached the ground, and ground-searching crews will likely never find it.

Mullen Pass—the last pass—came and went, and the Rockies were behind me. The remaining 40 minutes of flying over gradually lowering terrain into Spokane was anticlimactic. In a matter of just a few hours I had crossed snow-covered mountains, concerned that I had forgotten to consider cold weather survival needs. Now it was 85 degrees on the ground in Spokane.

Flight 16—Spokane to Pasco, WA
130 miles in 1 hour 32 minutes

Flying along the flat and increasingly hot country of Eastern Washington, I was in a world altogether different from the one I'd been in only a couple of hours before. The country under my monoplane was monotonous, with little in the countryside to catch my attention until I got within 30 miles of Pasco. Then I saw irrigation ditches, built in straight lines, miles and miles long. I came to understand that the land was very rich, but arid. Water is obtained from the Columbia and Snake Rivers and pumped through these concrete ditches, with apparently good results judging from the amount of farming I saw. The aridity became apparent close-up, too, when I landed for refueling at Pasco, a town at the junction of the Snake and Columbia rivers.

Flight 17—Pasco, WA to Portland, OR
190 miles in 1 hour 55 minutes

From Pasco, the navigation was quite simple—first climb to about 4,000 feet and then straight over a small range of mountains that separate the two ends of the U-shaped loop the Columbia River makes near Pasco. Within 20 minutes I was over this range and followed the Columbia River through the Cascade Mountain Range to Portland. The weather was fine and I picked up my ground speed, making about 100 miles an hour. This was particularly pleasing since this was the last leg of the trip to Portland. About 100 miles from Portland, Mt. Hood (11,245 feet) stuck her majestic head above the surrounding mountains, the whole top half covered with snow. As I began winding my way through the Columbia River gorge, this beautiful mountain came closer and closer and she was only about 20 miles from me as I passed alongside her. What a spectacle!

Fifteen minutes later I could see Portland. I landed in Vancouver, Washington, just across the Columbia River from Portland, at about 4:30 in the afternoon.

It had taken just 62 hours elapsed time since I left New Jersey, and some 35 hours flying time. I was very tired, but thrilled that I had been able to make the trip in the three days.

Monday, June 1, 1964

Flight 18—Portland to Corvallis, OR
80 miles in 55 minutes

My wife, Inge, had flown out on the airlines and she met me in Portland. She had not flown with me because of weight limitations of the plane, particularly with my survival kit. We had a good 11-day visit, first with my Grandmother Gross in Portland, and later with my Grandmother Henderson and other relatives in Corvallis. Inge returned home after I left Corvallis.

Short flight from Portland to Corvallis, 80 miles, 1 hour.

The flight to Corvallis was uneventful. Mt. Hood was on my left as I flew down the Willamette Valley, a rich valley formed by the Cascade Range on the east side and the smaller, but still impressive, Coastal Range on the west side between the Willamette Valley and the Pacific Ocean. Corvallis is the home of my maternal grandmother as well as my only uncle, aunt, and cousins.

Saturday, June 6, 1964

Flight 19—Corvallis to Eugene, OR
31 miles in 31 minutes

My return route was via a slight detour—El Paso, Texas, on the Mexican border. El Paso was about 1,600 miles from Corvallis, and it would take at least two full days of flying to get there. My return trip started out around noon on Saturday, June 6. Originally I had intended to get started early in the morning. However, a small mechanical problem worked against me.

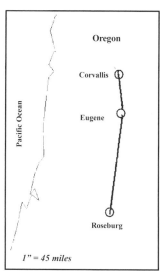

1" = 45 miles

Getting over the mountains proved to be a problem. Low clouds obscured the tops, stopping me at Roseburg.

A spring that held rudder tension on one of the two rudder pedals broke on Friday evening, and although it might have been possible to fly without repairing it, but then I would have had to keep constant pressure on that rudder pedal to counterbalance the spring on the other pedal. Rather than opt for that strain, I chose to locate a replacement spring and install it. This took until almost noon.

Meanwhile, by noon, the sunny weather had started to deteriorate. The ceiling was overcast at about 2,500 feet, with five to six miles visibility, interrupted by scattered rain showers in which the visibility was down to a mile or so.

Corvallis did not have a weather bureau, so I decided to fly to Eugene where I could talk with the weather forecaster located at the airport. In that way I could keep abreast of the latest weather reports from all over the west. Accordingly, even though the weather was far from good, I flew uneventfully to Eugene, dodging around a few scattered showers en route. A thousand foot ceiling and three miles visibility is the minimum needed for legal flight in "good" weather. I had this, but just barely.

Flight 20—Eugene to Roseburg, OR
68 miles in 48 minutes

The weather forecaster had little good to say about the weather. The entire region, from the Oregon coast inland to the Cascade Range, was covered with the same low overcast I had flown under getting the short distance from Corvallis to Eugene. If the Willamette Valley had continued south of Eugene perhaps I could have continued. But it didn't. The Willamette Valley ends at Eugene where the Cascade and Coastal mountains merge and the tops of these mountains were concealed in the overcast.

I had originally planned to fly from Corvallis to Eugene and then southwest across the Coastal Range to the Oregon Coast. I would then have followed the coast to San Francisco. In good weather that route would have made for easy navigation but this was out of the question. I could not get across the Coastal Range, and even if I could, the weather reports from the various airports on the Oregon and California coast showed ceilings of only four and five hundred feet with fog and rain.

At the same time, the obvious inland route, flying pretty much south of Eugene to the Sacramento Valley, had even higher mountains (Mt. Shasta was 14,162 feet). That route did not look promising either, because the overcast covered the tops of most of these mountains.

The obvious solution: I unpacked my James Bond paperback and spent the afternoon reading, checking the weather once an hour when the latest weather reports came in. At about six in the evening, it was obvious that I was not going to get very far that day and I needed a motel for the night. There were no hotels within walking distance of the Eugene Airport. My airport directory showed that Roseburg, Oregon had a motel adjacent to the airport. Roseburg is in a valley about 70 miles south of Eugene and on I-5, the main north-south interstate highway.

The Eugene weather forecaster assured me that I would have good visibility en route to Roseburg except in localized rain showers which I could fly around, and that the weather would not deteriorate on me. By this time he had also convinced me that my best bet for getting out of Oregon the next day was the inland route following the main highway south into California. So, off to Roseburg.

Actually there is little to tell about this leg of the flight. I flew generally about 1,000 feet above the ground and 500 feet below the overcast. The tops of many mountains were hidden in the overcast, but I followed the interstate highway as it snaked around the mountains, along valleys and rivers. There were a few isolated rain showers, but they didn't cause any trouble. In a little under an hour I was in Roseburg, and shortly thereafter was settled in a nearby motel for the night.

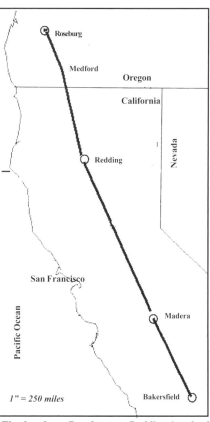

Sunday, June 7, 1964

Flight 21—Roseburg, OR to Redding, CA
221 miles in 2 hours 20 minutes

I walked (without breakfast) the mile-and-a-half to the airport before sunup. The weather, however, didn't look much different than it had the night be-

The leg from Roseburg to Redding involved getting across three mountain passes that were just barely below the overcast. The remainder of the flight was in sunny weather.

fore. The town and the airport, which were nestled among the mountains, had good visibility, perhaps ten miles, but the overcast still hid the tops of the mountains.

I called the weather bureau at Medford Airport, 100 miles south, and on my route. The forecaster expressed some doubt that I could get through the mountain passes. There were two passes between Roseburg and Medford, and a third one about 45 miles south of Medford. The route through the mountains in poor weather involved a weaving course, following I-5 through the valleys until getting close to a pass where mountains on both sides of the valley closed in. At that point the road steeply ascended, with many curves, up 1,500 or 2,000 feet from the valley, before going across the pass. Immediately on the other side of the pass the road descended to a new valley.

There was no weather bureau between Roseburg and Medford. However, the forecaster said an automatic weather reporting station at one of the two passes was reporting that it was in the overcast. He had no way of knowing how low the overcast might be at that pass. He did say that the visibility and ceiling over the valleys would remain about 10 miles, and overcast at fifteen hundred feet above the valley.

I had two choices: wait it out on the ground at Roseburg for better weather, or fly to the first pass, Canyonville, to see what the actual conditions were. I chose the latter. If I could not get over that pass I could always return to Roseburg.

The pass at Canyonville was relatively easy to get through. When I got within about five miles of the pass, I spent four or five minutes spiraling up to the bottom of the overcast, and then, ever so cautiously, flying along one side of the narrowing valley so I had room to make a 180 degree turn if I could not get across. When I got close to the pass, I could see across it and the valley beyond. I dashed across while I could.

After Canyonville, I had an easy 15-minute flight to Sexton Mountain Pass where I encountered much the same situation as at Canyonville, with no real problem. I then followed the interstate highway through the valleys to Medford.

Due south of Medford, however, I thought I might not be able to get through the third and final pass. This was the highest of the three, the Siskiyou Pass, at 5,200 feet above sea level, with mountains rising upward to 7,500 feet within two or three miles of the pass itself. As I approached the pass, I climbed and found myself touching the bottoms of the ragged overcast, which forced me several times to descend in order to stay below them. The valley at this point was about 2,000 feet above sea level, but rapidly rose to 5,200 feet at the pass. Three times I flew toward the pass at about 5,400 feet only to bump into the jagged bottoms of the overcast, which forced me to descend and turn around. On the fourth try, however, flying a little lower, 5,300 feet, I was able to see through the pass and the valley beyond, and I dashed across. On the other side, the terrain dropped off very rapidly and I was almost immediately over a valley, which was about 3,000 feet above sea level. I was also in California.

I continued to fly under the overcast, but because there were no more mountain passes to fly through, the height of the mountains on both sides did not bother me a bit. I continued to have good visibility and calm air. Fortunately, as I drew abreast and then south of Mount Shasta, about ten air miles from its peak, the overcast started breaking up. I was able to turn my head and see the whole south side of this magnificent, snow-capped mountain. After that the weather improved still further, but except for my backward glance at Mount Shasta, I had seen little of the immense mountain range through which I had threaded my way in a little more than two hours of flight.

As I flew into better weather, I came upon lower and lower mountains until the mountains became hills and lakes appeared. Soon I was over the rich Sacramento Valley. Redding, California, at the north end of the valley, was my refueling stop.

Flight 22—Redding to Madera, CA
276 miles in 2 hours 30 minutes

Unfortunately, Redding Airport had no restaurant open and so, as had happened frequently on the trip, I had no breakfast. The slight gnawing feeling in my stomach during the following two and-a-half hours was the only unpleasant aspect of my quick flight down the Sacramento Valley. I say "quick," for I averaged 110 miles an hour, which made it probably the fastest, or one of the fastest, flights of my trip. At last, a tailwind!

The Sacramento Valley appeared to be a rich valley with lush vegetation. The Valley itself is surrounded on its east and the west sides by mountain ranges, and on the north end by the mountains that I had just come through. Several hundreds of miles to the south, where it is called San Joaquin Valley, there is a fourth mountain range, just north of Los Angeles. My route took me down the center of this 100-mile-wide valley, passing near such well-known towns as Sacramento, Stockton, Fresno, and Bakersfield. I passed about 50 miles east of San Francisco and Oakland. The whole complexion of the valley was of active, rich, farming. This was one of the richest agricultural areas I had seen from the air. There were also a large number of airplanes flying around the area. At one point an old biplane from the era of the twenties flew alongside of me and then inched ahead. It seems there was an antique airplane fly-in at one of the airports along my route that day, which in part accounted for the activity.

Flight 23—Madera to Bakersfield, CA
133 miles in 1 hour 17 minutes

The flight to Bakersfield was uneventful. I made it a short one because of warnings of bad weather ahead. In checking with the weather bureau forecaster in Madera, I had found out that the weather around Los Angeles had deteriorated, and in fact was poor enough to raise questions as to whether I should fly further that day. Bakersfield was just north of the 8,000-foot mountain range at the south end of the valley. It seemed prudent to stop in Bakersfield to check the weather conditions again before going further.

Flight 24—Bakersfield to Blythe, CA
290 miles in 2 hours 53 minutes

The forecaster in Bakersfield said I could not fly into the Los Angeles basin because of low ceilings and visibility, both in the mountains and in the Los Angeles basin. So there went my beautiful plan to fly down the length of California to the Mexican border (at San Diego) before turning east and following the highway to Yuma, Arizona.

I had chosen that route for the safety factor—you can't get lost if you follow a highway. There is a lot of featureless desert ahead of me. I have heard too many stories about airplanes and pilots getting lost in the desert, and what usually happens to them. I didn't want to become a story myself.

But the forecaster, upon learning that my ultimate destination was El Paso, asked brightly, why I didn't just turn east about 25 miles south of Bakersfield and fly over the mountains, across the desert to Blythe, and then on to Phoenix, Tucson and El Paso. He assured me that although there might be clouds over the mountain range which separates the San Joaquin Valley from the desert on the east side, I could rest assured that once I was over the desert the clouds would dissipate and I would have no trouble flying. Well, that was all well and good, I thought, but how the heck do you navigate over a desert that stretches for miles and miles without any prominent landmarks. That was an important question, for Blythe was some 290 miles away and given a normal fuel range of only 350 miles, there was little safety margin if I got lost. The nearest airport of any significance to Blythe

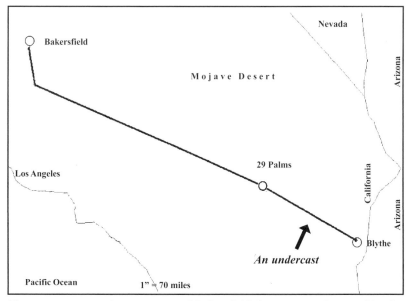

There was a mountain range east of Bakersfield, but a mountain pass 35 miles south of Bakersfield allowed me to get on the desert (and sunny) side. I was only 35 miles from Blythe (see arrow) when I encountered an unforecast surprise. See text.

was about 75 miles to the south of Blythe, and the only airport that I would pass over was at a town with the unlikely name of "Twenty-Nine Palms." I say unlikely, for, although I flew right over the place, I never saw anything that looked like palm trees.

The forecaster did have one favorable thing to say about that route. I would have strong tailwinds, particularly if I stayed up high. In fact he forecast that I would have a 50 mile per hour tailwind. I thanked him for his help and told him I wanted to think about this routing before deciding. But it didn't take long. The prospect of a significant tailwind was irresistible, and so I went that route.

Initially I had to climb up and cross a mountain range between Bakersfield and the desert on the east side. After crossing the mountains I was over desert for the next 240 miles. The route took me south of Edwards Air Force Base, although I was too far south to see it. I was concentrating on flying a straight compass course. Twenty-Nine Palms showed up below me at the expected time, and while I didn't see any signs of life, there was an airport. Blythe was 80 miles farther east.

There are many joys in flying but none surpass the intense satisfaction I felt in having flown 150+ miles over the blank desert on merely a compass heading and having hit my chosen landmark on the button. One of the pleasures of flying the old-fashioned way, as I was doing, was the constant challenge that it presented. I can't help feeling that pilots of today, with all of their expensive and accurate radio navigation aids, have missed the satisfaction of being able to navigate on their own. *[Author's reminder: this was written in 1964 decades before LORAN, GPS, glass cockpits and other modern navigation equipment.]*

The Last Thirty-Five Miles

About thirty-five miles from Blythe something happened to the beautiful, clear weather, something not foreseen by the Bakersfield forecaster. Suddenly, I encountered a low layer of clouds that extended ahead and to both sides of me. Since I was still at 9,500 feet, I was well above these clouds and not in immediate difficulty, but it was obvious there would likely be a cloud layer over the airport at Blythe, through which I could not descend without a radio.

I had been flying for almost two-and-a-half hours at this point. I doubted that I had enough fuel to get back to Twenty-Nine Palms, for if I turned around, instead of having tailwinds of perhaps 35 miles an hour or so, I would have headwinds of the same magnitude. Since my air speed seemed to be working out at about 90–95 miles an hour, with a headwind of 35 mph I would only be going 55 to 60 mph the other way. I would run out of fuel if I tried to get back to Twenty-Nine-Palms. Still, I couldn't fly above these clouds so I decided to descend along their edge and see if there was any chance of flying under them into Blythe. At the same time, I turned south, knowing that there should be a highway from Palm Springs to Blythe about 20 miles from where I thought I was.

When I got down to about 3,000 feet, I discovered that the clouds were not made of moisture, but of blowing sand. Apparently the same winds that had been helping me along were whipping up the desert into fierce and continuous clouds of flying sand. I descended still lower until I was about 500 feet off the desert floor, and then discovered to my relief that while the sand was blowing right on top of the ground up to perhaps 2,000 feet, it was possible to fly at 500 feet through the stuff and still see a mile or two ahead.

I continued to fly south until I hit the road which I had felt sure was there, and then followed the Sunday traffic into Blythe. Judging from the speed at which I was flying, compared with the speed of the automobile traffic, I seemed to be making good time. I soon started seeing the telltale signs of a town, billboards and motels. Then, off to my left, barely a quarter mile from the highway, I spied the main airport in Blythe about seven miles west of town. There was no control tower, and I could have used that airport. I intended, however, to use a smaller airport just on the eastern edge of Blythe which offered the advantage of being closer to motels and restaurants.

When I flew on to the smaller airport and tried to land, I discovered how strong the winds were. With only one runway, and a crosswind, I just couldn't get myself lined up with the runway. After one missed approach, I turned west and followed the highway back to the main airport which had three long runways, one of which would let me land directly into the wind. It took almost ten minutes to get the seven or eight miles back, for I was flying directly into the wind. When at last I had lined up with the runway and reduced power, I discovered what a helicopter pilot must feel like when he comes to land, for the wind was so strong I came almost straight down, with no forward speed. Once I had landed I could barely keep the plane on the ground standing still!

Unfortunately, no one saw me land because the visibility was perhaps only a half mile or so on the ground. It took me fifteen minutes to taxi the plane to the relative protection that the side of a hangar offered by breaking the force of the wind. Fortunately, the taxiway was directly into the wind, for I could not have taxied in any other direction. I did make it without further incident, and, much to my relief, there were tie-down ropes in the ground right next to the hangar which I quickly slipped onto the wing struts.

When I struggled over to the FAA flight service station, they were both surprised and pleased to see me. It seems that their winds at that time were blowing between 45 and 50 miles per hour on the ground! No wonder I had so much trouble getting, and staying down.

Conditions became so unfavorable for traffic that the State Police closed the highway down outside of Blythe that evening. The sand was almost as hazardous to cars as it was to airplanes. Oh, well. There is an old saying that any landing you walk away from is a good one. So I was not complaining.

There is also another saying that is both true and appropriate: "Flying is ninety-nine percent sheer boredom punctuated by a few seconds of stark terror!" The last 30 minutes of this flight qualified as that "few seconds of stark terror."

Comment About Flight Plans

This is probably a good place to digress and talk about flight plans and emergency planning.

In reading the account of the flight from Bakersfield to Blythe, one might wonder just what would have happened if I had not been able to land at Blythe and had to set down in the desert. Well, as you may recall, when I first ran into difficulty, I was fairly sure where I was, and I did not hesitate in what I did. I turned south. I knew that my route had taken me north of the main highway to Blythe and that if I did get lost, all I had to do was turn south and in due course I had to hit that highway. Then, even if the plane were damaged in the process, I could land on, or alongside, the highway and obtain quick assistance.

On every flight I have made over remote areas of the country, I have taken routes from which, if I had gotten into navigation or other difficulties, all I had to do was to fly to the right or the left and be certain of hitting known and conspicuous navigation aids. It is true, however, in the case of the flight to Blythe, that if I had gotten lost or hit a sandstorm 100 miles from Blythe, I would have had to fly south for perhaps 75 miles before I would have hit this highway. Still, at all times I knew my "out" if things did not go well. It is important for a pilot to always have an "out" in case of the unexpected, and to plan each flight with the recognition that something might go wrong. Complacency is a pilot's worst enemy.

All right, now, you might ask, what if the road to the south had been blocked by this same sandstorm? The answer is that I would have had to land in the desert. If the surface sand where I landed was fairly hard-packed, and the plane had not been damaged in landing, I might have been able to fly out later after the sandstorm stopped. Otherwise I would have had to wait for help to arrive.

About this time someone always remarks that, since I didn't have a radio, no one would have known that I was missing and down. The answer is that I had filed a flight plan and if I hadn't arrived within 30 minutes of my flight plan estimate, a well defined set of procedures would have been taken by the FAA to locate me. To be specific, before taking off from Bakersfield I had given the FAA the following information by telephone:

Air speed: 90 miles
Departure time: 2:50 Pacific Time
Cruising altitude: 9,500 feet
Route: Bakersfield to Tehachapi Pass to the southern tip of the
       Edwards Air Force Base restricted area, direct to Blythe
Estimated time en route: 3 hours
Fuel on board: 3 hours 30 minutes
Remarks: No radio
Name of Pilot: G-R-0-S-S
Address of pilot: Denville, New Jersey
Number of persons on board: One
Color of aircraft: Brown

Upon receiving that information, the FAA Flight Service Station office at Bakersfield had teletyped the pertinent information regarding my aircraft, time en route, fuel on board and "no radio" to the flight service station at Blythe. Then the responsibility to take action if I failed to get to Blythe shifted to the flight service station there. As I said, when I arrived in Blythe I went over to the Blythe Flight Service Station to close my flight plan. That was why they were so glad to see me. They were expecting a call from the other airport, and because of the heavy sand storm they were starting to worry about me. If I hadn't shown up within 30 minutes or so of my expected arrival time, the flight service station at Blythe would have started to make inquiries about me. Initially they would have contacted the control tower, or, as in the case at Blythe where there is no tower, they would have checked with local fuel operations and airport staff. They would have also phoned the other airport in Blythe to see if I had landed there. If I had radio, they would have tried calling me.

At the end of the first hour after I was expected, they would have sent a teletype request for information to all FAA stations along and to either side of my route for any information they might have regarding my flight. They would have also teletyped Bakersfield to make sure I had taken off.

They knew the time at which I would run out of fuel. At that time they would probably contact the State Police and have them check all airports within perhaps 150 miles of my route just to make sure that I had not landed elsewhere and failed to close my flight plan. If all of these efforts failed to locate me, they would notify the Air Force Rescue Service which then would have had responsibility to start an aerial search of my route. I might also add that as soon as I was missing they would have broadcast an alert to all aircraft flying along my route asking them to be on the lookout for me. Certainly, if I were anywhere near my planned route, I would have been found within a day or so of going "down." It might have been only a matter of hours.

All of this flight plan service is free and voluntary. I can file a flight plan or not as I want. It is up to me. If I do, my only responsibility is to stick to my flight plan, or if I deviate, to let them know. If one has radio in the plane, this is, of course, very easy. If one does not, then it means finding a phone right after landing and calling the nearest FAA flight service station. This is cheap insurance.

Monday, June 8, 1964

Flight 25—Blythe, CA to Tucson, AZ
255 miles in 3 hours 2 minutes

Bright and early the next morning, after a needed and restful sleep, I drove to the airport to resume my travels. I had been lent the airport courtesy car for the evening, but I had never driven a dilapidated car like this one. You had to push down on the brakes well in advance of wanting to stop, or you would just keep moving. Neither the headlights, nor the horn worked; the speedometer had long since stopped trying; the windows were cracked; the door tended to open without any help from the driver; and the fuel tank leaked when filled to the top. Still, there was no charge for it, so I guess I should not complain.

At about nine a.m., which was rather late for me, I took off once again across the desert. The wind had died and I enjoyed the beautiful scenery without incident. My route took me due east to Phoenix and then, via highways, southeast to Tucson. The flight was uneventful, except perhaps for flying pretty much to the limit of the plane's fuel capacity (11.6 of a 14.0 gallon capacity). It was not as close as it sounds

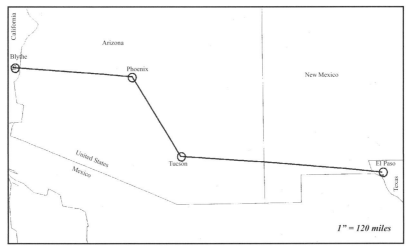

El Paso is right on the Mexican border, so this trip not only encompassed both coasts, it also included our northern and southern borders.

because there were numerous airports that I could have stopped at along the route if needed.

The scenery on this leg was fairly monotonous until I got to Tucson where I crossed over an airport which contained what appeared to be hundreds of swept-wing military aircraft—more planes than I had ever seen before. It was an impressive sight from 9,500 feet. I later learned that this was the Air Force graveyard for aircraft no longer being used. It is located in Tucson because of the dry climate.

Flight 26—Tucson, AZ to El Paso, TX
290 miles in 2 hours 46 minutes

Taking off from Tucson was somewhat nerve-racking. The temperature was close to 100°, it was a short runway, and an elevation of 3,000 feet. The performance of the plane was very marginal, and I did make it over the rooftops of low buildings at the end of the runway. However, for about ten seconds on takeoff, I had my doubts.

In the heat, the climb to 9,500 feet was a long, slow, grind, and I was almost 50 miles east of Tucson before I reached that altitude. My route was mostly east and later southeast along the railroad tracks going to El Paso. I'd had enough of dead-reckoning the day before, and this flight was strictly via iron compass (the railroad tracks). The plane bounced around somewhat in desert updrafts and downdrafts and I didn't try to fight it but just let the plane do whatever it wanted as long as I stayed on course. All in all, the highest the plane went was about 12,000 feet and the lowest was 8,500 feet.

The desert was mostly flat. Only an occasional small mountain or two stuck up, but I saw a long ridge of high mountains off to the north of me in the distance. At one point about 50 miles from El Paso I even noticed two craters which were marked on the map. I assume they were made at some long ago time by meteorites.

So it was a pleasant, relaxed flight to El Paso, arriving in the middle of the afternoon. Actually, I landed at a small airport in New Mexico. El Paso is on the Texas-New Mexico border and this airport was on the west side of El Paso, just over the state line in New Mexico. I used this airport since there was no radio requirement. There was a fairly strong wind on the ground which had been a tailwind for me.

Thursday, June 11, 1964

Flight 27—El Paso to Odessa, TX
246 miles in 2 hours 53 minutes

After a two-and-a-half-day visit in El Paso, it was again time to spend a couple of days sitting in the plane while it carried me back to New Jersey, home, and my pay check. Of course, the main question when it came time to leave was just exactly how I should return: via Chicago and the north, or by way of Memphis and the south. The decision was not altogether mine to make, for I told the flight forecaster at the airport to tell me which route offered the best chance of getting back to New Jersey without serious weather difficulty. This is, of course, the way to fly—to be covering enough distance so that you can pick your route in accordance with the expected weather. In this case, the flight forecaster suggested that I fly the southern route, and that I get started early the next morning. Even on this route, he said I

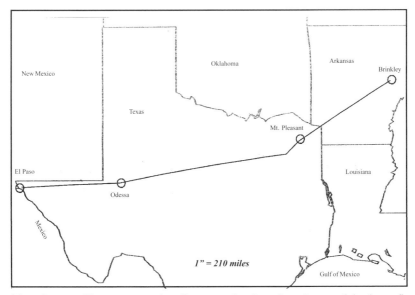

Texas is a very big state, even when flown over by plane. It took most of the day to fly from El Paso to the eastern edge of Texas. The slight jog shy of Mt. Pleasant was to ensure that I was flying far enough south of Dallas to stay out of its busy airspace.

might encounter weather problems. So once again at the crack of dawn I lazily spread my wings and turned eastward toward the Appalachian Mountains, and home, some two thousand miles away.

The first leg took me across more desert, but a highway provided easy navigation. About 75 miles from Odessa, I started seeing the first of many clouds. These were at about 2,500 feet above the ground, so I had no problem flying under them. I prefer to fly in the clear, open sky, but that is not always possible. By the time I got to Odessa, I had not only changed time zones, but I had also left the last of the high mountains and plateau behind me. I had mixed feelings to say the least.

Flight 28—Odessa to Cisco, TX
205 miles in 2 hours 33 minutes

Texas is a big state. Hour after hour I guided my small plane over its mighty lands, and while I was getting farther and farther east, I seemed to get no closer to the eastern end of Texas.

The weather held up for me. By "up" I mean that the clouds kept their distance above me, with an average ceiling of around two thousand feet. Since the mountains were behind me, this was more than adequate, and my flight was an easy one.

As I flew eastward, the towns became more numerous and I became aware that there are a lot of Air Force bases in Texas. Of course, they like the good weather there. Every time I came anywhere near one of these Air Force bases, I had to make a good-sized detour to avoid their flying area. For the most part their planes were flying below the overcast just as I was, and, given their fast speed, I was mighty wary of them.

I goofed in the selection of Cisco as an airport. It was not a large airport, and that was fine, but I do need certain facilities most of which are listed in my airport directory. However, who would think that an airport, even a small one, would not have a telephone? Well, this one didn't and I had a flight plan to close. So after refueling my plane, the manager of the airport kindly drove me the two miles to the nearest phone where I could call flight service.

Flight 29—Cisco to Mt. Pleasant, TX
240 miles in 3 hours

More and more Texas. I was getting rather tired of this big, sprawling state. I might not go any faster over the ground when flying over our smaller states, but it soothes the soul to cross a state line every couple of hours or so.

This flight took me just south of Fort Worth and Dallas. Just a little more than a year earlier, Inge and I had driven through this area on a return trip from Mexico City. That time we had lots of traffic jams. This time, I flew around the whole sixty-mile diameter metropolitan complex in less than 45 minutes.

I landed first for fuel not at Mt. Pleasant but at a paved airport, Sulphur Springs. The airport seemed deserted although I saw a couple of planes tied down. I looked around for someone to help me and realized that the airport was right on the edge of a farm. After about thirty knocks on the farmhouse door and a few shouts of "anyone home?" a farm woman came to the door. I asked her about fuel and she said fine, she would help me but I would have to wait until she finished dessert because she had company. I realized this would take some time, so, on not too much fuel, I took off and flew the forty miles to Mt. Pleasant where they were quite willing to sell me ten gallons of gas.

Flight 30—Mt. Pleasant, TX to Brinkley, AR
256 miles in 2 hours 40 minutes

At last, after 751 miles and nine hours of flying, I crossed the Texas border into Arkansas. It may seem illogical, but once I crossed into Arkansas, I felt that I was almost home. I still had 1,290 miles to go.

I seemed to be picking up a little more speed—up from 80 miles an hour to 89. The land beneath me seemed to change in character, too. There were many more farms and small towns, and everything was green and hot. I flew to within an hour of dusk, and then landed at the town of Brinkley, only to find that once again there was no one at the airport to give me fuel. It turned out that the airport was used primarily by two crop-duster outfits who started flying at daybreak and stopped fairly early in the afternoon. I found out the name of the owner of one of these outfits from the gas station across the street and called to see if he could send someone to refuel me since I, too, wanted to start out at daybreak the next day. In due course, the owner kindly came down and sold me ten gallons of gas. He certainly didn't make anything on me on that sale, but such is the flying fraternity, that a pilot will think nothing of helping another pilot out—be he flying a big DC-3 or a small Luscombe.

Friday, June 12, 1964

Flight 31—Brinkley, AR to Nashville, TN
263 miles in 2 hours 38 minutes

Up at 3 a.m. once again, I called the Memphis weather bureau long-distance to see if the El Paso forecaster had steered me in the right direction, weather-wise. They said he had and that I should have no trouble getting to New Jersey. I took off and was in the air at about 4 a.m. This is one of the nicest times of the day to fly—the air is calm and fresh. Unfortunately, the visibility between Memphis and Nashville was poor, and I had to work to keep on course.

Flight 32—Nashville, TN to Johnson City, VA
252 miles in 2 hours 43 minutes

The distances seemed to go by quite rapidly now. I was still averaging about 90 miles an hour, which, while faster than much of the trip, was still not very fast. Still, I flew 252 miles in 2 hours and 43 minutes, which isn't exactly slow. I started running into mountains again (figuratively speaking, of course) and the weather, while hot and sunny, started looking less and less like the good weather that had been forecast. Upon landing at Johnson City, which is right on the edge of the Appalachian Mountains, I called the weather bureau and found out that an overcast covered most of the mountains, and that I would have to fly low in order to get through to New Jersey.

Again I consulted local pilots who said I should have no real difficulty if I just followed the main highway into Roanoke which was on the other side of the mountains and on my route. I thanked them and took off for my now familiar road-following chore. In taking off I became somewhat concerned, for the plane did not want to climb in the heat, and I had to dodge a hill or two off the end of the runway.

Flight 33—Johnson City to Charlottesville, VA
254 miles in 2 hours 54 minutes

The weather on the leg to Roanoke was forecast to remain about the same or get better, not worse, so it was a fairly safe flight, but a lot of work. I had some fancy navigating to do in the Roanoke area. I wanted to fly around the city to stay away from the airport on the other side, but I didn't have enough visibility to navigate easily without following roads or railroads, which I did. This was not as easy as it may sound, because the roads were leading into and out of the city, not around it. I had to change highways and railroads several times. But this is part of the fun of flying, the challenging part of it. In less than 15 minutes, I was well on my way out of the Roanoke area. Even

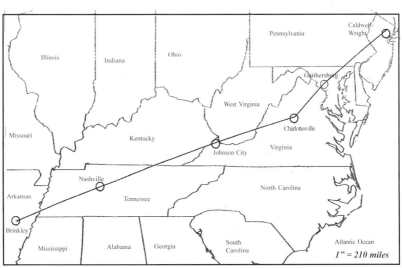

The last day, and a long one, 1,094 miles, in 11 hours, 45 minutes. I felt a real sense of satisfaction in having flown around the United States in an unsophisticated aircraft relying solely on my map-reading skills to make the trip. I had no radio, only 14 gallons of fuel, and no electrical system. This was not a barnstorming flight, but close to one.

though the mountains were now behind me, the visibility had not improved, and I had to continue the road-following technique until I later came across an electrical transmission line. The power line was also going to Charlottesville, and this made the rest of that flight a whole lot easier.

Flight 34—Charlottesville, VA to Gaithersburg, MD
115 miles in 1 hour 31 minutes

I seldom get discouraged, but at Charlottesville I hit a dispiriting snafu. They were out of the type of gas I needed! How can an airport run out of gas? I don't know, but once in a while they do—poor management, or because they didn't pay their gas bills. They did have some higher octane fuel that I normally shouldn't put into the plane, but considering it an emergency, I put 5 gallons in the tank which got me to Gaithersburg.

The visibility flying north from Charlottesville was generally four or five miles. I flew about ten miles west of Washington, D.C., to stay out of the flight patterns into and out of that city. Gaithersburg is located about fifteen miles northwest of Washington, D. C. and is one of several active general aviation airports in the area.

Flight 35—Gaithersburg, MD to Caldwell, NJ (home)
210 miles in 1 hour 58 minutes

The final leg was without incident, although I was getting very tired with these long days.

On arriving home, I reflected on the fact that I had managed to fly around the United States with the minimum of equipment and without getting lost. I ended up with a sense of satisfaction of having met all of the expected and unexpected challenges of this trip, and a deep feeling of being glad that I was alive and living in the United States where such an adventure is possible, even for someone on a modest budget.

PART III

THE MATURE YEARS
1972 to 1995

14

The Mature Years
An Overview
1972 to 1995

"Maturity" is defined as having reached full natural growth or development. In the aviation sense, it refers both to pilot skills and to the performance capabilities of the airplane. By the early 1970s general aviation aircraft had become far more utilitarian than when I first started flying in 1955. Avionic developments, coupled with modern aircraft design and larger engines, resulted in single-engine aircraft that could fly long distances under moderately bad weather conditions with almost airline-level dependability.

I believe my mature years started when we purchased our first well-equipped IFR aircraft (a Cessna 182) in 1972, and ended late in 1995, when my flying started to change with the purchase of a second aircraft, a single-seat Mooney Mite. During these intervening years I fully utilized the capabilities of, first, my Cessna 182, and after 1975, my Cessna T210.

Getting Back Into Aviation

Inge and I had stopped flying for financial reasons in March of 1969. I was advancing rapidly at Price Waterhouse and by 1972, our income had increased to the point where, with some struggle, we could take advantage of both my increased pilot skills and technological developments. As we considered getting back into aviation, I recognized it was essential that I relearn the skills needed to fly under instrument flight rules. There was little point in having a sophisticated airplane but be limited to flying only in VFR conditions.

The most important skill a pilot needs for flying in IFR weather is to automatically and continually scan the flight instruments, and then to adjust the flight controls as necessary. Driving requires similar skill. When a person drives down a highway, he is watching for traffic, curves in the road, and other potential hazards, without consciously thinking about it. A good driver automatically turns the wheel, puts on the brakes, or does whatever is necessary to stay safe. The same is true with flying under conditions where the pilot cannot see out the window. He needs to trust his instruments and react without thinking. This skill requires hours of practice because it has to become second nature.

While I had gotten my instrument rating in 1956, what little instrument flying I did stopped in 1959 when I sold my Cessna 170. The Aeronca, Luscombe, and Cessna 172 we had in the 1960s were good-weather-only planes.

In 1971, I purchased a desktop-size flight simulator in anticipation of my return to instrument flying. This was long before home computers had come on the scene, but this unit had a small computer in it and was the first personal simulator. It was rudimentary by today's standards but was very effective in helping a pilot develop basic instrument flight skills. The reader will recall that in 1956 I had used an Air Force simulator at Presque Isle Air Force Base when I got my instrument rating. It simulated a small military jet trainer and took up a whole room. I credit my new simulator with significantly helping me to jump-start my return to IFR flight, the key to fully utilizing both my Cessna 182 and later the Cessna T210. As I worked with this simulator to get back my skills, my desire to resume flying became stronger.

Cessna 182

Our family friends in El Paso, Noel and Mary Olmstead, owned a Cessna 182 which they had purchased new in 1964. Noel, who was now 70, had concluded it was time to close the hangar door on his flying, and in September of 1975, he sold us N3162S for $9,500 ($48,000 in 2008 dollars). It was a well-equipped plane by the standards of the

day. It had dual
transmitters and
dual navigation
receivers includ-
ing instrument
landing system
(ILS) capability. It
had a transponder
which continually
responded to radar
interrogation from
the air traffic con-
trol system. This
plane also had a
controllable-pitch
propeller, which
allowed more
control of the en-
gine power. The
Cessna 182 was a
much faster air-

This desk-size personal flight simulator allowed me to train myself to automatically scan flight instruments without consciously thinking about doing so. Simulated instrument localizer approaches could be made with variable cross-winds, and five-levels of turbulence. This really tested your skill. The control yoke would be attached to the tube in the bottom center (see arrow), removed here to better show the instrument and radio arrangements.

plane than the Cessna 172. The Cessna 172 had a 145 horsepower engine, whereas the Cessna 182 had 225 horsepower. The additional power increased cruising speed by 30 miles per hour, and also allowed the plane to carry more weight.

By the time we purchased the 182, I had perhaps a hundred hours on my simulator, but I still needed in-flight experience. I also had to be re-certified for IFR flight by an instructor. So when I went to El Paso to pick up the plane I arranged to have an instructor work with me to strengthen my instrument skills, and to check me out on this new, so-phisticated aircraft. When I left El Paso, I had eleven hours of flight time in the Cessna 182 and was certified as being IFR competent, and, for insurance purposes, qualified to fly this plane.

The rest of 1972 was spent getting used to the plane. Our first fam-ily cross-country trip was to Daytona Beach, Florida, for Christmas, 1972, with Inge's mother. The flying time from Morristown to Daytona was a few minutes less than 8 hours. After Christmas, we flew to Small Hope Bay on Andros Island in the Bahamas where we stayed for a

N3162S, a 1964 Cessna 182 on the tarmac in El Paso. With a 225 horsepower engine, this aircraft was an excellent plane in which to get back into serious flying.

week learning to scuba dive. This was also our first over-water flight. We rented a life raft and survival equipment in Ft. Lauderdale, but I was still uneasy flying over water. On one local flight while on Andros we observed in a bay what looked like a whole school of perhaps a hundred sharks. This was a vivid reminder of the importance of our engine.

I flew 81 hours in a little over the three months of ownership in 1972, and I felt that I was really back into flying, probably for good.

Flying Farmers Tour to Alaska

I flew 196 hours in 1973, mostly cross-country trips going places and doing things that we could not have done without our Cessna 182. The highlight was a trip to Alaska that involved 78 hours of flying.

We had joined the national organization of The Flying Farmers at the suggestion of our El Paso friends who were members. They had been on a Flying Farmers tour to Alaska several years earlier which they highly recommended. The real advantage of this organized tour was that the tour leader made all hotel and eating arrangements and knew out-of-the-way places that we would never have discovered. He was a retired farmer from Iowa and had led the tour annually for a number of years.

The tour began at Dawson Creek, British Columbia, which is the start of the Alaskan Highway. The flight to Alaska followed this highway for several reasons. It was easy to follow, and safer in the event of a mechanical or weather problem. This was a desolate wilderness area. Fuel had to be trucked in, and what few airfields there were with fuel had to be close to the highway. There were twelve to fifteen planes on the tour when we met at Dawson Creek on July 15.

We were living in Morristown, New Jersey at the time and decided to extend our trip at the front end by flying to Dawson Creek via our friends' home in El Paso, and the homes of some of my relatives in Corvallis, Oregon. This was an indirect route, but because we were flying, we looked on our plane as our "time machine." The deviations to El Paso and Corvallis added approximately 15 flying hours to the trip (but more than 1,800 miles). Try to do that by any other means of transportation!

All but one or two of the pilots were farmers, and flew off landing strips that were right on their farms. There was only one other pilot with an instrument rating, so all flights were under VFR rules. Generally that meant we were required to have three miles of visibility and fly free of clouds. There were several legs when the weather was marginal at best, and planes followed one another in single file. I remember one leg from Fairbanks to Palmer, Alaska where the weather was so marginal that 15 minutes out of Fairbanks everyone concluded they had better make a 180 degree turn and return to Fairbanks. The visibility was probably only a mile and the ceiling less than 3,000 feet. When we radioed the Fairbanks tower that we were returning, the tower con-

The Flying Farmers' planes at Circle Hot Springs, Alaska. We are 3rd from the left.

troller gave up trying to control the traffic. He just said over the radio: "All Flying Farmers. You are cleared to land. Don't run into one another."

We all made it, but I concluded that the next time the weather looked lousy I would file IFR, which I did later that afternoon when the group decided to try again to get to Palmer, about 200 miles south. They made it, but I felt a lot safer in the clouds and on the controller's radar screen than I would have if we had been flying VFR underneath the clouds.

This was a beautiful trip, and for the most part we had good weather. We resolved we would come back later, and we did so in 1976. The account of our 1976 trip is the subject of *Chapter 16, Top of the World, Mt. McKinley, and Point Barrow.*

One sad note. A year or two later, two planes on that year's tour flew into a mountain in very poor visibility. All persons were killed including the tour leader and his wife. Their luck had run out.

Move to Washington, D.C.

We moved in 1974 from Morristown to Washington, D.C., which meant moving our plane to Dulles International Airport. In those days, traffic at Dulles was fairly light, and small aircraft were welcomed. At that point Inge decided that she did not want to cope with the airline traffic at Dulles and essentially ended her flying as a pilot. Also influencing her was the fact that the children were then ages ten and seven and she had too little time to stay current with the Cessna 182.

12,000 Feet Was Not High Enough

By 1975, I was getting comfortable flying under instrument conditions and we were utilizing the plane to go places and see things that we could not otherwise have done. Our children were then 11 and 8 and good travelers. Between January and the end of August, we flew a hundred hours, making several transcontinental trips (Seattle, Washington and Long Beach, California). In May my logbook showed I had flown a total of 2,000 hours, another milestone.

The second half of 1975 turned out to be a turning point in our flying. I concluded that we needed to get a still higher-performance airplane. I reached this decision on June 19, 1975, while flying between Salt Lake City and Las Vegas. We were flying IFR on the airway at the minimum en route altitude (MEA) of 12,000 feet. The MEA is the lowest altitude you can fly on that route when you are in clouds to be assured that you will not hit a mountain or other obstruction.

With the whole family and luggage for four, the Cessna 182 struggled to get up to 12,000. I doubt that we could have flown any higher. What concerned me was that there were mountains on both our right and left sides that were higher than we were. We couldn't see them but knew they were there. If we had encountered turbulence, or down drafts, we might have had difficulty maintaining our altitude. We had no excess power.

I concluded that either we had to re-evaluate the risks of flying across the Rockies, and probably stop doing so, or we needed a higher-performance aircraft that could get to higher altitudes. The next chapter describes our decision, and the purchase of our Cessna T210. Chapters 16 through 25 detail the many adventures in this mature phase of my flying. By the end of 1995, I had accumulated more than 5,000 hours.

Retirement to Join NAA

In mid-1989, I took early retirement from Price Waterhouse at age 55 to assume the presidency of the National Aeronautical Association (NAA), which is discussed in more detail in *Chapter 26, NAA, The National Aero Club of the United States.*

While my full-time service at NAA only lasted through 1992, I served as president until 1995. During that period I actively used my Cessna T210 in traveling around the United States on NAA business. In the six years I was president, I flew eleven hundred hours, mostly on NAA business.

With my complete retirement in 1995 as president of NAA, I no longer had a reason to make as many long-distance flights, and, at age 63, I was slowing down as might be expected. In late 1995 I had also purchased a small aircraft, a single seat Mooney Mite which was a good-weather-only airplane. While I kept my Cessna T210 for another eight years it was no longer my only airplane. My focus started to change and I consider that the mature phase had ended.

15

A High-Performance Airplane
1975 to 2003

As I noted in the last chapter, I concluded that if we were going to be flying across the Rocky Mountains we needed to have the ability to fly higher. That meant I would have to either modify the engine by installing a turbocharger, or get another plane with a turbocharger already installed.

Turbochargers have been used for years on military and commercial aircraft, but in 1975, few light aircraft had them. Cessna Aircraft was just starting to make them available on the Cessna 210 as a high-cost option. I describe in detail in *Chapter 25, Turbocharger Failures,* the function and operation of the turbocharger. Let me just say here that a turbocharger allows an engine to develop power at much higher altitudes than one without.

On September 3, 1975, I picked up a brand new Cessna T210 from a Cessna dealer in Kalamazoo, Michigan. It had a factory-installed turbocharger, six-seats, retractable landing gear, and a built-in oxygen system. It came without avionics because I wanted to choose my own equipment. Its optimum flight altitude was 25,000 feet, far higher than any mountain in North America. This started a twenty-eight year love affair with a new mistress. At the time I purchased this plane I had 2,069 total flying hours. By the time I sold the plane in 2003, I had almost 6,500 hours, of which 4,000 were in this plane.

High Performance

The registration number (sometimes referred to as tail number) on this aircraft was N5119V. It was truly a high performance airplane. It was also a much more complicated plane to fly, particularly at high altitudes. Why fly so high? For a number of reasons. You are above most weather at 25,000 feet, and the air is usually smoother. There is less drag on the aircraft because the air is thinner. Less drag means that with the same engine power output, the higher you go, the faster you go. At 70 to 75 percent power, this plane flying at 10,000 feet travels 193 miles an hour but at 25,000 feet it travels 215.

A human being cannot live at 25,000 feet without supplemental oxygen. In fact if the oxygen system were to fail, the pilot would lose the ability to think straight within a couple of minutes. Loss of consciousness would follow, and then death. N5119V had a built-in oxygen system consisting of four inter-connected oxygen bottles, totaling 74 cubic feet and when the bottles were full, the oxygen was under eighteen hundred pounds of pressure. This oxygen fed individual face masks which the pilot and passengers wore above 12,000 feet. For one person there was enough oxygen for about ten to fifteen hours of use. In late 1976, I added an additional 72 cubic foot oxygen bottle, doubling the available oxygen. There is more discussion about oxygen and the hazards of high altitude flight in *Chapter 18, Thirty-Two Thousand Feet*.

Power Setting at Higher Altitudes

The Cessna T210 was a much more complex aircraft to fly than the Cessna 182. I had a great deal to learn, particularly at high altitudes. This was particularly true in power settings. In a normally aspirated engine, the power setting is straightforward. You push the throttle forward, and more fuel is fed into the cylinders, creating more power. In some aircraft, including the Cessna 182, the pilot also controls propeller rpm, manifold pressure, and mixture.

In a turbocharged aircraft there is an additional factor when the plane is at higher altitudes, say, above 17,000 feet. At these altitudes 100% of the exhaust gases from the engine turn the compressor blades of the turbocharger. Change the power setting and you change the tur-

N5119V in an aerial picture taken by a helicopter that was as close as it appears in this picture. San Francisco is in the background.

bocharger speed because the increase or decrease of power also increases or decreases the amount of exhaust gases. This change in the amount of exhaust gases results in a change in turbocharger speed. This affects the amount of compressed dense air going into the engine, further changing the power output and the speed of the plane. Likewise, a change in air speed also affects the turbocharger output.

This sounds complicated, and it is. Once at high altitude, it often took me 10-15 minutes before I was able to get the exact power output I wanted.

Avionics Installation

I mentioned that N5119V came, by my choice, with no avionics installed. Once I was checked out at Kalamazoo, I flew the plane to Columbus, Ohio where my avionics shop, Electrosonics, was located. I left the plane for two weeks while they installed a number of communication and navigation radios, including an autopilot. The plane as delivered at Kalamazoo had cost $50,000; this avionics installation added another $30,000, making a total cost of $80,000 in 1975 dollars ($315,000 in 2008 dollars).

I spent most of the balance of 1975 learning about this sophisticated plane and its capabilities. I flew about 80 hours, including trips to Phoenix, Arizona, Daytona Beach, Florida, and Kansas City, Missouri. My logbook for October 5 shows one flight leg between Nashville, Tennessee, and Washington, D.C. Dulles Airport at 23,000 feet with a ground speed of 268 miles an hour! That meant I had a tailwind of more than fifty miles an hour. It was a rare experience.

Time Machine

Over the next twenty-eight years I flew the plane some four thousand hours, almost all of which were flights that we could not have made with a lesser-performing airplane. We not only had a high altitude capability to allow us to get over the highest mountains, but we could often get above the weather. The plane had long legs and could fly almost six hours between fuel stops at speeds close to 200 miles per hour. We still encountered headwinds, but we could also encounter strong tailwinds, particularly on west-to-east flights.

N5119V became our time machine. We measured destinations not in terms of how far away they were in miles, but in terms of how many hours it would take to get there. Most of our flights were vacation trips, and pressures at work limited the time available. Our time machine effectively doubled the number of places we could visit in a two or three week period. We treated the plane in the same way most families treat their car—part of our routine life. Our two children grew up with a perspective of this country that few of their friends had.

I have long since lost mental track of the number of times we crossed the United States. In the pages to follow I will highlight a number of flights where I learned a lesson of importance, or traveled to a unique destination. For most flights, however, it was hours and hours of sheer boredom only occasionally punctuated by a few seconds of stark terror.

Instrument Flight

On almost every long flight, we were flying under IFR rules. Early on I found that during any flight of four or five hundred miles, or more, I was likely to encounter instrument weather conditions, regardless of what the forecast had been. Many times these conditions were storms that we were then flying above, "on top," in clear air. But we still needed to be on an instrument flight plan. Not only did I file IFR on virtually every cross-country flight, on most long flights I was, in fact, in instrument conditions for at least part of the time. I never really kept track of my total in-cloud IFR flight time other than to record instrument landings for FAA purposes. I suspect that I was in clouds less than 20% of the time. I became very comfortable flying IFR, and confident of my ability to make instrument landings even under "minimum" weather conditions, typically, a 200 foot overcast and landing visibility of half a mile.

Flying high, of course, was fine if you did so selectively. I found that the climb to 25,000 feet typically took 50 minutes, and the descent, another 50 minutes. I would start my descent for Washington's Dulles Airport while still 200 miles out. There was no point in using fuel to climb to 25,000 feet if the total flight was only three or four hundred miles. And if there were headwinds, I would never fly higher than I had to. Twenty-five to fifty mile an hour headwinds are all too common at high altitudes. The real advantage of a turbocharged aircraft is that, given a tailwind, you gain an advantage if you fly high, but, given a headwind, you can minimize its impact by staying low.

Boiling Point of Water at 25,000 feet?

Flying at 25,000 feet is flying in a different and dangerous world. Let me give you an example. We made many trips to Kansas City, Missouri, where two great-aunts were living. A flight to Kansas City, from our home in Washington, D.C. against the usual headwinds required one fuel stop, usually in Indianapolis. But returning with a tailwind, we often could make it nonstop, particularly if we flew at 25,000 feet and had a tailwind. It was on a flight home from Kansas City on a cold January day that I learned the hard way about the boiling point of water at 25,000 feet.

Just before leaving my aunts' house in Kansas City I had preheated my thermos and filled it with coffee right from the stove. Perhaps two hours later, I decided I wanted a cup of coffee. By that time I was at 25,000 feet and settled in for the flight home. I had the plane on autopilot and, of course, was wearing my oxygen mask. To drink or eat, I merely pulled the mask away from my face, took a sip, and then let the mask cover my face again.

I put the thermos between my legs and turned the cap to open it. The instant the thermos seal was broken, the reduced pressure at 25,000 feet entered the thermos and the coffee started boiling violently. Steam and liquid erupted through the partially opened bottle and my reflex immediately reversed the thermos cap to stop it. But in the split second that the seal was broken, half the coffee in the thermos had escaped, much of it in the form of steam. There was coffee all over the front of the instrument panel, and where the steam hit the windshield, it had instantly condensed and frozen. On the other side of the windshield the temperature was 35 degrees below zero Fahrenheit! While the plane's heater kept the cabin warm (I flew in shirt sleeves), the windshield, of course, was quite cold. I spent the next half hour cleaning up the mess.

After getting home, I did some research and found that at 25,000 feet water boils at 166 degrees. No doubt the coffee was much hotter than that, probably by thirty or more degrees. Clearly the atmosphere is very hostile to life at that altitude, and the pilot had better know what he is doing.

Additional Fuel Tanks

In November, 1976, I had wing-tip fuel tanks installed, each holding 14 gallons. I never again wanted to come close to running out of fuel, as we almost did in our 1976 Alaska trip. See *Chapter 16, Top of the World, Mt. McKinley and Point Barrow*. The plane's two original tanks held, combined, 90 gallons and by adding 28 gallons more I was adding 30 percent more fuel. That translated to a greater than 30 percent increase in range because on takeoff the plane needs fuel to taxi, take off, and climb to altitude; but once at altitude, the entire 28 gallons can be used to extend the range of the plane.

An additional reason for the tip tanks was that I wanted to set a speed record from San Francisco to Washington, D.C. for our weight category aircraft. The extra 28 gallons would make it possible to fly that route with a single fuel stop. I made that record flight with my son on January 1, 1977, as described in *Chapter 17, An FAI Speed Record.*

Lake Powell

In 1977, we discovered Lake Powell in south-eastern Utah. This was to be our vacation destination for a number of years to come. We landed at a remote landing strip at Bullfrog Marina and rented a houseboat, initially for just a week, but in later years for two weeks. This was a good example of how we used the long-distance capabilities of our

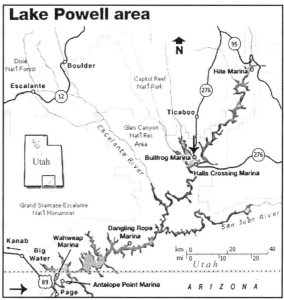

Beautiful Lake Powell was created when a dam was built across the Colorado River at Page, AZ (arrow left bottom). This canyon lake is 186 miles long and a wonderful boaters' paradise. It was our family's favorite vacation spot. It took a day-and-a-half to fly from Washington, D.C. to Bullfrog Marina, (1,800 miles), landing at an adjacent desert landing strip (arrow, center).

plane to do things that you could never think of doing if you had to depend on a car or even the commercial airlines. Airlines cannot fly into Bullfrog Marina. Lake Powell is a canyon lake and is surrounded by remote desert and Indian Reservations.

A footnote to history: The flight home from Bullfrog Marina in the summer of 1981 took place just after President Reagan had fired all of the striking air traffic controllers, making IFR flight very difficult; the only staff then on duty were nonstriking controllers and supervisors. I have long since forgotten the procedures we had to follow in order to fly IFR, but my logbook shows that on the return trip we did fly three hours under actual IFR conditions. The Air Traffic Control system, while hampered by the strike, was not totally shut down.

Facelift—N5119V becomes N210MG

In 1981, N5119V went into the paint shop for a face lift and name change. The plane had been sitting outside for its entire life and no longer had the pristine, racy look it had in 1975. I took advantage of this new paint job to request that the FAA change the registration number to N210MG. In radio communications the plane was referred to as "November-two-ten-mike-golf." For me, the letters "MG" stood for Mal Gross. Pilots have egos, too.

In October, 1981, I took the plane to RAM Aircraft in Waco, Texas for an engine upgrade and overhaul. We had decided to attempt a flight across the "big pond" to Germany and I wanted to be sure the engine wouldn't let us down. In addition we asked RAM to install a second vacuum pump on the engine in parallel with the factory-installed pump. The vacuum pump was used to power several of the instrument gyros. With only one pump, its failure meant that these instruments would stop functioning. We wanted a second vacuum pump for safety reasons. RAM designed and obtained certification approval from the FAA for this installation. Subsequently Cessna Aircraft started putting a second vacuum pump on their new aircraft. Once again, I was somewhat ahead of my time in the modifications I made to N210MG.

The Fastest Tailwind

Over the years I have experienced tailwinds of 30 to 50 miles per hour flying eastbound. On May 15, 1982, I picked up a 125 miles per hour tailwind at 25,000 feet. My ground speed was 315 miles per hour. The jet stream that day was much lower than normal, and was going in exactly my direction. This was the fastest ground speed I encountered in all my years of flying.

Orcas Island Property Purchase

In early February, 1983, we took a major step that influenced our flying for the next 24 years. We bought a five acre lot on Buck Mountain on Orcas Island in Northwest Washington State. We were not

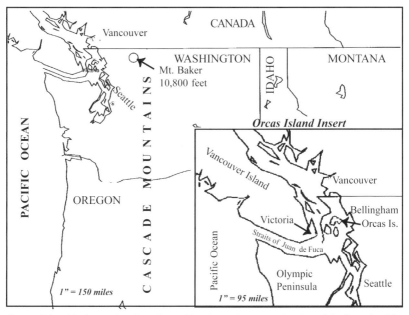

Orcas Island is located only a few miles from the water border with Canada. The ferry from the mainland was the only way to get to Orcas other than by plane. The ferry takes an hour-and-a-half, and there were only six daily sailings each way.

quite fifty years old but we were thinking ahead. From that point on, we had a destination that was uniquely suited for a family with an airplane—a destination 2,500 miles from our home, accessible only by an hour-and-a-half ferry ride, or by air. At the time we bought this lot I had my doubts that we would ever build or retire there. Inge, however, was excited. I agreed to the purchase largely because the aviation aspects attracted me. I would have a good reason to fly, some-times under demanding circumstances, because the Rocky Mountains were between our home and Orcas Island.

Ranchele Micro Flight Plan

In December, 1979, I purchased my first home computer, an Apple IIc. This was one of the earliest desktop computers. About the only programs then available, other than games, were a rudimentary word-processing program and a spreadsheet program called VisiCalc. However, a programming language called BASIC was installed, and computer owners had the option of learning this language and writing their own programs.

Over several years, I became reasonably proficient in writing computer programs in BASIC. My goal was to write a flight planning program for my personal use. Initially, this program was very limited in scope, dealing mostly with the calculation of the impact of winds on ground speed. Over time I added the ability to retrieve performance data from previously entered flight plans. By the time I had finished, the program code was huge—7,500 lines of BASIC. By today's standards the program was very rudimentary.

As I was developing it, I showed this program to several of my friends at the Aircraft Owners and Pilots Association (AOPA) and they encouraged me to make it available to their membership. I obtained a U. S. patent in 1983 and over two years sold about 1,000 copies through AOPA. I ended up with two versions, one for Apple IIc computers and the other for Radio Shack's TRS-80 computers.

The program was sold under the name "Ranchele Micro Flight Plans." We had two children, Randy and Michele for whom the program was named. It was not a commercial success because the data entry was very time consuming, and each copy of the program had to be tailored to the specific aircraft. It was a first, however, and pointed the direction that more capable personal computers would be playing in the future.

Autopilot Replaced

In 1984 I replaced the autopilot installed in 1975 with a more sophisticated one. This new autopilot could be programmed to follow instructions from the navigation computer. For example, after takeoff the computer would instruct the plane to climb to a pre-selected altitude. Upon reaching that altitude the autopilot would automatically level off and fly at that altitude. In the 1990s when GPS (Global Positioning Satellite) became available, you could preprogram virtually the entire flight before leaving the ground. When you got to your destination airport the autopilot could then fly the approach much more accurately than a human pilot. It was like having a copilot. My responsibility was to handle the engine and throttle controls, push the right buttons, and then monitor the flight to be sure nothing malfunctioned.

I made many flights to Columbus, Ohio, where Electrosonics had made the initial installation of my avionics. Columbus may seem like a long way to go for avionics—almost 300 miles each way—but I learned it was cheaper to fly back to the people that had installed the equipment. They knew the plane and could quickly identify and fix an avionics problem. I usually flew out in the morning to arrive about 9 a.m. and then returned in the afternoon.

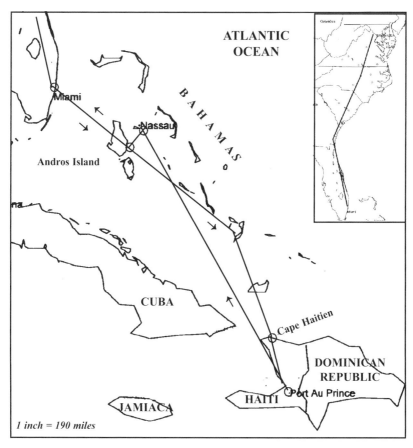

Our first long, over-water flight. Randy, age 16, and I flew to Cape Haitien and Port-au-Prince, in Haiti, and then to Nassau and Andros Island, in the Bahamas. We were gone ten days, flying twenty hours, half of which were over water.

STOL Modification

We made another significant change to N210MG. We had a STOL (Short Take Off and Landing) modification made to the leading edge of the wing to allow the plane to land and take off at a speed about seven miles per hour slower than before. It also changed the climb characteristics of the plane at lower speeds. Before this modification, once the plane broke ground on the takeoff run it really did not want to climb until the airspeed had increased to about 110 miles per hour. Then the plane would climb nicely all the way up to your desired altitude. After the STOL modification was made, once the plane broke ground it would immediately want to climb without first having to accelerate to the 110 miles per hour. This modification had no moving parts. At less than $2,000, it was an excellent investment.

Twenty-Eight Years

I kept N210MG for twenty-eight years, and it was part of the family. Our two children grew up with this plane and treated it pretty much as most children treated the family car. It was part of their life and, while they knew other kids did not have a plane in their family, they really did not fully appreciate that fact until years later. Our son soloed on his 16th birthday, but quit flying shortly afterwards. Our daughter had no interest in learning to fly.

We had a lot of adventures with this plane over the twenty-eight years, many of which are described in the following chapters.

16

Top of the World
Mount McKinley and Point Barrow
1976

In 1972, the family joined a flying tour to Alaska organized by the Flying Farmers of America, which was mentioned in chapter 14, the overview chapter. We flew our Cessna 182 on that trip, and it was a trip the entire family enjoyed. In 1975, we bought our six-seat Cessna T210, which had more speed and far higher altitude capacity than the Cessna 182, and the family decided they wanted to return to Alaska, but on our own rather than being constrained to follow a schedule set by others.

Ambitious Flight Plan

Our plan was first to fly from our home in Washington, D.C. to El Paso, Texas, to visit our friends, Noel and Mary Olmstead, for a few days. Then we planned to fly north to Calgary, Alberta, in one day (with fuel stops in Farmington, New Mexico, Salt Lake City, Utah, and Great Falls, Montana). The second day we would fly to Anchorage, following the ALCAN highway (with fuel stops at Fort St. John, Watson Lake, and Whitehorse). From Anchorage we would fly to Mount McKinley, Fairbanks, and Barrow. Barrow is the name of the village located on a point of land referred to as Point Barrow. This is the northernmost point of land on the North American continent. Then we would fly south from Barrow to Nome and then via Anchorage to Juneau. From Juneau we would fly south to Washington State on the coast, and visit the rain forests of the Olympic peninsula, before flying home. It was an ambitious trip involving 11,000 miles—about equal to halfway around the world at the equator. We planned on taking a month, leaving on July 12, 1976, just a week after the U.S. Bicentennial.

We made this trip, but there were a couple of surprises along the way.

El Paso Emergency

We arrived in El Paso on schedule, intending to stay two to three days. We actually left ten days later. On the last leg of the flight into El Paso, our son, Randy, was complaining about having a stomach ache. This was somewhat unusual because he had been flying all of his life and had never been airsick. We assumed that once we landed it would go away. It didn't, and by ten p.m. the pain had intensified enough that we decided we had better get him to a local hospital. Noel Olmstead immediately came over to our motel and drove Randy and me to the Providence Hospital emergency room. The emergency room doctor suspected appendicitis and tentatively scheduled Randy for surgery at eight in the morning. He was admitted, and Noel brought me back to the motel to rejoin Inge and Michele, since there was nothing I could do at the hospital.

No sooner had I gotten back to the motel, than the doctor called to say that Randy's condition had worsened and that they could not wait until morning. The doctor was sure the problem was his appendix and they needed to operate immediately, before it ruptured; he had already located a surgeon to perform the operation. By then it was one a.m. Noel took me back to the hospital where we stayed until after Randy was back in his room. The diagnosis had been correct, and it was fortunate that we had gotten him to the hospital when we did. If we had waited until morning the appendix would have ruptured, and threatened his life.

The doctor kept Randy in the hospital longer than he might have been kept if we had lived in El Paso because we were staying in a motel. We had, of course, told him of our travel plans to continue to "the top of the world" upon leaving El Paso. It was nine days later that the doctor said there was no reason not to continue our trip, and he released Randy.

A Second Stomach Ache

It took us three days to fly from El Paso to Anchorage, a distance of a little over 3,000 miles. We spent the second night in Whitehorse, Yukon Territories. Randy was again not feeling well. The following morning he was worse and seemed to have a fever. We arrived in Anchorage late that day.   I called one of my partners at Price Waterhouse—we had an office in Anchorage—and he immediately arranged for us to see a surgeon at Providence Hospital (coincidently, a hospital with the same name as the one in El Paso). It turned out that an infection had set in, and the doctors needed to operate once again. Randy then spent nine more days in the hospital, in isolation, before he was released on August 2.

During this period we stayed in a motel overlooking a float-plane base on Lake Hood. This lake had more float-planes than any other lake in the world. Between hospital visits we enjoyed watching the constant takeoffs and landings of these planes.

Top of Mount McKinley

Given these delays, we had to curtail our trip. Our return date was pretty well fixed since I had to be back at work. The two things that we most wanted to see while in Alaska were Mount McKinley, and Barrow, and before leaving home we had made arrangements for hotel accommodations in Barrow for the night of August 4. If we could not make this date, we would have to strike Barrow from our schedule. As it was, we would have little time to see Fairbanks or make side excursions to some of the glaciers south of Anchorage we had planned to fly over.

We also wanted to see Mount McKinley from the air. It was about a hundred miles north of Anchorage and on a clear day we could see it from Anchorage. We decided to make our flying trip over Mount McKinley without Randy because we were running out of time. So we kept watching the weather. We not only needed a clear day with good visibility, but also a day when the upper-level winds were minimal

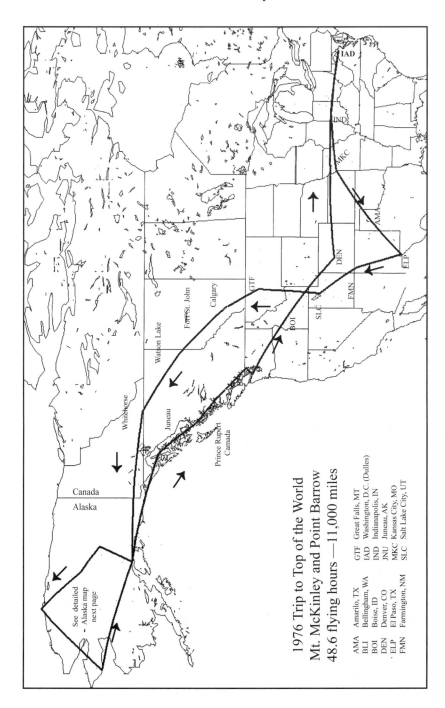

1976 Trip to Top of the World
Mt. McKinley and Point Barrow
48.6 flying hours —11,000 miles

AMA	Amarilo, TX	GTF	Great Falls, MT
BLI	Bellingham, WA	IAD	Washington, D.C. (Dulles)
BOI	Boise, ID	IND	Indianapolis, IN
DEN	Denver, CO	JNU	Juneau, AK
ELP	El Paso, TX	MKC	Kansas City, MO
FMN	Farmington, NM	SLC	Salt Lake City, UT

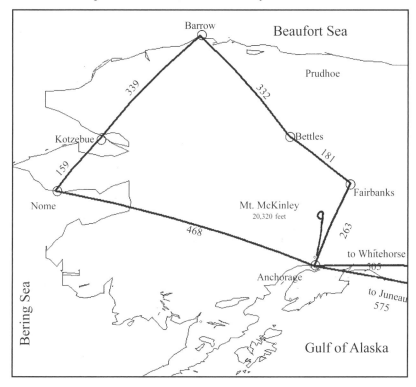

This enlarged map of Alaska shows our route, and distances in statute miles. Navigation was not easy. There was neither LORAN nor GPS coverage in 1976. VOR navigation was limited to Anchorage and Fairbanks because VOR used frequencies that were limited to line-of-sight operation. ADF (automatic direction finding) equipment was widely used, and a few low-frequency radio range stations were still in use. ADF was particularly useful because it could also show the bearing to commercial radio stations.

because our hope was to fly up to, and over, this highest of North American mountains.

August first was the day. It was clear, there were few clouds, and more importantly, there were no winds. Inge, Michele and I flew first to a small airstrip at the base of Mount McKinley, landed, and talked with a ranger to get information. Then we filed an IFR flight plan with Anchorage Center so that we could fly up and around Mount McKinley. It took the best part of an hour to climb to 23,000 feet but it was a perfect day and we saw the mountain as few ever see it, up close and from above. The pictures in this book do not do justice to the view.

We flew closer and closer to the top of Mount McKinley, cautious not to get too close until we were sure there were no strong up or down drafts. This shows the top portion of the mountain. This picture was taken from 23,000 feet.

I said we had to file an IFR flight plan. Flights over 18,000 feet require instrument flight rule clearances, and we were talking to Anchorage Center throughout the flight. No other planes were flying at that altitude—few private planes were able to fly this high in 1976. What little commercial aircraft traffic there was would be flying even higher than we were. We were far closer to the top of Mount McKinley than a commercial airplane would ever be.

What a view!

Randy, of course, missed out on this spectacular sight. However, the following day he was released once again and we left for Fairbanks, our jumping-off point for the northernmost settlement in North America.

Weather Problems at Barrow

Barrow is a little more than five hundred miles from Fairbanks, about three hours flying time. When I checked with Flight Service, I

The upper winds were almost calm and we came quite close to the top. Note the little cloud that was hanging over the summit like a halo (arrow). Those who risk their lives climbing Mount McKinley do not get as beautiful a view as we did.

found that Alaska Airlines, which flies several times a day into Barrow, had just reported that its morning flight had reached Barrow but could not land because of low clouds and was returning to Fairbanks. These low clouds might burn off about the time we would be arriving, but then again, there is nothing certain about weather in the Arctic.

What to do? If we were unable to get to Barrow on this day we would have to scrap going there. We did not have enough fuel to fly nonstop from Fairbanks to Barrow and back and back to Fairbanks if we could not land at Barrow.

There was a small field that had fuel just on the south side of the Brooks Range of mountains at the tiny town of Bettles, 180 miles north of Fairbanks. Flight Service confirmed they had fuel, albeit, very expensive. So we flew to Bettles and refueled. We then had enough fuel to fly from Bettles to Barrow, and if we could not land, return to Bettles, although with minimum reserves.

Once we were on the north side of the Brooks Range we flew over an undercast all the way to Barrow, never seeing the ground. Fortunately, the ceiling at Barrow was high enough that we could make an instrument localizer approach. It is always exhilarating to break out of the clouds and have the runway directly ahead of you with good visibility. This time it was especially thrilling. Our approach had taken us out over the Beaufort Sea. When we broke out, about a mile from shore, it looked as if the sea was frozen solid, with ice everywhere. A beautiful sight.

We Need Fuel

I was talking with a Flight Service station located at Barrow while making my approach. Once I saw the runway, I asked the flight service station: "Where do you want me to park," and told him "we will need fuel." He responded: "You can park anywhere you want, but we have not had any fuel for three years!"

No fuel? The FAA had told me at Anchorage that Barrow had fuel, and I had not bothered to double check in Fairbanks. Now what?

The Flight Service person did say that if it were a true emergency they could probably find a couple of five-gallon cans of fuel. That did not sound very attractive to me; we would have no way of knowing whether the fuel was contaminated or not. Besides, ten gallons would keep the plane aloft for only forty minutes. They did say that Prudhoe Bay had fuel, located about 200 miles east of Barrow.

The plane holds 90 gallons of fuel and the flight from Bettles to Barrow used about forty gallons. That left forty-five to fifty gallons. It would give me approximately two-and-a-half hours of flying time and would allow me to fly about 450 miles.

Our original plan was to fly nonstop directly to Nome from Barrow. There was one other option. Kotzebue was 339 miles on the direct route to Nome. If I flew to Kotzebue, I would have about 30 minutes reserve when I got there, which was cutting it pretty close. There were no other airports near Kotzebue. This would be an acceptable option only if I were sure of the weather, and winds. It was fortunate indeed that we had stopped for fuel at Bettles coming from Fairbanks. Otherwise we would have had even fewer options.

I decided to wait until the next morning, when we were ready to depart, to make the final decision. Then, based on the weather, I would either fly to Prudhoe Bay and then to Fairbanks, or to Kotzebue if the weather and winds were favorable.

Barrow

This was our first real experience of the Arctic, and there was no doubt that we were in the Arctic. Our first glimpse of the sea ice when we broke out on final approach testified to that fact. Once we were on the ground, looking out to the sea to the north, it appeared that the ice started about fifty feet from shore and was solid as far as we could see. We should not have been surprised. We had known that Barrow at 71 degrees north latitude was about 1,400 miles from the North Pole and 300 miles north of the Arctic Circle. Yet knowing this didn't prepare us for seeing the ice and the sunlight at midnight.

A celebration was going on when we arrived. By chance we had arrived on the day when the first ship in two years had made it through the ice, with an icebreaker's help, and reached Barrow. Everyone was celebrating. Barrow routinely gets its perishable foods, medicines, and lightweight provisions by air, but it is expensive to bring things in by plane and the village depends on a supply ship. Last year the ship had not made it through the ice.

Barrow is an Eskimo village. Fishing and hunting are very important food sources. Few tourists visit Barrow, and those that do, fly in by Alaska Airlines. Everything is extremely expensive because of the cost of transportation.

Tundra

The Brooks Range running east to west is some two hundred miles south of Barrow. North of these mountains there is tundra that extends to the northern coast and the Beaufort Sea. Here is a dictionary definition of tundra.

TUNDRA—A cold, treeless, usually lowland area of far northern regions. The lower strata of soil of tundras are permanently frozen, but in summer

"The Four Eskimos." This picture was taken at 11 p.m. August 4, 1976 at Barrow. It was cold! The permafrost was only two to three inches below the surface. Arctic ice was only fifty feet off shore.

the top layer of soil thaws and can support low-growing mosses, lichens, grasses, and small shrubs. (The American Heritage® Science Dictionary Copyright © 2005 by Houghton Mifflin Company.)

At Barrow, the top layer of the tundra is about three inches thick. Immediately below this top layer is permafrost which is permanently frozen soil. Because of the permafrost it is not possible to bury refuse, garbage, abandoned materials, cars, junk, and the like. Every house we saw had a junk heap in the back, and sometimes one in the front as well. The village we saw was not the picture that I had envisioned of an Eskimo village.

The Trip South

The next morning we were tired. We had been up to see the midnight sun, and so we had not gotten as much sleep as we normally would. Still, we had reservations for only the one night and had to get started south. We were due home in just a week.

The weather to and at Kotzebue looked quite good, and we even had a small tailwind. We double checked on fuel availability and were assured there was fuel. With that good news we decided to take that option, and the flight was made without any problems. We were on the ground at Kotzebue only long enough to refuel and eat chocolate bars from our survival pack. Nome was another hour-and-a-half due south, and we spent the night there.

I had not mentioned our survival pack before. Both Alaska and Canada strictly enforce survival food and equipment requirements for aircraft. My recollection is that we were required to carry food for two weeks for each person on board; we doubled that and carried enough for four weeks. Our food survival pack was professionally prepared and weighed about twenty-five pounds; we were also carrying an axe, knife, fishing gear, and other such things. We carried this same survival pack on all of our long flights for the next 25 years, and I am happy to say we never needed to use it, except for the chocolate bars at the Kotzebue Airport.

Juneau

Our flight from Nome to Juneau, with an intermediate stop in Anchorage for fuel, took all day. Juneau is located in an area where the mountains and glaciers come down almost to the water so the terrain is quite different from the tundra surrounding Barrow. There are no roads to Juneau; you get there either by air or by boat. It is 2,300 miles from the North Pole.

We stayed in Juneau for two days visiting a Price Waterhouse partner whose home was there. This gave us a chance to relax after the pressures of the trip north.

From Juneau we flew to Bellingham, Washington with an intermediate stop at Prince Rupert in Canada for fuel. That stop in Canada required us to get customs clearance back into the United States at Bellingham. If we could have flown without stopping in Canada we would not have had to stop in Bellingham (this was before the rules changed after 9-11).

The San Juan Islands

One of the legacies of this trip to the Top of the World came from the fact that on our return flight we flew directly over the San Juan Islands of Washington State. We were flying directly from Bellingham to Port Angeles on the Olympic Peninsula to visit the rain forest there. Inge fell in love with these islands from the air and could not get them out of her mind. Six years later we visited Orcas Island, eventually buying a lot, and in the early 1990s we built a retirement home in which we lived for fifteen years.

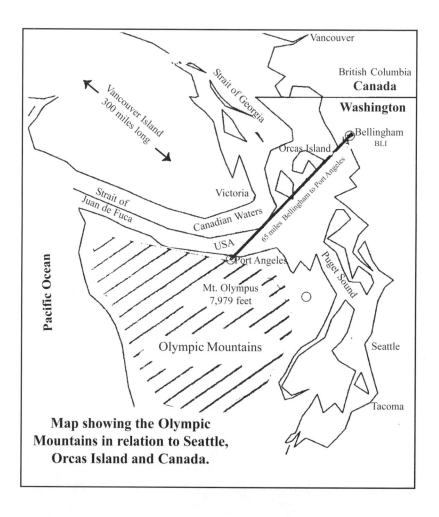

Map showing the Olympic Mountains in relation to Seattle, Orcas Island and Canada.

The Olympic Range of Mountains

The Olympic Range of mountains is on the Olympic Peninsula west of Puget Sound. These mostly snow-covered mountains stretch from just opposite Seattle to the Strait of Juan de Fuca in the north. The Strait is the connecting body of water between the Pacific Ocean and Puget Sound. Seattle and Tacoma are located at the southern end of Puget Sound. Vancouver Island (Canada) is on the north side of the Strait of Juan de Fuca, and stretches north for over 300 miles in the Strait of George.

The Olympic Range rises to almost 8,000 feet and acts as a barrier to storms rolling in off the Pacific. Winds are typically from the southwest and the storm clouds hitting these high mountain are forced to go up and over them. As the clouds rise, the temperature drops by three to five degrees for every thousand feet of altitude, causing the water vapor to condense and fall as rain. The western side of the Olympic mountains is one of the areas of greatest precipitation in the United States, averaging 130 inches a year. At sea level this results in a rain forest. At higher elevations the precipitation is snow and feeds sixty small glaciers resident in the Olympic Mountains.

We wanted our children to see the Hoh Rain Forest. The closest airport was at Port Angeles, a port town on the north side of the Olympic Peninsula. We rented a car to drive around to the western side and we were glad that we had made the trip. The forest was both lush and beautiful.

Back to Washington, D.C.

The trip home from the Olympic Peninsula was more or less without incident. I say this somewhat sheepishly. I had intended to land at Vail, Colorado, near the town of Eagle, to spend the night, but I ended up landing at Aspen, thinking it was Vail. You have heard stories about pilots landing at one airport, thinking it was another. Well, any pilot who says it can't happen to him has not been around very long. Vail and Aspen are about twenty-five miles from each other, up different valleys. I had made a wrong turn and followed another plane that I thought was also going to Vail. He was going to Aspen, so that was where we went. Vail did not have a tower; Aspen did, and I landed without realizing my mistake. The tower apparently did not notice I had landed, and when I realized my mistake I did not do anything to call attention to myself. I just parked at the fixed base operation and rented a car to drive to Vail, Colorado.

The next day we continued the flight home uneventfully. For Randy, however, this trip had been far from uneventful, and one he will never forget. He had spent more than half of the month in hospitals.

Never Again

One other outcome of this trip: I concluded that I did not want ever again to run low on fuel. If we had not refueled at Bettles we would not have had enough to get to Kotzebue. Once again, being conservative and always preparing for the worst had paid off. I looked into auxiliary fuel tanks, and soon had a pair of tanks installed as extended wing tips, giving me an additional hour-and-a-half flying time. There have been many times over the following years that I was thankful for the extra fuel. It allowed the plane to fly close to a thousand miles nonstop.

17

An FAI Speed Record
San Francisco to Washington, D.C.
January 1, 1977

On January 1, 1977, accompanied by my 12-year-old son, Randy, I set an official Fédération Aéronautique Internationale (FAI) speed record between San Francisco and Washington, D.C. which went down in the record book for my airplane's weight class. The 2,439 mile trip was made in exactly 11 hours, 7 minutes and 48 seconds, including a single fuel stop. The following account of this flight, compiled from recorded radio communications and detailed notes made during the flight, was published in 1977 in a Price Waterhouse in-house publication. It is reproduced below in its entirety.

High altitude flight is now fairly common, but at the time of this flight, turbocharged single-engine aircraft were just becoming available. Flight at 25,000 feet is far from routine, even today. Apart from the physiological aspects of high altitude flight, engine management is considerably more complex, and carelessness can easily result in engine detonation and destruction in just a few seconds. The extremely low temperatures create other problems—35 below zero Fahrenheit is typical at 25,000 feet. More than anything else, this was a flight that challenged my skills and knowledge, and was intended to demonstrate what a modern light aircraft could do: cross the country in a single day.

January 1, 1977

Minus 0:15

"This is San Francisco International Airport Information Zulu. One-two-five-zero weather, measured ceiling 2,000 feet broken, visibility one zero. Temperature four four, wind one three zero at five, altimeter 29.92. ILS 28 right approach in use, landing 28, departing runway 10. Advise you have Zulu."

Well, here we are at last, at the Butler Aviation ramp at San Francisco International Airport, about to start our long-planned attempt to cross the country in one day. Our plane, referred to as 5119 Victor, is a 1975 Cessna Turbo 210L, a six-seat, high-wing plane with a single, powerful, turbocharged 285-horsepower engine.

Our trip today promises to be a real adventure because we are going to try to establish an official world speed record between San Francisco and Washington, D.C. Perhaps it seems strange, 50 years after Lindbergh's flight, to be talking about establishing a speed record between these two cities, yet no one has ever done it officially in a light

This picture was taken from a helicopter the day before our departure. Price Waterhouse decided that they wanted to highlight this flight in a company magazine and arranged for these pictures to be taken.

aircraft. There have been official flights between other pairs of east and west coast cities, but not these two.

And there is a very good reason others have not set a record. The Sierras east of San Francisco on the direct route to Washington, D.C. are too high for all but a handful of single-engine airplanes to get across. The airway map shows a minimum crossing altitude of 15,100 feet—a barrier that would have stopped even Lucky Lindy in his "Spirit of St. Louis." But to 5119 Victor, 15,000 feet is child's play, an altitude that doesn't even start to test its capacity. On this flight we intend to fly at 25,000 feet—almost five miles high.

Minus 0:10

Engine started; time to request our clearance.

5119 Victor: *San Francisco clearance. Centurion 5119 Victor, IFR to Goodland, Kansas. Do you have my clearance? Over.*

Tower: *Centurion 5119 Victor is cleared to Goodland as filed, flight plan route, except after takeoff turn left to a heading of 080 for vectors to Linden, J–84, J–2 Coaldale, as filed. Maintain flight level two three zero; expect two five zero at Linden. Departure control will be 120.9, Squawk 3215. Over.*

I read back our clearance and they confirmed I had copied it correctly. I had pre-filed our flight plans shortly after getting a weather briefing by phone from the hotel and they went directly into the FAA computer. The computer will then give our routing to all of the controllers as we pass from sector to sector.

Minus 0:09

5119 Victor: *San Francisco ground control. Centurion 5119 Victor is ready to taxi, with information Zulu and clearance.*

Tower: *Roger 19 Victor. Taxi runway ten right. Call*
                  Tower 119.1 when ready.

Runway ten right seems like a long way from here, partly because of the darkness. But there's no other traffic and we have no real difficulty following the maze of taxiways.

0:00
(takeoff)

5119 Victor: *San Francisco Tower. 5119 Victor is ready for*
                  takeoff.

Tower: *Roger, 19 Victor. Winds 100 degrees at six.*
                  Runway ten right. You are cleared for takeoff.

5119 Victor: *19 Victor is rolling.*

0:01

Tower: *Cessna 19 Victor contact Bay Departure Control.*
                  Good luck!

5119 Victor: *Roger 19 Victor, and would you advise the exact*
                  time you show me off at?

Tower: *I show you off at 1339 and 25 seconds Green-*
                  wich Mean Time.

The clock has started! The time is 1:39 in the afternoon in Greenwich, England. This is the time system used in aviation to avoid the confusion of constantly changing time zones. There is an eight-hour difference in time, so here in San Francisco it is only 5:39 a.m., but already 8:39 a.m. in Washington, D.C.

Exact time is important, for this speed attempt has been officially sanctioned by the National Aeronautic Association (NAA) on behalf of the Fédération Aéronautique Internationale in Paris. The Fédération Aéronautique is recognized by all countries to oversee and certify all aviation records. When a Russian aircraft officially flies faster than one of ours, it is this organization that certifies that fact.

There are a number of classifications of aircraft. The one I am concerned with is for light aircraft weighing less than 1,750 kilograms, or 3,858 pounds. Back in September, I was granted an official sanction to attempt this flight anytime between December 15 and March 15. The date chosen was mine. To have the maximum tailwind dictated a winter flight when colder air generally brings high winds closer to the earth's surface. Randy's school vacation narrowed down the time even further to the Christmas recess.

To get this far has required considerable effort. Advance paperwork was necessary to ensure that an acceptable and official record would be made of our takeoff time at San Francisco, our landing and takeoff at our fuel stop at Goodland, Kansas, and our final arrival over Washington National Airport.

Prior arrangements with the FAA at each of

The plane has been refueled and is ready for tomorrow's flight. While confident, I am still apprehensive—and appropriately so. We will be flying over some high mountains and desolate wilderness, and in winter. We will be at an altitude that will not support life, and where the outside air temperature just a few inches outside our metal skin will be minus thirty-five degrees Fahrenheit.

these locations have been made. So far, all of this paperwork and coordination has gone without a hitch, but it is a constant worry. What would happen if someone forgets to record the time or send in the four copies of the certification forms? For us, that would nullify the record.

As partial insurance, I've hooked a tape recorder to the aircraft radio system so that I can directly record our radio communications and thereby record the exact times each facility tells me they've noted in their records.

0:03

We're established in our climb with the autopilot engaged. Bay Departure Control confirms "radar contact" and we turn on course.

We start to put on our oxygen masks even though we're only climbing through 1,500 feet. Might as well get that chore out of the way early. Our oxygen system is a permanently built-in one that contains 150 cubic feet of oxygen under 1,800 pounds of pressure. One hundred and fifty cubic feet may not sound like much oxygen but, under this pressure, it should last for over 12 hours of continuous use for both of us at 25,000 feet.

Oxygen is essential. Without it, an average person at 25,000 feet has only two minutes of useful consciousness. Fortunately, our oxygen system is virtually foolproof and, in any case, we have an emergency portable bottle that could sustain us for two hours if we had a problem.

0:08

Bay Departure: Centurion 5119 Victor, I see from the computer that this is a speed record flight. Is this something personal, or what?

5119 Victor: Strictly personal. It just seemed to us that it would be fun to see if we could cross the country in a light plane in a single day. Mountains are made to be climbed, and continents are made to be crossed, and I guess this is just something we thought should be done.

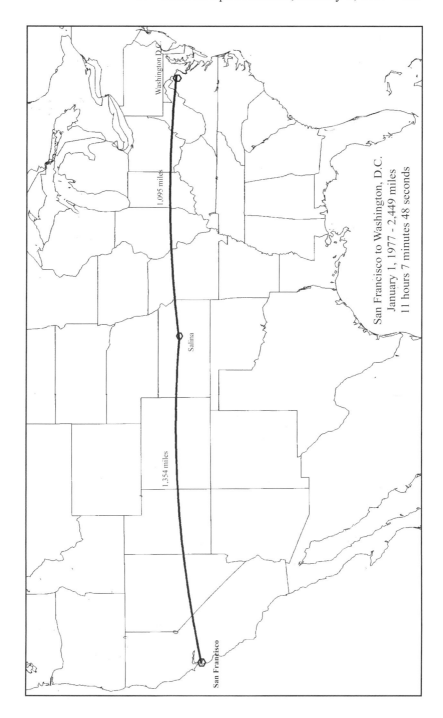

Washington D.C.

1,095 miles

Salina

1,354 miles

San Francisco

San Francisco to Washington, D.C.
January 1, 1977 - 2,449 miles
11 hours 7 minutes 48 seconds

*Bay Departure: Sounds like a great way to start out the New
          Year—doing something you really want to do.
          Have a good flight, and good luck.*

0:25

We're passing 15,000 feet and climbing at about 500 feet per minute. The lights of Stockton are up ahead. At 15,000 feet we're now higher than any mountain we will encounter on the trip.

It's getting cold in the cabin, so we put our coats on. While the heating system is quite effective once we get to our cruising altitude, this isn't true during climb. Because of our reduced forward speed in climbing, we have to leave the engine cowl flaps open to keep the engine from overheating. This means that all of the engine heat is washing out into the air. It's 12 degrees Fahrenheit outside.

0:53

Flight level two five zero—25,000 feet. It's now 35 degrees below zero outside, but because we can close the cowl flaps we now have enough heat to go back to shirt sleeves.

Twenty-five thousand feet is an unlikely place for a single-engine piston plane to be flying because of the lack of oxygen at this altitude––lack of oxygen for the engine, that is. The engine needs oxygen for combustion, and up here oxygen is in such short supply that most piston engine airplanes are unable to climb much above 10,000 feet.

But 5119 Victor is different: It has a turbocharger that takes the outside air and compacts it to sea level density, thus fooling 5119 Victor into thinking we're at sea level. The turbocharger is the heart of 5119 Victor's high altitude capability, and is presently spinning at an incredible 85,000 revolutions a minute to create this denser air.

00:55

We're 75 miles east of Stockton according to our distance measuring equipment (DME). The DME is a marvelous electronic device that continuously tells us the exact distance to or from certain ground stations along our route. It's accurate to the nearest tenth of a mile.

Besides giving us distance, its computer constantly calculates ground speed based on the rate at which we're approaching the station. The computer then calculates the time required to fly to the station. All of this information—distance, speed and time—is continuously displayed in digital readout on the panel.

01:03

Still dark, but with the moonlight it is easy to see that we're crossing both mountains and desert. There an occasional cloud layer beneath us, but it's very thin and easy to see through.

We switch from our left main fuel tank to our right main tank, Each tank holds 45 gallons of fuel, which feed directly into the engine. In addition we have two auxiliary tanks, each holding 14 gallons. The auxiliary tanks are at the wing tips and each has a small electric fuel pump to transfer the fuel into the main tanks. The auxiliary tanks aren't standard equipment. I had them installed in November so as to have sufficient fuel to make this transcontinental flight with just one stop.

The author and his son, Randy, age 12, the day after their record-breaking flight.

1:14

The oxygen pressure is down 300 pounds versus a normal 150 pounds for the one hour's use. Why? It is probably only the effect of the cold temperatures on the oxygen bottle back in the tail section. As the temperature decreases—and it's now 80 degrees colder than on the ground at San Francisco—the oxygen contracts, reducing the pressure.

This is my first flight at this altitude since the new oxygen bottle was installed last month, and so it's the first time I have had a chance to observe the effect of these extreme temperature changes on the tank. The other four oxygen bottles are built into the ceiling above our heads where the temperature is fairly constant. We must monitor our pressure carefully to be sure this conclusion is correct.

1:17

Sunrise

1:23

Over Coaldale VOR station (a VOR station is a radio navigation station for aircraft in the U.S.). There is nothing down there but desert. I can't even see the shack in which the station is located. I see no town. DME speed shows we are doing 238 miles per hour, which means we have a tailwind of about 20 miles per hour, just about as forecast.

1:33

My "steward," Randy, serves breakfast—a large cookie. It is a little hard to eat with an oxygen mask on, but it tastes good. We didn't have much breakfast before leaving. Not many eating places are open at 4:30 a.m.

1:45

Solid undercast ahead, but mountains are sticking up out of the clouds–otherwise we wouldn't know we were over the Rockies. Not much snow on the peaks. Seems warmer with the sun well up, but there's still frost on the right front window.

N5119V is not pressurized but its optimum operating altitude is 25,000 feet, the altitude we flew at on this flight. A person cannot live without oxygen at this altitude. If something happens to the oxygen system, a person has only about two minutes to recognize the problem and take corrective action. After that, hypoxia takes place and the person starts feeling euphoric, much as someone under the influence of alcohol, and is no longer capable of making good decisions. A few minutes later comes unconsciousness and, unless you get down quickly, death.

The plane has five built-in interconnected oxygen tanks that would last about 12 hours for 2 persons. Oxygen systems are very reliable, but a pilot needs special high altitude training. I regularly attended high altitude training programs for civilian pilots who fly at these altitudes. As part of this training you are put into a pressure chamber that simulates flying at 25,000 feet. Under close supervision you then remove your mask to experience hypoxia first-hand.

In the twenty-eight years I owned N5119V, the oxygen system never failed in flight; but it could have. If I recognized that a failure had occurred, the most important step was to immediately command the autopilot to descend to a breathable altitude, probably ten or twelve thousand feet depending on where we were. Once so instructed, the autopilot would do the rest even if I were no longer conscious.

This picture was taken with a photographer in the back seat the day after the record flight. You can see the oxygen lines and the masks we were wearing.

2:00

Salt Lake Center has now cleared us to use J-80 airway. This is an airway normally used only on a one-way, westbound basis. This will save us a couple of minutes because to get over to the eastbound airway, we would have had to fly a dog leg.

The airways are just like automobile highways—they have numbers and are well defined. They are fairly narrow, so if you stray off them you are likely to get a call from the air cop on the beat—the friendly radar controller. We're in continuous radio and radar contact with these controllers. About every 20 minutes we're told to switch frequencies as we pass from one controller's radar scope to another. This continuous contact is very reassuring as we cross the Rockies in the dead of winter.

Single-engine aircraft, properly maintained, are extremely reliable. I have no concern about 5119 Victor's engine stopping. The chances are so slim as to not constitute a significant risk. Still, I was a boy scout once and the "be prepared" motto is one of my maxims. If the engine were to stop, we could almost certainly glide the plane down to a landing from which we could walk away.

Should that occur, the problem would be to survive until we were located, particularly in winter. We carry survival equipment including sleeping bags, blankets, signaling devices, a stove, and food for four weeks. We hope never to use these things, but if we ever have to, we're prepared.

2:15

I call Cedar City Flight Service for the latest weather at Goodland and get this response:

> *6,500 feet scattered, 25,000 broken, visibility is 15.*
> *Forecast next three hours: 3,000 feet scattered to*
> *broken, 3 miles visibility in light snow.*

There should be no problem with that, even if the ceiling were to go to 3,000 feet broken.

2:37

We are 125 miles due south of Salt Lake City. Clouds are gone and visibility is between 50 and 100 miles. We're over the first small town we've seen since Stockton, although without checking a map I have no idea what town it is. We could pinpoint the name if we wanted to, since we know we're exactly 48.3 miles east of the Milford VOR. The DME is a lot more accurate than most sign posts on a highway.

3:00

We are about to get an undercast. The haze appears to come up almost to our level. This is probably the front that the weather bureau told us about before we left. Presumably this is causing the weather that is forecast later today for Goodland. We're 70 miles west of Grand Junction VOR.

3:32

We are directly over the Grand Junction VOR, but the DME distance shows 3.1 miles, indicating that we are 3.1 miles above the station. Our 25,000 foot altitude is above sea level, which means Grand Junction VOR itself must be about 10,000 feet above sea level.

3:34

I call for an update on Goodland's weather:

> *Measured ceiling 1,000 feet overcast, visibility 5, light snow. Temperature 15 degrees.*

Earlier, we had been led to expect a 3,000 foot ceiling. This was quite a change in a little more than an hour, and might cause us a real problem. Once a ceiling starts deteriorating as rapidly as this one has, it could get even lower than this reported 1,000 foot. Also, making the approach itself would cost us a lot of time in landing and then getting clearance to take off. Maybe we should start thinking about going to our alternative destination, Salina, Kansas. Let's wait another 30 minutes and then decide.

3:52

We're 60 miles east of Grand Junction, with breaks in the undercast below. Mountains appear high and rugged with lots of snow on them. This is what I envisioned the Rockies would look like.

4:06

It is 250 miles to Goodland from here, making good time. If I decide to overfly Goodland, at least fuel shouldn't be a problem.

4:09

Time to get the weather and make a decision on Goodland. It takes about 45 minutes to descend from 25,000 feet and if we're going to land at Goodland we must start our descent within the next couple of minutes.

Denver Flight Service gives us the weather as:

> *Goodland special observation—ceiling 500 feet, 3/4 mile visibility in snow.*

> *Salina, 10,000 overcast, 12 miles visibility. Forecast next three hours, 3,000 to 8,000 scattered to broken clouds with visibilities ten miles or better.*

We're now 437 miles from Salina which at our present speed should take about an hour and 45 minutes. We have a total of 260 pounds of fuel left, which at our present consumption of 95 pounds an hour would leave us a reserve of 100 pounds on landing. With the Goodland weather now down to 500 feet and plenty of fuel to get to Salina there's no question about what to do.

The instrument panel of 5119V at the time of this flight. Over the 28 years of ownership, I probably replaced all of this equipment every six to ten years as new generations of sophisticated equipment became available. Often I installed new technology equipment before the air carriers did.

5119 Victor: *Denver Center, Centurion 5119 Victor.*
                  Request. Over.

Denver Center: Go ahead 19 Victor

5119 Victor: *Denver, 5119 Victor would like to change*
                  our destination to Salina Kansas. From
                  present position direct to Goodland, J–80 to
                  Hill City, direct Salina.

Well, that decision is behind us. But now we have to worry about getting fast service at Salina. I had previously made a number of phone calls to Goodland to both the FAA and to the refueling people to ensure that we'd have fast service even on New Year's Day. They were really primed to do so. Even at this hour, Inge should be calling to remind them we're about to land (in case they have forgotten).

Now the problem is to get Salina up to speed and ready for us. And, of course, it isn't just the refueling that's important. We have four copies of a landing and takeoff form that have to be filed out and certified by the control tower. The Goodland FAA staff knew of the paperwork and were primed. Will the Salina Tower, on such short notice, be able to pick up the ball without a hitch? We can't afford any goofs on the paperwork. When we get closer to Goodland let's see if Goodland will call ahead for us.

4:22

We're solid IFR in clouds, but fortunately no ice. Ordinarily we would be above the clouds at this altitude; it's somewhat unusual to be in clouds at 25,000 feet. Ice shouldn't be a problem because at 35 degrees below zero there isn't enough moisture in the air to cause ice. Still, I have the prop deice heat on just in case we encounter some.

4:37

I call Goodland Flight Service and tell them of our decision to overfly Goodland. They're aware of our decision from Denver Center and say they will call Salina Tower for us to tell them of the special nature of the flight and our need for quick refueling. We're estimating Salina at 6:07 out of San Francisco.

4:47

Lunch (or is it breakfast?). It's now about 10:30 a.m. in San Francisco but 12:30 in Kansas. Take your choice. One sandwich for me and another giant cookie for Randy. Our speed is 262 miles per hour. At least the increasing speed trend is in the right direction!

4:54

I'm starting to relax with Salina now assured. Speed is up to 267 miles per hour. We are 42 miles west of Goodland and are above the storm. Unless we have a mechanical problem, we have it made.

4:55

Trouble! Vacuum suction gauge is reading 3 ½ rather than the normal five inches, with the needle fluctuating. I should never knock on wood.

The vacuum pump runs off the engine and provides suction for the two important flight instruments—the directional gyro and the artificial horizon. If the vacuum pump fails completely, we lose both instruments and the autopilot. While we could continue flight without these, it would be difficult in IFR weather. We'd have to revert to our backup, electrically-driven gyro—our turn-and-bank indicator—which, while adequate for safe flight, wouldn't be precise enough for a flight where every second counts. Also, I'd hate to fly after dark or in IFR weather with only the turn-and-bank indicator.

So, if we lose all vacuum, this attempt will end. We'll keep our fingers crossed. Perhaps it will hold. Perhaps it is the gauge that is off, and not the vacuum suction.

Dreamer?

5:10

Denver Center has cleared us to start down. We'll descend at about 500 feet per minute, allowing our speed to pick up in the descent. Suction still holding at 3 ½ inches. That's encouraging.

5:23

Passing 20,000 feet and the suction gauge is now starting to increase back toward a normal reading. Maybe it was just the gauge. We are back in the clouds.

5:32

We are now at 17,000 feet. Suction is holding at a full five inches. I guess that problem is behind us—whatever it was. Randy has taken his mask off, but I decide to keep mine on until we're below 10,000 feet.

5:45

We're at 11,000 feet, 52 miles from Salina. Salina confirms they have our request for fast fuel service.

5:57

Salina Tower tells us to land on the runway of our choice. We're now below the clouds, with visibility about ten miles. They are holding other traffic away from the airport to allow us to make a fast, straight-in approach.

6:04

Touchdown!

6:18

Airborne! Only 14 minutes on the ground. They were certainly ready for us. The tower had us land halfway down the runway so we wouldn't have to taxi so far. Then a "follow me" type vehicle appeared at the taxiway to lead us to the refueling area so we wouldn't lose any time trying to find our way. Two refueling trucks were waiting and they started refueling us even before we were out of the plane.

Randy and I made our pit stop and while Randy located the soft drink machine, I called Inge to tell her where we were and to give her our Washington, D.C. estimate–between 7:30 p.m. and 8:30 p.m. Washington, D.C. time. She said that several Washington, D.C. area radio stations had already broadcast news of the flight. Finally I gave the package of paperwork to a line boy to take up to the tower for them to complete and mail in. They assured us by radio that they wouldn't forget.

6:37

More trouble. Of all things, the lens of my glasses is coming loose. One of those tiny screws that you can barely see is wiggling around. Why now? My fingernail is not much of a screw driver but maybe I can keep it from loosening more. Fortunately I have a second pair with me.

6:40

Randy is reading again, as though nothing special is happening. I guess that is the result of growing up with airplanes. 5119 Victor is the fourth family plane he's known. Flying is part of his everyday life.

Our speed looks good. We have a 50-mile per hour tailwind. I'm starting to get elated. We have plenty of fuel, good winds, good weather ahead, and everyone is helping. We're going to make it!

6:58

Passing 23,000 feet. 50 miles west of Kansas City. Suction gauge again is low, but holding steady at 3 ½ inches. Must have something to do with the rarified atmosphere. In any case, it looks like it will hold as before. That should be enough vacuum to adequately drive the gyros.

We just overheard Air France calling the Kansas City Center. What's an Air France plane doing in the Kansas City area? It seems as unlikely to me as it must seem to him, that a single-engine aircraft is flying at 25,000 feet.

7:07

I confirm that Kansas City Center has my request for a radar fix over the Kansas City VOR. In addition to setting a speed record between San Francisco and Washington, D.C., I also want to set a record between Kansas City and Washington, D.C.

7:12

Over the Kansas City VOR. I tape record the conversation.

7:20

It's now clear, no clouds at all. The bad weather is behind us until we get into Ohio. Then there will be snow eastward across the Appalachian Mountains. East of the mountains is forecast to be good but with gusty winds around Washington, D.C.

7:34

Winds are pretty much as forecast: we have about a 50-mile an hour tailwind. It's now a little after 1 p.m. in San Francisco but 4 p.m. in Washington, D.C. We'll be getting darkness in another hour or so. A short day. I can already see the moon directly above the nose of the plane at about a 30 degree angle to the horizon.

7:58

Just crossed the Mississippi River. St. Louis is visible to the south, about 60 miles away. Speed 276. If winds hold, we could be over Washington, D.C. at about 7:15 p.m.

8:10

Still unable to tighten the screw on the glasses. Stupid thing! Why did it happen now, while I'm flying? We just passed over Springfield, Illinois.

8:19

Our speed is dropping off. It is down to 270. Looks like we're picking up a slight crosswind rather than a direct tailwind.

8:36

We're 136 miles due south of Chicago. Speed is down to 240, so it looks like our peak speed was when we crossed the Mississippi. Suction is still holding at 3 ½ inches.

8:46

Over Indianapolis. Lots of snow on the ground, and it looks like the start of an undercast up ahead. Probably the start of the bad weather forecast for Ohio eastward. The sun will set pretty soon. Randy has been reading almost continuously all day, but not for long now with the onrushing darkness.

8:55

Our oxygen supply seems to be holding well. We still have 600 pounds of pressure left, which is a four-hour supply. We should be on the ground in less than three hours, so we are ok. Our earlier abnormal drop in pressure was due, apparently, to the cold temperature.

9:06

Sunset. It's pretty but not as spectacular as some we've seen from the air. Perhaps our being above much of the atmosphere has something to do with it. Our day has been only 7 hours and 48 minutes long.

9:15

Our speed has dropped off further and now is only 220 mph— we've lost all of our tailwind. That's a disappointment, since many times in the past we've had a 50-mile tailwind all the way to Washington, D.C. from Kansas City.

9:27

Three hundred and eighty miles to go. At our present speed we should make it in less than two hours. Too bad our winds pooped out. Oh, well, as long as the suction holds. We can't have everything.

9:33

An Allegheny jet just expressed surprise to find us up here. He asked what we were doing and then wished us luck. There is a real bond between pilots. We share an experience that few non-pilots can comprehend.

10:07

Cleveland Center clears us to fly direct to Front Royal VOR. Front Royal is 30 miles west of Dulles Airport. Since we're too far out to pick up Front Royal, they give us radar vectors.

10:09

The start of the end of the flight! Cleveland Center clears us to start our descent. We're still 220 miles from Washington, D.C.

10:21

We're now down to 21,500 feet. Suction is returning to normal and the abnormal reading clearly appears to have been a function of altitude. We're 174 miles out and we allow the speed to build up in descent to try to pick up a couple of minutes.

10:26

I switch over to Washington Center. They confirm that they know the nature of the flight and our request for a time fix over Washington National Airport.

10:39

We're about 70 miles from our "home" airport, Dulles International, and I call Page Airways there to give them an estimate of my arrival time. The official trip is from San Francisco to Washington National, and not to Dulles, because Dulles is too far from Washington, D.C. to count for an official speed record between these two cities. So, we'll overfly Washington National to establish our time by radar fix and then fly back to Dulles.

10:43

I wake up the copilot and tell him to start appreciating the scenery—the lights of Washington, D.C. off in the distance.

10:51

We're in contact with Washington National Airport Approach Control. They confirm they're aware of the flight and are ready for us.

Inge brought the paperwork to them a couple of hours before. We're now at 8,000 feet, descending to 7,000.

10:54

Approach Control asks if we want to descend below our originally planned 7,000 foot passage over the airport in order to pick up more speed. I say yes, if it doesn't foul up their traffic pattern. They advise that they can work other traffic around us in view of the record we are trying to set.

11:01

Pass over Dulles Airport—30 miles to go.

To be accepted by the Fédération Aéronautique Internationale, an aviation record has to be well-documented. Our takeoff time at San Francisco was certified by the FAA control tower, and our arrival time over Washington National Airport by the FAA Approach Control radar facility. Our official record was from San Francisco to Washington, D.C. Our home airport of Washington Dulles was too far from the center of Washington, D.C. to meet the rules. That is why we flew over a specific point on Washington National Airport where our time was recorded. The picture above shows one of the Approach Controllers at Washington National Airport.

11:06

Approach Control tells me to advise them when I show "station passage" over the Washington, D.C. VOR. We're in a shallow dive losing altitude but building up speed to gain every second we can.

11:08

Station passage! We made it!

Approach Control acknowledges.

11:09

Approach Control gives us our official time as 0047 and 38 seconds, Greenwich Mean Time, January 2. That makes the total elapsed time from San Francisco 11 hours, 7 minutes and 48 seconds.

This is a picture of our actual arrival at Washington Dulles International.

11:10

As we turn back toward Dulles, an unidentified airline captain over-hears our conversation with Approach Control and asks where we started from. His one-word response seems to sum up our feelings and is the perfect ending to our flight:

"Beautiful!"

* * * * *

Inge was waiting, along with a number of other well-wishers at Dulles, including a photographer who recorded our arrival.

The Associated Press had picked up the story about the flight while it was underway, and the picture of a Father-Son team flying across the United States on New Year's Day—an unusual human interest story on an otherwise dull news day. As a result, this flight was widely re-ported throughout the country and we have a thick scrap book of clip-pings that friends have sent us, some even from Europe.

Records are, of course, meant to be a challenge to others to break them, and the amount of publicity this flight received was an invita-tion to others. Three years later, also in January, another pilot flew the same route in a Mooney aircraft, but without making a fuel stop. He put temporary fuel tanks in place of the rear seats and managed to knock three hours off my time. He was a professional pilot based on the west coast and the most important thing he did was to wait for the perfect day for tailwinds. I had not had that luxury with Randy having to go back to school on January 3rd.

I knew when this pilot was making his flight and I had the pleasure being at Washington National Airport when he arrived, and of person-ally congratulating him.

The Washington Post took the picture, above, which was picked up by the wire services and widely published. It appeared across the front page of their Metro Page under the caption:

What a Way to Celebrate the New Year!
McLean Man and His Son Set Speed Record
in Flight from San Francisco

But the article that I liked best was an editorial in The Arlington Journal, a local newspaper:

The Spirit of McLean

In these days when the pioneering spirit seems in dire danger of extinction, it is refreshing to hear about someone willing to accept the challenge of breaking new ground, seeking new horizons. And it is especially satisfying to us desk-bound types when the modern pioneer turns out to be one who normally makes his living working in an office.

We're talking about Malvern Gross Jr., of McLean who, on New Year's Day, set a speed record for light airplanes between San Francisco and Washington.

The 42-year-old certified public accountant covered the distance in 11 hours and eight minutes, for an average speed of 219 miles per hour. Flying a single-engine Cessna, Gross made only one refueling stop.

The record-setting flight was a family affair. Gross's 12-year-old son, Randy, accompanied his father on the long hop, serving as unofficial "copilot." And his wife, Inge, was in charge of "ground operations," taking care of countless vital details. For example, it was she who brought the necessary time forms to FAA officials at National Airport just before Gross was scheduled to arrive. Without precise official clocking, the record could not be certified.

Most of us sit in our offices and dream about exciting accomplishments. Mr. Gross dreamed, too, but then he went out and made his particular dream come true.

18

Thirty-two Thousand Feet!
August 19, 1978

I described in the last chapter the record-setting flight from San Francisco to Washington, D.C. that my then twelve-year-old son and I made on New Year's day, 1977. That flight was meticulously planned over a number of months. I was involved in another record-setting flight which was not so meticulously planned and that clearly held more risks than I realized at the time.

Highest Altitude In Level Flight

On August 19, 1978, I set a record for the "highest altitude in level flight" for an aircraft weighing less than 3,858 pounds on takeoff. My Cessna T210 had a maximum authorized takeoff weight of 3,800 pounds so we were within that category. The requirement was that the plane, once it reached its maximum altitude, had to remain in level flight for three minutes. You could not just zoom up and then fall back. You had to remain at that altitude. I reached 32,420 feet!

You also had to be able to independently verify the record. The most practical way to do this was to have an official observer on board to observe and take readings to validate the altitude claimed. It turned out that this was far more complex than just looking at the altimeter in the plane and noting the altitude.

I said that this flight had not been meticulously planned. In fact, it sort of just happened. But let me start from the beginning.

NAA Volunteer

After the record for our San Francisco to Washington, D.C. flight had been authenticated by both NAA and the FAI, I became involved as a volunteer with NAA, primarily in financial matters. It was a small organization with only half a dozen employees.

Early in the summer of 1978, NAA decided to sponsor an aviation event at the Gaithersburg, Maryland airport, to be held on August 19. (Gaithersburg is a suburb of Washington, D.C.) In order to promote the event, the president of NAA asked if I would be willing to set a "time-to-climb" record to 6,000 meters (19,685 feet) and another to 9,000 meters (29,527 feet). Apparently neither record had been set for my weight category, so if I made it to these altitudes I was assured that my times would then be the record. He also said NAA would waive the certification fees since they would be using the record for promotional purposes.

I had nothing to lose. I was sure that I could get to 6,000 meters since the plane's optimum altitude was 25,000 feet. I was not as sure of making 9,000 meters because I had never been that high before. It turned out that setting these records was the easy part; the hard part was calculating and substantiating the actual altitudes reached.

Measurement of Altitude

Every airplane has an altimeter, but unfortunately an altimeter does not measure how high an airplane actually is above the sea level. What it measures is the weight of the air that exists above the aircraft—that is, the weight of the air column extending from the plane up to the stratosphere. At a given altitude, the weight of that column of air can vary significantly depending on temperature and barometric pressure. I say significantly, because there was almost a 2,000 foot difference between what the plane's altimeter showed and the actual altitude above sea level on the day of our record flight.

How then do you accurately measure altitude? An aircraft altimeter is designed to display an altitude based on "standard" conditions.

Standard conditions have been defined by the International Civil Aeronautical Organization (ICAO) as sea level temperature of 59 degrees Fahrenheit, sea level pressure of the column of air above the altimeter expressed in the weight of 29.92 inches of mercury, and a temperature lapse rate of 3.5 degrees Fahrenheit per thousand feet, up to about 36,000 feet, the start of the stratosphere.

If all three standard conditions are present, the altimeter does measure altitude accurately, but that seldom happens. Barometric pressure at sea level changes continuously. The barometric pressure typically is between 29.5 and 30.5 inches of mercury. Each one-tenth of an inch of mercury is the weight of a column of approximately one hundred feet of air. A full inch is approximately a thousand feet.

So if you had an altimeter that correctly showed your altitude on the ground as 500 feet above sea level, and then the barometric pressure dropped two-tenths of an inch, the altimeter would read approximately 700 feet. If the temperature had also gone up or down the indicated altitude would also read higher or lower. On the ground, the pilot knows what the actual altitude above sea level is, and before takeoff, he will adjust the altimeter so that it reads correctly. In flight, he also adjusts the altimeter to sea level barometric readings based on reports he routinely receives from the Air Traffic Controllers.

Variations in Temperature and Lapse Rate

The actual variation from the standard lapse rate of 3.5 degrees Fahrenheit per thousand feet is much more difficult to determine because in the real world it is not a uniform rate, particularly under 10,000 feet. The higher you go the closer the actual lapse rate will be to this 3.5 degrees. In order to accurately factor in an altitude correction for such lapse rate variations, you must record the outside temperatures every thousand feet. Once back on the ground the variations from standard temperatures can be calculated for each reading. That is an onerous calculation and, except for official records, most pilots ignore this factor and use a single temperature at the highest indicated altitude based on the assumption that there is no variation from the 3.5 degree standard lapse rate between sea level and the indicated altitude.

At 32,420 feet (the record we set) the standard temperature is a minus 53 degrees Fahrenheit—112 degrees colder than at sea level on a standard day. But, like barometric pressure, a standard day temperature seldom exists. If the outside temperature of the air is either higher or lower than the standard temperature the actual altitude will be different than what the altimeter shows, sometimes by a significant amount.

Mechanical Errors in the Altimeter Itself

Like all sensitive instruments, altimeters have to be calibrated periodically, particularly just before a record flight is made. This involves putting the altimeter into a chamber, withdrawing the air in the chamber to create a vacuum, and then comparing the actual reading of the altimeter to the known pressure altitude within the chamber. This is done for each reading over the entire range of the altimeter—that is, from sea level to the high end of the altimeter range. The technician can then make small adjustments so that it will read accurately.

Hostile Environment for Human Beings

Another very important consideration in attempting the 9,000 meter (29,527 feet) record, was that it is a very hostile environment at that altitude, particularly in an unpressurized aircraft. The temperature is between thirty and fifty degrees below zero Fahrenheit, and the atmosphere is so thin that without a reliable source of oxygen you would lose useful consciousness within a minute or two.

The FAA requires a pilot flying above 12,500 feet to wear an oxygen mask. At 12,500 feet the air is only 70 percent as dense as at sea level which means that a person is getting only 70 percent as much oxygen unless he is using an oxygen mask to compensate for this reduced oxygen availability. At 25,000 feet that drops to 37 percent, and at 30,000 feet to 30 percent.

The oxygen system in my Cessna at that time was a continuous flow system which sent 100 percent pure oxygen into a breathing bag attached to a mask. The person breathing would exhale into the breathing bag where it mixes with the oxygen from the plane's system, and air from inside the plane. Then in breathing "in", the person would receive a mixture of new oxygen, the exhaled breath which was mostly nitrogen and carbon dioxide, and oxygen provided by the outside atmosphere.

This system was only certified to provide an adequate level of oxygen up to 25,000 feet because above this altitude the amount of oxygen in the atmosphere supplemented by the oxygen flowing into the breathing bag would not be adequate.

Oxygen was supplied by five interconnected tanks built into the cabin ceiling and behind the baggage compartment. The system provided 150 cubic feet of 100 percent pure oxygen initially pressurized to 1,800 pounds per square inch (psi). Depending on altitude, this system provided 20 to 35 man-hours of oxygen. There is a picture showing my son and I wearing our masks on page 193 in the previous chapter.

But flying even at 25,000 feet requires vigilance on the part of the pilot. Oxygen has no smell or taste, and if the oxygen system were to fail it would not be immediately obvious to the pilot. At 25,000 feet without oxygen, the period of useful consciousness is only two minutes (useful consciousness means the period when the person still has enough mental acuity to make reasonably intelligent decisions). After two minutes the average person may or may not immediately lose consciousness, but in any event will not be able to function effectively. Hypoxia is the term applied to lack of oxygen, and it usually gives the person a sense of calm and serenity similar to that which alcohol gives to an intoxicated person. People with hypoxia don't realize they have a problem.

At 30,000 feet this period of useful consciousness is even less. We would be venturing into a hostile environment and greatly increasing the risks if anything went wrong.

Atmospheric Pressure Needed to Absorb Oxygen

Major dangers attend high altitude flights above 25,000 feet. I did not fully appreciate this until long after this flight. Atmospheric pressure is needed to force the oxygen into the blood which carries it throughout the body. You could be breathing 100 percent pure oxygen but without sufficient atmospheric pressure this oxygen would not be absorbed adequately.

This absorption rate decreases the higher you go, and at about 35,000 feet the atmospheric pressure is getting so low that little, and or no oxygen gets absorbed. In fact, at some altitude, the opposite occurs. The oxygen and nitrogen in the blood starts to effervesce from the body. This is a form of the bends similar to what divers experience when they decompress too quickly. This is why military pilots wear pressure suits in high performance, high altitude aircraft. The pressure suit creates artificial pressure on the body so that oxygen in the lungs will dissolve and stay in the blood.

Airline aircraft are pressurized. The cabin is typically maintained at a pressure of about 8,000 feet. If a commercial aircraft flying at, say, 40,000 feet suddenly loses cabin pressure, the pilot will quickly descend to an altitude where there will be enough atmospheric pressure in the cabin to allow the oxygen from the masks, that automatically deploy in front of each passenger, to be absorbed into the passengers' bloodstream.

Hostile Environment for the Plane

An airplane is able to defy gravity and fly only because of the air passing over the wings and control surfaces of the plane which creates lift. The airplane will fly if the amount of lift created is more than the weight of the plane.

The significance of this is that it is not the speed which the aircraft is flying that is important, but rather the amount of air flowing over the wings. If the plane is flying near sea level, where air is dense, the speed the plane has to maintain in order to fly is less than where the air is thin. I have already mentioned that at 25,000 feet the air density is only 37 percent of sea level density. To sustain flight at that altitude the plane must be traveling 2.7 times the speed it has to travel at sea level. Or, said another way, the stalling speed—the speed below which the plane will not fly—is 2.7 times the stalling speed at sea level. If the stalling speed of the airplane at sea level is 50 miles per hour, then at 25,000 feet it will be 135 mph. At 30,000 feet the stalling speed increases to 166 mph, and at 32,420 feet (the record we set) to 188 mph.

The question is whether the engine can produce enough power to allow the plane to fly at this higher speed. The engine also needs oxygen. A normally aspirated engine—that is, one without a turbocharger––can produce full power only at sea level, and the total power the engine can produce drops as the plane climbs. By the time a plane with a normally aspirated engine is at 8,000 feet, the engine is only producing about 75 percent of sea level power. At 12,000 feet the maximum power output is down to 64 percent. Normally, one climbs at full power so it is extremely unlikely such a plane can get much above twelve or fourteen thousand feet.

My Cessna T210 had a turbocharger which compressed outside air for the engine, thus providing more oxygen to the engine than it otherwise would have had. I could maintain 100 percent power to approximately 17,000 feet, and 70 percent power to 24,000 feet. I would estimate that at 30,000 feet my plane's maximum power was 57 percent and at 32,420 feet, it was down to 42 percent.

Offsetting somewhat the reduced power above 17,000 feet, my Cessna flew faster on the same amount of power the higher I went because the air was thinner and there was a corresponding reduction in drag on the plane. For a fixed amount of power, the plane traveled faster the higher we went. This is one of the reasons for flying high.

There is a limit to how high you can go. Eventually the stalling speed increases to the point at which the speed of the aircraft is equal to the stalling speed. Attempt to climb higher and the airplane stops flying, that is, it stalls. In the case of this record flight that speed was 188 mph at 32,420 feet.

Precautions On High Altitude Flights

My autopilot had the capability to climb or descend to any specified altitude; that is, if I were at 10,000 feet and wanted to descend to 7,000 feet at, say, 500 feet per minute, I could instruct the autopilot to do so, and when the plane got to 7,000 feet the autopilot would level out the airplane and fly at that altitude without human intervention. It would also follow the flight plan programmed into its computer. On high altitude flights I made it a habit to preprogram the autopilot to descend to 10,000 feet. I would program it but not push the activation button. Once that single button was pushed, the autopilot would follow the programmed instructions.

Thus if I realized that the oxygen system had failed, or that I was becoming hypoxic, all I had to do was push this button to activate the descent instructions. I was then assured that the plane would start descending even if I lost consciousness. Once down at a lower altitude, I would presumably recover.

High altitude flights involve dangers and complexities that are not obvious. As I mentioned earlier, I attended courses involving an altitude chamber so that I could experience for myself what happens at 25,000 feet if the oxygen system fails. But 25,000 feet is not the same as 32,000 feet and, I really did not know what I might encounter.

Ground Preparation

August 19, 1978, was a perfect day for the record attempt. It was a bright sunny day with no clouds at all and good visibility. I'd had the altimeter calibrated to 30,000 feet on August 3 for the purposes of the flight, to insure there were no mechanical errors relating to the altimeter itself. I also filed an IFR flight plan with the FAA since I would be going into positive control airspace above 18,000 feet. The flight plan indicated I would take off and fly on a westerly course, or as instructed, once airborne. The purpose of the flight was also stated on the flight plan. If we needed government verification that the flight took place, the FAA would have a record of the flight and even a tape of the altitudes our transponder was transmitting. This would not be sufficient in itself to substantiate a record but would provide collaborative support if needed.

Official Observer

The NAA assigned an official observer (Mr. Cummings, if I recall correctly) to ride in the copilot seat. His job was to record time, the outside temperatures, and the altimeter altitude during the flight, and then eventually certify the data that supported the claim of a record.

We spent about fifteen minutes going over the procedures we would follow. I told him how the oxygen system worked, and what he should watch for in terms of hypoxia. I gave him strict instructions to advise me if at any time he felt uneasy, which might suggest hypoxia. I also indicated that we would be using the autopilot for the climb and would be controlling speed with fine adjustments of the electric trim.

In turn, he told me that he would be recording outside temperature and cumulative time since takeoff, using a stop watch, every thousand feet up to 16,000 feet and every 500 feet thereafter until he was sure we had reached an actual altitude of 9,000 meters. He confirmed that he would check to be sure the altimeter was set to field elevation (539 feet) and would then record the indicated barometric setting.

He reminded me that we would not know when we reached either the 6,000 or the 9,000 meter altitude until he had made all the calculations after the flight. It was for this reason that he needed temperatures and times for the altimeter-indicated altitudes above and below each of these two altitudes. He said that he hoped to make a rough estimate of the actual altitude based on the temperatures he observed.

I reminded him that I had never been as high as 9,000 meters and that I had no certainty that we would reach that altitude. I observed that the "service ceiling" of the plane was listed as 30,200 feet for 3,400 pounds (our weight) on a standard day, but that this was a summer day which could substantially reduce that figure. The service ceiling is the altitude above which the plane will no longer climb at least 100 feet a minute.

I showed him how to put on his oxygen mask, telling him I would check him once he had it on and confirm there was oxygen flowing to him. We would put our oxygen masks on once we were established in the climb.

Finally I showed him the button he should push on the autopilot control head to instruct the autopilot to make an emergency descent to 10,000 feet in case I lost consciousness or appeared to be obviously incapacitated.

The Climb

We took off about 9 a.m. Because it was still fairly early in the day, there was little traffic. I trimmed up the plane to fly at an indicated airspeed of 110 mph using full climb power. Not much traffic was anticipated and Center gave us a westward heading on which we would not likely encounter any other aircraft.

The climb to an altimeter reading of 6,000 meters (19,685 feet) took 21 minutes and 58 seconds. Later it turned out that we reached the actual height of 6,000 meters almost a minute earlier (20 minutes 55 seconds) when the altimeter read 18,800 feet.

Without any pause we continued climbing to 9,000 meters (29,527 feet) on the altimeter. Later, Mr. Cummings calculated that we actually reached this altitude in 23 minutes, when the altimeter read 27,900 feet.

Shall We See How High The Plane Will Go?

Once we reached an altimeter reading of 29,527 feet, it was obvious to Mr. Cummings that with the temperatures he was recording we must have been higher than this altimeter reading. That meant we had accomplished our objective of establishing "time-to-climb" records to 6,000 and to 9,000 meters.

At that point, I asked him how he was feeling, and if he had any uneasiness in terms of oxygen. When he said, "fine," I asked, "Shall we see how high the plane will go?" The plane still appeared to have some climb left in it. He said, "sure, and maybe we can establish another record."

We had been in continuous communication with Washington Center and later Cleveland Center and we told the controller of our intentions. All aircraft in that vicinity were on a common frequency. A few minutes later we heard the following exchange between a United Airlines jet and the Air Traffic Control Center:

Center: United 235, turn left 30 degrees. Traffic is a single-engine Cessna at your 12 o'clock position, five miles, your altitude.

United 235: Center, what kind of aircraft did you say?

Center: A single-engine Cessna 210.

United 235: And he is at my altitude?

Center: Yes. He is setting an altitude record.

United 235: Hard to believe.

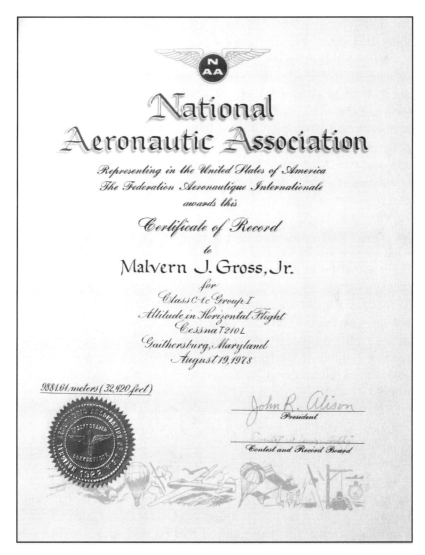

We received two certificates for each of our three records. The above certificate was issued by the National Aeronautic Association (NAA), the United States representative of the Fédération Aéronautique Internationale (FAI). The NAA is the sole representative of the FAI in the United States and is responsible for certifying all records originating in this country. Once the NAA certifies a record they forward all the documentation to the FAI which is then reviewed by that organization. If the FAI is satisfied that the documentation supports the claim for a "world record," they issue a certificate, in the French language, similar to the above certificate.

Both Mr. Cummings and I got a real kick out of that exchange. I think the Center Controller did too.

We continued climbing, although at a much slower rate of climb. After about eight or nine minutes, I sensed that the plane was approaching its limit and that we were getting close to its stalling speed. Still the plane showed signs of wanting to climb, albeit very slowly. The air was calm and the autopilot was doing a superb job of keeping the plane at the precise speed I wanted—just two or three mph over stall speed. If I had been hand-flying I could not have been that precise, and would not have been able to coax the plane as high as we did.

Fifty-eight minutes after we took off, I concluded that we were as high as we could get. We were right on the edge of a stall. At that point the plane would grudgingly gain fifty feet or so but then would settle back down about the same fifty feet. Mr. Cummings started timing our flight at that lower altitude, which we had to maintain for three minutes to establish the record. Our altimeter showed 30,600 feet.

We then headed back to Gaithersburg. It took us almost as long to get down as it did to get up. We landed at 11:10 a.m., two hours and six minutes after takeoff. In those two hours, we had established three records. It took Mr. Cummings several days to check and recheck his calculations. Both of us were surprised at how high we had managed to get—32,420 feet.

The three records are summarized at the top of the next page. The official times for the two time-to-climb records are shown in the third column from the left: 20 minutes and 55 seconds to 6,000 meters and 43 minutes and 55 seconds to 9,000 meters.

The third record was the unplanned "highest altitude in level flight." Look at the large difference between what the altimeter reading showed (30,600 feet) and our actual altitude (32,420 feet). The reason for this big difference was the temperature variation from standard. The outside temperature that day was minus 20 degrees Fahrenheit but the standard temperature for 32,420 feet is minus 53 degrees Fahrenheit. That difference—33 degrees Fahrenheit warmer than standard—required an eighteen hundred foot correction of the plane's indicated altitude!

The other thing of interest here is the average rate of climb for the three legs. Frankly, I am impressed that the plane climbed an average of almost 200 feet per minute between 29,527 and 32,420 feet.

Summary of Record Flights

Actual Altitude (meters/feet)	Altimeter Reading When at Actual Altitude	Actual Time (min: sec)	Rate of Climb (from sea level/ from previous altitude)
6,000/19,685	18,800	20:55	941
9,000/29,527	27,900	43:55	672/425
9,882/32,420	30,600	58:00	559/194

Some Reflections

After the glow of having achieved the highest altitude in level flight sank in, I tried to look objectively at what we had done and answer the question: "Should we have continued beyond the 9,000 meter record to see how high the plane would actually go?" It was a spur-of-the-moment decision without considering all the risk factors and without any planning. I concluded that the answer was clearly "no."

You may recall I mentioned earlier in this chapter that in addition to having oxygen to breathe, you had to have atmospheric pressure to force the oxygen into your blood. The 32,420 feet we had achieved is perilously close to 35,000 feet, the altitude where the pressure is so low that little if any oxygen gets absorbed.

We know the oxygen system is designed to be adequate at 25,000 feet. At that altitude, the atmospheric pressure is 37.1 percent of sea level atmosphere. The atmospheric pressure at 32,420 is only 26.5 percent. Note that this reduced pressure is only 71 percent of the 25,000 pressure. This can be seen in the chart at the top of the next page.

We were lucky not to have lost consciousness. We were not breathing 100 percent oxygen; our oxygen regulator system provided pure oxygen to a breathing bag which then mixed with the air we were exhaling. I am guessing that at very best the mixture we were breathing was 20 percent oxygen, but only a portion of this 20 percent oxygen was being absorbed into our blood. I must also note that I was 45 years old, and while I liked to deny it, I was certainly not in as good shape as a 19-year-old. The other factor was that I really knew nothing about Mr. Cummings's health, and whether I was putting him at risk.

In hindsight, then, the 9,000 meter flight was also probably mar-

Oxygen Availability Between 25,000 and 35,000 Feet
Using Oxygen Mask With Re-Breathing Bag, Certified for 25,000 Feet
And Showing Greatly Increased Risk Above 25,000 Feet

Altitude	Pressure (in. Hg)	Percent Of Pressure At	
		Sea Level	25,000 Ft
Sea Level	29.92		
25,000	11.10	37.1%	100.0%
30,000	8.89	29.7%	80.1%
32,420	7.94	26.5%	71.5%
35,000	7.04	23.5%	63.4%

ginal from an oxygen safety standpoint.

Test Pilot?

Aside from the oxygen issue, there was another risk that I have not mentioned. At 32,420 feet I was flying at a speed that was only one or two miles an hour faster than the plane's stalling speed. I had no way of knowing whether at this rarified atmosphere there would be enough air flowing over the control surfaces (ailerons and elevator) to allow me to recover from a spin or other out-of-control maneuver. If the plane had stalled, I would have become a test pilot since the plane was never designed to fly at that altitude.

Certainly I was violating the FAA limitations on this plane, and if something had happened it would clearly have been "pilot error." More importantly, I was responsible for Mr. Cummings. It was one thing to expose myself to a risky situation and another to expose a passenger.

Afterthought

After this flight, I purchased a different kind of oxygen mask, one that did not use a re-breathing bag but instead allowed me to breathe oxygen directly from the mask, either diluted or at 100 percent. It was a "demand regulated" mask. The oxygen would flow into the mask only when I inhaled.

By the mid 1990s, a pulse oximeter became available—that is an electronic device that you stick your finger into, which then calculates the amount of oxygen flowing to the finger expressed as a percentage of full saturation. It also shows a pulse rate. These units were designed for use by medical personnel for monitoring the respiration efficiency of hospital patients.

I purchased one, and thereafter found it almost essential for safe high altitude flights. I was surprised to see how much difference just a couple of thousand feet make in terms of blood oxygen saturation. At four or five thousand feet the saturation level would be in the mid-eighties, and by the time I was at twelve thousand feet it would be down to the low seventies. That made me a believer in always using oxygen above 5,000 feet.

One of the things that surprised me is how quickly our blood system transports oxygen throughout the body. If I checked my oxygen saturation level without oxygen at, say, 5,000 feet, and then put the mask on, I could see an increase in the oxygen saturation level back up to the normal level within 60 seconds. That seems incredible to me. The oxygen first has to be absorbed in the lungs, then has to be absorbed in the blood, and finally has to travel all the way to the tip of my finger, all within that short time span.

The conclusion I reached from this is that if the oxygen flow to the mask were interrupted, the pilot would be affected within a minute or two. At 25,000 feet the pilot must constantly be alert to the slightest indication of hypoxia, which can come on

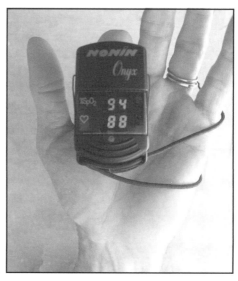

The pulse Oximeter shows a blood saturation level of 94 percent and a pulse of 88.

quickly. If I suddenly started feeling uneasy, I would quickly check my oxygen level with this oximeter device because it was foolproof. If the saturation level were low, I knew I was not getting the oxygen I needed and I had better react immediately.

I feel the need to stress the importance of pilots of high altitude planes attending a program involving an altitude chamber so they can experience firsthand the symptoms of hypoxia. Over the years I have met many pilots who flew turbocharged or pressurized aircraft, but very few had attended such a program. They are oblivious to the risks they are taking, much as I was in the flight described in this chapter.

19

Around-the-World
Without Refueling
December, 1986
9 Days, 3 Minutes, 44 Seconds

No, I did not fly around the world, either nonstop or with frequent stops. But I know the people who did, and in a minor way, I was a participant in this remarkable 1986 around-the-world flight of a home-built aircraft. An editorial which appeared in the *Washington Post* on December 24, 1986, is reproduced below to help refresh the reader's memories of this flight.

They flew at Lindbergh speeds and, in many respects, under Lindbergh conditions: a cramped little cabin, terrible noise, the pilots fighting fatigue hour after hour. Perhaps in some ways the flight of Dick Rutan and Jeana Yeager was not quite the leap into the dark that Charles Lindbergh made nearly 60 years ago when he flew solo from New York to Paris; the two who landed in California yesterday after flying around the world without refueling had the benefit of meteorological, technical and medical consultation not available to Lindbergh on his lonely flight. But in other ways, especially its length, the flight that ended yesterday was more grueling.

Ten days ago, you could have been pardoned for doubting they'd even get the strange, homemade plane called Voyager off the ground.

This beautiful picture of the Voyager was taken on an earlier test flight, probably their July, 1986, flight of 11,609 miles where they flew up and down the West Coast. Note that the wing tips in this picture are intact. On the round-the-world flight both wing tips were destroyed on takeoff because they dragged on the runway. The Voyager now hangs in the Smithsonian National Air and Space Museum.

The Post's reporter, Kathy Sawyer, described the revolutionary, featherweight craft as looking "like a fuselage dragging a fence." Its wingspan was greater than that of a Boeing 727, its weight about that of a very small car. At the start of its journey, almost every cubic inch was crammed with high-octane fuel.

On takeoff Dec. 14 the tips of the sagging, fuel-filled wings scraped dangerously on the runway as Voyager struggled for nearly three miles to get airborne. It finally made it into the air with 700 feet of runway left. Mr. Rutan maneuvered the plane to shake off damaged bits of wing, and off they went. "If it were easy," Miss Yeager radioed back for those who had just witnessed the harrowing takeoff, "it would have been done before."

Mr. Rutan, an experienced combat pilot, flew 55 of the first 60 hours (Lindbergh's flight took something over 33 hours in all). Then for the next week, in addition to the din and the exhausting routine of flying, the two endured endless buffeting as they were thrown about in their coffin-like confines by air turbulence, to which the Voyager is peculiarly susceptible. Late Saturday the plane was flipped on its side several times by an unexpected and terrifying thunderstorm over the Atlantic.

Dick Rutan's brother, Burt, who designed Voyager, said that by the time they reached the Western Hemisphere, the pilots were sometimes so tired and beat up they couldn't accurately relay to him the simplest flight data. But in the final hours, they were also alert and resourceful enough to restart an engine as their suddenly powerless plane dropped toward the sea.

The Voyager was a backyard sort of project in which the Rutan brothers and Miss Yeager were aided by volunteers and whatever they could scrounge in the way of money and materials from corporations and individuals. The plane cost about $2 million to build, a remarkably small sum when its implications for the future of flight are considered. A spokesman for the Voyager group speculates about using the strong, lightweight materials this plane is made of to construct jumbo jets that will fly three times as far as the present ones for half the money.

But even if there were no material payoff, this was something that was worth doing—"worth doing and worth remembering forever," as was written on this page the day after Charles Lindbergh's flight in 1927, "because it inspires mankind with fresh realization of its capabilities, and fresh resolve to break down the walls of ignorance that surround it."

As with the Lindbergh flight, the success of this impossible flight captured the imagination of people all over the world. The purpose of this chapter is not to relate the details of the five years of construction, or the flight itself, but to tell of my personal experiences. There is an excellent book that details the events, *Voyager: Jeana Yeager and Dick Rutan*, published by Alfred A. Knoff, 1987, ISBN 0-394-55266-0. Copies can probably be found via the Internet.

My Role

My role was a minor one, that of officially observing the landing and the exact time, and then presenting a certificate of accomplishment at a news conference later that morning. I had also been one of the thousands of pilots who had contributed to their request for financial support. For the last 20 years since this flight I have seen Dick

Rutan routinely at EAA's AirVenture each year. I have lost contact with Jeana Yeager.

In 1986, I was volunteer Treasurer of the National Aeronautic Association (NAA). NAA was the official record keeper for all aviation records originating in the United States. I was at Edwards AFB as NAA's representative when the Voyager touched down after their nine day, three minute and forty-four second flight, officially recording the time they landed. I then presented the two pilots, Jeana Yeager and Dick Rutan, with an NAA Certificate acknowledging the flight.

This incredible flight should not by any logic have taken place, but it did. I have two scrapbooks full of evidence. And, I was there (along with 40,000 other people) when they landed and can personally attest to the exact time. I also inspected the sealed recording barograph which ran throughout the flight, recording the plane's altitude. If the flight had landed for fuel somewhere it would have shown up on this recording.

As the treasurer of NAA, I had an opportunity to meet with Dick and Jeana several times in Washington, D.C. after the flight. I was also present in Stockholm in October, 1987, when the FAI awarded them the FAI gold medal, and I served on the Collier Selection Committee

I presented the certificate about three to four hours after Dick and Jeana had landed. After landing they were examined by medical personnel, and although they were exhausted, they were otherwise in good shape.

that selected this flight as "the greatest achievement" in 1986. The Collier Trophy has been the nation's highest aviation award since 1911.

Wing Tip Damage on Takeoff

The *Washington Post* editorial made reference to the wing tips scraping the runway on its 14,200 foot takeoff run. It was not until the plane landed nine days later that the extent of the damage was evident. I took the picture on the right. It is hard to see on this small picture, but the wing from the stained

area (see arrow) all the way out to the tip seems to have been affected. It turns out that the fuel cap on that section of the wing was damaged and that about 20 gallons of fuel leaked out over the course of the flight. That doesn't sound like much, but when you realize Voyager landed with just 18 gallons remaining, it is clear that every gallon counted.

Flight Statistics

The gross weight of Voyager at takeoff was 9,694 pounds, of which fuel was 7,012 pounds. The aircraft itself weighed 2,250 pounds; the crew and provisions, 432 pounds.

The Voyager flew over four specific locations where an observer could verify its passage: Hawaii, Thailand, Kenya, and Costa Rica. The total distance between these flight turn-points was 24,987 statute miles and is the official NAA/FAI distance flown. The actual distance flown is calculated to have been 26,359 miles, with the difference accounted for by deviations primarily for adverse weather. If there had been no adverse weather they could have flown directly between the turn-points.

The average altitude flown was 9,063 feet, the average ground speed was 122 mph, and the average tailwind was 9.8 mph. The fuel remain-

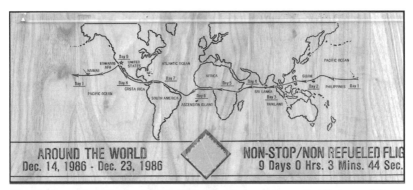

The above map is actually a photo of a wood-engraved plaque that Rutan and Jeana gave to a number of supporters. The bottom center rectangle is a sample of the materials the plane was made of. I treasure this plaque.

ing at landing amounted to 109 pounds, or 18.3 gallons. The plan had been to have 400 pounds, or 69 gallons of fuel left on landing.

One other fuel statistic is important. For every gallon you want to have available at the end of the flight, you must start out with three and-a-half gallons. That is because you use fuel to carry the extra weight of the gallons you want left at the end. By this reasoning, the miserly 18.3 gallons actually left in the tanks started out as 64 gallons.

The wings, fuselage and booms were essentially fuel tanks. Their interiors were partitioned to form tanks and the tops and bottoms of the tank were the skin of the plane. There were sixteen such partitions holding the seven thousand pounds of fuel. There were no fuel gauges on these tanks. The only fuel gauge was on a header tank in the fuselage from which the two engines drew fuel. There was an accurate fuel transducer that recorded fuel pumped into the header tank. The pilots kept track of the remaining fuel in the tank from which it had been transferred by way of a handwritten fuel log.

After the flight the engineers concluded that 109 pounds were lost from the left tip tank (see the picture on the previous page). In addition, 190 pounds of extra fuel were used on the last few hours of the flight when both engines were running to speed the return. This occurred just a little more than five hours from Edwards AFB when the rear engine—the only engine running—stopped due to a vapor lock in the fuel line between the header tank and the engine. It occurred when the Voyager was at 8,000 feet over the Pacific flying north, parallel to the Mexican coast, but too far out over the Pacific to be able to glide to land. By the time they got the front engine running, they were down to 3,500 feet. Once the front engine was running, they could stop the descent and when the plane was flying level, the vapor lock dissipated and the rear engine started. As Dick said to me later, "there were teeth marks on my heart" from that episode.

There were about a dozen such incidents during the flight, each one of which could have spelled disaster.

Rare Opportunity to Question Dick and Jeana

On February 3, 1987, a little more than a month after the Voyager landed at Edwards AFB, I attended a small luncheon at the National Aviation Club at which Dick and Jeana were present. Only half a dozen people were there, and both Dick and Jeana were obviously relaxed. I asked them many questions, and after the luncheon recorded the following summary of their comments. I have edited these comments in a few places to provide some background, but they are largely as written more than twenty years ago.

Fuel on Landing

I asked Jeana how much fuel there was left on landing—both usable and unusable. In the hours leading up to their landing it had been reported to the press that there were several hundred gallons and they had enough fuel to fly to New York. Her answer: 18.3 gallons, total fuel on board. The earlier report of a large quantity of usable fuel had been incorrect.

Fuel Pump Failure

We discussed the fuel pump problem that occurred about eight to ten hours before landing. There were only two fuel pumps, one for each side of the wing. All of the fuel tanks in each side of the wing were connected to their respective fuel pump. Through a complex valve system, they could select the individual tank they wanted to transfer fuel from. The fuel pump would then be turned on to pump fuel into a header tank located in the cabin. When the fuel pump in the right wing failed, they were able use the engine-driven fuel pump to pump fuel directly from tanks on the right side. The problem with this arrangement was that if they allowed the engine-driven pump to empty the tank to the point that it started sucking air, the engine would stop. As discussed below, that happened.

After the engine failure, they were able to physically modify the fuel system (under the instrument panel) so that the left side pump could pump from the tanks on the right side into the fuel header tank which supplied fuel to both engines. However, when they made these plumbing changes, fuel leaked into the cabin. This had been reported to Mission Control at the time.

It was also noted that the fuel pump had a statement right on it not to run a tank dry; that the pump needed fuel in it at all times to keep it running. But they intentionally allowed the pump to empty each of the tanks as they were using them, trying to get the last bit of fuel out of each tank. After they ran the right pump dry about 35 times, it failed. I asked why they had not used a pump without this limitation. Dick said such pumps were not available.

Engine Stoppage

I asked why, when the engine stopped, they didn't just use the engine starter to get it going again. Dick noted that there was no starter on the rear engine because of weight considerations. Besides, they had never intended to shut the rear engine off during the flight. The front engine did have a starter.

When the rear engine quit, they put the plane into a shallow dive (they were at 8,000 feet) to keep the propeller on the rear engine windmilling. They then switched to a fuel tank with fuel in it, expecting the engine to catch from the windmilling propeller. It didn't. An air bubble had gotten into the fuel line because the pump was sucking air from the empty tank.

Four minutes later, and down to 3,500 feet, they managed to start the front engine. With the front engine running they raised the nose allowing fuel to flow to the rear engine and it started by itself. This was just five hours before they landed at Edwards AFB.

Lost Fuel From Tip Tank

Jeana indicated that they lost about 20 gallons from a fuel cap leak in the left wing as a result of damage on takeoff. She also said that they lost about three percent efficiency as a result of the wing damage.

When asked why, with the takeoff damage, they did not land and make repairs, she stated that they would have had to fly 28 hours before their weight would be low enough as a result of fuel burn-off to allow a landing.

Rutan Relinquishing Controls

I asked Jeana if she had been concerned because Dick had flown most of the first three or four days. There had been press accounts of difficulty in Mission Control getting Dick to relinquish the controls to Jeana.

She stated that they had both known before the flight that this would be a problem. The plane was so unstable with its very heavy fuel load that Dick felt that only he could handle the controls. She observed that he got more rest than the press accounts would

The Collier Trophy is awarded annually "for the greatest achievement in aeronautics or astronautics in America, with respect to improving the performance, efficiency, and safety of air or space vehicles, the value of which has been thoroughly demonstrated by actual use during the preceding year." The trophy has been justly called the greatest and most prized of all aeronautical honors in America. This trophy was awarded to Dick Rutan, Jeana Yeager and Burt Rutan, Voyager Aircraft, for the successful nonstop of the Voyager around the world.

suggest since he could doze with the autopilot on. She, in turn, could monitor and make adjustments from her position.

Autopilot

I asked about the reports that they had two autopilots. She said they had only one, but they had a replacement "black box" which they could plug in if the main box failed (which it did). She also indicated that because of the inherent instability of the plane, constant autopilot adjustment was necessary to keep the plane trimmed properly. She emphasized that the plane was terribly unstable, that the autopilot had been designed specially to deal with that, but that it required constant monitoring.

Exit From Aircraft

I asked Jeana whether they really expected to be able to get out of the aircraft in an emergency. She said they were wearing parachutes and felt that the person in the pilot seat could definitely get out even in a structural failure situation. The other pilot would have more difficulty—but she observed with a smile—if an exit had become necessary she was sure that the second person (meaning, probably, herself) would have been able to find a way.

If the plane lost power but did not come apart, she said they would have ridden the plane down. She felt comfortable that they could have gotten out unless they were in very heavy seas.

East To West Direction

I asked Jeana why they flew from East to West, noting that some commentators had suggested it might be for psychological reasons: they would have longer days rather than shorter ones. She said, "No, winds were the consideration." Later, Dick stated that at the Equator at low altitudes the prevailing winds are from the East, although the higher you got the more the winds tended to reverse direction. Hence they stayed low. Dick also emphasized there was less turbulence at low altitudes than at high altitudes, contrary to how it is at U.S. latitudes.

Structural Limits

Dick was asked what "G" load the plane could take and he said, "none." He indicated that the issue was not "G" load but wing deflection. They were concerned about the wing snapping in two from being bent too high or low about the wing chord. I asked whether the wing spar—which is the structural part of the wing—was a single piece that went from wing tip to wing tip. Dick said no, that there were actually four sections, bolted together.

Weather Assistance

Apparently Dick and Jeana had used the volunteer services of three meteorologists, including one who had been the top man in the Western United States before his retirement. Dick said that Mission Control was receiving all worldwide weather satellite pictures on a real-time basis. The pictures were so good that Mission Control staff could easily see what Dick and Jeana were seeing at any given time.

Dick indicated that because of this, Mission Control could give him detailed instructions with course headings and distances to get him around weather. He implied that these detailed instructions were quite specific and involved distances as little as ten miles. Mission Control also gave them latitude/longitude data which they put into their computer. He also said that he could describe what they were seeing to Mission Control, and that the meteorologists could look at their detailed satellite pictures and see the same thing.

Availability of Weather Data

Dick said they had had great difficulty in getting both planning and current information on ocean weather, particularly over the Indian Ocean at lower altitudes. There were no weather reporting ships such as were once on the North Atlantic. Still, they usually chose to fly over oceans because if they were flying over land, and then encountered bad weather, it was often difficult to get permission from local governments to deviate from their flight plan.

Leigh Wade In Attendance

General Wade, age 90, was also at the luncheon. General Wade was the last surviving pilot of the first round-the-world flight in 1924. Dick expressed considerable interest in Wade's flight, and it was obvious that he had done some research about it. I was impressed by Dick's sincere interest at a time when you might have expected him to be interested only in his own flight.

Jeana Yeager

Jeana was very alert and very much the interested, good guest. She gave no signs of fatigue or boredom at having the same questions asked again and again. I mentioned to her my instant impression on seeing her at the Press Conference at Edwards AFB that she looked like Anne Lindbergh. She replied that no one had ever told her that before, and she seemed pleased at the comparison.

Summary Observation

Both Jeana and Dick came across as very ordinary but dedicated human beings. It is somewhat trite to say so, but they are the type of people you would expect to find "hangar flying" around almost any small town airport in the heartland of the United States on a bright sunny day. Very fine people.

20

Anne Morrow Lindbergh
North to the Orient
1981

In December, 1980, I was the president-elect of the National Aviation Club in Washington, D.C. (not to be confused with the National Aeronautic Association). Each year the Club presents its prestigious "Award for Achievement" to a deserving individual who made a difference in aviation. As I pondered whom we should select for the 1981 and 1982 awards, I thought about the influence of the Lindbergh flight to Paris on the world, and the subsequent exploration flights the Lindberghs had made.

Then I remembered a book I had once read that exerted a tremendous impact on me as a young man—Anne Lindbergh's account of their epic flight from New York to the Orient via the great circle route that took them across the arctic. That account was chronicled in her first book, *North To The Orient*. It became a best seller throughout the world and greatly influenced the public's impression of the future of aviation.

She Graciously Said "No"

I wondered if we could get Anne Lindbergh to accept our award? I had my doubts. Both the Lindberghs had shunned all public functions for many decades, and Charles Lindbergh had died six years earlier. I

239

didn't even have an address for her, but one of the National Aviation Club's members was a long-retired officer of Pan American Airways. Charles Lindbergh had had a close relationship with PanAm and this member had Anne's address. So, with nothing to lose, I wrote to her. I received a most gracious reply which said in part:

> *I am troubled about the response I feel I must give to your invitation to attend the award luncheon in Washington in the fall of 1981. For five years after my husband's death, I attended many public occasions honoring him (and in some cases myself also), which I was happy to do and felt was proper for a widow.*
>
> *I feel, however, that my true profession is writing, and I came to realize that any public appearances, such as dedication ceremonies, formal speeches, and large receptions, greatly increase the pressures in my life. The resulting publicity brings more invitations and demands to participate again, and these interrupt and distract from the quiet life necessary for a writer. I have therefore been forced to the decision that I must avoid as much as possible all public occasions.*

HARBRACE PAPERBACK LIBRARY HPL 5
50¢ SLIGHTLY HIGHER IN CANADA

NORTH TO THE ORIENT
ANNE MORROW LINDBERGH

"One of the most beautiful and great-hearted books that have ever been written."
—Sinclair Lewis

The cover of the paperback edition

What a gracious way of saying "no."

My Response

I wrote back to her, and I consider my reply to her to be one of the best letters I have ever written, because she then said "yes." Here is that letter.

Dear Mrs. Lindbergh:

I am not sure that my earlier letter adequately described the basis for our "Award for Achievement." This award is being given to you for your role as a writer, not for your role as an aviator. As you point out, your true profession is writing, and this is an award for the tremendous impact your first book had on your readers.

Perhaps you have had no reason to reread *North To The Orient* in recent years. I have. Your final chapter is one of the most eloquent descriptions of the feelings and emotions of pilots that I have read. Forgive me for quoting the last three paragraphs:

One could sit still and look at life from the air; that was it. And I was conscious again of the fundamental magic of flying, a miracle that has nothing to do with any of its practical purposes— purposes of speed, accessibility, and convenience—and will not change as they change. It is a magic that has more kinship with what one experiences standing in front of serene Madonnas or listening to cool chorales, or even reading one of those clear passages in a book—so clear and so illuminating that one feels the writer has given the reader a glass-bottomed bucket with which to look through the ruffled surface of life far down to that still permanent world below.

For not only is life put in new patterns from the air, but it is some-how arrested, frozen into form. (The leaping hare is caught in a marble panel.) A glaze is put over life. There is no flaw, no crack in the sur-face; a still reservoir, no ripple on its face. Looking down from the air that morning, I felt that stillness rested like a light over the earth. The waterfalls seemed frozen solid; the tops of the trees were still; the river hardly stirred, a serpent gently moving under its shimmering skin. Everything was quiet: fields and trees and houses. What motion there was, took on a slow grace: the crawling cars, the rippling skin of the river, and birds drifting like petals down the air; like slow-motion pictures which catch the moment of outstretched beauty—a horse at the top of a jump—that one cannot see in life itself, so swiftly does it move.

And if flying, like a glass-bottomed bucket, can give you that vi-sion, that seeing eye, which peers down to the still world below the choppy waves—it will always remain magic.

This description is as beautiful today as it was 50 years ago. It is for this capturing of some of the feelings of those of us who are privi-leged to see through "glass-bottomed buckets" that we want to honor you. We sincerely hope that you can reconsider our request. I can assure you there will be no publicity outside of the Club.

As I said, she wrote back promptly:

"...I was very touched and surprised by your reference to and quotation taken from my first book, North To The Orient. *Your consideration of my life and understanding of my problems in regard to writing and publicity have certainly made me reconsider your very cordial invitation. I would very much like to accept your invitation..."*

Mrs. Lindbergh normally spends the summer in Europe with several of her children, and we agreed on a date in October. I then proceeded to let the Club's members know of this wonderful opportunity to honor one of the pioneers of aviation.

I also got in touch with her publisher and asked if they had any copies of *North To The Orient.* At first her publisher would not believe that she had agreed to speak, and I had to fax a copy of her acceptance letter before they would. At that point they discovered they had 500 copies of the book in paperback published in 1963 that they would be willing to sell to the Club for 25 cents a copy, half of the price shown on the cover. We distributed copies to all the members so they could read this beautiful book for themselves.

October 17, 1981

Mrs. Lindbergh took the train from her home in Connecticut and stayed with her daughter who lived in Washington, D.C. Inge and I met her at her daughter's apartment and then arranged for a limousine to drive us to a back entrance of the hotel so that if any reporters had gotten wind of the event she would not be spotted.

She had said that she did not want to give a speech, and so in my introduction, I quoted from her book and told the audience of the impact it had in 1935 when the book was published. I then asked if she wanted to say a few words. She did, and she talked extemporaneously from notes she had made on the back of an envelope. The audience listened to every word; they were as beautiful as her writings. Fortunately we were able to record her remarks.

Anne Lindbergh's Remarks

First of all, thank you Mr. Gross for such a perfect takeoff. I can remember how cheered I felt in the old days at some small airport on one of our transcontinental survey flights when the mechanic, after pulling away the blocks from the wheels, shook a goodby to us with both hands clasped above his head. This meant good luck and happy landings.

I have been thinking about flying as it used to be when I first started before North To The Orient *was written—the book that Mr. Gross has resurrected for you. That flight started just fifty years ago in 1931. My thoughts went back to early flying after reading Mr. Gross's account of his record-breaking flight with his son in a single-engine plane, across the country in 1977 in, I believe, 11 hours, 8 minutes, and 48 seconds. As I read, I remembered a flight my husband and I made in 1930. Also a record-breaking flight "Dawn to Dusk" as it was called, from Los Angeles to New York in the Lockheed "Sirius" in 14 hours and 45 minutes. No one counted the seconds, not then! We refueled in St. Louis, taking the southern route, not over the high Rockies.*

Our motive, to establish a new record, and our reactions to the excitement and the beauty of the flight, were very parallel, but there were enormous differences. The Lockheed Sirius, which you know of, was just then built to my husband's specifications. It was a wonderful plane, but its performance was not up to the Grosses' 1975 Cessna turbocharged plane. The Sirius was a single-engine, low wing, open monoplane with sliding cockpit covers. It was not comfortable. It was wonderful, but... no radio on that particular flight, no automatic pilot, no radar contact, no oxygen masks. We also went to high altitudes to take advantage of the tailwinds in the upper air but nowhere near 25,000 feet. We had perhaps ten or fifteen thousand feet at most. We had no airways to stick to, and no scoldings if we detoured.

Comparing our flights, I began to think about what flying used to mean fifty years ago. Flying in the 20s and the 30s was an intermediate period, long after the pioneers and the experimenters, and after the heroic knights of World War I. This was the era of long-distance survey flights and not just for the prize of breaking records, but for pragmatic reasons, to prove that worldwide air transportation was a practical working proposition. These were the rational motives, but I

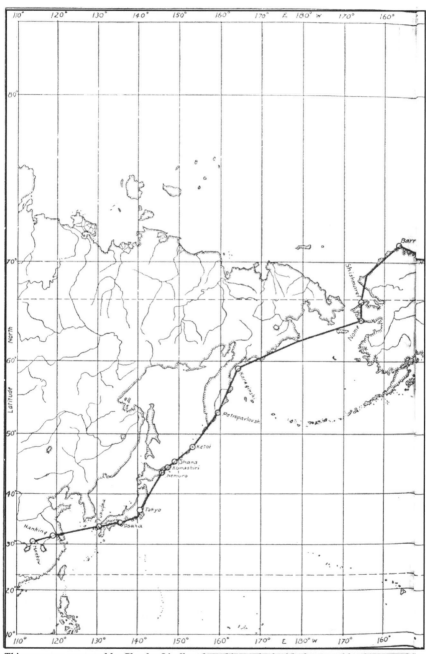

This map was prepared by Charles Lindbergh and is on the inside front and back cover of the hard-copy book. The flight started in Washington, D.C., but first they flew to North (next page)

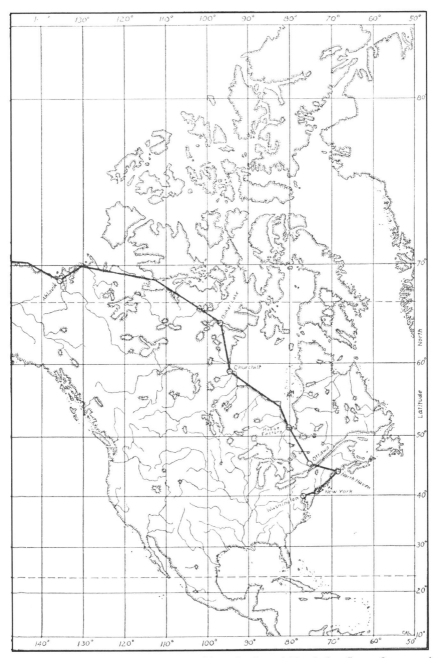

Haven, Anne's family home. After a good-by to family and friends they flew to Ottawa and points north and west. The flight ended when the plane capsized in the Yangtze River.

believe what drew adventurous men and women into this new profession was something far more emotional, perhaps even romantic.

Flying meant freedom; freedom to leave the earth; freedom to go anywhere; freedom to land anywhere—like a bird—even in a tree! My husband once bought a plane for me to fly. It was called the Bird Airplane. It was a biplane. And he said he bought it because he was sure I could land it in a tree.

A Special Breed

Pilots then were a special breed. They were adventurous, yes, and certainly courageous, and usually stubbornly independent. They often flew alone, and they were great dreamers. Flying was more of an art, not as much of a science or a profession in those days. Because of the many unknowns of machines, weather, and territory, the pilots relied much more on their instincts and their experience than on the meager instruments of the day.

Flying, of course, also meant danger, but the men and women who were drawn to it were not in love with danger. They were in love with life. They wanted to expand life's possibilities to the limit of their dreams. And their dreams and aspirations have to a large extent come true.

Today, inevitably, much of the freedom has gone. Flying has become disciplined and regulated, which was inevitable and necessary with its tremendous growth. It has also become infinitely safer.

There were still dangers on the Gross' record-breaking flight. Wind, weather, cold, and technical breakdowns were not completely in control. They had vacuum pump trouble; light snow impaired their vision for a night landing; ice might have formed on their wings or propeller, although they had something called prop deice heat, which was unknown to us.

I Remember Every One!

Despite their reliable engine, they had carefully considered the possibility of a forced landing. I was delighted to read that they were well prepared by carrying "survival equipment." My husband would have approved. In our time, a forced landing was a possibility we always had to consider, and my husband, as an old barnstorming pilot, prepared for them. We had emergency equipment for forced landing at sea, and emergency equipment for forced landing over land. We had emergency equipment for landing on the Greenland Ice Cap, including snowshoes and a sledge. And, emergency equipment for a parachute jump. We didn't have many forced landings, but I remember every one!

One I remember vividly was on a survey flight from New York to the west coast in a single-engine Monocoupe in 1934. That was rather an unlucky trip. First, we ground-looped in the middle of Wichita airport. No one was hurt but the landing gear was smashed and the wing was slightly damaged, and my husband was terribly humiliated. "I'm afraid we have a ground-looper," he said glumly. He discovered later that the brake was put on backwards on one of the wheels, which made him feel a little better. But we had to wait two days in Wichita.

On the third day, we started west again in a second Monocoupe. We hummed along quite nicely for about an hour and-a-half and we had just passed Waynoka, Oklahoma, when suddenly there was the most terrible knocking and grinding noise and the whole plane started to vibrate.

"What is it, Charles?" I shouted, expecting a wing to fall off at any moment.

"Just the engine." he said glumly. "Just the engine!" I knew what that meant. Soon there was no more noise at all. He turned the ship slightly, and we floated down practically perpendicularly against a strong headwind and landed gently on the slope of a plowed field. No bumps, no skids, no tail up in the air, just a perfect three-point landing. "Wouldn't you know it," said my husband, "I would smash a landing gear and damage a wing in the middle of Wichita airport and then, with a forced landing and engine failure, put the plane down in a furrowed field without even blowing a tire!"

By this time the farmer who was plowing another field came up to us. "Having trouble?" "Just a little engine trouble," said my husband. "We kind of thought so," said the farmer, "when we saw that Air-o-plane up there it looked like it was coming right down on top of us, but why did you pick that field?" We didn't explain that we didn't have much choice.

Anne Lindbergh sitting in the Sirius. Referred to in the thirties as the "First Lady of the Air" she held both a pilot's and radio operator's license. She was the first woman to earn a first-class glider license. She was the radio operator on the Lindberghs' survey flights, as well as copilot.

He asked what he could do to help, and, with some trouble, hitched up the plow horses to the poor Monocoupe and dragged it up to the farmhouse and staked it down for the night. Did they have a telephone? Yes, they did. The farmer's wife came out on the back stoop with her apron on and her hair done up in pin curls. I can see her now. "Well, you folks did pick a godforsaken spot to land in. Where are you headed? You can stay right here until you get all fixed up. We got room and plenty of food." And out she ran after a chicken. The chicken knew what was coming. And it took off, flapping its wings and squawking like mad. But she ran after it shouting, "don't squawk now, you're Lindy's dinner!"

It was a very good dinner, too. We were there three days waiting for the third Monocoupe. When it arrived, my husband took the whole family up for their first airplane ride before we took off again for the west coast. Actually, we only got as far as Roswell, New Mexico.

Those were the days of unexpected delays and happy surprises. Fortunately, the element of danger has diminished today, and perhaps some of the fun. The practicality of aviation is never questioned.

We Live Today In The Dreams of Yesterday

As my husband said over twenty-five years ago: "We live today in the dreams of yesterday." But all of his dreams have not materialized. In some of his early crusading speeches made after his first Paris flight, he voiced the hope that aviation would be one of the forces of the future to bring nations together. Once people traveled freely and swiftly, he argued, we would have more communication, greater understanding, and less strife in the world. He was young and he was overly optimistic. Swifter communication does not necessarily mean deeper understanding. The world is now webbed with air routes, but wars have continued, more terrible than ever before, partly through the advances in aviation.

Bond Between Flyers

However, despite his unfulfilled dreams, what has endured, I think, has been a bond between flyers. Those of us who had that early experience of seeing the world from above, are perceiving the earth as a planet, of sensing the air, not as passengers, but as pilots, immersed, held up by another element. We have an unforgettable common background. We remember the heady excitement of climbing up through pillars of clouds, or the beauty of being on eye level with a sunset or a sunrise, or the surprising sense of tenderness we feel toward earth itself, looking down on its neatly combed fields, its velvet forests, the gleaming curves of its rivers, the twinkling towns seen from above at night.

Our first impressions have remained with us. Our eyes have never lost the early vision or the instinctive bonds between others who have shared it with us. That is why I am so honored and happy today to have from you a tangible expression of this bond, which is, I think, unbreakable.

Mrs. Lindbergh captivated that audience as I have never seen before. We were in the Mayflower Hotel with probably 250 Club members present. You could have heard a pin drop.

My parents were seated next to Mrs. Lindbergh's 40-year-old daughter. She told my mother that she had never heard her mother give a speech before. That testifies to the rarity of this talk. There was even a reference to it in *Time Magazine*.

The next day, Mrs. Lindbergh called me at my office before starting home to thank me for inviting her. She was not saying this to be polite; she truly enjoyed being here.

A week later, I received from Mrs. Lindbergh a book written by a British aviation pioneer, John Grierson, titled: *I Remember Lindbergh*. She told me that this book provided the most insightful description of Charles Lindbergh of any book yet written. John Grierson had met the Lindberghs in Iceland in 1933 on their Atlantic survey flight, and became lifelong friends.

Mrs. Lindbergh had written the introduction to this book. After the manuscript was already at the publishers it was necessary for her to insert the following just before the title page:

John Grierson died the night of May 21, 1977, after giving a lecture at the Smithsonian Institution in Washington, D.C., in a commemorative symposium for the fiftieth anniversary of Charles A. Lindbergh's first solo transatlantic flight to Paris. The lecture was a recounting of the ordeals of the flight itself, much as they are told in this book. He had arrived at the point in the story where Lindbergh had reached Ireland. He was unable to continue his speech, sat down quietly, and died a few hours later of a cerebral hemorrhage. His death is a great loss to his family and friends and to those who knew of him as one of the early pilots of a heroic period in aviation. His last act was to pay tribute to a fellow airman and to the profession in which he himself had devoted his life.

Anne Morrow Lindbergh
June, 1977

I treasure this book, and the memories of having had an opportunity of meeting, and, in a small way, honoring Anne Morrow Lindbergh.

21

Atlantic Adventure
1982

I think I first started dreaming about making the ultimate flight——the one across the big pond—while I was still at Presque Isle AFB, with perhaps 200 flight hours then behind me. Private planes were not allowed to use Presque Isle AFB, but a pilot could usually get a one-time permission to use the base when flying across the Atlantic. Presque Isle was the northernmost U.S. airport with long runways. There were few private plane flights, particularly single-engine flights, across the Atlantic around 1955. But a few pilots made the flight and when they took the northern route, they likely stopped for fuel at Presque Isle.

I remember one gentlemen who came through Presque Isle. I didn't meet him, but I saw him from a distance, and he started my imagination going. He was flying a Cessna 195—a four-seat, single-engine aircraft, then the top of the Cessna line. He was a jeweler from San Francisco, and was referred to as the "flying jeweler." Most of the people I talked to thought he was crazy to attempt such a flight. I don't recall his route, but he fired my imagination.

Later, when I had my first flight in a single-seat Mooney Mite in December, 1955, I wondered if you could cram enough fuel into it to somehow get across the ocean. It had a miserly fuel flow of less than 4 gallons an hour and cruised at 105 mph. I don't think my dreaming was at all realistic—but dreams have a way of staying with you.

Fast Forward to 1981

Once I had purchased my brand new Cessna T210 in 1975, my dream started coming closer to the surface of my consciousness. By then, the preferred route for those with limited range was to fly north in Canada to just about opposite Sondrestom, Greenland, then turn east to Greenland, Iceland, and finally to Scotland. The map on the opposite page shows the route and distances between fuel stops, the longest of which was 850 statute miles. In theory, an aircraft with a thousand-mile range could hopscotch all the way across with reasonable fuel margins—at least in the summer months. Fall and spring months, and particularly winter months, were almost impossible because of strong headwinds and storms.

My Cessna T210 as it came from the factory would carry 534 pounds of fuel—89 gallons, at 6 pounds per gallon. The Cessna pilot's operating handbook indicated a no-reserve range at 24,000 feet and 75 percent power of 1,170 miles. In 1976 I had added tip tanks, holding an additional 168 pounds which increased my range by 400 miles, all at long-range power settings. This modification gave my Cessna the necessary range to make this northern crossing without having to add extra tanks just for this trip.

By 1981, a number of other private pilots had crossed the North Atlantic, and it was no longer the rare event that it had been in 1955. Pilots are glad to share their experiences, and several had written about their flights and the lessons learned. It was then that I became convinced that I wanted to make the crossing, but I wanted to do it with a twist: for Inge's sake, as well as my own, I would make our final destination Berlin, her hometown. This would involve political problems since it was still a divided city, and the Russians controlled the airways into Berlin.

So I got out a map and started to look at what the distances actually were. As you can see on the polar map on the opposite page, the longest leg was from Sondrestrom, Greenland, to Reykjavik, Iceland—850 miles. The total distance to Berlin from Washington, D.C. was 5,351 miles.

The next question to answer was what would the fuel range be given the most economical power settings. By 1981, I had considerable experience with my Cessna, and with the extra capability that the long-

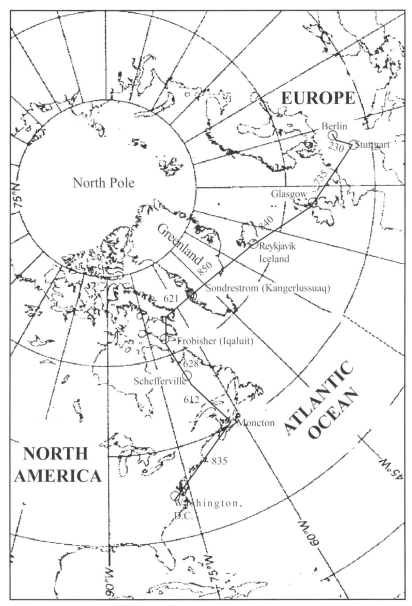

This was my initial plan: to fly across the big pond with our final destination being Berlin, Inge's home town. Going east we could expect some tailwinds, but returning we would be faced with headwinds. This flight could only be undertaken in the summer months because of fuel limitations. As the reader will find, we did not make it, but we are here to tell about it.

range fuel tanks added.

But many variables enter into the calculation of the range of an aircraft, some under the pilot's control, and some not. The biggest variable over which the pilot has limited control is wind. Generally in the northern hemisphere winds blow from west to east, and the higher one flies the greater their velocity. Wind speeds are much less in the summer than in winter.

I constructed a chart based not only on the Cessna aircraft manual data, which tends to be overly optimistic, but also on my own experience with six years of flying my Cessna. While I could not control the winds, I did have control over my power settings and over the altitude at which the flight would be made. The higher the altitude the more efficient a turbocharged aircraft becomes. In a tailwind that is fine, but in a headwind the pilot had better stay low where the velocity of the

Percent Power	Fuel Flow/Hr (gallons)	Speed		Range (miles)	
		10,000'	25,000'	10,000'	25,000'
75	18.0	185	212	1,112	1,204
70	16.7	180	207	1,165	1,262
65	15.7	176	200	1,213	1,293
60	14.7	170	190	1,251	1,310
55	13.7	160	180	1,264	1,329
Assumes no headwinds or tailwinds, and includes fuel for taxi, climb to altitude, and reserve fuel for 90 minutes at 70% power.					

winds would usually be slower. Here is the chart.

I concluded that my Cessna T210 definitely had the potential fuel range to make it over and back. Once I reached that conclusion, I had effectively made the "go" decision. I had heard the Siren of the Sea, and I was hooked.

Navigation

The next issue I tackled was navigation. Could I find my way from airport to airport? Although I was going the northern route and would be over land much of the way, there were few landmarks, and still fewer airports. Historically, on long-distance flights over oceans or desolate areas, pilots had depended on a combination of dead reckoning and low-frequency homing beacons located at airports. Few remote airports had VOR navigation, and those that did were usable only when you got within fifty miles.

New technology helped solve that problem. For many years the Coast Guard had operated a marine navigation system referred to as LORAN (**LO**ng **RA**nge **N**avigation). This system picked up very-low-frequency radio signals from three stations plus a "master" station, each often a thousand miles away, and, through triangulation, a boat could pinpoint its position within a couple of miles. The receivers were bulky, and until the early 1980s, involved the user having to interpret the signals received and then to plot them on a map to determine where he was. This was not practical for small aircraft.

But microcomputer chips were being developed in the late 1970s. This made it possible to reduce the size of the receiver, and made the output more user friendly. In 1981, Texas Instruments developed the first airborne LORAN receiver, and in April, 1982, I had one installed. I believe that my unit was one of the first twenty-five produced, so I can claim to be a pioneer in the use of airborne LORAN. This was a great advance, although the unit was crude and rudimentary by comparison to the equipment that became available five and ten years later.

LORAN coverage was spotty because each "chain"—as the three stations and the master station were called—covered an irregular, albeit specific geographic area. To illustrate, flying from the east to west coast would typically require using three or four chains. Coverage was good in the United States, but coverage pretty much ended at the St. Lawrence River when flying north until you got close to Greenland.

My LORAN unit always selected the appropriate chain since it knew at all times where we were, and therefore when to change to another chain. When I turned off the unit at the end of the flight, it kept track of where we were, and the next time I turned it on, it hunted for the chain appropriate for our location based on its stored memory from the last flight. When flying from coast-to-coast, it automatically switched from one chain to the next. If two chains overlapped each other I could tell it which chain I wanted it to use.

There was no permanent data base of airports and their latitude and longitude in the LORAN receiver. To select a destination you had to enter its latitude and longitude. It had a very limited memory and could store only ten destinations. By departure date, I had flown almost 80 hours with the LORAN and thought I understood how to use it.

Engine Overhaul

Another issue I had to address was the condition of my engine. You cannot pull over to the side of the road if your only engine stops in flight. If you are above the icy water of the North Atlantic, your odds of survival are zero. The normal overhaul period for my engine was 1,400 hours at that time. I then had almost 1,000 hours, which while within the 1,400 hours, was outside my comfort threshold, given what I was going to attempt.

Two periods in an engine's life appear to be most risky. First, as the engine approaches the recommended overhaul time. Of course the engine keeps going when it reaches this 1,400 hour number, but historical records suggest that the risk of failure increases.

An engine is also at higher risk in the first hundred hours after the overhaul. In a comprehensive overhaul, many new parts are used, often including new cylinder assemblies. Until the engine has run long enough to have broken in these new parts, there is an elevated risk of failure.

I decided to have the engine overhauled early enough to be sure I was past this initial break-in period—that is, until I had at least a hundred hours of flying after the overhaul. I also wanted the best overhaul I could get, regardless of location or cost. I quickly settled on RAM Aircraft in Waco Texas. They specialized in the specific engine I had, and were known for the quality of their work. They had also developed a modification to convert the engine from 285 horsepower to 310 horsepower on takeoff. Cessna T210s produced after I had purchased my aircraft had this larger horsepower engine installed at the factory.

I called the folks at RAM and told them why I wanted an overhaul at that time to be sure they understood what a major flight I would be undertaking. They agreed with my reasoning and I took the plane to Waco in October, 1981, for the overhaul. It took about a month.

Planning for July, 1982

Then we started planning in some detail for this big adventure. We decided to make it a family visit to Berlin. Inge and I would fly the Cessna, and the two children would fly on the airlines, meeting us in Frankfurt. The children were not enthusiastic about the Atlantic crossing in the Cessna, and I did not want to push them, nor did I want their weight and baggage. We would be carrying survival equipment which would take up both space and weight, and I didn't want to be too heavily loaded.

I looked into the requirements for the 100-mile flight through Russian-occupied East Germany into Berlin. Because of the political and military risks, the Air Force required a face-to-face detailed briefing at an Air Force base in South Carolina, which I agreed to. Unfortunately, at the last minute the Russians said "nyet" to allowing a private single-engine aircraft fly the corridor. I guess I was a casualty of the cold war. I concluded that, instead, I would park the plane, probably in Stuttgart near relatives, and we would then take the train into Berlin.

A number of other things had to be arranged, including a special international aviation credit card for fuel purchases. Even with my years of flawless credit, it took some time to convince Exxon to issue this type of special card. If they hadn't, we would not have been able to make the trip because few airports on our route were equipped to take cash.

I also did a lot more research on the flight plan. This was still during the cold war, and we would be flying near a number of U.S. radar sites. I was able to get the radio frequencies for these sites through my aviation connections. They were not generally available to private pilots but they provided additional backup in case of problems. As it turned out, this was extremely valuable.

Gremlins

During the spring of 1982, the plane was plagued with one little mechanical problem after another. None was major, but this was unusual in that most of these mechanical problems were with things that seldom failed or required attention. It seemed that the gremlins were after me.

I also became concerned with the oil consumption on the overhauled engine. Normally after an overhaul, it takes a while to stabilize at about nine or ten hours per quart. Throughout the spring, with close to 100 hours on the overhauled engine, it was burning a quart of oil every four or five hours. I talked with the folks at RAM several times about this and finally they had my mechanic make a borescope inspection of the insides of the cylinder walls. This revealed that the chrome cylinder walls had not broken in as well as they should have. RAM assured me that while the oil consumption was higher than normal, the engine was perfectly safe to make the crossing. At the same time they recognized my concern, and in May, they suggested that they replace the cylinders with new ones. They did so in June, without charge, and even flew the plane back to me in Washington, D.C., knowing how tight time was getting. Oil consumption returned to the more normal levels.

I had an annual inspection made of the plane in late June, with a scheduled departure date on Monday, July 19. With all the little problems that we had had that spring I was on edge as we approached departure day.

I made a last check of the plane the Saturday before our Monday departure and found evidence that the alternator was starting to fail. My mechanic had no replacement alternator available on Saturdays, and it would be Tuesday at the earliest before a replacement could be installed. But we had to depart on Monday because the children had airline reservations for a specific day and we needed to be in Germany in time to meet them. If we left late we would also have fewer days for possible weather delays en route.

I called Summit Aviation in Middletown, Delaware that Saturday. They had worked on the aircraft in the past and I told them of my problem. They told me to fly over on Sunday afternoon, and they would replace the alternator first thing Monday morning. So they did, and we started out on our big adventure at about 10 a.m. that Monday, as scheduled. Middletown was on the direct route from Washington, D.C. to Moncton so we did not lose any time.

Middletown to Moncton

It was 731 miles from Middletown to Moncton, New Brunswick. We flew pretty much directly to Moncton, with a jog to the east to avoid air traffic around New York City. Probably a third of the trip was over water. This was good because we needed to get used to flying over water.

We used the LORAN navigation radio on this part of the trip, and it worked well until we were about 50 miles from Moncton. At that point we ran out of LORAN signals. The LORAN system was still primarily used for high density marine use. Consequently, we had no signal while flying over Canada, but knew we would be able to pick up a signal again as we crossed the Davis Strait to Greenland, almost fifteen hundred miles north of Moncton.

Moncton was our first stop because the Canadian Government required all small, private aircraft that are departing Canada for Europe to stop there and be inspected. It seems the Canadians are responsible for search and rescue efforts if a plane's last departure point is Canada, so they have a vested interest in being sure that people attempting this type of flight know what they are doing, and are well-equipped with the required survival equipment.

The inspector looked over the plane's papers, took a quick look at the plane, and talked with us for about fifteen to twenty minutes asking questions about our experience and plans. He even asked us a number of trick questions designed to test the depth of our knowledge. After passing this inspection, we spent the night in Moncton.

Moncton to Schefferville to Frobisher Bay

The weather was good the next day, and we both enjoyed the flight to Frobisher Bay. The 612 miles to our fuel stop, Schefferville, took a little less than four hours; the 628 miles from there to Frobisher took four hours and fifteen minutes. Schefferville is a tiny village located on the northeastern part of the Province of Quebec near the northwest border of Labrador. I doubt that more than a hundred people live there, but the airport had a good runway and sells fuel. There appears to be a road from Sept-Iles on the Gulf of St. Lawrence—five hundred miles to the south—to Schefferville, but it goes no further north. It must be how they get aviation fuel to this remote part of the world. The line boy was efficient and got us on our way quickly.

The landscape for hundreds of miles around us was populated with thousands of lakes and, as Inge remembers, billions of mosquitos. From Schefferville on, we were over the Province of Quebec until we reached the Hudson Strait; after that we were over the Northwest Territories. The town of Frobisher Bay—now known as Iqaluit—is at the northwestern end of Frobisher Bay on Baffin Island. We spent the night there.

Frobisher Bay has access to the sea, and appeared to be a major town. It had all of the trappings of an Eskimo village, and reminded us of Barrow, Alaska. The natives are called the Inuit. Inuit means "people" in Inukitut, their language. Although tired, we did walk around after dinner to get an impression of the town.

Frobisher Bay to Sondrestrom

The next morning we got up at 4:30 a.m. in order to get an early start. When we got to the plane we found another minor mechanical problem that needed fixing—the gremlins would not leave us alone. I don't even recall what the problem was but we managed to fix it ourselves, and were on our way by 7 a.m.

Our route from Frobisher took us northeast to Cape Dyer on the east coast of Baffin Island, opposite Sondrestrom Fjord, on the other side of the Davis Strait. It was 284 miles to Cape Dyer and then 337 miles more to Sondrestrom Airport at the head of Sondrestrom Fjord about a 100 miles in from the coast. As with most fjords, mountains rose steeply on both sides of the fjord. The safest approach when there was an overcast is to fly from the coast directly up the fjord underneath the overcast. This is what we did.

The reason we made a dog-leg north to Cape Dyer rather than going direct is that we wanted as little over-water flight as possible. We

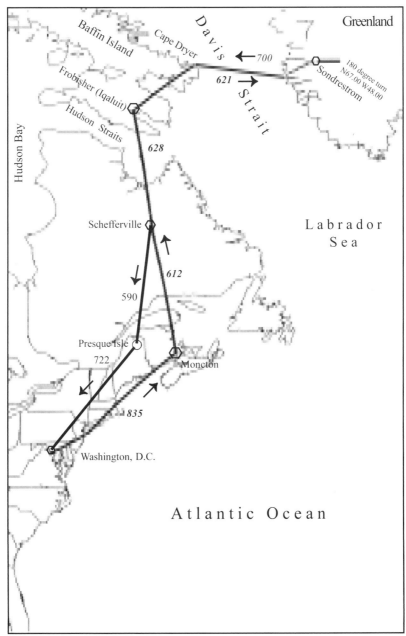

This was the actual route we took, out and back. At Sondrestrom we were about 30 miles north of the Arctic Circle. We didn't see the Greenland Icecap because of the cloud cover. We made our "180" turn just to the east of Sondrestrom where shown.

were now just about at the Arctic Circle and we expected to find icebergs in Davis Strait, and we did. It was on this leg that the first inkling of real trouble appeared.

We were close enough to the north magnetic pole that magnetic variation becomes a major factor in navigation. In this situation, the compass may read "north" but if it is corrected for magnetic variation you may find that you are actually flying thirty or forty degrees to the west of north. I was, of course, fully aware of this and all of our compass headings properly took this into account.

So when I routinely contacted the Air Force early-warning radar site at Cape Dyer, they indicated that I needed to make a further, significant correction, saying that I was off course for Sondrestrom by perhaps thirty degrees. This puzzled me because I rechecked the compass. I was on the proper course. Of course, I also rechecked my original calculations. Nevertheless, the radar at Cape Dyer had to be believed and we followed their instructions and made the correction. They followed us across the Davis Strait to Greenland.

We knew that once we got part way across the Davis Strait, we should be able to pick up a LORAN signal. We turned on the LORAN receiver but it gave no indication that it was receiving a signal. I as-

These ice floes in the Davis Strait would not make a very good landing area in the event of an engine failure. The water temperature was reported as 30 degrees F.

sumed that we were just outside the LORAN coverage and left the unit on. But it never seemed to pick up a signal, even when we got over the Greenland coast. I began to think something must have failed within the LORAN unit.

We had clear skies across the Davis Strait. Once we got to the Greenland coast, however, there was an overcast at twenty-five hundred feet or so, but with good visibility beneath. We followed the fjord to Sondrestrom and landed uneventfully, three hours and forty minutes out of Frobisher Bay.

Greenland is Danish territory, but the ground crew and weather staff spoke English. I eventually got a bill from the Danish government for about $50 for the landing fee and services. Fuel was several times more expensive than at home, but considering where we were, it did not seem unreasonably expensive.

The weather picture ahead of us was less pleasant. We would be flying at 13,000 feet over a storm until we were about 100 miles from Reykjavik, Iceland. I was now concerned about the apparent failure of the LORAN unit. Looking down at the tops of clouds does not tell a pilot much about where he is. I had forgotten about the magnetic compass deviation question raised by the Cape Dyer radar site.

The entrance to the fjord that led to Sondrestrom. We had to descend to about 2,000 feet, and the mountains rose above us on both sides of the fjord.

The Sondrestrom airport can be seen on the left center (arrow) and we are headed for a straight-in landing. The airport is located in the village of Kangerlussuaq, population about 500. The airport is run by aviation authorities in Denmark since Greenland is part of Danish territory. They had a comprehensive weather service in 1982, with most planes landing there being business aircraft en route to Europe. The officials all spoke fluent English. There was far more traffic in 1982 than at present because of the rapid growth in the number of business jets that fly across the Atlantic nonstop or with only one stop, therefore not needing Sondrestrom.

Sondrestrom to Reykjavik

We took off, and this time we had to go into the clouds at about 2,500 feet. We climbed in the departure corridor between the mountains, and found ourselves in rain, but little turbulence. I don't recall at what altitude we got on top but probably about 10,000 feet. We leveled off at 13,000 feet.

The LORAN was still not picking up a signal so we were truly "dead reckoning."

We had been in moderate rain on our climb in clouds which was not a problem. The top of the windshield occasionally leaked a little water—a drop or two every second—and it had done so during this climb. I don't know to this day what made me reach down with my finger to touch the drip of water on the floor, and then to smell it. It was not water! It smelled like kerosene. There was only one possible source of kerosene, and it helped explain the earlier mystery—the compass deviation.

The compass sits directly in the center of the cockpit just under the top edge of the windshield, about where a rearview mirror is located in a car. The compass consists of a sealed container with a glass plate on the side through which you can see a compass ball floating in kerosene. Apparently the compass seal had started leaking earlier in the trip.

Normally we don't directly use the compass because it bobs around in turbulence. Instead we have a directional gyro which is not subject to turbulence. The autopilot gets its instructions for keeping us headed in the right direction from this directional gyro. The directional gyro has to be aligned with the compass periodically, and on the leg from Frobisher we had to continually adjust our heading because of the magnetic deviation, so we were constantly referring to the compass. Once the leaking kerosene fluid level started to go down, the compass ball became unreliable. There was enough kerosene in the jar to allow some turning of the compass ball but obviously it was not turning freely.

Time for Action

Pilots learn to be pragmatic, and they seldom call a committee together to make a decision when flying. As soon as I smelled the kerosene I started a one-hundred-and-eighty degree turn back towards Sondrestrom. There comes a time when one has to cut his losses, and the leaking compass clearly indicated that the time had come. The gremlins had won.

N210MG: Sondrestrom Departure, November two ten mike
             golf, over.

Sondrestrom: Go ahead, mike golf.

N210MG: Sondrestrom, two ten mike golf would like to
             change our destination from Reykjavik back to
             Frobisher. Present position direct Sondrestrom,

direct. Twelve thousand. Over.

Sondrestrom: Understand two ten mike golf you want to go from
present position, direct Sondrestrom, direct
Frobisher. Is that correct?

N210MG: Affirmative.

The rest was anticlimactic. Once we reached the Greenland coast, we had clear skies all the way to Frobisher Bay. We called the kids from Frobisher Bay, and had them cancel their airline reservations. There were a few tears, but we had made the right decision. We spent the night in Frobisher. The next day we flew to Presque Isle where the dream had started twenty-five years before. We spent the night there and arrived home at noon the following day.

LORAN Mystery Solved

The LORAN started working again once we got back into the States. Eventually we figured out what the problem had been with the unit in Greenland—in a nutshell, pilot error. The LORAN unit lost its signal approaching Moncton, New Brunswick, and therefore recorded where it was at the time of that loss. When I turned it on approaching Greenland, it still thought it was near Moncton and kept searching for a signal on the frequencies applicable to the Moncton area. Neither it nor I, had any idea that it was looking for the wrong frequency signals.

What I should have done in turning on the LORAN receiver near Greenland was to start a re-initialization procedure to tell it approximately where we were. It would then have looked for the Greenland chain on the correct frequency. The unit had been installed only three months earlier and I had not encountered this situation before. I had flown eighty hours with this unit including a coast-to-coast trip, and a trip to Denver, all without this situation coming up. It had worked fine, of course, because every time it needed to change frequencies it knew where it was and made the change automatically.

Eventually I found the answer in a fine-print footnote prepared by some engineering-type person who was clearly not a pilot. I had not done my homework to the necessary level of detail. This is a good lesson that is particularly applicable these days for pilots with complex GPS units and "glass cockpits" that do virtually anything you want, provided you know which buttons to push or turn.

Self-Evaluation

As I have mentioned elsewhere in this book, I automatically evaluate my performance on every flight, hoping to learn from my experiences. Obviously, with all of the emotion and energy that went into the year-long effort to make this flight, I looked back and evaluated my performance on this "Atlantic Adventure."

Overall, there is no question I made the right decision to turn back. Given that I did not have LORAN coverage, my navigation ability was limited until I got close enough to Iceland to pick up an ADF radio signal. With the compass out of commission, I could not even be sure of flying a straight course. There really was no other decision to make.

I asked myself if I had been wise to overfly Sondrestrom and continue on to Frobisher. There the answer is "yes." I knew how good the weather was once I was west of the Greenland coast, and the landmarks between Cape Dyer and Frobisher were very obvious. I also could get help from the radar site at Cape Dyer if I really needed it. There was a small risk that the weather might deteriorate below IFR minimums, but that was very unlikely.

Landing back at Sondrestrom would have risked the possibility of getting stuck. It was not the kind of airport where I would have expected much in the way of maintenance, and the authorities might have grounded me. Overall, I have no regrets. I wish we had made it; we didn't—but we are here to tell about it.

Unanswered Questions

Two lingering question remain twenty-five years later. First, were the gremlins trying to tell me something? If one were superstitious, it would not be hard to imagine that they were. I had never had such a long streak of maintenance issues come up either before, or since that flight, and they stopped once we got home.

Second, what prompted me to reach down with my finger and touch the rain drops coming from a leaky windshield seal? This water leaking into the cabin was not new. I had several times tried to get the windshield resealed so it would not happen. It didn't happen on the ground, only in the air, and only in heavy rain.

I had ended up just learning to live with this situation which occurred perhaps two or three times a year. Certainly seeing a couple of drops of water during that climb-out was not unusual.

So what set off the alarm bells and caused me to smell one of the drops? I will never know, but if I hadn't, we would likely have flown past the point of no return with a leaking compass, twenty or thirty or more degrees off course, and never found Iceland. Sobering.

22

Freedom To Fly
1989 to 1995

Career Change

A major life event took place on June 30, 1989—the end of my career as a CPA and a partner in Price Waterhouse. I had joined the Firm in 1954, just out of college. We had a mandatory retirement age for partners of 60, but with an option of early retirement at 55, which I took advantage of. Frankly, I was pleased to start a new career: the presidency of the National Aeronautic Association (NAA). Private aviation had become a focal point in my life, and this gave me a chance to pursue this interest. I could now use my plane to travel on NAA business which I was not able to do while I was with Price Waterhouse. I now had the freedom to fly, and July 1, 1989, started a much more intensive period of flying.

Recurrent Training

Once I had accepted the invitation to become president of NAA, I had to be mindful that if I were involved in an aviation accident, both NAA and I would be in the spotlight. I concluded that I should have formal recurrentcy training every year to ensure that I remained competent to fly, particularly under IFR conditions. Such training is not mandated by the FAA for private pilots, although commercial airline pilots are required to have such training every six months.

This was one of the simulators. It was very realistic and I always came away totally exhausted. The company was run by an air traffic controller who had many years of observing where pilots get into trouble when flying IFR: poor organization, and failure to be in a "go-around" mental state when making an approach. Both were emphasized by the instructors.

So, on July 1, the day after my retirement, I flew to Champaign, Illinois, where a small company, Recurrent Training Center Inc., offered a two-day program combining ground school and simulator training. I was in the simulator for a total of eight hours and "flew" with three different instructors. It was a very intense experience, but at the completion, one of the instructors signed me off as having passed an IFR competency check. This is the same standard of competency that is required to initially obtain an instrument rating.

Almost every year after that, right up to 2003 when I sold the Cessna, I went back to Champaign to repeat this recurrent training. At the beginning of each year's training session, I told the instructors that I was looking to them to make sure that they had no reservations about my competency to continue flying IFR. I recognized that I was probably too close to be totally objective. I was also aware that as one "matures" both their mental and motor skills slow down, and I didn't want to make a fatal mistake of flying beyond my level of competency. At the same time I recognized that I was my own harshest critic and I didn't want to quit flying prematurely. I needed an independent evaluation. *Chapter 33, Decision Time,* describes the eventual decision on my part to stop IFR flying.

Glider Private License

My new job as president of the NAA did not start until the end of September. I wanted the summer off, and after the recurrentcy training in Champaign, Inge and I continued west to Orcas.

I also wanted to get my glider rating. The Soaring Society of America was affiliated with the NAA, and each organization had a representative on the other's board of directors. I had already been appointed to the Soaring Society Board and I felt that getting my private license in gliders was appropriate to be credible in that role. On an earlier trip to Orcas I had found that the Bayview Airport, about 15 miles from Orcas on the mainland, had several two-place gliders and gave lessons.

I already held a commercial license to fly single-engine land aircraft, so a good deal of the ground school training I would otherwise have had to take was not required. But I still had a lot to learn, particularly how to locate and stay in thermals, which are upward moving columns of air, that would lift the glider higher. I also had to learn how to judge how far away from the airport I should go, considering my altitude and the level of thermals available that day.

Tow aircraft were used to pull the glider to two or three thousand feet, at which point the glider pilot releases the tow rope. He was then on his own. Western Washington (west of the Cascade Mountains) is not a very good place to learn to fly gliders because there were few thermals to allow you to climb and remain in the air. The countdown to landing started almost immediately after release from the tow plane. I had to judge my altitude carefully because without power I didn't get a second chance if I ran out of altitude. I had to be at the airport or I would be faced with an off-field landing. Touchdown speed was only 30 or 32 miles per hour, and I usually landed on the grass beside the paved runway. The sink rate for the glider was between 100-200 feet per minute. This compares to close to 700 to 1,000 feet per minute in the Cessna T210. Most of my training flights were only about twenty minutes long.

By early August, I had flown 38 flights and had total glider flight time of fourteen hours. I easily passed my check ride and received my private license endorsement to fly gliders.

Soaring versus Gliding

I would characterize my glider experience as training in gliding, but not in soaring, which is where the real fun is. What is the difference? In gliding you are trading altitude for distance; in soaring you are trying to find updrafts that will lift your glider, perhaps thousands of feet, and your objective is to stay aloft until you are ready to land. There were very few thermals in western Washington, and therefore little soaring.

Minden, Nevada is often referred to as the soaring capital of the United States and many world soaring records have been set there. Minden is located about 30 miles south of Reno, and just a couple of miles on the eastern side of the Sierra Nevada Mountains (9,000 feet). Minden is in a valley at an elevation of about 4,700 feet. These mountains, coupled with the hot desert air, create updrafts that the glider pilot can use to keep airborne for hours at a time.

In mid-September, 1990, I attended a board meeting of the Soaring Society of America being held in Minden, and I arrived for the meeting three days early in order to learn about soaring. I found out.

There were several small FBOs with gliders for rent. I had to be checked out by an instructor before they would let me fly by myself since I would be using one of their gliders. I also needed instruction in soaring since I had never experienced strong thermals.

What a difference from my earlier experience! The tow plane released the glider at about two thousand feet over the ground, and then I quickly located some updrafts and soared. During these several days, there was lots of lift off the mountains. My log book shows that on that first checkout flight my instructor and I reached 16,500 feet. Later that same day, flying alone, I reached 11,300 feet and stayed aloft for three and-a-half hours! In total, I flew nine hours while in Minden. More importantly, I came away with an understanding of the difference between gliding and soaring.

I am sorry to say that was the end of my glider experience. I had accomplished what I set out to do, namely to get an understanding of this sport so that I could better represent this segment of sport aviation at the world aviation body, the Fédération Aéronautique Internationale.

Aerobatic Training

Besides my other board memberships, I was also on the board of the International Aerobatic Club (IAC). As with gliding and soaring, so, too, with aerobatic flight—I could be a more effective representative if I had some rudimentary experience in the sport. The Bayview Airport also had a Cessna 152 Aerobat which was Cessna's aerobatic basic trainer.

I took five lessons with an instructor practicing spins, rolls, loops, and two or three other aerobatic maneuvers. This gave me a slight taste of aerobatic flight, but I didn't take to it enthusiastically. Perhaps I was intimidated by the parachutes we had to wear, and the quick hinge-release handle on the door in case the wings fell off. I don't know. I am not sure how much insight my few lessons gave me because the IAC board members were real pros, flying high performance,

This is the Grob 103 two-seat glider I trained in. The silence and low sink rate took some getting used to. I was surprised how quickly I learned to locate thermals that would delay my inevitable return to earth. I came away with great respect for glider pilots, many of whom travel great distances in their gliders over forbidding terrain.

aerobatic aircraft in world-class competition. They were also flying very complex maneuvers that I could not visually picture.

Flying for NAA

I used my plane on NAA business for the first time in January, 1990. On that flight I flew to Hobbs, New Mexico, and then on to San Jose, California. Hobbs was the home of the Soaring Society of America. The San Jose area is the home of the United States Hang Gliding Association, and, while not on their board, I became active helping these sports men and women obtain approvals to use public lands as launching sites.

During the spring and early summer of 1990, I flew to Indianapolis, Indiana; Savannah, Georgia; Miami and Vero Beach, Florida; Birmingham, Alabama; Oshkosh, Wisconsin; and Montreal, Canada, all on NAA business. By April 10, 1990, I had accumulated 4,000 hours of total flight time, another milestone.

For the next few years I frequently used my plane to attend sporting events, conventions, and other NAA business throughout the United States. I now had the freedom to fly on business, which I was not able to do for my 30+ years with Price Waterhouse because of their concerns with potential liability.

United States Parachute Association

I also served on the board of the U.S. Parachute Association. At the first board meeting I attended in late September, 1990, I was asked the expected question: "Mal, how many parachute jumps have you made?" I confidently replied that I had not made any but that I was an instrument-rated, commercial pilot, had a private license for gliders, and that training for and keeping up with these activities was a major job. I thought I handled that question with skill until a voice piped in: "Mal, how about your first jump this afternoon, say about 3?" I am not sure what I said, but I still have not jumped out of a perfectly good airplane.

Fuel Leak In The Engine Compartment

My NAA flights did have some anxious moments. I remember one trip where I was headed for Denver. I had overnighted in Salina, Kansas, on March 6, 1991. The outside temperature was a cold 10 degrees when I departed Salina the next morning for Denver. I had been airborne for about 15 minutes when the fuel line fitting on cylinder number two came loose (but not totally off), allowing fuel to spray into the engine compartment. I could tell because my fuel flow computer was showing abnormally high flow, and the cylinder head and exhaust gas temperatures for cylinder number two were lower than they should have been. This suggested the potential for fire in the engine compartment and demanded quick action.

I was about 30 miles from the Wichita Mid-Continent Airport, Kansas. I called Wichita Approach Control, declared an emergency, and told them I was proceeding directly to the airport and wanted fire trucks to be standing by. I didn't touch the throttle for fear of making the situation worse. I did open the cowl flaps to get the maximum air circulation going across the cylinders. I also mentally prepared to make an emergency landing in a farmer's field if it became apparent a fire had started. Fortunately it didn't.

Two fire trucks were waiting at the approach end of the runway when I landed 10 to 12 minutes later. As soon as I was on the ground and off the runway, I quickly shut down the engine, closed the fuel lines from the wing tanks, and got out of the plane. Cautiously I touched the cowling above the engine. It was hot, but no more so than normal. The firemen helped me remove the top of the cowling and confirmed that there was no fire.

Why was I so lucky? To this day I can only speculate, but I suspect that the cold temperature of the outside air was a factor. If it had been a hot summer day the outcome might have been far different.

So, why was the fuel line fitting at cylinder number 2 loose and spraying fuel? Just before leaving Leesburg, Virginia, my home airport, the two magnetos had been removed and replaced. In order to get to one of these magnetos the mechanic had removed the fuel line to cylinder number 2. Then when he had reinstalled the magneto he must have failed to tighten the fitting. On the flight to Salina vibration gradually loosened the fitting. Given enough time, it would have totally come off.

Check Gear!

If there is a guardian angel, then in a commanding tone, he once urgently spoke two words to me: "CHECK GEAR!"

I had just about completed the short 35 minute flight from Orcas Island to SeaTac International Airport in Seattle. The weather was beautiful and I could see forever. I was at 200 feet and just about to touch down when a voice in my headset said those two words. There was no reference to my plane or anything but the urgency of the command caused me to look, and sure enough, my landing gear was still retracted. Another 30 seconds and I would have landed gear-up at one of the busiest airports in the country. I immediately leveled out, put the gear down, and then landed.

There is an old saying about pilots who fly retractable-gear aircraft. "There are those who have landed wheels up, and there are those who will." I had never thought I would fall into either category, but that day I came very close. To this day, I can only speculate that an airline captain on the ground, perhaps waiting to take off, happened to be watching and was my guardian angel. Whoever he may be, he has my eternal thanks.

Coast-to-Coast In One Day

I have made only five coast-to-coast flights all in one, long day. I made my fourth such flight on January 28, 1990 when I flew from San Jose to Leesburg with an intermediate stop for fuel in Garden City, Kansas. I flew both legs at 25,000 feet. The last one-day flight was on August 10, 1991, this one from east to west. I left Leesburg at 6:30 a.m., and 12.5 hours flying time later, I was over Orcas Island, Washington. With the three-hour time difference it was about 7 p.m. I had made quick fuel stops in Rockford, Illinois, Sheldon, Iowa, and Billings, Montana. My flight logbook indicates that there were thunderstorms over Montana and ice on descent at Orcas.

I have summarized the pertinent data for these five flights on the next page, taking the liberty of considering Leesburg as Washington, D.C. (Leesburg is a suburb, 31 miles from Washington) in order to simplify the presentation. Note that the westbound flights were in the

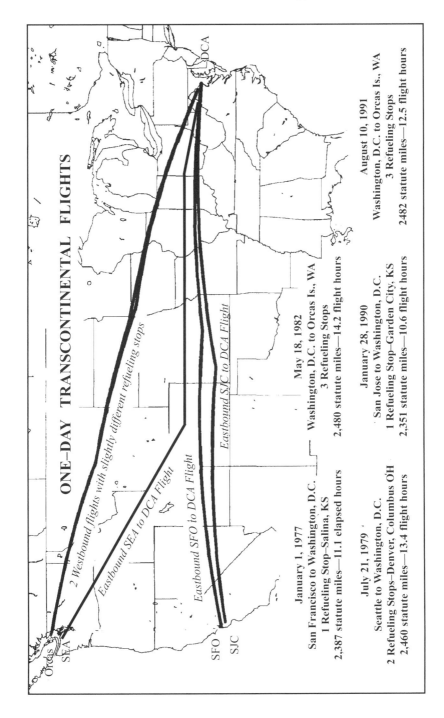

ONE–DAY TRANSCONTINENTAL FLIGHTS

2 Westbound flights with slightly different refueling stops

Eastbound SEA to DCA Flight

Eastbound SFO to DCA Flight

Eastbound SJC to DCA Flight

Orcas
SEA
SFO
SJC
DCA

January 1, 1977
San Francisco to Washington, D.C.
1 Refueling Stop—Salina, KS
2,387 statute miles—11.1 elapsed hours

July 21, 1979
Seattle to Washington, D.C.
2 Refueling Stops—Denver, Columbus OH
2,460 statute miles—13.4 flight hours

May 18, 1982
Washington, D.C. to Orcas Is., WA
3 Refueling Stops
2,480 statute miles—14.2 flight hours

January 28, 1990
San Jose to Washington, D.C.
1 Refueling Stop—Garden City, KS
2,351 statute miles—10.6 flight hours

August 10, 1991
Washington, D.C. to Orcas Is., WA
3 Refueling Stops
2482 statute miles—12.5 flight hours

summer, with long daylight and minimal headwinds. By contrast, two of the three eastbound flights were in January with strong tailwinds.

To a large extent there really is no significance in flying something over 2,000 miles in a single day; it is largely a matter of pilot endurance. However, that is only partly true, since one can seldom travel such a distance without encountering weather conditions that can tax both plane and pilot. That I managed it successfully five times rewarded me with the "magic" of being able to tell earthbound beings, "Yes, I have flown from coast-to-coast in one day. How long does it take you to drive that far in your car?" Being able to state that claim helps to dispel the notion that all I do is to fly around the local pea patch.

Retired from NAA and Moved to Orcas

In December of 1992, I retired from the NAA and we moved permanently to Orcas Island. The stress involved of being president of a small, nonprofit organization, and its constant money issues, had started to undermine my health. My priority was to fly in retirement and I was afraid that staying with NAA could put my FAA medical certificate in jeopardy. NAA subsequently hired a full-time executive director to handle the day-to-day affairs. I continued as volunteer president for two more years, mostly in a ceremonial capacity. I did continue to fly my plane on behalf of NAA.

1995 was also significant because I had occasion to make a number of long trips in which I fully utilized the capabilities of N210MG. I made fourteen such flights in 1995. Looking back on my fifty plus years of private flying, clearly 1995 was the year where my flying reached its apex, both in terms of number of flying hours (237) and the full utilization of the capabilities of the plane.

23

Mayday at Flight Level Two–Five–Zero
March 1993

As I relate elsewhere in this book, I became president of the National Aeronautic Association in the fall of 1989. In this role I wrote a column titled "From the Cockpit" for a bimonthly newsletter which went to all of the Association's members. Reprinted below, is a vivid description of a flight I made in the Spring of 1993 in my Cessna T210.

From the Cockpit

Flight Level Altitudes

Flying in a non pressurized aircraft at "flight level" altitudes presents unique problems. The obvious one is that the pilot—and the passengers, too—are somewhat inhibited by the "elephant trunk" oxygen masks that permit life to be sustained at that altitude. An oxygen mask is awkward, but comfortable enough in view of the alternative—namely, descending to a lower altitude and then being in weather, perhaps bouncing around or picking up ice.

There are other unique problems of flying at these altitudes that complicate life. Engine controls with a turbocharger are not easy to adjust and I find that it often takes 10 to 15 minutes to get the engine power adjusted exactly to the setting I want. It is also very easy to

This type of mask provides life-supporting oxygen to the pilot and passengers when flying at high altitudes. I call it an "elephant trunk;" it inhibits turning your head. The oxygen is stored in five, high-pressure bottles at 1800 psi.

abuse an engine at these altitudes. Another complication is that there is little margin for error—if something happens to the oxygen supply, the time of "useful consciousness" is just two minutes. You do not have much time to consider alternatives.

All of this by way of background.

Night Flight over Missouri

It was night, and I was at FL250 (25,000 feet) en route from my home on Orcas Island in Washington State to Memphis, Tennessee, to attend a board meeting of the International Aerobatic Club. I was then just a little over an hour out from Memphis on the second leg. It had been a good flight up to that point.

I had started out from Orcas in the morning, flying nonstop to Rapid City, South Dakota, for fuel. There had been a lot of weather over the Rockies, but at 25,000 feet I had been comfortably above it. I made a routine instrument approach into Rapid City, with no ice on descent, and—best of all—a good tailwind the whole way.

I had lost an engine-driven vacuum pump on the first leg, but I have two vacuum pumps, and there was no reason for concern. I only needed one, and I would get the first pump replaced at Memphis. I also have a backup battery system that powers only the GPS navigation system in an emergency, and that battery system, too, had failed for no apparent reason on the first leg to Rapid City. But since that was only for emergency use, it seemed of little consequence at the time. With a sophisticated aircraft it is not unusual to have failures, and that is why the plane has backup equipment.

With just an hour to go, the flight seemed serene enough to go down into the log book as another "uneventful" flight—the kind I like. But suddenly, warning lights started flashing, and my computer instrument monitoring system spelled out the problem in English: "Low voltage." That was an understatement: there was no voltage! The alternator must have failed.

Mayday!

"Kansas City Center —Centurion N210MG— I have just lost my only alternator. The battery and all communications are likely to be

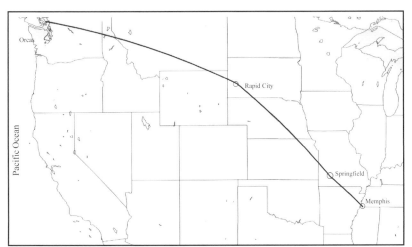

Orcas Island to Memphis. Note on the Orcas to Rapid City leg that our route actually was not a straight line. The on-board computer calculates and tells the autopilot to fly a Great-Circle route.

lost very shortly. I need an immediate descent from flight level two five zero."

"Two ten mike golf—are you declaring an emergency?"

"Affirmative!"

I didn't wait for the clearance to descend, but immediately extended the landing gear and ten degrees of flaps because I wanted to get down quickly—far more quickly than the maximum allowable air speed would have permitted without the drag of the landing gear. That prompt action, while I still had power, also saved me from later having to lower the gear by hand—a time consuming process, particularly in a stressful situation. The downside of this action, however, was, once lowered, the gear could not be raised again.

Fortunately, I had passed over Kansas City just a few minutes before and had listened to the recorded weather at Kansas City International Airport (ATIS), and knew the ceiling was high—7,500 feet. I told Center I wanted a heading for Springfield, Missouri, which I knew was about 50 miles away. They gave me the heading and told me to call Springfield Approach directly. Springfield didn't respond to my call, and I went back to Kansas City Center. They told me to try again. The second time Springfield did respond, and I made sure they knew that this was an emergency.

Meanwhile I had pulled back the throttle and was descending at about 35 percent power. I was also getting additional alarms from the computer about shock cooling on the engine. Shock cooling occurs when the temperatures within the engine are cooling too quickly which could damage the engine. I ignored these warnings because I wanted to descend to at least 10,000 feet so I could take the oxygen mask off. Keep in mind it was night, I was flying in clouds, IFR, and I had only two hands.

Then, as I descended through 17,000 feet, the battery gave out and the panel lights, radio and everything powered by electricity except the engine went dead. The ignition system on the engine is a dual-magneto system that is independent of the electrical system, so I continued to have engine power.

Hand-Held Transceiver

I have carried a hand-held transceiver for many years for just such an emergency, and only three days before had replaced the three-year-old nickel cadmium battery to make sure I had plenty of power in case of need. I even had an outside antenna installed, with a coaxial cable inside the cabin to hook this transceiver into. Connecting the outside antenna to the hand-held sounds like a simple thing to do and, in daylight with no distractions, I guess it is. But it seemed to take me forever. I also had to fumble to set the right frequency for Springfield Approach. Eventually I did. I also found out how awkward this setup is in the dark because I had to lean over to reach the hand-held radio—the mike and speaker are in the radio and the coaxial antenna cable was too short to hold the hand-held up to my face. It probably took only a minute or so to do all of this—it seemed like forever—and communications were re-established.

When the lights went dead, so, too, went the autopilot and all navigation equipment. It was then that I wished the backup battery for the GPS navigation system was working. Fortunately, while the directional gyro and the turn and bank were electrically driven, the artificial horizon was vacuum-powered and the second vacuum pump was working perfectly. Springfield Approach gave me a heading to fly and the magnetic compass—the same instrument that had guided Columbus 500 years ago—became my eyes, telling me where I was headed as I descended through the dark, overcast night.

And it really was dark, and I really was in clouds. I didn't need lights outside the cockpit, but I still had to see the artificial horizon, altimeter, airspeed indicator and compass to keep the plane heading in the right direction, and without building up excessive speed on the long, five vertical mile descent. Holding a flashlight by hand would be problematic under such circumstances, but I have long carried a flashlight that was originally designed for people wanting to read in bed. It hangs from a strap around the neck and it can be adjusted to shine on a good part of the instrument panel. I routinely strap this light around my neck on every night flight because I find it more useful for reading charts than the plane's lights. So it was on and working before the emergency, and it was a godsend. It meant I didn't have to waste one of my two hands to hold a flashlight; I could use both to fly the airplane. With only one hand, it would have been easy to lose control of the plane and tear the wings off. This $14 light was worth its weight in gold on this flight.

Finally, beneath the Clouds

Finally, at about 7,000 feet, I broke out of the clouds and found the lights of two towns perhaps 25 to 30 miles ahead of me. One was Springfield, and Springfield Approach guided me to a routine landing, complete with fire engines escorting me down the runway.

I am not sure exactly how long all of this took—probably less than 15 minutes although it seemed much longer. While a great deal of adrenaline had energized my body, the flight ended without incident and no one from the FAA has since asked me for an explanation. These were tense minutes, but everything basically worked as it was supposed to. Had the weather below me been much lower, or even at minimums, I had fuel and could have flown the plane for another three hours. I am sure that with the help of ground radar I could have continued on to Memphis or found another airport with adequate ceiling and visibility.

After landing, I taxied to what looked like the maintenance hangar of the local fixed base operator and shut the engine down. Now the engine could not be restarted until the battery was charged. The next morning I was at the maintenance shop when they opened at 7:30. I have always found that transient pilots get the highest priority when they have problems, and that was the case here. By noon I was on my way to Memphis.

Plenty of Margin

I relate this incident because I think it shows how a well-maintained aircraft—even when things go wrong—has plenty of margin. Even when things were very tense, there was no question that the outcome would be successful.

Incidentally, for those who may wonder what caused the electrical failure, it was a broken voltage regulator that sensed a high voltage condition and—as programmed—dropped the alternator off-line to protect the electronics. There is some question in my mind whether I might have been able to get it back on-line, but I was so intent on starting the descent and letting Center know of the problem before the battery went dead, that I did not do all of the troubleshooting that hindsight suggests might have been possible.

Self-Evaluation

Over the years I have tried to be honest with myself, and during or after each flight I critique it and my performance. On a scale of one to five, I rate this flight only a "three" in terms of my reactions at the time, but probably close to a "five" in terms of being prepared and having an "out" when things started deteriorating. So overall, I guess it was possibly a "four," but certainly not a "five." But then, there have been very few flights in my 38 years of flying on which I haven't learned something, or found that I could have done something better. This time, the lesson was especially deeply etched into my memory.

I wouldn't fly in any other way. When the time comes that I stop critiquing and learning, that is the time to close the hangar door for good.

Mal Gross
June, 1993

What Was Not Published

At the time I wrote the above "From the Cockpit" column, I wrote the following addendum which was not published. It provides more insight and more of the drama of this incident. As the president of NAA, I was mindful that I needed to cast the flight in a positive light, stressing that while it was a tense situation, safety was never in doubt. However, the following additional comments, which were written at the same time as the above narrative, are part of that tense fifteen-minute situation.

Fifty Degrees Below Zero

I had another problem which I did not mention in my "From The Cockpit" column, and it could have had very serious consequences. The outside temperature was the coldest I have ever seen it at 25,000 feet—minus 50 degrees Fahrenheit—some 82 degrees below freezing. I know this to be a fact because my engine monitoring computer also records outside air temperatures, and the record was there when I looked at the data after the flight. Minus 35 degrees is normally what I see at this altitude.

When I pulled back the throttle to slow the plane down to allow the landing gear to be extended, this also, of course, reduced the engine-generated heat inside the engine compartment. At the time I did not realize how cold it could get in the engine compartment in a very short time. Data I retrieved later showed that in a little more than six minutes the cylinder head temperatures dropped from the normal 350 degrees to about 150 degrees Fahrenheit. With that rapid a drop in cylinder head temperature, the bitterly cold air entering the engine compartment dramatically cooled everything else.

Throttle Control Stuck

The engine throttle control is a stiff, solid cable that moves back and forth from the cockpit inside a flexible tube. After I had gotten the landing gear down, I left the engine power set at about 35 percent power in order to descend fairly rapidly.

I do not recall precisely when I tried to add power to the engine but it was probably when I passed through 20,000 feet. But whenever it was, the throttle would not move. I pushed it in much harder than normal but it would not budge at all–either in or out! I could not vary engine power at all; it was stuck at 35 percent.

At the time, I was struggling to regain radio communications with the ground using the hand-held radio, and most of my attention was directed to this. When I finally got through to Springfield Approach I told them my throttle cable seemed to be stuck, although I am sure they did not appreciate the significance of that statement.

Descent into the Ground?

My first concern when the alternator failed had been—and it was a correct concern—to get down from the oxygen-starved altitudes, and below the overcast without losing control of the plane or allowing the plane to speed up and possibly exceed its design limits. I had deliberately extended the gear and flaps to get enough drag for the plane to descend quickly, but once the battery was drained I could not retract the gear or the flaps to get rid of the drag. The problem I faced was that I was pretty sure that I could not level out and maintain a given altitude with only 35 percent power. The plane would continue to slowly descend until it hit the ground.

I had no way of knowing what was causing the throttle problem, so I didn't know whether I would be able to regain power control. It was a dark night and with the cloud cover there was no moon. While I thought I was mostly over farm land, I knew there were also rolling hills, and the likelihood of landing in a smooth farmer's field was remote. I concluded that I would be lucky even to see the ground in any detail until just a few seconds before hitting the ground. All of these thoughts flashed through my mind.

As it turned out, by the time I was down to about 8,000 feet the outside temperature had risen to a *plus* ten degrees Fahrenheit, and enough heat was being generated even at 35 percent power to warm up the engine compartment. Almost as suddenly as the cable had frozen tight, it loosened up and I had power control again. Then as I described, the flight proceeded normally after that, and I landed without difficulty at Springfield.

Apparently there had been a little bit of moisture in the throttle cable, and when the temperatures in the engine compartment went well below freezing, this moisture froze. Normally there would be no moisture in this cable. At the time, I had no way of knowing what was causing the problem. Needless to say, I replaced the throttle cable shortly afterward.

Once I got back home, I ran some tests to see what power setting I needed with the gear and flaps extended to be able to fly in level flight. I concluded that I would have needed 45 percent, almost a third more power than I had.

What If?

What would have happened if my throttle cable had remained frozen? It is unlikely that I would have reached Springfield or another airport with lights. I would have had to make a forced landing into, hopefully, some farmer's plowed and smooth field, a chilling thought.

Equally chilling is the thought of what would have happened if I had still been over the Rockies instead of over the Midwest with numerous airports and flat terrain. The throttle did not thaw until I got down to 8,000 feet. Most of the mountains are higher than this.

Once again "luck" was on my side!

24

Synthetic Oil and the Class Action
1995

Mobil AV 1 Oil

In the early 1980s, Mobil Oil developed a 100 percent synthetic engine oil and marketed it for automobiles, apparently with good success. In 1987, they introduced this synthetic oil to the aviation market under the name "AV 1," touting it as an oil that, because of its high temperature tolerance, and other characteristics, needed to be changed only every 200 hours. This contrasted to every 25 to 50 hours for petroleum-based aviation oils. Mobil AV 1 was expensive—$6 or $7 a quart, whereas petroleum-based oils were in the $2 to $3 range. Mobil claimed that with the longer time between oil changes the cost per hour of flying was actually less.

Their advertising also stated:

It is a man-made 100% synthetic. Therefore it is more chemically perfect. This and our unique additives result in little or no sludge, acids, or lead deposits...Mobil AV 1 comes to you with an extra margin of performance superiority other aviation oils don't offer. That margin is always there for you if you need it.

Abrupt Withdrawal

Abruptly, in June, 1994, Mobil issued a statement withdrawing the oil from the market. In their announcement they stated:

During the past month, Mobil's technical staff determined that...the lubricant is not dispersing lead from the fuel as well as had been predicted on the basis of original flight and factory tests.

They went on to say:

It's not merely this potential performance question regarding AV 1 that leads us to discontinue production... It's also the limited market for this product and the distribution inefficiencies we were encountering since getting out of the fixed base operator business in 1991.

Reading between the lines, this last statement was saying they were not selling enough Mobil AV 1 to warrant keeping it on the market: they were losing money. Most pilots using Mobil AV 1 took in the profit reason for the discontinuation and overlooked the "not dispersing lead from the fuel" statement. Certainly, that is how I initially reacted to their announcement.

My Use of AV 1

I had, of course, seen the Mobil AV 1 ads repeatedly in the years following the oil's introduction in 1987. It was touted as the best, al-

This was an ad from 1990. Note how Mobil specifically says the oil produces "little or no sludge, acids or lead paint deposits." If Mobil had run extensive flight tests they would have found this statement was not true. The pilot is left with the impression that this oil would prolong, not reduce, engine life. That is why I switched to this oil. As a result, I came close to a catastrophic in-flight failure.

beit perhaps the most expensive oil, and an oil that would provide an extra margin of engine safety.

I had long before been taught not to change oil types except at the time of a major overhaul because one could never be sure what impact a new type of oil might have on the engine partway through its overhaul cycle. Wait until you overhaul the engine and then switch; but don't switch in-between.

So when I had a complete engine overhaul in December, 1991, I switched to what I thought was a superior engine oil, one that would help ensure my getting the now rated 1,600 (previously 1,400) hours between overhauls. Mobil had advertised 200 hours between oil changes, but I didn't buy that. I changed oil on average every fifty hours. As soon as I received the "discontinuation" notice from Mobil in June, 1994, I had the oil changed back to petroleum-based oil, even though the oil had just been changed and had only two hours on it. Clearly I was being conservative.

During the period I was using Mobil AV 1, the compression on the engine cylinders deteriorated much more quickly than what one would have expected from a high-quality overhaul. Cylinder compression is only one indicator of engine health, but it is easily measured and commonly used.

I had been concerned for some time about the engine's falling compression, and now Mobil's notice of possible sludge problems caught my attention. In November, 1994, I put Mobil on legal notice that I might be making a claim for damages although at that time I was really just protecting myself. Mobil had arbitrarily established November 30, 1994, as its deadline for submitting claims.

My engine overhaul shop at that time was Victor Aviation in Palo Alto, California, a five-hour flight from Orcas Island. I decided I would take the plane to them to check out the engine in January, 1995.

Engine Inspection

Victor Aviation initially looked at the insides of the cylinders using a borescope. They found evidence of excessive wear and saw that the oil control rings did not appear to be functioning properly. They removed one cylinder and found a groove worn in the cylinder wall, and confirmed that the oil control rings were clogged with sludge and not functioning. They suggested removing the propeller and rear oil-transfer plug from the crankshaft. It is in these two areas that, if there were sludge problems, it would likely form first. These two areas also can be inspected relatively easily. Sure enough, an examination of both areas disclosed massive sludge, most likely from lead deposits formed in the combustion process.

The sludge accumulation was particularly damning because less than 200 hours before, the propeller had been removed and whatever sludge was in these two areas was cleaned out at that time. The sludge we were finding had accumulated in less than 200 hours. This raised an alarm. Where else in the engine might sludge be accumulating? Could it be choking off any of the oil galleys (passageways) within the engine?

I called Mobil Oil from Victor's office, told them of our findings, and expressed concern that the problem was potentially far more serious than they had initially thought. I indicated that it looked to me as if I might need to have the engine totally torn down, and I would look to Mobil to reimburse me for the damages. The designated Mobil representative stonewalled me. Clearly, they were not about to acknowledge any financial responsibility. So I needed to document everything we found because we were talking a significant amount of money: Victor's 1991 overhaul had cost close to $50,000.

Engine Expert

At that point, Victor Aviation's owner, Victor Sloan, put me in touch with a recognized engine expert at a local university, Dr. Michael Wood. He had recently been successfully involved in a class action suit against another oil company over contaminated aviation fuel. I asked Dr. Wood to come to Victor Aviation when they removed the remaining five cylinders so that he could inspect them and the engine and give me his conclusions based on what he saw. Was the engine damaged, was Mobil AV 1 oil likely the cause, and finally, should we tear down the engine completely?

Dr. Wood was present when the cylinders were removed. He concluded that the cylinders were damaged, and that there was excessive sludge in the parts of the engine he could examine without tearing the engine completely down. Everything he looked at showed signs of the sludge. He stated the problem was that synthetic oil was so slippery that it did a very poor job of picking up the lead deposits formed in the combustion process. A standard petroleum-based aviation oil has the ability to pick up such deposits in the oil , and when the oil is changed, such deposits are removed with the oil. Synthetic oil just does not have that ability.

I asked him if we should completely tear down the engine, noting that I fly over water at low altitude and safety was my foremost concern. Initially he was hesitant because we were talking about ten to fifteen thousand dollars. I then asked him a specific question: "If this were your airplane, would you tear the engine down?" He immediately answered "Yes."

"Imminent Danger"

The engine was torn down. It turned out that the sludge had migrated throughout the engine oil galley passageways and was blocking the flow of oil to critical parts, the most important of which were the bearings. Dr. Wood told me on February 15 that I was a very lucky man. I had been in imminent danger of suffering an in-flight catastrophic engine failure. The decision to have the engine inspected probably saved my life.

I told Victor to go ahead and completely overhaul the engine. Not only did we need to get rid of the sludge and damaged parts but we also needed to eliminate any question or cloud that might hang over the engine. If we performed a complete overhaul, all parts would then be within new-part tolerance, and good for 1,600 hours.

Stonewalled Again

I informed Mobil of the results of the inspection, but again they disclaimed any responsibility.

I now had two concerns. Initially, I was concerned about getting Mobil to accept the financial responsibility for my overhaul. I knew the final cost would be at least $30,000.

But in thinking more about the stonewalling I had experienced, I started worrying about the number of pilots who had used this oil but were totally ignorant of the time bomb this sludge inside their engines represented. I was mindful that relatively few pilots would have been as aggressive as I was in following up and inspecting their engines. Mobil's stonewalling really bothered me because they knew I was president of the National Aeronautic Association, vice president of the Fédération Aéronautique Internationale, and a member of the board of directors of the Experimental Aircraft Association. I put this concern in writing on February 21, 1995, as follows:

Because of these national and international leadership positions, I believe it is my responsibility to urge Mobil to immediately alert all pilots that used Mobil AV 1 to the potentially serious problems that have surfaced, and to encourage pilots who find sludge in their engines to tear down the engines, remove all sludge and repair any lubrication-induced problems that have occurred. To do otherwise is to potentially jeopardize the lives of those who have placed their trust in Mobil.

I sent this letter by UPS and have certification that it was delivered. I never received a response from Mobil.

Time for Legal Action

Dr. Wood put me in touch with a one-man law firm that he had worked with earlier in connection with a fuel contamination problem. In turn, that firm introduced me to a major San Francisco law firm that specializes in class action litigation. I talked at length with them about my options, and then agreed to file a class action suit against Mobil Oil as the fastest way to get national (and international) attention focused on the risks of having used their oil.

Events followed quickly. On April 12, 1995, we filed a national class action in federal court in San Francisco. On April 18, we filed an "Application for Emergency Notice To Class Members" requiring Mobil to notify affected owners of the allegations in our suit. Mobil had no list of customers of Mobil AV 1 but they had already conceded that, at a minimum, all owners of the same engine I had in my Cessna T210 were potentially at risk. A list of such owners was available from FAA records. Mobil was initially opposed to this emergency notice but the Court made clear that, based on the declarations we had filed, there was a reasonable basis to assume that lives might be at stake.

The notice went out early in May to some 20,000 aircraft owners, and full-page ads were placed in selected aviation publications.

Most people think it takes a long time for a court to act. This suit has to have been a record—from the initial filing it was less than three weeks before the Court issued its emergency order directing Mobil to notify 20,000 owners.

Legal maneuvering went on throughout the summer of 1995, with Mobil objecting to virtually everything. An expedited trial date was set for fall, which Mobil opposed. I spent most of the summer advising the attorneys and reviewing documents obtained through discovery. During this period I was the subject of misinformation probably fomented by Mobil.

Settlement

A compromise was worked out by October, under which Mobil would admit no fault, but would agree to pay for a several-stage inspection protocol under which individual owners could have their engine inspected by one of six special masters appointed for this purpose. These special masters were appointed by the Court and were all licensed mechanics with aviation shops in various sections of the country. If the inspection by the special master found no evidence of damage in the first stage of inspection, then Mobil would pay for that inspection but nothing further. If there was damage, this would authorize the special master to take the inspection a step further. If the damage was as extensive as mine, the entire engine would be torn down.

This compromise was agreed to by both sides and ratified by the Court. The elapsed time from the initial filing to court-approved resolution was just a little more than six months.

I had mixed reactions to this compromise. On the one hand I believed the evidence was all on our side and that we were likely to prevail in any legal action. But as my able legal counsel pointed out, even if we won, Mobil would appeal and the issue might not be resolved for many years. In the meantime, some pilots would be unconvinced of the threat and, might not be willing to have the appropriate inspections made if they had to pay for them. Some of the at-risk pilots were skeptical, having been taken in by some of the misinformation Mobil had put out. I would have liked to have had the vindication of a court decision, but my original objective was to alert pilots to the risk, getting inspections and repairs made, and saving lives. In that I was successful.

"Undoubtedly Saved My Life.. "

I was deeply moved by an e-mail I received from one aircraft owner, Earl Jordan, on June 1, 1997. The inspection of Earl's engine under the program disclosed that it was close to failure, but Mobil would only make limited repairs. He then took up the battle and helped a number of other Mobil users whose engines were also affected. Eventually he gave up trying to get Mobil to do the right thing. His message to me read in part:

> *Regrettably, I must throw in the towel on chasing Mobil...Mobil won by dragging this thing out. For myself, I can't do any more. Thankfully, and I know I speak for all of us who were involved with this matter, you did the right thing by settling for the inspection program which undoubtedly saved my life. If you had gone for more, Mobil would have dragged it out. In the end, they have lost monetary damages but we would have lost our lives. Please accept my deepest thanks and be assured that you did a noble and great service to your fellow airmen. You truly did a great thing. — Earl Jordan*

In November, 1997, I checked with my attorneys to see what the final outcome had been. At that time there had been 662 claims submitted, of which 612 had been closed. Mobil paid out an average of $10,000 to class members for each of these closed claims. So I think it is fair to say that our allegation of engine damage had been vindicated. I am sure that Mobil fought every one of these 612 claims, but in the end made payments of over six million dollars. They also had legal bills that probably exceeded this amount. Mobil also paid several million dollars to my attorneys.

One of My Finest Hours

During the course of the summer, my attorneys obtained boxes and boxes of documents under discovery procedures. I looked at a great number of these documents since I knew more about aviation matters than their legal staff. There was evidence that the Mobil staff had been aware of the sludge problem long before their June, 1994, notification letter. Virtually none of the Mobil staff were pilots and I have to assume that they really didn't appreciate that you can't just pull over to the side of the road if an aircraft engine quits.

If Mobil had done its homework before trying to adapt their automobile synthetic oil (Mobil One) to aviation uses, they would have learned that the Army Air Force had experimented with synthetic oils during World War II. They had much the same sludge problem. Eventually they issued a report in 1950 describing this experiment and concluded that synthetic oil was "not satisfactory as an aircraft engine oil." I picked that information up from the internet back in 1995.

Incidentally, part of the reason Mobil was blind to the sludge issue is that automobile fuel is unleaded. There is no lead oxide sludge to remove. The problem with aviation use is that we use leaded fuel and the lead oxides formed in combustion create sludge. Unfortunately, synthetic oil is very slippery and would not remove the sludge. Ordinary aviation oil does.

1995 was both a very difficult year and a very satisfying one for me. Difficult because of the stonewalling and misinformation put out by Mobil about me and my motives. This was totally overshadowed by our success in forcing this issue into the aviation limelight and getting inspections and repairs. I know that lives were saved. One of those lives was probably mine.

Looking back, clearly this was one of my finest hours!

25

Turbocharger Failures
1993 and 2002

A turbocharger is a device that compresses outside air for use in the engine combustion process. Just as an individual needs oxygen when climbing a mountain, so, too, does the aircraft engine. Without a turbocharger most aircraft have to struggle to get much above ten or twelve thousand feet. The turbocharger uses exhaust gases from the engine, that are close to 1,600 degrees Fahrenheit, to turn a small turbine shaft with compressor blades that turn at very high velocity to compress outside air into denser, sea-level air.

On my Cessna T210, my optimum altitude was 25,000 feet. That is, the highest altitude under standard atmospheric conditions at which my engine can produce 70 percent of sea level power. By contrast, without a turbocharger, the plane would probably produce 70 percent power only up to about eight or nine thousand feet. This is a significant difference, particularly if you fly in mountainous areas of the country.

Consequences of a Turbocharger Failure

A well-maintained turbocharger does not stop without a reason. Most typically, it fails only when an object gets past the air filters and into the turbocharger itself, or, more commonly, when the oil supply to the bearings in the turbocharger is interrupted, causing the bearings to overheat and fail.

299

Most pilots assume assume that in the event of a turbocharger failure all that happens is that the engine will become a normally aspirated engine since the turbocharger is no longer compressing the air going into the engine. If a plane is flying at 25,000 feet and the turbocharger fails, the engine will still produce power, but because of the thin air at that altitude, probably will produce only about 35 percent, or less, of full power. One might think, then, that the result of a turbocharger failure would be the inconvenience of having to descend to ten thousand feet, but not a threat to life except over mountains that were higher than that.

But that assumes that the turbocharger failure has not also caused damage to other parts of the engine, and that is a very big assumption.

Ninety Thousand Revolutions a Minute

The turbocharger on my Cessna at 25,000 feet rotated upwards of ninety thousand revolutions per minute. Stop and look at that number. It is not ninety thousand times an hour—it is per minute, fifteen hundred times a second, and close to forty times faster than the propeller is turning. Can you imagine what happens if something causes the turbocharger to suddenly stop? The blades can disintegrate and be thrown outward by an unimaginably powerful centrifugal force. The turbocharger can literally explode, throwing blades through the turbocharger casing out into the engine on a random trajectory, destroying anything in its path. Equally serious, the oil system for the turbocharger is likely to be breached, allowing the oil to gush out of the oil system. Once that happens the engine life is mere minutes.

I had two in-flight turbocharger failures in the twenty-eight years I owned N210MG, one on September 13, 1993, and the other on May 24, 2002. I remember both times clearly because each was an emergency.

September 13, 1993

I had been at Galvin Aviation at Seattle's Boeing Field that day, partly for some routine maintenance on the aircraft, and partly because I had also been having difficulty getting normal high altitude performance out of the plane. Galvin checked all the obvious things in the turbocharger system, but everything appeared normal, at least on the ground.

They were wrong. I was on climb-out from Boeing Field en route back to Orcas Island in perfect VFR weather. At about 3,000 feet I heard a single "thud" in the engine, and my engine computer immediately indicated that power had dropped abruptly from the climb power setting of 92 percent down to about 70 percent.

I immediately started a 180 degree turn back towards Boeing Field, and then advised Departure Control that I had an emergency and thought the turbocharger had failed. I was probably eight to ten miles from the field, but over water and beyond gliding distance from land. The controller cleared me back to Boeing, and told me to descend to 2,000 feet. I told him "negative," that I would stay at my present altitude until I was within gliding distance of the field since I could not be sure that the engine would continue to run.

I had taken off on runway 31, toward the northwest, but requested a landing on the same runway in the opposite direction so that I could make a straight-in approach. The winds were minimal and I did not want to run the engine any longer than absolutely necessary. The landing was completed uneventfully and I returned to Galvin Aviation.

The Reason For The Failure

As it turned out, the bearings had failed and the rotor shaft had seized. Fortunately, both the rotor shaft and the attached blades stayed intact. The failure had probably been taking place over a period of time and must have accounted for the sluggish high altitude performance I had been complaining about. The turbocharger was not turning at its full speed at the time of the "thud" because I had just taken off and it takes a good deal of time for the turbocharger to get up to its maximum rotational speed once the plane gets off the ground. There was no damage outside of the turbocharger.

It turned out that the cause of the failure was the incorrect installation of an oil line to the turbocharger when the engine had been overhauled two years earlier. A single oil line is connected into the engine block oil system. This single oil line has a "Y" fitting to which two oil lines are connected. One line goes directly to the turbocharger, and the other line, which has a constriction in it to reduce the oil flow, goes to the oil pressure gauge on the instrument panel. Outwardly both lines look the same. If you are an expert mechanic and familiar with that engine model you can tell from looking at the "Y" split which line should go to the turbocharger and which to the instrument panel, but the difference is very subtle. The "Y" split is located at a nearly inaccessible place and you have to be lying on your back underneath the engine to see it. These oil lines are never disconnected from the "Y" except when you take the entire engine out of the plane. If you need to change the turbocharger, you just disconnect the oil line at the turbocharger, replace the turbocharger, and reconnect the oil line.

In 1991, when the engine was reinstalled after an overhaul, the two lines were reversed, and as a result, for 394 hours the turbocharger had been receiving oil from the constricted line, perhaps 20 percent of the oil it should have.

How did the turbocharger last so many hours with the reduced oil? I had started using straight 100 percent synthetic oil (Mobil Av 1) at the time of the overhaul. One of the strengths of synthetic oil is that it can withstand much higher temperatures than ordinary aviation oil, so that less oil is required to lubricate the bearings. It took almost 400 hours of operation before the cumulative impact of reduced oil flow to the turbocharger caused the bearings to fail. More typically—as you will see below—ordinary aviation oil would have kept a turbocharger going under similar circumstances for only twenty-five to fifty hours.

I was, of course, very lucky that this failure occurred in good weather, near an airport, and that it was not a catastrophic event where the blades exploded outward into the engine. In the 394 hours since the oil lines were reversed, I had flown many flights over high mountains where a failure could have been very serious indeed. I had also flown a great deal over water where a water landing would result in hypothermia in ten or fifteen minutes, and probably, death.

May 24, 2002

On May 23, 2002, Inge and I had returned nonstop from Oakland, California across the Siskiyou Mountains of Northern California to our home on Orcas Island on the Canadian border. It had been IFR almost the whole trip, and we were flying "on top" above a widespread storm system at 19,000 feet. It was an uneventful flight almost all the way.

We were making a 100-mile-long descent just east of the Olympic Range of mountains. About 30 miles from landing I felt two momentary "hiccups" in the engine rhythm, so slight that Inge did not feel a thing. I instantly went on full alert—we still had twenty miles of open water to cross—but when the hiccups did not repeat I assumed that a drop of water in the fuel had passed into the engine. This would have been unusual since I check for water in the fuel very carefully, but it seemed like a possible explanation. The flight proceeded uneventfully to a landing at Orcas fifteen minutes later.

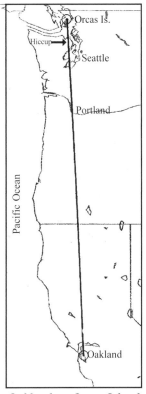

Engines Should Not Hiccup

The next morning I was still somewhat troubled by the "hiccups" on the previous flight. One of the advantages of flying the same aircraft for more than a quarter century is that you get to know what is normal

Oakland to Orcas Island, showing our route and where the engine "hiccupped."

and what is abnormal. Hiccups were not normal. I went down to the airport and ran the engine at length on the ground, but the engine sounded OK and all temperatures in the engine were normal. I took off and flew within gliding distance of the Orcas airport for about ten minutes. Then, since everything continued to seem normal, I flew the 14 miles over water to the Bellingham airport.

When I got to Bellingham, I decided to make a couple of practice simulated instrument approaches. In a practice approach you fly the plane by reference to instruments and navigation equipment in the plane, descend as though you are going to land, and then make a "missed approach" if you want to make another practice approach.

Failure!

While I was making my first practice approach, I heard and felt nothing unusual until I added power to make the missed approach. Then I realized that I did not have normal power. A quick check showed that with full throttle I had about 70 percent power, enough to climb slowly, but clearly something was very wrong. As soon as I was established in my climb, I informed the Bellingham Control Tower that I had an emergency and would level off at 1,000 feet and immediately turn downwind for a landing. At that point I did not know what the problem was, but I had to assume it was serious.

I landed without further incident and taxied to the transient parking ramp. Once I got out of the plane I did not have to look into the engine compartment to know that the turbocharger had failed. Oil was already running out of the engine compartment, and the sudden loss of power was exactly how a turbocharger failure affects the plane.

An inspection of the engine compartment and a subsequent teardown of the turbocharger showed that the bearings had overheated, and that, as they started to fail, they had allowed the rotor shaft to start wobbling. In the process, the outer portion of the blades started grinding themselves into very small pieces against the side of the turbocharger case. Eventually, one of the blades must have jammed into the side of the case, which caused the shaft to stop and shear off. With the

This is the rotor and shaft from the hot side of the turbo. Note the metal at the ends of the blades has been ground off. These blades are made of very hard metals and tiny particles can do great damage to the inside of an engine.

bearing failure, the oil seal also broke, allowing oil to escape into the engine compartment. This was the worst possible scenario since it would take only a few minutes to lose all of the engine oil, and then the failure of the engine was imminent. There was also a fire hazard. It was a mess.

I called my mechanic on Orcas Island, who flew over to look at the damage. We then made arrangements for the local fixed-base operator at Bellingham to obtain and install a replacement turbo-charger. I flew back to Orcas with my mechanic.

The repair took four days because the replacement turbocharger had to come from California. When I returned to pick up the plane, I cross examined the mechanic to make sure that the steps he had taken to wash out the metal pieces had been adequate. He had also changed the oil in the engine to get rid of any metal pieces that might have gotten into the oil system of the engine itself. I ran the engine at various power settings on the ground for about thirty minutes, monitoring carefully the temperature and engine instruments. I then made the ten-minute flight back to Orcas.

But Why?

With the plane back on Orcas, I then had to answer the most important question—why had the turbocharger failed? Engines and turbochargers don't fail without a reason. I knew my turbocharger had been overhauled only 200 hours before by RAM Aircraft, one of the most respected engine shops in the country. My past experience was that turbochargers last the life of the engine between overhauls—1,600 hours. It was Memorial Day weekend, and I grounded the plane pending answers.

Tuesday morning, I contacted RAM Aircraft and after just a few minutes' discussion we concluded it had to be an oil problem. RAM had been involved the previous September when a major FBO in Wichita inadvertently had retracted the landing gear while my plane was in their hangar for maintenance. This necessitated a complete engine tear-down and inspection since the propeller had banged into the ground and could have bent the engine crankshaft. I insisted that the engine be sent to Waco, Texas where RAM Aircraft was located. After they tore the engine down and checked for damage, they reassembled the engine and shipped it back to Wichita for reinstallation on the plane.

Thinking alike, both the RAM technician and I wondered out loud whether the Wichita FBO had reinstalled the oil lines correctly. Could the mechanic have reversed the oil line connections as had happened in 1991? This was a large Cessna FBO, and surely such an error would have been caught by their inspector. Still, it had happened before.

As you have probably guessed by now, we found that the Wichita FBO had made this same cardinal error upon reinstalling the engine, so the turbocharger was only getting about 20 percent of the oil that it should. This time, the oil was regular aviation oil, not synthetic oil, and it had taken only 44 hours to destroy the turbocharger.

Metal In The Engine

If that had been the end of the story, the cost to the FBO's insurance company would have been about $7,000, but the worst was yet to come. When the original turbocharger started coming apart the hot and cold compression blades were partially ground up into tiny pieces not much larger than small grains of sand by the wobbling of the rotor shaft before it broke. Probably 50 percent of this gritty material was immediately dumped overboard at the turbocharger itself; some, however, managed to get into the engine through the air induction system that runs between the turbocharger and the cylinders.

The final failure sequence must have started on the flight from Oakland the day before. The two "hiccups" I felt just before landing at Orcas Island were undoubtedly tiny pieces of metal from the compressor blades that had gotten into the cylinders and then momentarily blocked one of the intake valves. It turned out that a great deal of metal managed to get into the cylinders, and, that some of it had migrated into the oil system.

The RAM technician suggested we change the oil again even though the present oil had been used for less than an hour. We did so and found a lot of metal particles in the oil. This could mean that these particles had damaged the main bearings. If so, the entire engine would have to be overhauled. I grounded the plane and called the insurance adjuster for the FBO who had installed the engine. He flew up from Seattle that same day, and quickly agreed it was a valid insurance claim.

Now what? The insurance adjustor and I both agreed that we should fly the plane for five hours, and then change the oil again and check for particles.

At that five-hour point we still had metal particles showing up in the oil, but far fewer. We continued this routine of changing the oil every five to ten hours for the next fifty hours. While the number of particles decreased with each oil change, at fifty hours I concluded that we had to have RAM Aircraft again tear the engine down to get rid of the remaining particles and to make sure that there had not been damage to the bearings, camshaft, and other parts of the engine.

The tear-down by RAM Aircraft did disclose some damage, and all questionable parts were replaced. When all the bills were added up they came to $20,000, all of which were paid for by the Wichita FBO's insurance.

Some Reflections

So far I have described in somewhat clinical terms what happened on both turbocharger failures. Luck was very much with me on both. I had been at the right place in the right weather when each failure occurred. In the 1993 failure I would have been able to continue to fly as long as necessary to get to an airport, but if I had been over high mountains, I would have had a problem.

The second failure was more sobering since the turbocharger was badly damaged in the failure process, and oil was then being pumped overboard. Engines won't run without oil.

The hiccups I experienced the day before pretty much established that the turbocharger was failing during our flight from Oakland. If the turbocharger had totally failed just a few hours earlier while we were flying at 19,000 feet over the Siskiyou Mountains, it is very unlikely that we would be here today. From the damage we saw after the failure over Bellingham, the engine would have run out of oil, and stopped, in just a few minutes.

The Siskiyou Mountains are rugged and snow covered. A survivable forced landing would have been unlikely. The storm clouds over the mountains probably extended right to the ground. There were no airports along our route. If the worst had happened, no one is likely to even have known the cause of the accident—the failure of the mechanic to reinstall the engine correctly, and the more serious failure of the inspector to catch this error. A crash site in the mountains is hard to find, and in many cases the wreckage is never found. Once it is obvious that there are no survivors, the search is likely to be abandoned after a few days. If the accident site were located, a trained accident investigator would probably never visit the site, and even if one did it is unlikely that he would have seen the fatal switch of oil lines. The Wichita FBO would then never have been called to account for their fatal error.

Many times over my fifty plus years of flying, "luck" or "fate," or call it what you want, was on my side. I cannot take any credit. It had nothing to do with my flying experience or skills. The timing of this failure was not under my control.

26

National Aeronautic Association
The National Aero Club
of the United States
1989 to 1995

I took early retirement from Price Waterhouse on June 30, 1989, to assume the presidency of the National Aeronautic Association (NAA). I had first been introduced to NAA back in 1976 when I applied for a sanction to attempt a record flight from San Francisco to Washington, D.C., described in Chapter 17. I became the volunteer treasurer of this small, Washington-based nonprofit organization in 1983, and six years later, when its president retired, I agreed to assume that full-time responsibility.

History of the NAA

NAA is little known in the aeronautic world today. It started out as the Aero Club of America in June, 1905, as an offshoot of the Automobile Club of America, an exclusive organization of some of the most powerful men in America—Astor, Vanderbilt, Glidden and Dodge. Initially, the Aero Club was looked upon as a "gentlemen's club" for the wealthy balloonist, but within just a year or two became the center of all aviation in the country. Federal government involvement did not occur until the 1920s.

The founders stated in their Certificate of Incorporation that the overall objectives of the Aero Club were:

To advance the development of the Science of Aeronautics and kindred sciences.

To encourage and organize aerial navigation and excursions, conferences, expositions, congresses, and races.

To hold, maintain, and conduct games, meets, contests, exhibitions, and shows of airships, balloons or other inventions or contrivances designed to be propelled or travel through the air or otherwise.

These were lofty goals considering that it was barely a year-and-a-half after the Wright Brothers' first flight. Most people in this country still doubted that the Wright Brothers had actually flown, and few saw any future in flight even if they had.

Fédération Aéronautique International

One of the first acts of the Aero Club of America was to authorize one of its members, who happened to be in France at the time, to represent the Aero Club of America at an initial meeting in Paris of the world's leading aeronautical associations. Representatives of the Aero Clubs of France, Germany, the United Kingdom, Belgium, Switzerland, Italy, and America met in October, 1905, and agreed to form an international organization of aero clubs, The Fédération Aéronautique Internationale (FAI). Membership was limited to a single national aero club from each nation. Today there are close to 100 countries represented.

The FAI's objectives were similar to that of the Aero Club of America, shown above, except on an international scale. Over time, as individual categories of air sports evolved, the FAI oversaw the competition rules for these sports both on a national and international basis. The FAI has also become the official sanctioning body for all international aviation, and now space, performance records, with the respective Aero Clubs taking on the role of supervising all record attempts originating in their country.

Dominated American Aviation

The Aero Club of America dominated aviation in the United States for the next 17 years before evolving into the National Aeronautic Association (NAA) in 1922. The history of the Aero Club, and, later the NAA, is a history of early aviation in America. The Aero Club focused on aviation competition, record-setting, and recognition as the primary means of encouraging aviation advancement. That role continues today with NAA.

The Aero Club required pilots participating in aeronautic sporting events or record-setting activities to have a pilot's license issued by the Aero Club. As a result of this requirement, the Aero Club set training standards and oversaw civilian flight training in the United States until 1926. Chapters of the Aero Club were established throughout the country and virtually every pilot or would-be pilot became a member.

There was no federal oversight at all over flying rules and licensing requirements until the mid-twenties and the public looked to the Aero Club of America for leadership. Congress saw no reason to become involved in regulating what they saw as a rich man's sport. At one time the Aero Club, and later NAA, issued an annual report to the President outlining their view of the nation's aviation priorities.

The Army and U.S. Government were slow to recognize the potential military role of the airplane, whereas European nations early on embraced the aeroplane and its military potential. This potential was obvious to Aero Club members because of their interactions at the FAI with the aero clubs throughout Europe. The Aero Club became a very vocal advocate of military air power, particularly as this country faced the prospects of World War I. In fact, a national campaign was undertaken by the Aero Club to raise funds from the public for both flight training and the acquisition of aircraft for the Army. This helped galvanize the nation.

Air Commerce Act of 1926

After the explosion of flying precipitated by World War I, and the availability of cheap, war surplus planes, a number of states started establishing their own rules in the early 1920s, with no uniformity between states. Pilots in New Jersey flying to New York could have different rules to follow when they crossed the state border.

NAA saw the need for a single set of federal rules that were applicable to all states, and started lobbying Congress and the President. Finally after several years of effort by NAA, Congress passed The Air Commerce Act of 1926. NAA's legal counsel became the first Assistant Secretary of Commerce for Aeronautics.

Some of these early roles have long since been eclipsed by a mature industry now employing millions of people, and by a government that not only issues all pilot licenses but itself has a staff of thousands regulating the industry. NAA's lone voice advocating the nation's priorities has been largely replaced by those of a dozen aviation organizations whose functions are to lobby for the specialized interests of individual sectors of this vast industry.

October, 1989

So, what was the mission I inherited when I joined NAA as president in 1989? I put that question to the Board of Directors. After a lot of discussion, the Board concluded that NAA's mission had changed very little from that of the Aero Club of America's statement in its Articles of Incorporation in 1905. Here is a one-paragraph summary of NAA's mission today:

NAA is the National Aero Club of the United States, and is the sole United States member of the FAI. Its primary mission continues to be the advancement of the art, sport, and science of aviation and space flight by fostering opportunities to participate fully in aviation activities, and by promoting public understanding of the importance of aviation and space flight to the United States. NAA represents United States sport aviation organizations at the FAI, and oversees all record-setting that originates in this country.

There are three major elements in this mission, each of which I will offer comments on below:

☐   Fostering opportunities to participate

☐   Overseeing record-setting

☐   Promoting public understanding of the importance of aviation

Fostering Opportunities to Participate

As the National Aero Club of the United States, NAA has as its members each of the autonomous air sport organizations that NAA represents at the FAI. Here is a current list, both as of 1989 and 2009:

The Academy of Model Aeronautics
The Balloon Federation of America
The Helicopter Club of America
The International Aerobatic Club
The Soaring Society of America
The United States Hang Gliding and Paragliding Association
The United States Parachute Association
The United States Ultralight Association

These eight organizations each promote their air sport through active participation by both experienced and inexperienced sports men and women. Over the years competition has become a focal point locally, as well as nationally, and internationally.

One of the most important functions of the FAI is to establish competition rules and oversee world and regional international competition. Most of the work of the FAI is carried out by individual commissions that are established for each discipline, on which representatives from each of the countries involved in that sport serve.

Whenever a multinational group comes together, it is likely there will be considerable debate, and a need for negotiation and compromise. Furthermore, establishing rules and procedures for world aviation championships is a never-ending process because as the equipment being used improves, new rules and procedures, or at least modifications of old rules, become necessary. Then, too, within certain disciplines rules and procedures for competition must be established for a number of sub branches of the discipline. Aeromodeling, for example, has aerobatic championships, free-flight championships and helicopter championships, to name a few.

Reciprocal Board Seats

NAA has a seat on the board of directors of each of these air sport organizations (other than the Helicopter Club of America), and in turn, they have a seat on the NAA board. During my tenure as NAA president I served on the boards of The International Aerobatic Club, The Soaring Society, and the U.S. Parachute Association. Other NAA personnel served on the other boards. Obviously I was not an expert in these disciplines, but, instead, brought a broad perspective with an emphasis of encouraging participation by sports men and women of all skill levels. The more insight I had into these sport organizations, the more useful I was in promoting their interests at the FAI.

I also served on the Board of the Experimental Aircraft Association (EAA) starting in 1989. For the first several years thereafter, EAA was also a formal member of NAA and had a seat on NAA's board. Early in the 1990s, EAA concluded they did not really fit into our organization, and this board-seat arrangement was terminated. At the same time, I was asked by EAA to stay on their board. I agreed, and served until August, 2009.

General Conference

The FAI holds an annual meeting called a General Conference at which representatives of all national aero clubs attend to deal with top-level policy issues of FAI. As the president of NAA, I was the United States "head of delegation" to these General Conferences. These typically two-day conferences were far more complex than this might at first suggest. With so many countries involved, different languages, customs, and politics, there were many barriers to getting agreement. During the cold war, international politics often intruded, and in many ways the FAI annual General Conferences were a miniature U.N.

These General Conferences were held in a different country each year, hosted by the aero club of that country. During my tenure, I attended General Conferences in the following cities:

1987–Stockholm, Sweden   1992–Athens, Greece
1988–Sydney, Australia   1993–Tel Aviv, Israel
1989–Varna, Bulgaria   1994–Antalya , Turkey
1990–Budapest, Hungary   1995–Sun City, South Africa
1991–Berlin, Germany

In addition to these General Conferences, the FAI also had an executive Council that handled matters between the annual General Conferences. The United States was part of this Council and we met in Paris once or twice a year.

I developed good relations with most of my counterparts. I was particularly pleased with the rapport that I had with General Karmalof of the U.S.S.R. If he said he would support a U.S. position, I could depend on his doing so. The same was true when he asked for the United States support. While our two countries were at odds with each other internationally, we trusted each other. This was not true with respect to certain other European countries.

Keeper of Aviation and Space Records

The FAI, like NAA, has other roles, the most visible of which is to establish the rules under which "world" aviation and space records are established. The FAI is recognized as the world's keeper of such records. In the United States, the NAA serves as the FAI's agent in connection with overseeing and certifying world records that originate or terminates in this country. The world records I set before joining the NAA, described in Chapters 17 and 18, are examples of this dual certification—first by NAA and then by FAI.

There are two major categories of aviation records: absolute world records, and records by weight class. Absolute world records are without regard to the weight category of the aircraft, and obviously there are only a handful of such records. Almost all other records are established by various weight categories. There are about 20 weight categories, starting at "less than 300 kilograms" all the way up to "more than 500,000 kilograms."

NAA encourages pilots of all levels of experience to set speed records between any two recognized cities within the United States, or from the United States to any major city abroad, or even around the world. These records are set by weight category to permit the owner of a small two-seat aircraft to set records in the same way as could the pilot of a larger, more advanced craft. In the case of the records I set, my plane was in a category "more than 1,000 kilograms but less than 1,750 kilograms." (2,205 pounds to 3,858 pounds).

Many ask, why establish records by weight category between two cities; what purpose does that serve? Record-setting, and the recognition it provides, spurs technological advances. When Dick Rutan and Jeana Yeager flew around the world without refueling in 1986 in "Voyager" (see Chapter 19), many asked what that proved. Yet about twenty years later the same people who designed the Voyager, designed "SpaceShipOne," the world's first successful civilian-built spacecraft. SpaceShipTwo has already been built and is expected to carry tourists commercially within a few years. See the colored picture of SpaceShipOne in the folio of pictures following page 394.

Record Documentation

Setting a record and having it recognized, is a several step process. The first step is to obtain an official sanction to attempt to set a record. You cannot just go out and set a record and worry about the paperwork later. The sanction application spells out the specifics of what you are going to attempt, and your qualifications for doing so. You must hold a pilot's license and the appropriate ratings. NAA will look carefully at your qualifications, and if there is any doubt, will deny the sanction request.

Two examples come to mind. We denied a sanction application from a 12-year-old child whose parents wanted this child to fly across the United States as pilot in command, with an instructor accompanying the child. This child did not have a pilot license (age 16 is the minimum age) and so could not legally make this flight. We denied the request. In another sanction application, we felt the pilot with barely 100 hours total time had too little experience to fly across the North Atlantic.

Record attempts must be overseen by qualified, objective individuals without any perceived conflict of interest. NAA's Contest & Records

Board is comprised of individuals who specialize in observing record attempts. In some instances, air traffic control personnel are used. With respect to my 1977 transcontinental flight record, the control towers at San Francisco International, Salina, Kansas Airport, and Washington National Airport all provided written statements to NAA as to my take-off and landing times.

Heritage

Another major function of the NAA is what is often referred to as our "heritage" role. The NAA is the custodian of many of the nation's most prestigious aviation awards. In recent years the NAA has annually been involved in presentation of awards and honors to more than fifty individuals and organizations. The early pioneers of aviation strongly believed that public recognition of aviation achievements was a major factor in encouraging others to excel and make advances, and this function continues to be an important one for NAA.

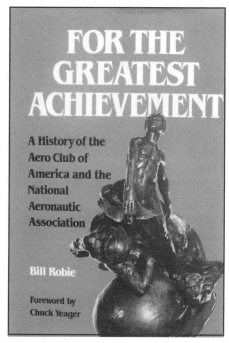

Before I joined NAA, I was only vaguely aware of the rich history of the Aero Club of America and the National Aeronautic Association. All of NAA's historical records had been given to the Smithsonian and were not readily available. I needed to find someone who could write a history of the two organizations. Bill Robie was referred to me by the National Air & Space Museum, and he agreed to do so. He had already researched some of the early history of the Aero Club because of his own love of early aviation. The above book was the result. Included in this scholarly, 380-page book are the names of all the pilot licenses issued by the Aero Club from 1905 to 1919. These were our early aviation pioneers. The picture on the jacket cover above is of the Collier Trophy. This trophy weighs over 600 pounds and resides in the National Air and Space Museum. Recipients are presented with small replicas.

The most famous of these awards is the Robert J. Collier Trophy, which was established in 1911, and first presented to Glenn Curtis. It is awarded annually for the greatest achievement in aeronautics or astronautics in America as demonstrated by actual use during the previous year. A list of the recipients of this, the most prestigious of all aviation awards, is also a history of aviation, as perceived by the leaders of that time.

NAA's heritage function embraces more than the Collier Trophy. Included in the awards are: The Brewer Trophy, Harmon Trophies, Henderson Award, Katharine Wright Award, Mackay Trophy, Stinson Award, Wesley L. McDonald Elder Statesman Awards, and the Wright Brothers Memorial Trophy. As with the Collier Trophy, several of these awards date back to the early days of aviation. No other aviation organization has this unique mandate to maintain and perpetuate the heritage embodied in these awards.

* * * * *

Small and Financially Strapped

NAA is actually a small nonprofit organization, and has all of the financial problems such organizations often have. When I joined NAA in 1989, we were in a financial crisis and I had to appeal to our aviation corporate members to each make a special contribution of $5,000, which all of them did. It was probably good that I had a financial background.

Our major sources of income during my stewardship were corporate members, membership fees from the air sport organizations, sanction and record-setting fees, and membership fees from a small number of individual members. Our major expenses were salary for our four or five staff, rent, fees to FAI, and travel expenses. We also had a newsletter which during my tenure was subsidized by one of our corporate members, AVEMCO Insurance Company.

It was a small operation, and money was always an issue. By late 1991, I found that the financial pressure was starting to affect my health, and I became concerned that I could lose my FAA medical certificate. I concluded that I needed to withdraw as full-time president, which I did in 1992.

On December 15, 1992 the Administrator of the Federal Aviation Administration presented me with their Award for Distinguished Service "...for his insight, leadership, and promotion of air transportation in the U.S. and for being an effective advocate of U.S. aviation interests in the international arena."

I continued to serve as a volunteer president until 1995, with an executive director being hired to handle administrative and fund raising functions. My tenure was short but personally very rewarding, particularly in my role in representing United States sport aviation in the world arena at the FAI.

PART IV

THE LONG DESCENT
1996 to 2008

27
The Long Descent
An Overview
1996 to 2008

It took 50 minutes in my Cessna T210 to climb from sea level to the plane's optimum altitude of 25,000 feet, and just about the same time to descend back to sea level. This required me to start my descent several hundred miles from my destination, particularly when flying west-to-east where I usually had a good tailwind. When en route to Washington, D.C. I would usually start my descent just to the east of Columbus, Ohio.

By 1996, I had been flying some forty plus years. I was then 63 and no longer president of the National Aeronautic Association. Except for trips to see my parents and family on the East Coast, I had little other reason to fly Coast-to-Coast. I also recognized that I was slowing down and at some point would need to stop flying. Like descending from 25,000 feet, it was getting to be time to start my own descent.

I would still fly about 1,650 hours before I closed the hangar door for the last time in late 2008, but 1996 was the year that I recognized that this time would come. Like others, I was subject to the laws of gravity, and needed to make a graceful, and equally important, a safe, final landing.

These in-between years were not without their challenge, and, as it turned out, also full of risks. Again, I was lucky, as you will read in subsequent chapters.

My Mooney Mite Infatuation

Many decades ago, in December, 1955, a friend let me fly his very small, single-seat aircraft called a Mooney Mite. I flew a little more than an hour and when I landed I knew that someday I would have my own Mite. I never forgot that first flight. It was almost exactly forty years to the day before that dream came true. *Chapter 28, The Mighty Mite, A Log of the Trip Home* describes this earlier 1955 flight, and the renewal of my love affair with this mistress.

The plane itself was forty years old at the time I purchased it, but its total flight time was only a little over 2,000 hours. In the following ten years, I flew it 525 hours. That may not seem like a lot of hours, but keep in mind how small the cockpit is. It was a fun plane to fly, but not very practical for traveling. I did fly it to AirVenture in Oshkosh, Wisconsin twice during this period, and to southern California probably four or five times to attend Mooney Mite gatherings. You could go a long distance only if you were willing to make frequent fuel stops; it carried only 13 gallons of fuel. When I went to Oshkosh I had to ship a box of clothes by United Parcel Service because I didn't have enough room in the plane. The fuselage was so narrow that before getting into the plane I had to be sure my handkerchief was in my shirt pocket because once I got into the plane I could not get my hand into the pants pocket to retrieve it.

Engine Overhaul

The plane had a small, 65-horsepower engine. While the engine log book had an entry in the late 1960s indicating that the engine had been overhauled by a local mechanic, there were no details, or indication of any parts being replaced. I was trusting this engine with my life and decided to have a complete overhaul by the same company that had overhauled my Cessna T210 engine, Victor Aviation in Palo Alto, California. They were able to get new cylinders and other parts, and when they finished the engine was probably as good or better than new.

Restoration

That took care of the engine, but what about the airplane itself? It is made of very high quality plywood (I believe mahogany plywood) that is covered with fabric. It has a wood spar which runs from wing tip to wing tip. The wing is one piece, with the fuselage bolted on top of it. It is inherently very strong, but in the fall of 2002, I concluded that with almost fifty years on the plane, it was time for a total restoration. The wing had been re-covered with new fabric over the mahogany plywood in the 1980s, but the fuselage had never been re-covered. While I had no reason to believe the structure was not sound, it seemed prudent to tear the plane apart and make sure termites had not gotten into it.

This restoration was a big, labor-intensive job. My mechanic started work on the plane full time in the fall of 2002. It was completed in

This is the fuselage from the rear of the cockpit to the tail section, but with the tail cone removed. You are looking at mahogany plywood which has been formed into curved surfaces. This wood was in excellent condition, very strong, and only minor repairs were required. The fuselage, wings and all surfaces were recovered with Poly Fiber fabric, and then painted with a number of coats of two-part epoxy paint. It should last for another fifty years, if hangared.

May, 2003. Before this restoration was completed, and minor repairs made, I had spent close to $60,000. This was in addition to the engine overhaul mentioned above. We replaced the aluminum fuel tank, propeller, canopy, radio, and brakes. I enlisted the help of a professional aircraft paint designer to create a new paint scheme.

Without question the plane then was better than new. I proudly flew it back to Oshkosh that summer where it received a trophy for the quality of its workmanship (see picture page 328). The Mooney Aircraft Company asked if they could display the Mite next to their new aircraft exhibit under the banner: *Fifty Years and Still the Fastest In Its Class.* It received a lot of attention and the Company could have sold a dozen Mites if they were still in production. *Chapter 30, Mooney Mite Fuel Leak* details a close call on this trip to Oshkosh.

The leading edge of the wing is pointing downward toward the floor in this picture. The wing spar runs from wing tip to wing tip, and the fuselage is attached to the center section (see center arrows). The leading edge of the wing is formed by mahogany plywood which actually forms a curved, four-sided long box. In the event of a water landing this boxed area would probably help keep the plane afloat. I never tried it. The area where you can see the wing ribs will be covered by fabric. The fuselage can be seen in the middle, right side of the picture (arrow).

The Decision

During the years between 1996 and 2003, I flew close to nine hundred hours in the Cessna T210, largely on cross-country trips. Almost all of these trips involved flying at least part of the time under instrument flight conditions. I continued to return annually to the Recurrent Training Center in Champaign, Illinois for two days of intensive training. It was just after one of these sessions that I made the decision to sell the Cessna. *Chapter 33, Decision Time, April 23, 2003* discusses this decision.

After selling the Cessna, I was then down to just one aircraft, the

This cockpit section is formed with metal tubing, with a fabric covering on the outside, and black, padded panels on the inside. The seat has been removed in this picture. This section is bolted onto the fuselage section shown on the two other pictures, and then both sections are secured to the top of the wing.

Mooney Mite. I also was 70 years old and getting uncomfortable flying the Mite. On a calm day without winds, it was a fun plane to fly. It was so small that when looking through the windshield you could see out of both sides of the plane at the same time. It was responsive to the slightest pressure on the control stick.

But it was not an easy plane to fly compared to the Cessna T210, mostly because it was so small and light. The gross takeoff weight was 870 pounds, and that included the plane, engine, 13 gallons of fuel, and pilot. The Cessna, by comparison, had a gross takeoff weight of 3,800 pounds, a 310 horsepower engine, and 116 gallons of fuel. Because it was so light, the Mite got knocked around in the air by every little gust of wind. That was most noticeable in landing, particularly

The inscription reads: "Classic Aircraft, Best of Class, (0-80 HP), Malvern Gross, Mooney M18, N4187." Awarded by EAA at AirVenture in 2003, the bronze casting is of Lindbergh and was awarded for the quality of workmanship and attention to detail in the restoration of this classic aircraft. Hundreds of aircraft are judged and this award is highly coveted.

on Orcas Island where the landing turbulence could be severe. I was mindful that you can be killed in the Mite as easily as in any other plane. By early 2005 I was getting more uncomfortable, particularly during landings in gusty wind conditions, and I started wondering if I should really be flying it. I was no longer 22 years old.

The decision was really made for me because by then I knew we were going to move to New Jersey in two or three years, and that I would not be able to get hangar space for it. That was essential because this airplane would quickly deteriorate sitting out in the open. With mixed feelings, I sold the plane for top dollars, $32,500. I had invested close to $90,000 in the restoration, and major engine overhaul, but I have no regrets. The plane, if well cared for, should last another fifty years, and I have the satisfaction of knowing I have done my part to keep a beautiful plane from being lost to history.

Back Surgery

There was another reason for selling the Mite. On Father's Day in June, 2005, I ruptured one of the disks in my back by improperly lifting a 40 pound bag of salt to put into the water softener. I had five hospital-administered epidural injections without success, and finally had back surgery just before New Year's Day. I was grounded for almost seven months.

During this period of inactivity I became very much aware that getting my next FAA medical certificate could be difficult, if not because of this back problem, then for other medical conditions that at my age could unexpectedly pop up. I already had the Mite up for sale, and decided the answer to this medical concern was to fly a new category of aircraft that did not require a medical certificate. *Chapter 34, –A New Sport Aircraft* discusses this new category and the benefits to pilots concerned about getting their FAA medical renewed. I ended up buying an Italian, all-metal, two-seat plane, a Tecnam Bravo. I picked up this new plane in Atlanta in March, 2006.

The Landing

For a while I thought my decision to buy this plane was a good one. But along the way several things happened. First, early on I had an engine failure and, luckily, survived. This experience made a deep impression on me. I had known for fifty-plus years that an engine can fail in flight but that didn't really sink in until I actually experienced one. I am sure that my age magnified that experience. If I had been 22 years old, I suspect I would have taken this more in stride.

The second thing that happened—and I should have realized this ahead of time—was that this new plane had a takeoff gross weight of 1,320 pounds, more than the Mite's 870 pounds, but still subject to the same gusty wind conditions. Finally, after moving to New Jersey in May, 2007, I found that I was flying less than fifty hours a year, and having to force myself to fly even that number.

It was time to close the hangar door for the last time and quit while I was ahead. As with the Cessna T210, I called an aircraft sales broker and he came and took the plane back to his airport. It was the right decision, at the right time.

The descent was over. The final landing uneventful. As they say, "any landing that you can walk away from is a good landing." I did, and I am grateful. My luck held out to the end. 6,850 hours over 53 years and ten months.

28

The Mighty Mite
A Log of the Trip Home
December, 1995

December 18, 1955—"THEN"
Houlton, Maine

I was a young, 22-year-old pilot in 1955 when I climbed up on the wing of N4146 for my first flight in a Mooney M-18C. With barely 250 hours, less than a year's total flying, and most of it in a Cessna 140, I was about to have an experience that I would savor for the rest of my life.

The Mooney "Mite," as it was commonly known, was a small, single-seat aircraft that looked more like a miniature fighter than a civilian aircraft, and certainly not at all like the high wing Cessna or Aeronca Champs that I had previously flown. Sporting all of 65 horse-power, this retractable landing gear aircraft—built of wood and fab-ric—was a beautiful, low wing aircraft that you entered by climbing up on the wing and then over the side.

There was no electrical system in the plane. I had to start the en-gine the old fashioned way—by hand. I stood behind the propeller with the backs of my legs firmly placed against the leading edge of the

---

Note: This account was written in December, 1995.

wing to keep the plane from moving. Then, with one hand in the cockpit to manipulate the throttle and magneto switches, I spun the propeller from the rear and was rewarded instantly with the roar of the four-cylinder Continental engine. Then, carefully, so as not to lose my balance in the propeller wash, I climbed up on the wing and over the side of the cockpit, letting myself down into the seat before pulling the canopy closed above my head. I was 6 feet 2 inches tall and weighed 185 pounds and there was no room between my shoulders and the sides of the cockpit. It was more as though I had strapped the plane onto myself rather than having climbed into the plane.

With a grin and a wave at the friend who had lent me his Mite, I was then on my own—to learn to fly a new aircraft type, to learn to handle a retractable landing gear, and to experience flight as never before. After an hour and 20 minutes I landed back at Houlton airport.

But something had happened during that short flight; I had fallen in love with the Mite. In the decades that followed I could not forget that first love. The entry in my log book summarized the experience completely but simply, with just two words: "What fun!"

I never forgot that flight. Forty years later, almost to the day, I became a youth of 22 again when I purchased a Mooney Mite of my own. This is the story of my flight home to Orcas Island just after the purchase in Augusta, Kansas, 15 miles east of Wichita. I believe it conveys the fun and excitement I felt.

November 30, 1995—"NOW"

Augusta, Kansas

I was in Augusta, Kansas to take delivery of N4187, a 1955 model Mooney Mite. When N4187 rolled out of the factory and was flown by test pilot W. W. Taylor on March 10, 1956, there would be only five more Mooney Mites produced before the Kerrville, Texas, factory would stop manufacturing this aircraft. In total, 287 Mooney Mites were made. I had just purchased one of what many felt was the Ferrari of its day.

I have flown almost 5,000 hours since that first flight in the Mite, much of it in instrument weather conditions, over mountains, and across continents, to the farthest reaches of Alaska, and to central Greenland. I have set five internationally recognized FAI speed and altitude records for my weight class, and I have owned seven other aircraft. But the excitement and exhilaration cruising through my blood that morning in Augusta was just like the excitement of that 22-year-old youth back in Houlton, Maine.

I was also apprehensive. I was not 100 percent sure I was up to the task of soloing a new aircraft type, and then flying it in early December close to 2,000 miles across the Rocky Mountains to my home on Orcas Island. My well-meaning friends had told me that I would soon feel cramped and uncomfortable, and that an hour out of Augusta I would likely conclude I had made a mistake. They gently suggested that my recollections of my first "affair" would fade like the puppy love of a teenager as he becomes more mature.

They were wrong, but I was right to be apprehensive, not because I was not up to the task of soloing a new aircraft—I was—but because it was winter, and I was flying a plane that was only one fifth as heavy as my Cessna T210, had one fifth the horsepower, and was strictly a VFR aircraft. And as I found out, it is much easier to fly a heavier airplane than a lighter one in windy conditions. For all practical purposes, all of my hours and years of flying since the first flight counted for little. I was again an inexperienced pilot learning to fly a new and different airplane.

As I eased the throttle forward for my first takeoff that morning, a memory came flooding back: the sound of the four-cylinder Continental 65-horsepower engine that had powered my first training aircraft––an Aeronca Champ. There was something magical about the sound of that engine, a hoarse roar coming out of an engine that had virtually no muffler system and into an airplane that had no sound insulation. At once, barely 100 feet down the Augusta runway on my takeoff run, I was transported back more than forty years to my first training flights. Almost immediately, I felt at one with the Mite.

And so, with the confidence and the enthusiasm that only youth can have, I again learned to fly a light airplane. Even at 8:30 in the morning, there was a Kansas wind blowing across the runway, and as soon as N4187 had literally jumped into the air as I pulled back on the stick, I found myself bobbing in a sea of troubled air above the runway. I had my hands full trying to tame the Mite and making it go where I wanted. Because it weighed just 574 pounds empty, every air current caused it to bob and turn. I felt like a rodeo cowboy on a bronco;

it took me almost half an hour to get N4187 to understand that I intended to be the boss. Gradually, we seemed to make peace with each other, and I began to feel comfortable.

The landing gear took some getting used to. It is a mechanical gear operated by a long handle that—with the gear down—runs along the side of the cockpit from just forward of the seat up toward the right rudder pedal. To raise the gear, the pilot reaches down and grabs the forward end of the gear handle and slides a spring-loaded, one-inch-diameter knob down and out of a solid ring attached to the side of the fuselage. He then moves the lever about 150 degrees toward the rear, where a similar ring is also securely fastened to the side of the fuselage, and places the spring-loaded knob into that ring. The movement of the lever raises or lowers the tricycle-like landing gear mechanically. As long as the handle-knob is securely inserted into a ring, the landing gear is locked into place, either up or down. If it is not locked securely, however, the gear will collapse on landing or extend while flying. It is critical for the pilot to ensure that the knob is securely in place.

The Mite is a small airplane with not much wiggle room. The engine is started by hand-pulling the prop from the rear. Once the engine is running smoothly, I climb up on the wing and lower myself into the plane. Getting into this plane is like strapping wings onto your body. Note that the engine is wider than the cockpit.

The pilot, of course, must learn to raise the gear after takeoff and ensure it is locked into the retracted position while keeping his full attention outside the aircraft. Two hundred feet above the runway is no place for the pilot to forget where he is! The number one rule of flying is the same, whether flying a 747 or a Mooney Mite: fly the airplane, then worry about everything else when you have time.

I made three takeoffs and landings at the Augusta Airport before feeling comfortable enough to start the long trip home. I topped off the fuel tank, filed a VFR flight plan, propped, the Mite and climbed aboard. Then, in my only concession to modern technology, I strapped onto my knee a cigarette-package-sized, hand-held GPS receiver. The antenna was fastened to the front windshield with a plastic suction cup. Two minutes later it had acquired seven satellites and knew within 100 feet where I was. Furthermore, the position was displayed on a rudimentary but effective moving map display, with bearing and distance to my first refueling stop, Woodward, Oklahoma, clearly displayed. This certainly beat navigating the old fashioned way with sectional maps that were individually twice as wide as the inside of the cockpit. I had the maps, and I did use them, but only to confirm that the GPS receiver did, in fact, know where I was.

Flight Planning for the Trip Home

My planning for the flight home had started two weeks earlier when I had agreed to buy N4187 and sent off a check for full payment. I had been looking for a 1955 Mite for the better part of a year. There were only twenty-two 1955 Mites left on the FAA registry, and I wanted to take no chance that the seller, Sam Mitchell, might change his mind. This had happened earlier in the year when another owner had agreed to sell me his 1955 Mite, but then changed his mind.

I had three concerns while planning for the flight—weather, fuel range, and high altitude performance. Weather was a major factor, particularly this time of the year. I planned to allow ten days for the flight back since bad weather could ground me for a number of days. Weather planning, however, cannot be done ahead of time.

An equally important factor was that I needed to plan a route where the distance between airports was not more than 200 miles, and airports where I could be sure of getting fuel. N4187's fuel tank could hold only 13.5 gallons, and until I had some experience of my own, I could not be sure exactly how much fuel the plane would use in an hour. Prior discussions with Sam had suggested slightly under 4 gallons an hour, but it was difficult to be sure if that is accurate since each pilot tends to lean an engine differently, and run it at higher or lower power settings than others. All I could really be sure of, until I had personal experience, is that the fuel flow would probably be between 4 and 5 gallons an hour. At 5 gallons an hour, I had a theoretical range of 2 hours and 36 minutes. At 4 gallons an hour the range would be 3 hours and 20 minutes. Based on these numbers, I concluded I should assume, at least until I had more experience, that I only had a two-and-a-half hour range. The 200 miles between airports would be approximately two hours of flying without headwinds.

Of course, the distance actually traveled is a function of fuel consumption, air speed, and winds. In theory, the plane would travel 105 miles per hour, but I also knew I would likely have a headwind traveling west. I used 95 miles per hour in my planning. This meant that 2 ½ hours at that speed gave me a range of 235 miles; hence my estimated 200-mile maximum between fuel stops. As it turned out, fuel consumption ended up being 4.3 gallons an hour, so I was actually able to fly for a little over three hours.

The third factor in the planning process was a desire to minimize the use of high altitude airports. The Mite has a theoretical service ceiling of 19,000 feet, but I just didn't know what the actual performance would be at an airport with, say, an elevation of 7,000 feet. For this reason, I decided that in crossing the Rockies at their midpoint north/south (just north of Denver) I should use only airports with long runways—5,000 feet or longer.

I mapped out three different routes taking into account altitude and airports not more than 200 miles apart:

Route #1—The northern route across Montana, Great Falls, Montana, Coeur D'Alene, Idaho, and Spokane, Washington. This is a relatively low level route, and while I would have to get up to 10,000 feet at one point on the trip home, I would only have to fly that high for an hour or so and would have no airports higher than 4,500 feet in elevation.

Route #2—The mid-continent route, across Cheyenne, Rock Springs, Boise, and Yakima. This is the route with the highest alti-

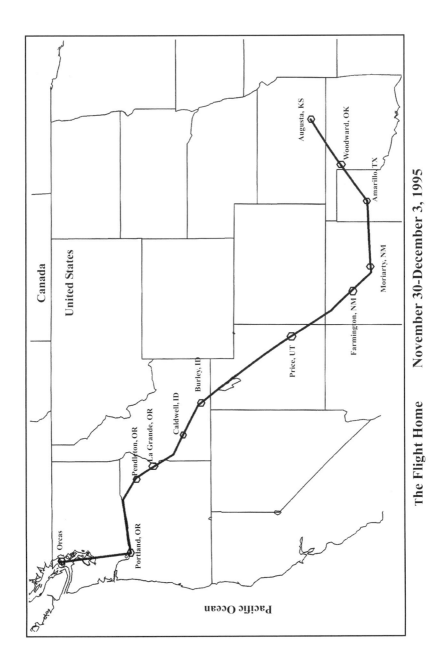

The Flight Home   November 30-December 3, 1995

tudes, and several airports were located at elevations well over 5,000 feet. This was also the shortest and most direct route.

Route #3—The southern route, across Albuquerque, Salt Lake City, Boise, and Yakima. This route involved crossing mountains at about 9,000 feet near Albuquerque, and again near Provo, Utah. Generally this route could be expected to have better weather than the other two, but it is several hundred miles longer.

In each instance, I checked published data on availability of fuel at each of the proposed fuel stops both on weekdays and on weekends. Where smaller airports were involved, I telephoned to confirm the information I had; I would be in a real bind if I landed with, say, only 3 gallons left and found that there was no fuel available. Also, smaller airports tend to have shorter hours in winter months, and sometimes were closed all winter. I carefully inserted all of this advance planning into a binder and consulted it that gusty morning in Augusta when I finally had to decide which route to take.

In point of fact, there was no real decision to be made because when I arrived in Augusta a large storm system coming down from Canada had settled in the northern plain states and the Rockies. A high pressure system in the central plains was keeping this storm system to the north, and spreading good weather in the southern plains and south-western states. With it, however, were strong winds, mostly from the southwest. So the choice was clear—take the southern route via Albu-querque and deal with the potential of strong headwinds as necessary. The extra distance and slower speeds would be offset by my not being grounded, perhaps for days, by bad weather.

Leg #1—Augusta, Kansas, to Woodward, Oklahoma

Augusta, Kansas, is 15 miles east of Wichita, and just east of McConnell Air Force Base. Flying on the first leg involved flying due south until I was south of the Class C restricted airspace surrounding the Wichita area. The first 15 minutes suggested that this was going to be one heck of a long trip home, for I was headed directly into a headwind. My ground speed dropped to barely 65 miles per hour. I had planned the entire flight to average 95 miles per hour so this first indication of the Mite's speed was not reassuring. Yet one of the ad-vantages of my thousands of hours was that I had learned not to draw conclusions too quickly about headwinds when traveling cross-country. Strong headwinds frequently peter out, and sometimes even turn into tailwinds. So while I was initially dismayed at my slow progress flying south around the Wichita airspace, I was still making progress, and with patience would eventually get home.

Woodward, Oklahoma, was about halfway to Amarillo, Texas, my planned overnight stop, and just 155 miles as the crow flies from Augusta. I wanted several shorter flights to get some fuel consumption experience before trying a 200-mile leg. The weather, aside from the winds, was perfect VFR weather, with not a cloud in the sky, and with record high temperatures for the last day of November.

Fortunately, once I got far enough south that I could turn southwest, toward Woodward, the wind was no longer directly on my nose, and my speed picked up. One of the nice things about my GPS receiver was that it continually calculated ground speed and I could see what even a slight change in direction, or altitude, did to my ground speed. I stayed low—probably about 500 feet or perhaps a tad less—and was careful to avoid all towns and even farmhouses. Then one hour and 42 minutes from takeoff I was over the Woodward airport.

Most of the airports I used on the trip home were near smaller towns and did not have control towers. This meant it was up to me to overfly each airport, look at the wind sock from the air, and decide which runway to use. If there were other planes in the pattern at the time, I joined the pattern they were using. There was no one in the pattern at Woodward and looking at the wind sock, I quickly saw why. It was standing straight "out" and whipping from side to side, indicating that the wind was quite gusty on the ground. And, yes, it was ferocious! I picked the runway aimed most directly into the wind and set up my approach. As I approached the ground, N4187 started bouncing around like a wild colt. Yet, at the last minute, just before touching down, I managed to get the plane lined up with the center line of the runway and the Mite touched down just as gently as a kitty cat.

It is funny, but until the moment I landed, I had given no consideration to needing to answer a call of nature. But while I was taxiing in, nature called and I learned that when you have to, you can get out of the Mite fairly quickly, albeit in an undignified manner. It was good that I was on the ground. In my Cessna T210, I have a container that can be used for emergency calls of nature. However, in the small space in the Mite I am not exactly sure how you would handle this problem. The stick is directly in front of the seat. The seat does not move backward (or forward, for that matter). You can't turn sideways in the seat; the side of the plane prevents that. So if you have to unzip the front of your pants I am not exactly sure how you do it. Pushing the stick forward would cause the plane to go into a dive, and that would be strictly a "no-no." In any case, I am happy to report that I did not have to find an answer to an in-flight "call" on the trip home. Just as well.

I had landed at about twelve o'clock. I pulled out my lunch bag and went into the FBO building where I found a place to make a cheese sandwich using a bottle of pimiento cheese spread and some sandwich rolls. I had brought along enough sandwich makings to last four or five days because I had learned a long time ago that you can seldom get more than a cup of coffee at most airports.

Leg #2—Woodward to Amarillo, Texas (Tradewind Airport)

My ground time was probably less than 45 minutes, even with lunch. Taking off in gusty conditions is far easier than landing, so I lost no time in getting back into the air.

As before, I flew low to minimize exposure to headwinds, and also to see a bit of the countryside. Suddenly, the ground looked quite different than from the Cessna T210. In the Cessna you can see out the front of the airplane, and down on the pilot's side. But you cannot see out of the copilot's side without leaning way over or tipping the aircraft 45 degrees. But in the Mite, you can see out of both sides at the same time. That is a different perspective.

I have flown a lot in Aeronca Champs, a two-seat, high wing aircraft with one seat behind the other. In that plane, you can look down out of either side window quite easily, but not out of both sides at the same time. The Champ is much wider than the Mite. In the Mite you really do feel suspended in midair, not by a solid airplane, but by a set of wings attached to your body—and the Mite responds to your slightest wish to turn, almost without your awareness.

The difference between my Cessna and the Mite is the same order of magnitude as that between a 727 and the Cessna. Few airline passengers have any comprehension of this difference, and likewise, those flying a Cessna can't know the sense of flying that the Mite provides.

This leg was about the same distance as the first one, but took about 15 minutes longer. I guess the afternoon had brought slightly stronger winds, or the winds had shifted so they were more on the nose. Also, as I approached Amarillo, I detoured to the south around the city; Tradewind Airport is on the western side of town. That may have added 5 or 10 minutes.

It was obvious as I got closer to Amarillo that I would still have two or three good hours of daylight flying if I wanted to go on, rather than spending the night as I had originally planned. Moriarty, New Mexico, 206 miles down the road was my next planned stop.

As I refueled the plane it occurred to me that I had not seen any tie-down rings on the wing where I could fasten a rope to tie the plane down at night. I got down on my hands and knees and looked and looked but I could find no tie-down ring on either wing. That seemed too incredible to be true. All airplanes have tie-down rings. I sheepishly called Sam Mitchell and asked him where the tie-down rings were. "There aren't any. That is the way the factory built them," he responded. I then asked the obvious: "How do you secure the plane at night when you are traveling cross-country." "You put it in a hangar," he answered. I thanked him, but as I hung up I was dumbfounded. Getting hangar space while traveling cross-country is extremely "iffy," but leaving a plane outside without being tied down in uncertain weather is even iffier. So I now had an unexpected additional factor to consider in my flight planning. I had to make sure I stayed overnight at an airport where hangar space would be available.

Leg #3— Amarillo, Texas, to Moriarty, New Mexico

I knew I could get the Mite into a hangar in Amarillo, but what about Moriarty? I telephoned ahead and explained the problem, and the listener went off line to talk with someone. Back on the phone he asked how long the Mite was. I told him I wasn't sure but that I knew the wings were about 26 feet wide. He said he thought they could handle the Mite and to come on.

I left as quickly as I could because I knew I would be fighting the loss of daylight. Moriarty is on Mountain Time, but it was almost 3 p.m. by the time I got airborne, Central Time. That meant I had actually departed Amarillo at 2 p.m. Moriarty time. I figured that the sun would probably set about 4:30 at Moriarty so that would give me about two and-a-half hours to fly the 206 miles from Amarillo. In fact, the flight did take 2 hours and 30 minutes, and the sun was barely above the horizon when I landed.

The flight itself was delightful. I stayed a little higher because the terrain was gradually sloping upwards and higher hills started appearing ahead and on both sides of the route. As I passed Tucumcari, New Mexico, and later Santa Rosa, I checked my ground speed and "time to go" against the available daylight and decided to continue. Had higher headwinds reduced my forward speed, I would have overnighted at either of these two airports.

Moriarty was easy to find with the aid of my GPS, but without the GPS I would have had trouble finding it quickly. The 8,000-foot runway blended into the surrounding desert and was hard to pick out, particularly with the sun getting lower on the horizon. I landed without incident and then tried to find Sundance Aviation, the FBO I had talked with from Amarillo. They had told me they were at the east end of the field, but when I taxied by the only hangar I could find, there was no name on it and no sign of activity. Three or four gliders were tied down outside, and the place looked deserted. By this time the sun had set and it was starting to get dark. I resorted to calling Sundance on the unicom frequency. Sure enough, Sundance Aviation was actually a glider FBO, and "yes," it was the hangar without any sign on it.

It was good that I got there when I did because they had about given up on me and would have gone home in a few minutes. They said they thought they could get me into their hangar, which was stuffed full of gliders of all descriptions. But first I had to pull the Mite from the hard surface area across about 250 feet of relatively smooth dirt to the hangar. I did not dare try to taxi; there were too many small rocks, and the landing gear on the Mite is very short, in proportion to the Mite's size. This means that when taxiing, ground clearance is at a minimum—about eight inches from the tip of the propeller when it is turning. The real advantage of such a light-weight aircraft is that it is relatively easy to move on the ground. If the plane is on level and smooth ground you can move it with only one hand. Here the ground was slightly uphill, but even then I could do it by myself.

They squeezed the plane into the hangar, with only about six inches clearance when they closed the hangar door. The tail section of the

Mite was right by a beautiful glider with less than an inch clearance. Still, an inch is as good as a mile as long as there is no movement. So, the first night out from Augusta, N4187 spent the night in a hangar, as apparently it has been used to doing for most of its forty-year life.

December 1—Day #2

Leg #4—Moriarty, New Mexico, to Farmington, New Mexico

Moriarty is only 35 miles east of Albuquerque, but you would certainly not realize how close it is when you were flying over Moriarty. Between Moriarty (elevation 6,200 feet) and Albuquerque there is a mountain range which goes up to 12,000 feet at various places. The mountain pass that the highway follows is at about 9,000 feet.

I was airborne at about 8:30 a.m., later than I would have liked, but I was dependent on others for a ride from the motel. This first leg of the day was planned to take me due west over the mountain pass to Albuquerque, and then northwest across the top of the Class C restricted airspace over Albuquerque.

The beautiful weather I had enjoyed the previous day was to stay with me until late in the afternoon. VFR, visibility was fifty to a hundred miles, and the winds had died down so I was no longer being bounced about or fighting a headwind.

Like most Mites, N4187 had no electrical system, but it did have an aircraft battery that powers a communication radio. The battery is recharged on the ground with a 110 volt battery charger.

While a pilot is not required to do so as long as he stays above the restricted airspace around major airports, he is always wise to let the radar controllers know that he is there, and listening to them. To stay above restricted airspace in the Albuquerque area, I needed to fly at 9,400 feet, or higher. This is particularly true with the Mite because it has no radar transponder that would help the radar operator see the plane on his screen. Being a wood and fabric airplane, it has few structural elements that reflect radar energy, so I was practically invisible, or as I like to say, stealthy.

Shortly after taking off from Moriarty I tried to contact Albuquerque Center to tell them of my presence. I got no response. Then I realized that I was getting no feedback of my voice over the headset, although I could hear the hum of the transmitter "carrier." Normally when you transmit you can hear yourself.

My headset has a boom mike attached to it which is positioned in front of my mouth at all times, and both the mike and the headset wires are plugged into the panel of the Mite. There is a button on the top of the airplane control stick. To transmit, the pilot only has to push this button. So, when I tried to call Albuquerque and could not hear myself I realized that either my radio or my headset/mike was not functioning. I tried several more times as I got closer to Albuquerque. But each time I could hear the "carrier" portion of the transmitter, but not my voice. This presented no real problem, since I was not required to contact Albuquerque Center.

With clear weather, I climbed to 10,500 feet to cross the pass. Once on the west side of the mountains, and just east of Albuquerque, I turned north and stayed as close to the mountains as I could while flying around the east and then the north side of the city. Once northwest of the city, I let down to about 1,000 feet over the desert for the direct route to Farmington, another hundred miles to the northwest.

But that still left the question of how I was going to land at Farmington without a radio. Farmington is an airport with a control tower and you can't just barge in and land without permission. As I got within about 25 miles of Farmington I again tried the radio, but while I could hear the transmission carrier, there was still no voice on it. Farmington tower could hear the transmission carrier, too, but likewise could hear no voice. After I had tried several times, Farmington broadcast in the blind: "Aircraft on the Farmington tower frequency, receiving carrier but no voice."

I then had two choices. Since I could still hear the Farmington tower, I knew in what direction planes were landing and which runway was in use. By listening carefully I could determine whether or not there were other aircraft in the pattern. I could enter the pattern in the normally prescribed manner, and fly at pattern altitude until the tower saw me. The tower would then likely either broadcast in the blind, assuming that I was the aircraft which had broadcast a transmission carrier but no voice, giving me landing permission or other instructions which I could acknowledge by rocking my wings.

My second alternative would be to find another airport in the Farmington area to land at and get fuel, and bypass the main Farmington airport. I looked at the map. There was another airport—Aztec Airport—about 15 miles away. That looked like the best bet since there were two hard-surfaced runways, and it was likely there would be both fuel and people to service the Mite. So I changed my course slightly and headed for Aztec. When I got over Aztec, however, there didn't seem to be any aircraft activity on the ground. I needed fuel and I didn't want to waste time landing at an airport where there was no one around, so I decided to fly back to the Farmington airport and get in the pattern.

I did so, and I flew the pattern twice at pattern altitude, all the time rocking the wings up and down trying to attract attention. The control tower personnel must have had their heads in the sand because they never knew I was there. Yet I also kept transmitting the carrier without the voice since I knew they could hear it, and one would think this would cause them to look up and outside. After all, that is what a control tower operator is supposed to do—look outside and make sure one airplane doesn't hit another. But no luck. I was reluctant to just land without permission, so I flew back to Aztec and landed there. As I suspected, there was no one on the ground, and no fuel. Effectively the airport was closed.

However, I was carrying a hand-held radio which was in a small baggage compartment behind my seat, and not accessible in flight. I got it out, fired up the Mite once again, and headed back to the main Farmington Airport. This time my hand-held radio was effective, and I called them just after taking off from Aztec. "Farmington Tower. November 4187. I am a very small, single-seat aircraft. I have just taken off from Aztec Airport where no fuel is available. I am low on fuel, landing Farmington with information Yankee (the ATIS identification)." "Roger 4187. Do you need priority handling?" "Negative Farmington, I still have 4 to 5 gallons left."

I am not sure what the tower operator thought. Certainly it has to be unusual at the very least for a pilot to report he is down to 4 gallons, but is not declaring an emergency or requesting priority treatment. But the tower didn't say a thing and I landed without further difficulty. After I landed and was in the FBO terminal, I called the tower on the phone and respectfully asked what I should have done the first time I was over their field without radio. The tower operator said that after two or three circuits of the field, I should just have carefully landed since I knew the runway being used and could see and listen for other aircraft. I never had the guts to ask him why he wasn't looking out his window. No point in pushing my luck.

I said before that the weather was beautiful. That was certainly correct, but in one significant respect the weather was not as good as it had been the day before. While over Kansas and Texas, the temperature had been unseasonably warm—I believe parts of Kansas reached 70 degrees on the ground. It was much colder in Farmington and the temperature gauge showed the low 30s while I was flying at higher altitudes.

The Mite has an "idiot" knob labeled "heat," but I can assure you that a 65-horsepower engine has no extra heat to spare for a hapless pilot. This is particularly true with the Mite which has all four of its cylinders sticking out the side of the airplane in the slipstream of the propeller. Heat is simply a joke. The only heat you have in the Mite is the body-heat that you bring with you when you embark.

This is the type of hand-held radio every pilot should carry on every flight. This one provides not only communication but also VOR bearings for navigation use.

My 5,000 hours in mostly heated, comfortable airplanes had not obscured my memories of the early days of flying in northern Maine in drafty, unheated airplanes. I had brought along a pair of insulated overalls, the type that construction workers put on over their ordinary overalls in freezing temperatures. The flight from Moriarty to Farmington was so cold that it was with relish that I got these overalls out of the baggage area and put them on in the Farmington FBO's lounge. They looked silly with the straps over my shoulders, but boy, did they feel good. My legs did not get cold again all the way home.

The Mite attracted a good deal of attention at Farmington, for this is a major refueling stop for both private and corporate aircraft. Sitting in the lounge of the FBO were perhaps half a dozen corporate pilots in their sharp uniforms, many of them young enough never to have seen a Mooney Mite before, and most of them younger than the Mite itself. They all trooped out to look in the cockpit, and then proceeded to ask me the usual questions about the plane. I like to think they were all a little envious.

Leg #5—Farmington, New Mexico, to Price, Utah

I had lost nearly an hour going back and forth between the Farmington and Aztec Airports. This became a concern because once again I had to consider the absolute need to be on the ground once it got dark. It was close to noon before I got airborne for only the second flight of the day. Flying north meant that I would have a shorter day, perhaps offset by the fact that I was also flying farther west. I was concerned because I knew from the forecast that somewhere north of Salt Lake City I could expect to hit bad weather. My objective was to fly as close as I could towards the easternmost edge of the storm, land, and spend the night. Since the storm was moving to the east, I might not have to wait too long until it blew past me, hopefully by morning.

The two hour and twenty-four minute flight to Price, Utah was spectacular. I was flying fairly low over country that Inge and I knew well from both our many auto and flying trips. It was exciting to identify places where we had been. The experience was enhanced by spectacular visibility, and I could see Navaho Mountain which had to be at least 100 miles away.

The winds were relatively calm. I found that I could let go of the stick and the Mite would fly straight and level without any help from me. This is remarkable in an airplane that is forty years old, and a testament to Sam Mitchell's care during the past five years.

I had chosen Price, Utah as my destination because it was the last airport before the Wasatch Mountains, which run north-south just east of Provo, where I intended to cross them. The landing at this 5,600 foot elevation airport was as routine as if it had been at sea level. I was becoming quite comfortable that the Mite truly did have high altitude capability and could handle any airport I was likely to fly into.

Leg# 6—Price, Utah, to Burley, Idaho

The flight through the mountain pass was more difficult than I had expected. All I had to do was to follow a divided highway, gaining enough altitude to comfortably cross the mountains. Gaining altitude was the easy part because it was a CAVU day (Ceiling And Visibility Unlimited). I guess I was getting complacent, though, because another highway branched off of the one I was following, and for a couple of minutes I was not sure which highway I was to follow. I had my sectional maps out, of course, but the 60-mile route from Price to Provo requires three separate maps to cover that short distance (the Denver, Las Vegas, and Salt Lake sectional maps). I had not really studied all three maps carefully enough, thinking, I guess, "How can I go wrong when all I have to do is follow a highway?" What I overlooked was that unfolding a single map in the confines of the Mite's cabin and finding a small section on it is a major challenge, and it's a bigger one still to open three maps and line them up so I could really see where I was. Obviously I managed to get back over the right highway and a few minutes later crossed over the pass into the incredible beauty of the Salt Lake valley.

I was enthralled. Provo and Salt Lake City lie snuggled right up to the Wasatch Mountains. They are at an elevation of about 4,500 feet, but the Wasatch Mountains extend up to almost 12,000 feet within 10 miles of the heart of both cities. I had crossed the mountains at 10,000 feet, and then turned north, hugging the mountains. The westerly wind created an updraft as it hit against the side of these mountains, and almost immediately lifted me in level flight to 12,500 feet, much as it would a glider. Not wanting to go higher because I didn't have oxygen, I kept the nose pointed slightly downward to offset further updraft, and in so doing picked up speed. I also realized, thanks to the GPS, that by turning north, the headwind I had been experiencing had became a crosswind.

I had another reason for hugging the mountains. While I was flying above the Salt Lake City Class C restricted airspace, and thus was legal, I was also flying within 5 miles of the busy Salt Lake City airport. I certainly did not want an encounter with a 747. Indeed, as I flew north, I could see three or four airliners on the approach to Salt Lake City. Fortunately, the runways run north-south, which meant that the planes I saw were flying south, and their pilots certainly had no desire to fly as close to the Wasatch Mountains as I was. I felt quite comfortable with my perch which provided almost a 360 degree view of the airspace. It was only when I was about 15 miles north of the Salt Lake City airport and had to turn more to the west that I really needed to watch for other traffic.

Once I had crossed to the west of the north-south approach path, and outside the restricted airspace, I let down once again to about 1,000 feet over the ground. The headwinds were not entirely gone, but more importantly, looking ahead, I could see the start of the buildup of clouds that signaled the storm I had been told I would meet. I could not fly into these clouds but the forecasts had suggested that it might be possible to fly beneath them at least as far as Burley, Idaho.

However, just to the east of Burley was one final hurdle: a mountain range that rises to over 9,000 feet within 10 miles of the airport. Fortunately, Interstate 84 from Ogden to Burley goes through some fairly wide valleys that allowed me to fly around and through these mountains at about 6,000 feet, which on that day was just below the clouds and about 1,000 feet above the ground. So once I had turned northwest I followed the eastern edge of the Great Salt Lake and then continued pretty much in a straight line until I hit Interstate 84. At that point, I followed the Interstate to Burley.

I was again faced with the necessity to land before the sun completely set. By the time I got to Burley the sun was just below the horizon and I was in the twilight zone. It was not hard to tell that the storm was rapidly approaching the airport. The winds started whipping around on the ground, and when I got over the airport, the wind sock was twisting and turning almost violently in the gusty winds that were probably 40 to 50 miles per hour. That was no time to hesitate. I lined up the plane with the runway as best I could, and I had my hands full in landing safely.

Taxiing in from the runway to the FBO was even more tricky. In gusty winds, the secret to taxiing is to do so slowly, using the ailerons and elevator to keep from getting a gust of wind under either the wing or the horizontal stabilizer. By the time I got up to the FBO's hangar (I had made prior arrangements for hangar space) a downpour began. The hangar doors were closed. I looked at my watch and it was close to 5 p.m. Fortunately the FBO personnel were still there, and we got the Mite inside just as the full fury of the storm hit.

They told me that they were expecting snow that evening, and I guessed my good weather was a thing of the past. Well, that is why I had allowed 10 days to get home. I could hardly complain, since in the first two days I had managed to come two-thirds of the way.

December 2—Day #3

Leg #7—Burley, Idaho, to Caldwell, Idaho

I couldn't believe my eyes when I looked out from my hotel room in the morning. Not only was there no snow on the ground, but the rains had stopped and the sun was shining. I had expected to spend at least a day waiting for the weather to pass, but it was already gone. What a good omen.

The flight to Caldwell was a short one, only 142 miles. Located just northwest of Boise, Caldwell is an uncontrolled airport. The weather seemed especially beautiful, maybe partly because I'd expected it to be a day in which I was grounded in Burley. I hardly noticed that I still had headwinds, and it was quite a bumpy flight, which is typical just after a cold front has passed. The winds, however, were a warning of what was yet to come.

Leg # 8—Caldwell, Idaho, to La Grande, Oregon

I had not intended to go to La Grande, Oregon. I had intended to fly to Pendleton, Oregon. But one of the things you learn early on in flying is that sometimes things don't work out as planned.

The route to Pendleton goes across a mountain range, most of the peaks of which were in the 5,000 to 6,000 foot range with an occasional peak that was higher. From the moment of takeoff at Caldwell, the plane was bouncing all over the sky. As I approached this mountain range, it was obvious that there was a layer of clouds perhaps 2,000 to 3,000 feet above the mountains that I was going to have to fly under. The mountains were on a largely north/south line and my flight path was largely in a northwest direction, so I approached the mountains from an angle, not head on. As I got closer, the winds became even more gusty.

As I crossed the first ridge of this range, I started hitting my head on the top of the canopy, and I began to ask myself about the structural integrity of this 40-year-old wooden aircraft. Could the gusts become severe enough to damage it?

Once I crossed the first ridge, I was over the valley, where it was smoother, but still bumpy. Ahead was an airport (La Grande), and beyond the airport and east of my course, perhaps 15 miles, was a wall of snow showers that seemed to extend down to the valley floor. I was not headed in that direction, but I didn't know enough about the weather over the mountains to Pendleton, 45 miles away, to want to go further without a weather update. I couldn't be sure that once I started over the mountains from this valley toward Pendleton I wouldn't find impenetrable snow showers right down to the mountaintops.

So, I landed at La Grande, but not without considerable difficulty, because below the tops of the mountains surrounding the valley the winds became even more gusty. The saving grace was that one of the runways was directly lined up into the wind.

Leg #9—La Grande, Oregon, to Pendleton, Oregon

When I landed, I had about concluded that I should spend the night at La Grande. The winds had bounced me around a lot, and the wall of snow showers to the northeast suggested more problems over the mountains. Even before I called the FAA Flight Service Station to check on the weather, I confirmed that the FBO could get me into a hangar if I decided to stay. But the FBO also told me that the forecast for the area was for snow that evening and that I might get stuck for a couple of days.

Flight Service was more encouraging. They indicated that Pendleton had ceilings of about 3,000 feet above the ground and that their weather observer in the Pendleton tower reported that the clouds over the mountain range toward La Grande were well above the mountains, at least as far as he could see. Based on this information I decided to try to make the 45-mile flight to Pendleton and then re-evaluate the weather and decide whether to go on. It was too early in the day to stop flying, but I was apprehensive.

This leg of the trip was bumpy, no question about it. But it was not as bumpy as it had been just an hour before. I stayed about 1,000 feet above the terrain, and still had about 1,000 feet of ceiling above me, with good visibility (20+ miles).

Leg #10—Pendleton, Oregon, to Portland (Troutdale), Oregon

My original flight plan had assumed that from Pendleton I would fly north to the Yakima, Washington area, refuel, and then hop over the Cascade Mountains, flying directly to Orcas Island. This is a fairly straight route, and the one we normally take in the Cessna T210 when we refuel in Boise. Of course on those flights we can easily fly non-stop and at altitudes far above the 10,000 foot peaks of the Cascades.

But N4187 had neither the fuel nor the altitude capacity of the Cessna T210. The weather report indicated that the clouds over the Cascades were right down on the mountains, and even the road passes were socked in. This had been the case for most of the past week.

I had started asking pilots at my fuel stops which route they would take to get over the Cascades and to Seattle. Their unanimous answer was: "Don't go over the Cascades this time of year, go through them via the Columbia River Gorge to Portland, and then up Interstate 5."

And that is what I did. I checked with Flight Service at Pendleton and they said I could expect an overcast at about 2,000 feet over the entire Columbia River Gorge, but that except for an isolated snow shower, the visibilities were 10 miles or better. They also gave me the weather at The Dalles, an airport located alongside the Columbia River about 50 miles east of Portland. Flight Service also indicated further bad weather was coming in off the Pacific, and that, if I didn't depart right away, I might have to wait a day or two before conditions would again be this good.

A phone call to the airport at Portland's Troutdale Airport confirmed that there was hangar space. I had been lucky on getting hangar space on this trip.

It was 150 miles from Pendleton to Troutdale Airport. Did I still have enough daylight left? Barely. But if headwinds slowed me down I could always land at The Dalles. With this in mind, off I went.

Navigation on this leg was easy. I took up a northwest heading to intercept the Columbia River, then turned west and followed it to Portland, flying about 1,000 feet above the river. Although the sky was overcast and dreary, the flight was beautiful. The Columbia River Gorge is truly spectacular, particularly when viewed from an eagle's perspective, 1,000 feet above the river.

Troutdale Airport is right on the Columbia River, just a few miles west of the mountains that form the Columbia River Gorge. It has a control tower, but it is located under the Portland Class C airspace, so I could land without a transponder. I used the hand-held radio to communicate. Again, I landed just before the sun went down. I had been having full and satisfying flying days.

As on the previous night, the weather forecast for the next day was poor and it looked likely that I would have to stay in Portland for at least a day. Too bad, I thought, since I was so close to home. But I had been incredibly lucky so far, so I could hardly complain.

December 3—Day 4

Leg # 11—Portland, Oregon, to Orcas Island, Washington (via Bellingham)

After a good night's sleep, I found that once again the weather forecaster had been wrong. The weather system moving in off the Pacific had slowed down and was lagging at least 12 hours behind the original forecast. The forecaster told me that if I left promptly I would be able to stay under the overcast at about 2,000 feet above the ground. The preferred route is following Interstate 5, which wanders through a valley, with the Cascades Range on the right, and the lower, coastal mountains on the left. The valley is fairly wide and you are 25 or more miles from either of these mountain ranges if you stay over the Interstate.

So, off I went that early Sunday morning, full of anticipation at the possibility of getting home. The weather was pretty much as advertised, except for one thing. I had a tailwind! The GPS was showing a fairly consistent 145-miles per hour ground speed for a good part of this leg. What a delightful way to end a long trip!

Alas. Never knock on wood, particularly the wood in a wood airplane! I made it back to Orcas Island in good time. The 190-mile flight took barely an hour and-a-half. But as I approached Orcas Island I realized that it was starting to get more than just a little bumpy. This often happens when southwest winds hit mountains on Orcas Island (Mt. Constitution on Orcas is 2,500 feet high); they create a great deal of local turbulence. These winds wreak havoc with landings at my home airport, the Eastsound Airport.

I was high on my first attempt to land, and that was a mistake. I have since learned that the Mite likes to do things by the numbers. With the gear retracted it does not slow down very quickly, and in this instance I tried to enter the downwind leg for a landing to the south about two miles out, but from 2,000 feet I never really got down to the pattern altitude of 1,000 feet until I was on base leg. Then I had trouble slowing down so that I could lower the landing gear. I aborted that attempt to land even before turning final.

The Mighty Mite is shown here beside one of the largest aircraft in the world. Taken in 2003 at AirVenture in Oshkosh, Wisconsin, the plane was being moved to The Moony Aircraft Company exhibit where it was displayed under the banner: "50 Years and Still the Fastest in its Class." I had just completed a major restoration of the plane, the first in its 50 year life. It should be good for another 50 years.

Sheepishly, I went back and entered the traffic pattern in the conventional manner, slowed the plane down properly, and lowered the gear while on downwind. The Mite was bouncing around a good deal on downwind but I still felt I had it under control. The bouncing increased as I got lower on base leg. Then, once I turned final, the Mite bounced so dramatically that I wasn't sure I could control it. Then a gust raised one wing, and even with full opposite aileron, the plane continued to roll. It did right itself, but not before I wondered how well the Mite would fly upside down.

I decided at that point to break off the approach. Perhaps if I had continued, and flown lower, the gustiness would have abated and I could have landed. However, I was reminded of the old adage: "He who runs away, lives to fight another day." While I had been enthusiastic about my transformation back to being a 22-year-old for four days, I decided that it was time for the "real me" to run away and execute Plan B.

I headed for the mainland and the Bellingham airport with its 5,000-foot runways and clean approaches with no mountains nearby to disturb the airflow. The landing there was without incident although there was a strong wind blowing. I managed to find hangar space to get the Mite in so that both of us could fly another day.

Bellingham is only 14 miles from Eastsound, but the flight there is all over water, so having called it a day in Bellingham presented certain logistical problems in terms of my getting back to Orcas Island. I could rent a car and drive the fifty miles to Anacortes where I could get a ferry to Orcas. That would take between three and five hours depending on when the next ferry was leaving.

Once again, luck was with me. West Isle Air, the local commuter airline, had three flights a day to Eastsound from Bellingham. I landed at about 10:30, and their next flight was a little after 11. I was the only passenger, but I was back on Orcas Island by noon, exhausted. I was exhilarated at having completed the trip in just a little over three days, but was disappointed that I had not been able to land at my home airport.

The next morning I took an early West Isle Air flight back to Bellingham, retrieved the Mite, and landed uneventfully on Orcas mid-morning.

The Mighty Mite was home.

29

The Southern Alps of New Zealand
January, 2002

In early January, 2002, I noticed a small ad in a magazine published by the Cessna Pilots Association:

> Pilots! Fly yourself on a wonderful vacation in New Zealand. Check out our unique website **www.flyinn.co.nz**–lots of great information and photos. Plan your N.Z. adventure now!

This ad caught my attention because my wife and I were leaving just ten days later for a two-month vacation in New Zealand. I immediately emailed to get more information. It turned out that Matt and Jo McCaughan were New Zealand sheep farmers with a love of aviation. Located near Wanaka on the South Island, they had their own 3,000 foot landing strip on their five thousand acre sheep station they call Geordie Hill. They had something like 7,000 Merino sheep and 200 cows. Flying was part of their lives and they had a small family business assisting pilots from other countries to see New Zealand by air. They arranged for these pilots to obtain their New Zealand private pilot's license, and then rented their aircraft to these pilots, but accompanying them as their guide.

This sounded intriguing. While I really had no compelling interest in getting a New Zealand license, I was certainly interested in seeing

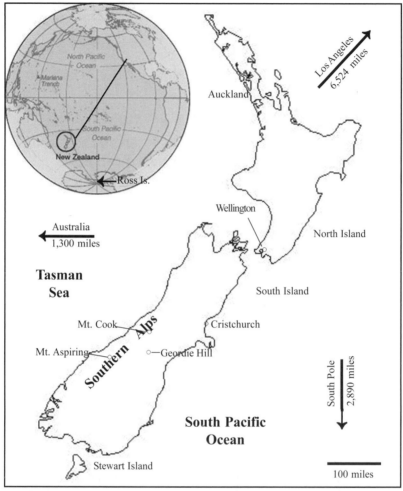

New Zealand is located in the Southern Hemisphere where summers and winters are reversed, and is becoming a popular destination for Americans. While most think of New Zealand as being composed of two islands, there is actually a third—Stewart Island—at the very south end of the country, which we have visited several times. New Zealand was the departure point for all of the early expeditions to Antarctica. Note on the globe insert that there is nothing between New Zealand and Antarctica except for a handful of Sub-Antarctic islands. Even today, U.S. scientific expeditions to Antarctica leave from Christchurch. The year after this trip we, too, went to Antarctica from New Zealand. For about 45 days a year the ice breaks up enough for a ship to get through to Ross Island which is only 800 miles from the Pole. It is a hard trip, taking ten days each way through some of the roughest seas in the world. The Russian ship we were on carried only forty other "adventurers."

the Southern Alps—as the mountain range on the South Island is known. We had visited New Zealand in the late 1980s and had seen the Alps from the ground. Now was a chance to see them from the air.

Geordie Hill is located on the eastern side of the Alps, less than 100 miles from Mount Cook, the highest mountain in New Zealand (12,315 feet). It sounded to us like an ideal place from which to fly. Matt said he could squeeze us into his schedule if we could do so at the beginning of our trip.

Time was short because in order to fly his aircraft I needed to have a New Zealand pilot's license. There would be another New Zealand pilot with us at all times. I believe this requirement for a license had something to do with in-

Geordie Hill is a working "station" with 7,000 Merino sheep whose wool is world renowned. The grass landing strip is 3,000 feet long, shown here with two planes getting ready to take off.

surance or New Zealand pilot license requirements to rent aircraft.

There were two parts to the process of getting a license. First I had to complete the necessary paperwork and get it to the aviation authorities. Normally this paperwork was submitted well in advance, usually before the prospective pilot arrived in New Zealand. That was not going to be possible in our case, but Matt dropped off the necessary forms at our bed-and-breakfast in Christchurch. When we arrived on January 20 we completed the paperwork and mailed it directly to the authorities.

The second phase of getting a license was to have an authorized inspector fly with me to make sure that I was current and competent. This second phase took place once we got to Geordie Hill.

Getting to Geordie Hill

We flew 6,524 miles from Los Angeles nonstop to Auckland, the country's largest city, located on the North Island. We immediately transferred to a direct flight to Christchurch on the South Island. We spent five days in Christchurch getting acclimated to both the time zone changes, and driving on the wrong side

This was the bed-and-breakfast where we stayed for 5 days after arriving in New Zealand. We also stayed here the following year.

of the road in our rental car. The bed-and-breakfast we stayed at was on the edge of the downtown area.

Geordie Hill was about 250 miles from Christchurch and it took us about six hours to drive there. New Zealand is a long, fairly narrow country, and the distance across the southern part of the island probably averages about 100 miles as the crow flies.

The Southern Alps are located in a 50 mile wide band on the western side of the island from about opposite Christchurch southwest to close to the southern end of the island. The land on the eastern side of the Alps away from the foothills is mostly farmland with a few rolling hills. Geordie Hill is located in the foothills of the Alps and is in sheep country. It is too mountainous and rocky for farming. You can get a sense of the country from the pictures on the previous page.

An off-field landing in a meadow near a friend's house. I let the inspector make this landing.

Cessna 172

Matt had two 180-horsepower Cessna 172s available, and with the help of another pilot-guide could accommodate two couples. This was the first time I had flown in a 180-horsepower Cessna 172, but almost all of my flying had been in Cessna aircraft. I felt at home with this one.

We arrived mid-afternoon at Geordie Hill. Inge had done all the driving since she handles the "wrong side of the road" driving better than I do. About 5 p.m. Matt arrived from a day's flying with another couple who would also be flying for several more days in another aircraft. John Penno, the inspector from the Civil Aviation Authority of New Zealand, flew in about the same time. It was his job to determine if I was competent to fly in New Zealand and should be issued a New Zealand license. That evening he spent time talking with me about regulations and general aviation flying in New Zealand.

The following morning John was in the right-hand seat of the plane while I was flying. Both planes were traveling together over and through the Southern Alps. I say "through" because during the morning hours we had an overcast that kept us from flying over the mountains and we followed valleys and roads to get from the east side of the Alps to the west side. Once on the west side, we were at the coast of the Tasman Sea. We landed to visit a relative of Matt and Jo's who lived in a house on the coast. There was no airport so we landed in a meadow which they use for that purpose. I wisely suggested that John make that landing, which he did. We stayed about an hour

The rest of the day was spent landing at several paved strips and flying along the western side of the Alps. The highlight of the day was the flight over Franz Josef Glacier, and then past Mt. Cook. By the end

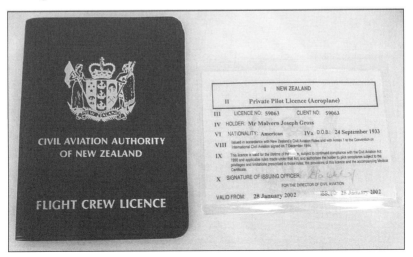

of the day we had flown 3.3 hours. John Penno signed off on my New Zealand license and then departed.

Pilot-in-Command

Davida Mead joined us the next morning. She was a longtime instructor-pilot and knew the Alps as few people did. I was officially the pilot-in-command of the flight but I asked Davida to sit in the left front seat, and do all the flying. I wanted to enjoy the spectacular scenery without being distracted by having to fly. That was a good decision because she was far better qualified than I was to be flying near rugged, glacier-covered mountains.

We flew with Davida for two days over other parts of the Alps, and to several towns on both sides of the Alps. At one point we landed on a deserted section of beach so Davida could show us a "getaway" cabin she and her husband had built, and which was not accessible by road. Each evening we returned to Geordia Hill for the night.

It is hard to describe the extraordinary views we had. They say a picture is worth a thousand words, and so, I leave readers to form their own opinion from the several pictures that follow.

continued on page 368

Milford Sound, showing the airport where we landed. This fjord extends about 10 miles to the Tasman Sea. New Zealand has many fjords that reminded us of Norway. To the south of Milford is a huge national park named "Fjordland National Park" with what looked like dozens of much longer fjords, most of which were not accessible by roads.

Mt. Cook, 12,316 feet, is the highest mountain in New Zealand.

Mt. Aspiring, 9,941 feet, is known by mountain climbers as "The Matterhorn of the South."

Solid mountains, up close!

Another view of Mt. Cook.

Sutherland Falls, 1904 foot waterfall, the highest in the Southern Hemisphere. This picture shows the source of the falls.

Two-Month Tour

These three days were the highlight of our two-month trip to New Zealand. After we left Geordie Hill we toured all three islands—the South Island, the North Island, and Stewart Island. It is a hospitable country, and we were made to feel welcome. They have one bad habit, however—they drive on the wrong side of the road.

Christchurch became the focal point of our trip. Not only is it the major city on the South Island, but it remains the southernmost port city for travel to and from Antarctica. All of the early explorers—Shackleton, Scott and others—provisioned their ships in Christchurch before leaving for McMurdo Sound adjacent to Ross Island in the Antarctic. Their winter huts were on Ross Island which was the southernmost point on the Antarctic continent that ships can reach, but then only two months a year because of solid pack ice. Once at Ross Island these explorers were still almost eight hundred miles from the South Pole, which they reached on foot.

Today virtually all travel to this area of Antarctica is for scientific reasons, and the United States maintains a research base at both McMurdo and at the South Pole itself. The U.S. Air Force services these bases from Christchurch using ski-equipped aircraft. There is one ship that carries 40 tourists on a month-long trip from New Zealand to and from Ross Island in January and February of each year. We returned the following January, 2003, to join this tour.

Highly Recommend

New Zealand is a beautiful country, and appears all the more spectacular when seen from a small plane. Matt and Jo McCaughan do a wonderful job of showing pilots their country from the air. I recommend them. They have been attending AirVenture at Oshkosh and have had a booth in one of the Exhibit Halls for the last five years. Their website (www.flyinn.com.nz) has many pictures and information.

30

Mooney "Mite" Fuel Leak
July 21, 2003

Kalispell

It was a hot day, and my Mite was not particularly anxious to climb. Yet I had to climb. I had just taken off from the Kalispell Airport in Montana, just south of the Canadian border. Kalispell is located in a valley to the west of Glacier National Park, whose 10,000-foot glacier peaks blocked my way to the East.

I was en route from Orcas Island to Oshkosh, Wisconsin, where the largest aviation event in the world, AirVenture, takes place each summer. It is about 1,800 miles from Orcas to Oshkosh, and for my little Mite this was a long trip. It was made longer by the plane's miserly fuel tank—just 13 gallons. This was enough to fly three hours at about 120 mph, but if you flew for a full three hours you would be in danger

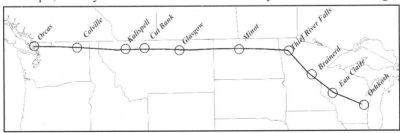

This is the route I took from Orcas to Oshkosh. I stayed close to the Canadian border to keep cool and avoid the higher mountains farther to the south. I stopped at each of the towns indicated, typically at about 200 mile intervals.

369

of running out of fuel. I find that I sleep better at night when I figure that the Mite has a two-hour range; that gives me some leeway in the event of headwinds or unexpected weather requiring me to land elsewhere than where I had planned.

With just 65-horsepower and fully loaded, the Mite was not happy to fly above about 8,000 feet, particularly on this hot day, but I had to do so. Winds hitting the mountains that I had to cross could create downdrafts and turbulence which could be very serious if I were flying close to these mountaintops.

So, after takeoff, I looked for some rising air thermals, created by the heated air one often encounters on hot days in mountainous areas. The Mite is so light—850 pounds—that it acts like a glider, and an updraft or thermal can help the plane gain altitude.

Just like a bird, I located half a dozen thermals, and circled tightly in each one to stay within their rising currents of air. It took about 30 minutes but I got up to 13,000 feet, well above the nine-and ten-thousand-foot mountains I would encounter. I didn't have supplemental oxygen, but I would be at 13,000 feet for only thirty minutes. That is about the limit at that altitude.

I headed east over Glacier National Park which is only 50 miles from the west side to the east side. Once across, I was over a flat plateau and there were no more mountains between me and Oshkosh. I like this northern route for that reason—there are fewer mountains to cross compared to the southern routes.

It was a beautiful crossing—good visibility, and fairly smooth air. It was cold, and there is no heat in the Mite so I dressed accordingly, regardless of what the temperature is on the ground. Once on the east-

The map on the opposite page shows Kalispell on the west side of Glacier National Park, and Cut Bank on the high plateau east of this forbidding mountain range. Most of the peaks are in the nine to ten thousand foot range. There are glaciers in these mountains, and a single road that weaves through these mountains on a southeast to northwest orientation. It is possible to follow this road through the mountains in poor weather, provided the visibility is good. There is no place where you could land a crippled aircraft. The straight line distance between Kalispell and Cut Bank is 90 miles. The actual route of flight was longer because of the need to climb to 13,000 feet before turning east.

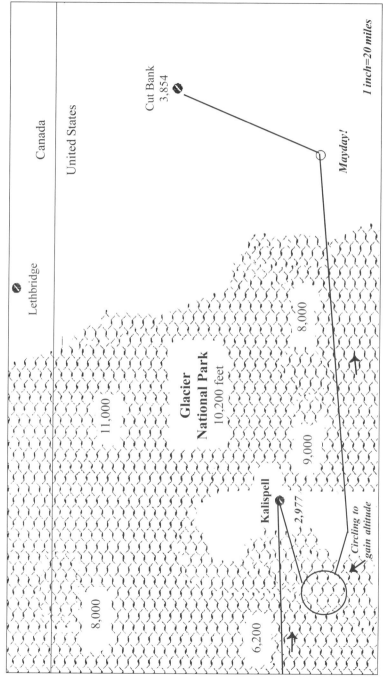

Kalispell across Glacier National Park to Cut Bank where we made an emergency landing.

These glacier-covered, rugged mountains are among the most beautiful mountains in the United States. The view from the ground is also spectacular, but it pales in comparison with the aerial view which a pilot sees up close.

ern side of these mountains, I started to let down to a lower altitude primarily to get to warmer temperatures and more oxygen.

It was then when some instinct caused me to look at the fuel gauge behind my head. Now the Mite fuel gauge is one of the most foolproof fuel gauges there is—it is a sight gauge. The fuel tank itself is right behind the pilot's head at the top of the cabin. In fact, the pilot's head leans against the fuel tank, albeit protected by a padded bulkhead. But on the pilot's side of this bulkhead is a long plastic tube that attaches to a brass 90-degree fitting on the top side of the tank, and the other end of the tube is attached at the bottom in the same way. The fuel in the tube is always at the same height as the fuel in the tank. The tube is recessed into the bulkhead so it does not protrude on the pilot side. It is truly a foolproof system with no mechanical parts or things to go wrong. What you see is what you have.

Emergency!

But when I looked at this plastic tube I saw that a fine mist of fuel was spurting from the bottom of the tube at the lower fitting—and this fine mist was, of course, spraying into the cockpit. Given enough time, I would be soaked in flammable fuel.

Now flying is considered pretty safe if you follow all the rules, have good weather, and use common sense. Even if the engine stops, the plane becomes a glider and you have a pretty good chance of telling about it if you keep your head.

But fuel in the cockpit—that is a no-no, and the very thought of it runs chills up and down a pilot's spine.

The cockpit of the Mite is so narrow and small that I could not turn around and touch the plastic tube in flight. Out of the corner of my eye, twisting my head as far as I could, I saw the fuel level in the plastic tube, and the misting fuel coming out of the bottom of the tube, but I could not reach back to touch the tube itself. That inability to get to the tube is probably what saved me.

Get on the ground! And get on the ground fast! A fire in the cockpit is not survivable in the air!

Fortunately I knew the area. I was probably 20 miles from the Cut Bank Airport. I was still at eleven thousand feet, and even in a glide, the plane cannot descend at more than about 700 feet a minute without over-speeding. I turned immediately toward Cut Bank. I was using a GPS strapped to my knee and instructed it to amend its destination to take me to the Cut Bank airport. I didn't want to waste any time looking for it visually. From ex-

Shown here is the plastic tube that is recessed into the bulkhead behind the pilot's head. The level of fuel in the tube equals the level in the tank. The arrow is pointing to the fuel level.

perience, I knew that this airport blends in with the desert until one is almost on top of it.

I then called the FAA Flight Service Station in Great Falls, Montana and told them I had fuel leaking into the cabin and would make an emergency landing at Cut Bank. That got their attention. I didn't have to use the emotion-laden word: Mayday! They understood, and treated it as the life-threatening emergency that it was. When a pilot declares an emergency all the resources of the FAA are brought to bear.

They said they would advise the Cut Bank Fire Department and get equipment there as quickly as possible. Normally, there is no one at the Cut Bank Airport; there is only self-service fuel. Then I told them I was turning off the radio for fear a spark from it would ignite the fuel.

I kept monitoring the fuel flow, and it remained what I can best describe as a mist spurting out about three to four inches from the tube. The cockpit is not airtight and I believe the airflow through the cabin was taking most of the mist out with it. I was not terribly troubled by the fuel smell but, of course, was very concerned over what if the fuel flow increased to a gusher.

It took about ten minutes, but luck was with me and I made it to the airport where a runway directly in front of me allowed me to make a straight-in approach. I did not bother to check the winds because I needed to follow that first, second, and third rule for fire-related emergencies—get on the ground, now!

Bad, Safe Landing

My landing was one of the worst I have made, and I almost lost the plane because of crosswinds, but I had other priorities on my mind. I then taxied directly to the parking area near the terminal building and shut the engine down. The airport was deserted. Once out of the plane I called the FAA to tell them I was safely down. The Fire Department had not yet shown up—the town is three miles from the airport.

From outside the plane, I then examined the plastic tube and saw that it was leaking where it connected to the bottom 90-degree brass fitting. I reached in to push down on the plastic tube to see if I could get a tighter fit, but in doing so the tube came completely off the fitting and the misting turned to a gusher, spurting upwards 6 to 8 inches.

Finger in the Dike

I have never been to Holland, but I remembered the story of the boy with his finger in the dike. Like him, I quickly stuck my thumb on top of the brass fitting, stopping the flow completely, and that is how the Cut Bank Fire Department found me about five minutes later when they showed up. My thumb was in the dike.

From that point on, things went well. One of the fifteen responding fire fighters traded places with me and put his thumb on the tube. Then we unloaded the baggage compartment which is underneath the fuel tank so that if any fuel leaked it would not saturate the assorted bags and sandwiches that I had stored. Afterwards another fireman disconnected the top end of the plastic tube from its 90-degree brass fitting, and since it was at the top of the tank, no fuel came out. Then they slid the plastic tube securely onto the bottom fitting so that there was no further leak. As long as the top of the tube was held upright, no fuel would come out.

The plastic tube seemed to have shrunk. It was just barely long enough to be clamped at both the top and bottom fittings but not securely at both ends. Clearly I needed a longer plastic tube. The Fire Chief then went into town and procured several lengths of plastic tube from the local NAPA automotive parts store. One of these tubes was exactly the right inside diameter and this was fitted onto both the top and bottom 90 degree fittings and clamped tightly.

Problem fixed. No fire. The Fire Department left, and I was again alone.

I had probably lost only a quart of fuel, not very much, thank goodness. It did not take long for all of the fuel fumes to dissipate. I put the baggage back in the plane, used the self-service pump to refuel, and got back in the air.

Hindsight

Why was the plastic tube short? I had recently had the plane overhauled and had also replaced the fuel tank with a newly manufactured tank made by a local tank shop using the old one as a model. Apparently, the two fittings were not precisely the same distance apart on the new tank as on the old one, but instead of putting on a new plastic tube, my mechanic had reinstalled the old one, which was about an inch too short to fully cover the two brass fittings securely.

It was a very lucky happenstance that I could not reach the plastic tube in flight. Judging by how easily the tube came off when I did touch it, I would surely have had a serious problem if I had done this in the air. I could not have reached back and played "Dutch boy" in the air.

Given the diameter of the fittings, I would guess an unimpeded flow would have emptied the eight or nine gallons remaining in ten or fifteen minutes. Once that happened, there would be no fuel for the engine, and I would have had to land wherever we were. Although the ground was fairly level east of the mountains, the plane would surely have been destroyed by the rocky terrain on landing, and I could have been badly hurt, or worse. Being soaked in fuel added a dimension; I don't know what might have happened. Even on the ground fire can be very serious.

So, luck was with me. I had already crossed the Glacier mountains. As the picture of these mountains shows, if the tube had come off over these peaks I would have found no place to land that was survivable. The luckiest part of all was that I could not reach the fitting while in flight.

So much for a fuel gauge system that is "foolproof."

• • •

Postscript—Eventually I got a bill from the Cut Bank Fire Department for their services and gladly paid the $150.

31

AirVenture
The National Air Show
of the United States

For twenty years I was privileged to have been a member of the Board of Directors of the Experimental Aircraft Association. EAA, as it is commonly known, is a unique nonprofit organization that has become the center of sport aviation not only in the United States, but in the entire world. In late July it holds an annual, week-long event in Oshkosh, Wisconsin, called AirVenture, which is attended by seven hundred thousand people including visitors from seventy plus countries.

But it is not only people who attend AirVenture. Upwards of ten thousand airplanes will land at the Oshkosh Wittman Regional Airport during this week, twenty-five hundred of which are "show planes" whose owners proudly display and compete for awards. There will be "vintage" aircraft, World War II warbirds, ultralights, light sport aircraft, and yes, even float planes that land at nearby Lake Winnebago. The Air Force usually has several of their latest aircraft on display, and as the pictures in this chapter show, several of the major aircraft manufacturers will have aircraft on display. Until the Concorde was removed from service, it attended every couple of years—and gave subsonic rides. Every few years a Boeing 747 flies directly from Australia with a plane load of Australian aviation enthusiasts.

During this one-week period the Wittman Regional Airport becomes the busiest airport in the world. The FAA has more than fifty tower and traffic controllers to handle this air traffic. Almost forty-thousand campers will use the fly-in, drive-in, and camping areas. There will be more than eight hundred media representatives from five continents.

National Air Show of the United States

AirVenture is unique, and while not promoted as the National Air Show of the United States, it clearly has reached that status. Mac McCellan, Editor-in-Chief of Flying Magazine, in an editorial back in 2001, was probably the first journalist to express this view. Here are his words:

"What makes AirVenture a truly national show is that it now represents all facets of American aviation activity. No other show can make that claim, no matter how successful it may be in showcasing one segment or another of U.S. aviation. AirVenture is different because it was founded to attract and intrigue anybody who is interested in anything that flies. Yes, homebuilders were the core of the EAA, and remain one of its more important elements, but they did not exclude others, they included them. By treating all aviation activities equally, AirVenture was able to grow into our national air show."

It All Started with One Man—Paul Poberezny

AirVenture did not just happen. It took one man's vision, energy, and hard work, but he could not have done it alone. He also had to become the Pied Piper of Aviation. His charisma attracted thousands of other aviation enthusiasts to volunteer their time and money to make it happen. It all started in 1953. Here is an excerpt from the EAA website:

January 1953. Paul Howard Poberezny, the leader of a small group of aviation enthusiasts who had been assembling at his home on an irregular basis, founded the Experimental Aircraft Association and was elected its first President. On January 26th, 1953, Poberezny called the first official meeting of the EAA at Curtiss-Wright (now Timmerman) Field in Milwaukee. The group originally gathered together to aid and assist amateur aircraft builders. However, its purposes quickly encompassed the promotion of all facets of aviation—especially sport aviation, the preservation of America's rich heritage of personal flight, and the promotion of aviation safety. The organization derives its name from the Experimental Aircraft category, which is assigned to airplanes used for recreational and educational purposes only. One of the keys to the Association's constant growth is the fact that its membership is open to everyone interested in aviation.

This small group of aviation enthusiasts has grown over the years to 170,000. The annual fly-in of members outgrew the airport facilities first in Hales Corner, Wisconsin, and then Rockford, Illinois. In 1972, EAA moved to Oshkosh, Wisconsin. The members committed the funds to build both EAA's new headquarters, and its world-class Museum.

Paul's son, Tom Poberezny, ably took over the reigns as President in 1991, while Paul continued his leadership as chairman of the board.

There have been several books written on the history of EAA which I highly recommend. It is not my purpose to summarize EAA's rich history, but instead to highlight AirVenture, the biggest aviation event in the world.

AirVenture Is Unique

Let me just make some observations about AirVenture that I believe make this week-long event so unique. As Mac McCellan so succinctly summarized above, AirVenture appeals to "anybody who is interested in anything that flies." That means not only pilots, and aircraft owners, but the millions of people who have always dreamed of learning to-fly, but, as yet, have not done so. It means the kids of all ages who have never experienced a flight in a small plane. It means those who served in military aviation in earlier wars and then relive their experience by seeing aircraft from that era; in short, it means millions of people from all walks of life and all economic brackets.

AirVenture is attended in substantial number by key staff of government agencies dealing with aviation—FAA, NASA, Homeland Security, NTSB and Congressional committees dealing with aviation issues.

AirVenture could not exist without the more than three thousand members who volunteer their time and talents each year to make it work. Many arrive in Oshkosh a month ahead of the opening date to handle the thousands of logistical and maintenance jobs that an undertaking of this size requires. Others serve as registration, sales staff, and announcers. All of the members of the board of directors have responsibilities; I served in the Finance Office as a cashier. If you had to hire people to perform these functions the cost would be prohibitive, and AirVenture could not exist.

The EAA museum in Oshkosh is the finest aviation museum in the world, built entirely with private donations. In addition to a huge Warbirds Hangar, the Museum houses full-scale replicas of the Wright Flyer, and Lindbergh's Spirit of St. Louis. It has a full-scale replica of the fuselage of Voyager—see Chapter 19—as well as Rutan's Spaceship One, the first privately-financed and built vehicle to reach suborbital flight. The museum has hundreds of exhibits, and one could easily spend several days without seeing everything.

But this museum is not just a collection of exhibits. It also has its own active airport within Wittman Regional Airport. Next to the museum, Pioneer Airport is a replica of a 1930s-era small airport with its own runway, hangars, and exhibits. During AirVenture, sight-seeing rides in a vintage aircraft are available.

In addition to Pioneer Airport, there is also another active runway within the Wittman Regional Airport for ultralight aircraft. Located near the south end of the main north-south runway, this runway is quite active throughout AirVenture. Planes using both Pioneer airport and the ultralight runway have a special traffic pattern which allows them to fly even while the main Oshkosh runways are also in use.

Every afternoon the Wittman Regional Airport is closed to all air traffic during a two-hour air show by the top aerobatic pilots in the world. Often the Blue Angels perform, and on several days the warbird pilots take to the skies and fly formation over the field. Nowhere else can you see so many vintage World War II planes in the air at one time.

Throughout the rest of each day, other aircraft arrive or depart, enthralling the crowd. AirVenture is where aviation companies introduce new aircraft and equipment designs. With eight-hundred-plus members of the press in attendance, there is no higher visibility aviation venue.

Education

EAA started out as a group of amateur aircraft builders, and right from the beginning the annual fly-in (now known as AirVenture) was intended to be an educational experience for EAA members. The more experienced aircraft builders would pass on their knowledge to others. Over the ensuing 55 years this educational function has become a major part of AirVenture. More than five hundred speakers are scheduled to make presentations at the 2009 AirVenture. Some are so popular that they will make their presentation two or three times during the week. Most of these will take place at Forum Plaza, a collection of twelve buildings of various capacity. These presentations will start at 8:30 a.m. and continue until late in the afternoon, with each presentation typically lasting an hour. In addition to the Forum Plaza, there are also other workshops demonstrating various skills, presentations at the Museum, and Theater In The Woods. Nowhere else in the world can you find this much aviation knowledge available at one time.

Commercial Exhibitors.

More than eight hundred commercial exhibitors attend AirVenture, displaying their latest product, or service that they hope to convince the attendees they cannot live without. Virtually every general aviation and business aircraft manufacturer will have flown their latest design to AirVenture for display. This includes the latest single or twin-engine business jets costing in the millions of dollars each. At the other end of the spectrum, both ultralight and light sport aircraft will also be displayed.

In recent years, integrated glass cockpits have become increasingly available, and many exhibits deal with such sophisticated electronic equipment. AirVenture is where you want to go if you have an aircraft and want to see the latest equipment available for it.

A Picture Is Worth a Thousand Words

It is difficult to fully describe AirVenture in words. In the remaining pages of this chapter I have reproduced a number of pictures that hopefully will give the reader a glimpse of AirVenture, showing why it is truly the National Air Show of the United States. And, for many of us, it is also the mecca of sport aviation that calls the faithful to Oshkosh year-after-year.

Satellite Picture

A satellite picture of AirVenture from space. Pioneer Airport can be seen in the upper-left side (arrow). The EAA Headquarters and the Museum are just below the arrow. The Ultralight runway is at the bottom, center (arrow). If you look closely you can see rows and rows of planes parked alongside both runways. The north-south runway is 8,000 feet long and the east-west runway is 6,170 feet. See also the aerial picture in the color folio following page 394.

Craig VanderKolk–EAA

Aircraft-type Clubs often arrive together. This picture shows some of the 100 Bonanzas that arrived together, as they taxied to their group parking.

Jim Koepnick–EAA

Hotel space is both sparse and expensive. Most of those flying to AirVenture bring along camping equipment and camp beside their aircraft.

Top picture: "North 40" airplanes and tents. Bottom picture: Campgrounds with recreational vehicles of all sizes. Many arrive a month early. Without such volunteers AirVenture could not exist.

DeKevin Thornton–EAA

Cindy Luft–EAA

The F-22 Raptor is a fighter aircraft that uses stealth technology and is highly maneuverable at both supersonic and subsonic speeds. It is able to achieve a high angle of attack due to thrust vectoring, a design unique to the F-22. It was displayed on AeroShell Square for visitors to check out.

Nowhere else will you see so many warbirds in the air, in formation, at one-time.

The AV-8B Harrier's most famous feature is its vertical takeoff and landing capability. Although this jet has only one jet engine, it has four nozzles that direct the jet engine thrust downwards for vertical maneuvers. Here the Harrier is "hovering" and starting to make its descent, with no forward speed. The pilot often makes a 360 degree turn before descending. The sheer brute force of the engine also creates a roar unlike any other plane I know of.

Jim Koepnik–EAA

Jim Koepnik–EAA

The U-2 spy plane is seen here taking off. The car on the runway will recover the wing-tip wheels which are used only on takeoff (see arrows top picture). On landing there are wing-tip skid plates. The U-2 was on static display in AeroShell Square, and can be seen in the bottom picture (see arrow top left) and while roped off to keep spectators back from the plane itself, it was an impressive plane. An earlier model flown by Gary Powers was shot down in Russia in 1960. See page 81 for a picture of the wreckage. The U-2 is still used for intelligence gathering missions.

The AirVenture Seaplane Base, located on the west shore of Lake Winnebago, becomes the destination for those who prefer to "splash-in." Located about five miles from Wittman Regional Airport, almost 150 planes will make it their home for the week. There is a shuttle bus service between the two. It is a favorite attraction for those interested in water-based aviation.

Craig VanderKolk–EAA

Craig VanderKolk–EAA

Author Photo

Boeing uses the Dream Lifter to transport aircraft sub-assemblies between factories.

Jim Koepnick–EAA

The Concorde was a frequent visitor to AirVenture, and provided sightseeing rides.

The Ultralight runway is between the two arrows. They have their own traffic pattern and operate even when there is traffic on the main north-south runway.

Jim Raeder–EAA

Mike Steineke–EAA

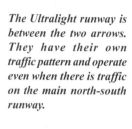

Jim Raeder–EAA

Jim Koepnick–EAA

EAA's Headquarters, Museum, and Pioneer Airport.

The top aerial view shows the 12 dedicated educational forum buildings. More than 500 speakers will make hour-long presentations starting at 8:30 a.m. to 6 p.m, and will continue for the entire week. The forum buildings vary in size. The bottom picture is of the largest building. The sides are open recognizing the hot Wisconsin summers. Nowhere else in the world can a pilot find such a concentration of aviation expertise.

Jim Koepnick—EAA

A night view of the EAA Headquarters, Museum, and front pond.

Author Photo

A full-scale replica of SpaceShipOne which rocketed into history by becoming the first private manned spacecraft to exceed an altitude of 328,000 feet twice within the span of a 14 day period, thus claiming the ten million dollar Ansari X-Prize.

Notes on Full-Page Folio Color Pictures

This complete aerial view of AirVenture was taken look-ing to the east. The water at the top of the picture is Lake Winnebago, a thirty-mile long lake. If you look closely you will see aircraft parked on the west side of runway 18/36, and on both sides of 9/27. Pioneer Air-port and the Ultralight runways are clearly visible. Pedestrian trams oper-ate continuously along the major routes. (Photo by Jim Koepnick-EAA)

This view of SpaceshipOne, riding on the top of its mother ship, White Night, was taken at AirVenture 2005. On October 4, 2004, SpaceShipOne rocketed into history, becoming the first private manned spacecraft to exceed an altitude of 328,000 feet twice within the span of 14 days, thus claiming the ten million dollar Ansari X-Prize. Shortly after this picture was taken the White Night carried Spaceship One to Washington, D.C. to be placed in the Smithsonian Air and Space Museum. (Photo by Jim Koepnick-EAA)

Airplane #7: 1975 Cessna T210L, 6-seat, turbocharged Continental 310-horsepower, retractable landing gear, optimum altitude 25,000 feet, 215 mph at that altitude, purchased September, 1975, sold October, 2003, Flown 3,998 hours. This plane set an FAI speed record for its weight category from San Francisco to Washington, D.C. (11 hours 8 minutes) in 1977 and "highest altitude in level flight" record of 32,420 feet in 1978. See chapters 17 and 18. Our children grew up with this plane being part of the family.

Over the 28 years of ownership of my Cessna T210, the instrument panel was upgraded with the latest avionics four or five times. This picture was taken in 2003, shortly before I sold the plane. It looks complicated, and it was. There were a total of 273 knob positions, switches, warning lights, controls, as well as both analog and digital information on instruments. I not only had to know what each was for, but also be able to instantly respond as appropriate to the displayed information.

Airplane #1: 1946 Cessna 140, Continental 85-horsepower, 101 mph, 2-seat side-by-side, purchased March, 1955, sold September, 1956. Flown 432 hours.

Airplane #2: 1951 Cessna 170A, Continental 145-horsepower, 120 mph, 4-seat, purchased September, 1956, sold February, 1959. Flown 471 hours.

Airplane #3: Aeronca 7AC "Champ," Continental 65-horsepower, 80 mph, 2-seats in tantum, purchased May 1963, sold October 1963. Flown 170 hours. Inge soloed in this plane. I learned to fly in a similar plane in northern Maine, 1955.

Airplane #4: Luscombe 8A, Continental 65-horsepower, 90 mph, 2-seats side-by-side, purchased October, 1963, sold July, 1967. Flown 428 hours. Inge got her private license in this plane.

Airplane #5: Cessna 172, Continental 145-horsepower, 124 mph, 4-seats, purchased July, 1967, sold March, 1969. Flown 251 hours.

Airplane #6: Cessna 182, Continental 230-horsepower, 156 mph, 4-seats, purchased September 1972, sold September 1975. Flown 562 hours.

Airplane #8: 1955 Mooney M-18C-55, Continental 65-horsepower, retractable landing gear, 120 mph, one-seat, purchased December, 1995, sold June, 2006. Flown 530 hours. Restored, 2003. "Best of Class, less than 80 hp" AirVenture, 2003.

Airplane #9: 2006 Tecnam Bravo, Light Sport Aircraft, Rotax 95-horsepower, 135 mph, seat side-by-side, purchased March, 2006, sold May, 2009. Flown 180 hours.

32

Emergency Landing at Madison
October, 2002

It was raining that Thursday morning in Milwaukee as Inge and I prepared to start the 1,750 mile trip to our home on Orcas Island, Washington. Not hard rain, but enough to make you wet if you stood out in it for more than a few minutes. The ceiling was a ragged seven or eight hundred feet, visibility one to two miles, and the forecast was for pretty much the same conditions for the first half of the flight to Pierre, South Dakota, our first refueling stop.

It was our last day of flying on a long, two-week trip that had started in Waco, Texas. From there we had flown to Champaign, Illinois for two days of intensive recurrent instrument training, and then on to Baltimore, Maryland, to visit my Mother. From Baltimore we had flown the long way to Shreveport, Louisiana. I call it the long way because we had to stay north of a hurricane that had come ashore in Louisiana earlier in the day and was itself proceeding on a northeasterly course. Instead of going directly, we crossed the mid-section of the country before turning south on the west side of the hurricane. From Shreveport we had flown to Milwaukee to attend an EAA board meeting.

Alternator Failure

We had arrived at General Billy Mitchell International Airport in Milwaukee, Wisconsin, Tuesday afternoon. About fifteen minutes be-

fore landing, a warning light indicated that one of the internal compo-
nents in the alternator had failed, and that the alternator was in danger
of complete failure within the next several flight hours. Upon landing,
my first concern had been to arrange for the alternator to be replaced,
which I did. I attended a meeting the following day at the airport hotel,
but in the middle of the afternoon I excused myself to make sure the
alternator had been replaced, and the plane was ready for flight. It was.
I checked the oil level, added a quart, and then returned to the meeting.
The mechanic promised to have the plane brought up to the Executive
Terminal the next morning for our return flight to Orcas Island.

Preflight

As I said, it was raining, and I was in a hurry. We had a long day
ahead of us if we were to get home before dark. While the airport on
Orcas had runway lights, I had stopped flying at night when we moved
to Orcas in the 1990s. There are mountains on Orcas that rise to 2,600
feet, and only three miles from the Orcas Airport. On a dark night that
can be deadly.

The preflight was routine except that I didn't check the oil level. I
had done so the previous afternoon, and I had added a quart. I was in a
hurry, and it was raining.

Flight Misgivings

We took off uneventfully, climbed to our cruising altitude of eight
thousand feet, and proceeded westward in clouds and light rain. The
outside temperature was well above freezing, the air was smooth, and
the autopilot was flying the plane on a great circle route to Pierre,
South Dakota.

At first it was perfectly routine. Soon something didn't seem quite
right. I saw very tiny droplets on the windshield, pretty much what
you would expect when flying in light rain. The droplets are small
because the propeller is in front of the windshield and its force, plus
the 180 miles per hour the plane was moving, would break up the
biggest raindrops into small droplets.

I kept looking at the tiny drops. They did not seem to be acting the
way rain droplets usually act. I had flown this plane for twenty-seven

years through lots of rain. I can't explain what it was that made me uneasy. Perhaps the droplets did not run together or off the windshield the way rain normally does. Then I asked myself: Could they be oil droplets, not water? The droplets seemed too small for oil, and the droplets appeared clear, not brown like oil. But there was still a doubt. Over the years I have learned to trust my instincts. No matter what was making me uneasy, it was time to get on the ground.

Get On the Ground

Landing when the weather is IFR is not always as easy as it may sound. First you have to find an airport with an instrument approach. Then you have to make sure that the weather is above minimums. Ideally, you want to choose an airport with an ILS landing system and approach control, but you don't always have that option.

By this time we were getting close to Madison, Wisconsin, seventy miles west of Milwaukee. While I had never landed at Madison, I knew they had an ILS and approach control. To check the weather, I located their approach chart (see next page) and found the frequency for their recorded weather.

Madison Dane County Regional Airport, ceiling six hundred feet, visibility two miles, light rain, winds zero-three-zero at five.

Good. I needed at least 200 feet and half a mile, so the approach should not be tight. It was time to let the Chicago Air Traffic Control Center know I had a problem and needed to land.

N210MG   Chicago Center, November two ten mike golf. We are four miles east of Madison and may be having an engine problem. We need expedited handling for an approach to Madison.

Chicago Center Roger two ten mike golf. You are cleared to descend to six thousand feet. Turn left heading one eight zero. Contact Madison Approach on frequency 124.0.

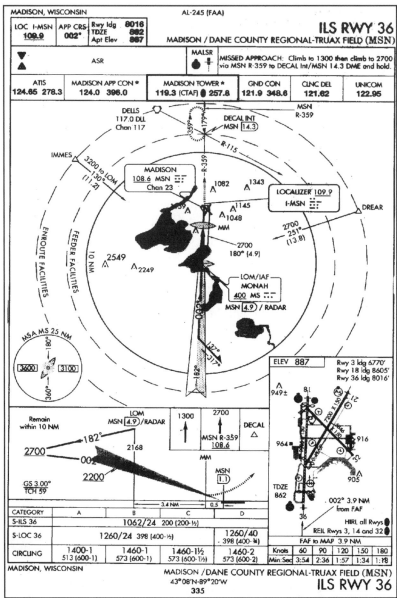

We carried approach plates for the entire United States. There are more than 10,000 plates and they are bound in books. In an emergency I had to be able to locate the correct approach plate, while still flying the airplane, communicating, and dealing with the emergency. I then had to absorb key information on the approach plate. Here is the Madison plate. The landing was routine, the pressure was intense.

N210MG	Madison Approach, November two ten mike golf with you, descending to six thousand, turning to heading one eight zero. Requesting lower. We want to remain within three miles of the airport in case we have an engine problem.
Madison	Roger two ten mike golf. Descend pilot's discretion to two thousand seven hundred. Expect vector to ILS runway three-six. Are you declaring an emergency?

I told Madison Approach "negative." The engine seemed to be running fine and I still did not know if there was oil on the windshield. From that point on everything worked as it should. We were vectored to the ILS, close in, and made an uneventful landing. Taxiing in, we still did not know what the problem was.

The Answer

We pulled up to Wisconsin Aviation, the local FBO. When I opened the pilot-side door and looked at the left side of the plane, I was shocked. The side of the plane from the front of the cowling back almost to the tail was covered with oil—not tiny droplets of oil, but a thick coating. It looked at first glance as if we had lost all ten quarts of our oil. It turned out only to be four quarts, but even so it was a mess.

What had happened? Pilot error. After I had put the quart of oil in the top of the engine the previous afternoon in Milwaukee, I either had not put the oil cap back on, or had not screwed it tightly. The cap is secured to the engine by a short metal chain, and when I looked into the engine compartment, the cap was off, and hanging on the chain. It is hard to believe, but the airflow over this open neck had created a vacuum that literally sucked the oil out of the engine. Once the oil was sucked out, it was forced out of the engine compartment where the cowling attaches to the plane. I would have expected the oil to show up first on the windshield, but, in fact, instead of coming out at the top of the cowling, it came out of the side where it could not be seen in flight.

Wisconsin Aviation's mechanics were a big help. First they cleaned both the engine compartment and the side of the plane. Then they carefully checked the amount of oil remaining to determine if the engine had enough oil to have escaped damage. They checked several other things and, indeed, concluded the engine was undamaged. The pilot's ego, however, certainly was.

What If?

What would have happened if we had not landed but continued on toward Pierre? It is hard to say. The engine could have run safely on the five quarts left in the engine, but still more oil might have been sucked out. Some have suggested that we had probably already lost all the oil we were going to lose since the air flowing over the open neck can only create a limited vacuum (venturi effect). The more oil that has already been sucked out, the more suction is required to suck out the rest. Others have said they didn't see how we could have lost as much oil as we did.

Two hours later, we took off for Pierre, tired, wiser, and deflated. We spent the night in Billings, Montana instead of making it all the way home.

Reflection

I always review my performance after a flight in an effort to learn from my mistakes. On this flight I was, of course, critical of my pre-flight inspection. If an accident had resulted, the NTSB would have clearly said the problem was "pilot error."

At the same time, I gave myself a "star" for my decisiveness in taking action once I sensed there was a problem. I certainly did not know that I was seeing very tiny oil droplets but something looked odd, so, in the absence of knowing, I did what had been drummed into me over fifty years of flying. I got on the ground as quickly as I could and let both Chicago Center and Madison Approach know that I needed expedited handling. It was probably only ten minutes from my deci-sion to land, to touching down, but they were intense minutes.

If I had been wrong and there had been nothing amiss, I would not have been embarrassed. My job as pilot was to minimize risk, which I had done.

One final note. It is a good thing I did not have any way of seeing what the side of the plane looked like while flying. I would probably have had a heart attack.

33

Decision Time
April 23, 2003

Every mature pilot is aware of the vulnerability of his license to fly. He may have great piloting skills, many hours of flight, and many past aeronautical achievements, and he may hold as many ratings as the FAA issues, yet these can be but memories if he loses his FAA medical certificate. Without a medical certificate his license to fly is not valid.

Even with a valid medical certificate, a pilot before each flight must confirm to himself that he is physically and mentally fit to make the flight safely. Only the pilot can make this determination, although in the event of an accident, the FAA may second guess the pilot if medical incapacity appears to have been a factor.

Maturity Takes A Toll

Our physical capabilities, reaction times, and mental acuity deteriorate as we age. Most pilots recognize that by the time they are ninety years old they should not be flying under the same demanding conditions they did when in their twenties. When, then, should a pilot start to pull back and fly only under less demanding circumstances, or perhaps stop flying altogether? When is the magic date?

Alas, there are no rules of thumb. The FAA mandates that airline pilots retire at a specific age, but even then they can continue to fly as commercial or private pilots. Private pilots face no mandatory retirement date as long as they can pass their FAA physicals and biennial flight reviews. For some, failing to pass their medical examination settles the question. Given a heart attack or other serious illness, they can be pretty sure that they will have trouble getting the FAA doctors to say they can fly.

Many decades ago I was told by an older pilot that I didn't have to worry about knowing when the time had come to pull back from flying under demanding situations. If I became an old pilot, it would be because I had become very pragmatic in my flying, and had learned that the laws of physics and gravity that govern flight make no exceptions and accept no excuses. That same pragmatic discipline would tell me when to quit.

Decision Time

I made my decision at 9:30 a.m. on the morning of April 23, 2003. I was not quite seventy at the time. I was flying in good VFR conditions about twenty-five miles south of Oshkosh, Wisconsin. The details are not important but the gist was that I was not "connecting the dots." I was in good weather, there was no crisis, and eventually I did process all of the information available to me. But I realized that if I had been on final, with an approach to minimums—say, 200 feet and-a-half mile—I might have faced disaster.

What do I mean by "connecting the dots?" On my Cessna T210, I had a total of 273 knobs, toggle switches, push buttons, warning lights, instrument displays, and circuit breakers. It was my job to process what my instruments and signal lights were telling me, and then react by taking the appropriate action. On top of that, I had to listen for my radio call sign, and respond correctly when instructed to do so. Not connecting the dots was failure to react in a coordinated manner to all of this data.

As I have said before, I always made it a practice after every flight to ask myself the question: "how could I have performed that flight more professionally?" Over the previous year or so I had caught myself in more than the usual number of situations where I had given myself a low score. Fortunately in each instance I was either in good weather or I managed to salvage the situation before it got out of hand.

In each of these incidents the only embarrassment was to my ego—I knew what I had done or not done. No one else did. But I was the one that counted.

That April morning I made an instant decision. I would no longer fly under IFR conditions. From then on I would fly only in good weather.

The irony was that my flight that morning was from Champaign, Illinois, where I had just completed two days of recurrent IFR training, using sophisticated simulators that fully tested my flying skill. I had come through that annual experience with a log book endorsement stating that I had met all the FAA requirements for IFR flight, and assurance of the instructors that I was safe to fly for another year. At 9:30 that morning I concluded otherwise.

Rational vs. Emotional Decision

I made a rational decision quickly and firmly. But like most people, I have an emotional side to me, too. I knew that my emotional side would rationalize that I was still capable and could fly safely under IFR conditions. The training I had just had testified to that. But I knew that as long as I continued to own N210MG my emotional side would challenge the rational side of me. N210MG was meant to be flown long distances under moderate IFR conditions, at high altitude. I knew I would have to sell this plane.

That morning I was going to Oshkosh to attend a board meeting. I used that occasion to ask Tom Poberezny, President of EAA and one of the statesmen of general aviation, whom he would recommend to handle the sale of N210MG. He recommended Courtesy Aircraft in Rockford, Illinois. I made the initial call to them that same day and they agreed to sell N210MG for me.

I did fly back to Orcas after the board meeting, but I made only one more flight after getting home. I had asked Courtesy to send a pilot to pick up the plane, and my final flight was to Seattle to pick up the ferry pilot who would take the plane to Rockford for sale. I knew that I had to get N210MG out of my sight; but it was like losing a child after twenty-eight years. It was a very sad event.

I still had another plane, one that could be flown only in good weather—my Mooney Mite. Having the Mite helped me in the healing process.

N210MG about to take off with the ferry pilot at the controls. I took this picture with tears running down my face.

It has been more than six years now since I saw N210MG take off from Orcas Island for the last time. I still miss that beautiful plane, and the wonderful times we had as a family with it. On many occasions since, I wished I still had N210MG.

But I know that it was the right decision, even though there are tears in my eyes as I write this.

34

A New
Light Sport Aircraft

Life is full of surprises and turning points. A significant turning point for me took place at 2:25 p.m., on Father's Day, June 19, 2005. That was the moment I realized I was no longer a youth of nineteen, but a man who had aged as the years rolled past.

I was in our utility room that Sunday afternoon, and noted that our water softener was getting low on salt. Without giving it a thought, I reached over to the side of the softener, twisting my body to the right, and picked up a forty-pound bag of salt. I had lifted it about halfway up to the top of the softener when an excruciating pain shot through my left leg just below the knee.

The subsequent details are not terribly important except to note that I have had two back operations and still have some residual back pain. Sitting and moderate walking has not been a problem since the first surgery, so my flying continued until November, 2008.

FAA Medical Implications

As a private pilot, I am required to hold a "third class" medical certificate which must be renewed every two years. I had been sailing through the FAA medical examinations for more then fifty years without any real concern. Now, suddenly, there was a cloud on the horizon. I did not think this back injury would disqualify me at the time of my

405

next medical in 2007, but I could not be sure. More to the point, my back injury reminded me that I could no longer assume that I would be able to pass these physicals as I grew "more mature."

I was now face-to-face with every pilot's biggest concern after age fifty—passing the bureaucratic FAA medical where even the simplest medical problem can potentially ground you.

All of this is by way of background.

New Category: Light Sport Aircraft

In mid-2004, the FAA established a new category of airplane—the "Light Sport Aircraft" and the related new pilot license, the "Sport Pilot." The purpose of this new category was to address the rising cost and complexity of modern small aircraft. Both factors were making it increasingly difficult to attract young people into flying for recreational purposes.

Over the fifty years I have been flying I have seen an immense increase in aircraft complexity and capability, but these new aircraft have also become prohibitively expensive and required skills far beyond those required to fly a simple airplane like the famed J-3 Piper Cub, or even my Cessna 140. The FAA, at the urging of the Experimental Aircraft Association (EAA), concluded that what was needed was a category of airplane that was simple to fly and did not require all the skills now required for someone to get a private pilot's certificate. Thus was born the concept of a Light Sport Aircraft and a Sport Pilot Certificate, and with it, a change in medical certification.

The FAA defines a Light Sport Aircaft as an aircraft that meets very specific standards to ensure that it is easy to fly and requires only moderate training. The plane is limited to two-seats, a maximum gross weight on takeoff of 1,320 pounds, a maximum speed of 120 nautical (138 statute) miles per hour, and a maximum stall speed of 45 nautical (51 statute) miles per hour. In addition, the plane cannot have either retractable landing gear or a controllable pitch propeller. The plane cannot be used for commercial purposes, other than for flight instruction.

The pilot holding only a Sport Pilot's License can fly only a Light Sport Aircaft, is limited to daytime VFR flying, and is not allowed to fly into certain high-density airports and airspace. If the sport pilot takes further instruction after getting his Sport Pilot's License, certain of these limitations can be eliminated with an instructor's endorsement.

Sport pilots can upgrade their skills and obtain private, commercial or even airline transport pilot's licenses. All of their flight experience in Light Sport Aircaft can be used to meet the requirements of these higher license ratings.

It is intended that this category of license be an entirely new entry-level license to encourage young people to get into aviation. The minimum flight time before being issued this license is only twenty hours which compares to a forty-hour requirement for a private license. Both numbers are the minimum and most student pilots actually have 25 percent or more time when they take their flight check ride.

Driver's License Medical

Someone already holding a private license can fly a Light Sport Aircraft without any paperwork. Accordingly, I am automatically entitled to fly one of these new aircraft, and if the airplane were appropriately equipped, I could fly it anywhere I wanted within the United States, with only a few restrictions.

Why would a private pilot want to fly a Light Sport Aircraft? For several reasons, but for us "maturing" pilots, the major reason is that no FAA medical certificate is required. The only medical requirement is that the pilot have a valid driver's license, and that before each flight he self-certifies that he is medically qualified. These regulations solve the problem for "maturing" pilots such as myself who are concerned with passing an FAA third-class medical examination.

Some have questioned whether this is prudent. What is to keep a pilot from flying when he or she is incapacitated? Self-interest. The pilot knows that he

Here is my "light sport aircraft medical certificate." I still have to self-certify that I am medically fit before each flight, but I am no longer required to have FAA medical examinations.

will be the first person to arrive at the scene of an accident. That is a powerful motivator, and one that applies even if the pilot has an FAA medical certificate. Further, medical issues seldom are the major factor in aircraft accidents, and even when they are, the medical causes are not likely to have been identified in an FAA medical examination. There is also a precedent. Glider pilots have never been required to have an FAA medical examination, although all glider accidents are investigated by both the NTSB and the FAA.

Purchase of N144MG

Unfortunately, my Mooney Mite was not qualified as a Light Sport Aircaft because it had retractable landing gear. If I wanted to avoid future FAA medical issues I needed to purchase a Light Sport Aircraft.

In March, 2006, I did so. I purchased a new Light Sport Aircraft made in Naples, Italy by Costruzioni Aeronautiche Tecnam (referred to as Tecnam). This beautiful two-seat airplane flies at 115 nautical (132 statute) miles per hour, carries almost five hours of fuel, and stalls at only 35 nautical (40 statute) miles per hour with full flaps. It is a high wing airplane and weighs, empty, only 760 pounds, only about two hundred pounds more than my single-seat Mooney Mite.

A Modern Engine

Perhaps the most unusual aspect of this Tecnam plane is that it has an entirely new type of aircraft engine. The Rotax engine, made in Austria, is a light, modern, four-cycle aircraft engine that incorporates modern automobile engine technology of the 1990s. It has dual electronic ignition, the cylinder heads are water-cooled, and the balance of the engine is air-cooled. Existing aviation engines incorporate 1930s technology. It is also a lightweight engine, approximately half that of existing engines of the same horsepower. Most of the Light Sport Aircaft manufacturers are using this engine.

Why does this engine have modern technology whereas almost all other aircraft engines are built with ancient technology? It is because the FAA has delegated to the manufacturers of a Light Sport Aircraft, Tecnam in my case, responsibility for certifying the airworthiness of both their airplane and the engine it uses. By contrast, all other catego-

The Rotax 912 ULS engine is used in most of the Light Sport Aircaft. It produces 95 horsepower, and uses 1990s automobile technology. Designed to run on auto gas, it will also run on 100 low-lead aviation fuel. One of the biggest advantages of this engine compared to traditional aviation engines of the same horsepower is that it weights only 120 pounds, about half the weight of a Continental 0-200 engine. With an FAA mandated maximum gross weight on takeoff of 1,320 pounds, the lighter engine increases the useful load.

ries of aircraft engines have to conform to very specific and detailed standards established by the FAA specifications. Meeting these FAA specifications is both time consuming and expensive. That is why the delegation of that responsibility to the Light Sport Aircaft manufacturer is such a major breakthrough. It cuts through the bureaucratic red tape and places the responsibility where it belongs, on the people making and selling the aircraft instead of on the FAA.

This is an oversimplification. Actually the Light Aircraft Manufacturers Association (LAMA), an association of the Light Sport Aircaft manufacturers, working with the FAA, has created broad standards to which each of the individual manufacturers must adhere. The FAA has reviewed these broad standards and said that planes meeting these standards can be certified as "airworthy" by the manufacturers themselves. It is up to LAMA—rather than the FAA—to police adherence to these

N144MG on the tarmac on Orcas Island after its flight from Atlanta. A high-wing aircraft without wing struts, it has a fixed landing gear and seats two people. An all-metal aircraft, its empty weight is 760 pounds as equipped. It carries 26.4 gallons of fuel and burns about 5.3 gallons an hour. It uses a water/air cooled Rotax engine, which turns at 5,000 rpm. The propeller is geared down to about 2200 rpm.

standards. Further, any modification that an individual owner wants to make to his Light Sport Aircaft must be approved by the manufacturer, and not by the FAA.

Avionics Installation

Each purchaser decides what avionics and instruments he wants. If the plane were a standard category airplane, the pilot would have to specify FAA-approved equipment, referred to as TSOed equipment. But for Light Sport Aircaft the FAA is not involved since the aircraft manufacturer is the only party that has to approve such equipment. The result was that I was able to install a very sophisticated flight instrument referred to as an EFIS—electronic flight information system. Essentially it is a modern electronic flat screen which shows a wealth of information that previously would have required many sepa-

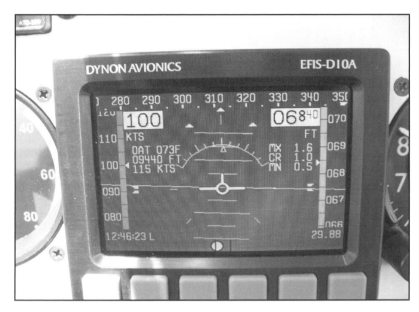

This is the EFIS installed in N144MG. The display is a color monitor and very easy to read. When I took this picture I was at 6,840 feet, traveling at an indicated airspeed of 100 kts (112 mph) but a true airspeed of 115 kts (129 mph) on a heading of 312 degrees. It also incorporates an artificial horizon, and a turn and bank without the need for old-fashioned gyros.

rate instruments. Look at all the information it provides in the illustrations on pages 412 and 413.

This type of equipment is available for standard category aircraft but costs in the neighborhood of ten thousand dollars, or more. My unit, installed, was less than three thousand dollars.

I also had a single-axis autopilot installed. This computer-controlled autopilot receives instructions from flight plan information in the GPS navigation receiver. As with the EFIS, the autopilot is state-of-the-art electronics and has bypassed FAA bureaucratic approval. As a result it was modestly priced, again, at less than three thousand dollars installed. A similar but FAA-approved single axis autopilot for a standard airplane with similar capabilities would cost several times that amount.

The plane also has a standard transponder, altitude encoder, intercom, and traffic advisory receiver. In short, N144MG came with a lot of fine equipment.

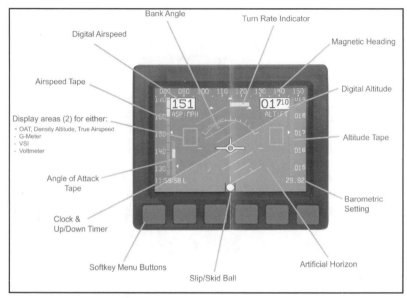

The illustration above shows all the information that can be displayed. It is worth studying because virtually everything the pilot needs to fly either VFR or IFR is on this single four-inch screen other than engine and avionic information. The installed cost was less than $3,000 in 2006, but it was not FAA approved so I could not have installed it in any of the other airplanes I have owned.

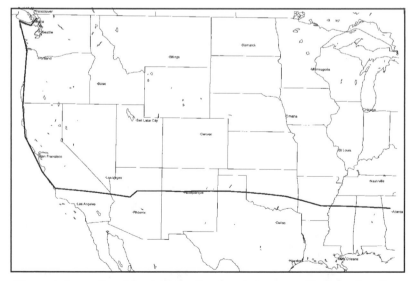

The route home. I could not fly the direct route because of bad weather. From south of San Francisco until I got to Orcas I flew just offshore.

This picture of the panel was taken while flying at 12,380 feet en route to Oshkosh. The large, center screen display is the plane's GPS which has been programmed with the route to Oshkosh. Immediately below this display are the transmitter and transponder. The autopilot control head is located below the EFIS. The rectangular unit above the airspeed indicator is a unit that warns of nearby aircraft.

Delivery in Georgia

As I mentioned, the plane was manufactured in Naples, Italy, and first flown by Tecnam's test pilot there. The wings were then removed and the airplane put in a forty-foot container (actually they were able to put two planes into each container), and then sent by ship to Savannah, Georgia. Once inspected by Customs and Homeland Security, the container was trucked to Atlanta. The Tecnam importer had the wings, control cables, and avionics installed, and the plane test flown and inspected by the FAA. It was then my aircraft.

I traveled to Atlanta where I received extensive indoctrination and about five or six hours of flight instruction over a three-day period before I was certified as competent to fly the plane.

Then came the long trip back to Orcas Island. It was mid-March with plenty of snow and storms on the direct route. I chose to stay south and flew straight west through Oklahoma, northern Texas, New Mexico, and Arizona to the coast south of Santa Barbara, California. The weather over the mountains of northern California was lousy, so I flew just offshore up the Pacific coast to the Canadian border, turned right and flew over the Strait of Juan de Fuca for about seventy-five miles until I reached Orcas. It took 28 flying hours and about a week to make this trip. By the time I reached Orcas, I felt comfortable with N144MG.

Two months later I experienced my first in-flight, total engine failure, described in the next chapter.

35

Then There Was Silence!
An Engine Failure
May 18, 2006

I decided to fly from Orcas to Porterville, California, to attend the annual Mooney Mite get-together of .West Coast owners, all of whom were friends. I intended to fly my new Tecnam Light Sport Aircraft to show it off, but the plane never quite made it to Porterville.

It is about nine hundred miles from Orcas to Porterville and the direct route goes through the mountains of southern Oregon and northern California to the Sacramento Valley. I had another pilot friend with me, Dave Rutherford of Abbotsford, British Columbia. The flight went well until just south of Mt. Shasta in northern California. We were at 8,500 feet and suddenly I felt a slight vibration in the engine of a kind I had never felt before. It lasted only a few seconds, but Dave also felt it. It was not terribly pronounced and would have been easy to miss. But since I had flown for fifty-plus years, my ears were sensitive to new sounds, and this slight vibration was certainly new to me.

Precautionary Landing #1

When we felt this vibration, we were about forty miles from Redding, California which is just south of the mountains at the north end of the Sacramento Valley. I called Redding Tower and said we were going to make a precautionary landing because of the vibration.

415

We stayed at 8,500 feet until we were close enough to glide to the airport in the event that the engine were to stop. It didn't, and we landed uneventfully.

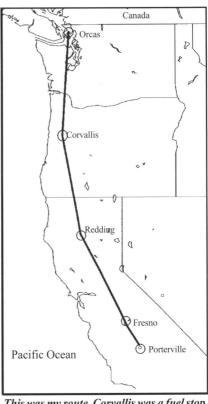

The shop manager at the Jet Center FBO carefully inspected the engine, removed the spark plugs, and looked for any sign of a problem. He could not see any, although he pointed out he had not worked on this type of engine before. I called Geoff Schussler, my mechanic on Orcas, to see if he had any suggestions. I was carrying four spare spark plugs with me and he suggested that they be substituted for the lower plugs in each cylinder even though the existing plugs looked fine. I then ran the engine on the ground for about 15 minutes and there was no sign of a vibration. At that point we decided to continue south.

This was my route. Corvallis was a fuel stop. Redding and Fresno were precautionary landings. The next day I started for home because I was uncomfortable with the way the plane was behaving, and I also wanted to get ahead of the weekend weather.

Precautionary Landing #2

Everything went smoothly for the next two hours. Then I noticed that the oil pressure gauge showed the oil pressure needle "pinging" at the very top, high end of the scale. The oil temperature was well within the "green," the engine was running smoothly, and there were no vibrations or other abnormalities. This appeared to be a problem with the oil pressure gauge itself. Still, this had not happened before, and coming on the heels of the earlier vibration, I decided we needed to get back on the ground.

At this point, we were about thirty miles from the Fresno, California airport, a much larger airport than Redding with lots of airline and business jet traffic. I called the tower and, as at Redding, said we needed to make a precautionary landing. Again, we did so, without incident but I was pleased to see that the airport emergency fire trucks had been alerted and were alongside the runway as we landed. They followed us to the parking ramp where we shut down the engine.

Once the engine was shut down, the oil pressure should have gone to zero, but it stayed at the high end of the scale. That suggested we had a defective gauge since there could be no oil pressure when the engine was not running. I again called Geoff Schussler and he confirmed my "gauge problem" conclusion.

By this time it was 6 p.m., and the maintenance shop was closed. We decided to call it a day. Unfortunately, there were no hotel rooms available in Fresno because it was Graduation Weekend. Since we had reservations in Porterville which was only sixty miles further south, I decided to leave the plane in Fresno and drive to Porterville. That way, Dave would at least have arrived in Porterville and could join the group. I could sort out the plane problems the next day.

Back to Fresno

Next morning I left Dave in Porterville and drove back to Fresno, where I got the service manager of the FBO maintenance shop to look at the engine. He agreed with my assessment that it was probably a faulty gauge and not something more serious. That appeared to be confirmed when he found a loose wire on the oil pressure "sending" unit which provides input to the oil pressure gauge in the cockpit. Sure enough, after he reattached the wire, the gauge behaved properly.

After running the engine for ten or fifteen minutes on the ground I concluded that this wire had been the problem and that the airplane was now airworthy. However, I had been traumatized the previous day by having two precautionary landings. I had made only a dozen precautionary landings in my fifty-plus years of flying, and I felt uneasy flying on to Porterville because I still had no answers to the "why" of these two incidents. Call it intuition.

It was now Thursday noon and the weather forecast for the weekend suggested the weather would be marginal over the mountains on the scheduled return flight to Orcas on Saturday. Having learned to listen to my intuition, I decided to start north towards home while the weather was good. I would not be able to get all the way home, but at least I could fly north of the mountains, probably to Eugene or Corvallis, Oregon.

There was another factor. I felt uncomfortable flying with a passenger, and possibly putting him at risk. I called Porterville and left word for Dave that I was headed home and that he would have to find his own way back.

I left Fresno at noon and my uneasiness became justified about an hour-and-a-half later.

Smoke In The Cabin!

I was flying north, on the direct route from Fresno to Redding at 6,500 feet. This route took me over the rocky foothills of the Sierra Nevada Mountains, which paralleled my course. The sky was clear and visibility was ten or fifteen miles. I was northeast of Sacramento, and southeast of Beale AFB, when at about 1:20 p.m., light smoke started seeping into the cockpit from the engine compartment. The engine was running smoothly but the oil pressure gauge needle was again "pinging" at the high end of the scale. After about ten seconds of disbelief, I realized that I needed to get on the ground quickly. An in-flight fire is one of a pilot's worst fears.

The rock-strewn foothills below me were not suitable for an off-field landing. An attempted landing would almost certainly result in a non-survivable crash. I immediately turned west toward what looked like farmland, then switched to the emergency frequency and broadcast a "MAYDAY" in the blind. I don't know which facility responded––perhaps it was Sacramento Approach—but whoever it was, they responded immediately. "Mayday" calls galvanize attention. I advised them that I had smoke in the cockpit and very high oil pressure and expected a total engine failure shortly. Just as I told them this, the engine shuddered for perhaps two seconds, and the prop stopped!

The engine had "seized!"

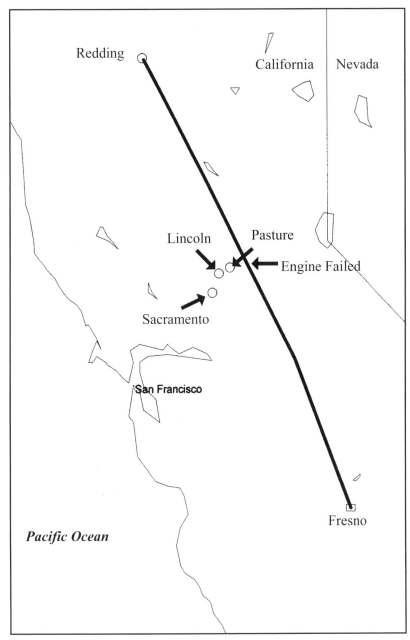

This was the route north from Fresno. The engine failed about an hour and-a-half into the flight over the foothills of the Sierra Nevada Mountains.

And Then There Was Silence!

I told the controller. He asked me where I was and I gave a very general description (northeast of Sacramento). He had me enter the emergency code in my transponder (7700), and almost immediately, confirmed they had radar contact with me.

I was on my own. The controllers could do nothing until after I had landed, wherever that might be. My first priority was to fly the airplane, which had become a glider.

I trimmed the plane to glide at 70 miles per hour, the speed that is most efficient in terms of distance traveled when you have no power. I believe my descent rate, once the plane slowed to that speed, was about 750 feet per minute. I noted on the GPS display that there were several airports pretty much ahead of me. Lincoln Airport turned out to be the closest but it looked too far away.

My mind is vague as to the details of the next several minutes, and who said what to whom. I know they had me switch frequencies. The smoke stopped shortly after the engine seized and I concentrated on finding a suitable field west of the rocky foothills to land on. I remember being told at one point that Lincoln Airport was only two miles ahead of me, but my responding that I could not make it, that I was already down to about 800 feet and lining up to land in what looked like a fairly flat field.

I used full flaps to both slow the plane and to lose altitude so I would not overshoot the field. On "final approach," I saw that there were about fifty cows under a grove of trees that I had not seen before, but I easily steered away from the cows. I landed at about 45 mph into a very light wind, and stopped in about 300 feet without any damage to the airplane. For all intents and purposes it was a routine landing. But I knew instinctively that the engine was "junk" without even having to look at it.

Safely On the Ground

Once I was on the ground I lost radio contact with the FAA controllers because aircraft radio transmissions travel along lines of sight. I assumed that other pilots flying in the area were likely monitoring my frequency so I radioed "in the blind" that I was down and OK, and to relay that information to the controllers. An unidentified voice said "Stay with the aircraft." I do not know whether that was a relayed message or not, but I had long ago learned that almost without exception the pilot should stay with a downed aircraft.

I inspected the outside of the plane and confirmed there was no damage. A few drops of oil dotted the windshield and streams of oil appeared on the passenger side of the aircraft, running from the cowling back toward the tail. There was oil on the belly and wheel pants, particularly on the nose wheel. Later, I found oil inside the belly of the cockpit under the two seats. The inside of the engine compartment had a lot of oil on the passenger side and some, but less, on the pilot side. It looked to me as if oil must have baked onto the exhaust pipe coming from the cylinders, and that was probably the source of the smoke.

About 50 cows occupied the pasture, mostly in the shade of the trees you see here. I came to a stop fairly close to them. This picture was taken from the front of the plane and the propeller is in the foreground.

There was loose hardware in the engine compartment towards the front of the engine near the oil radiator.

About 20 to 25 minutes later a helicopter circled high overhead and a couple of minutes after that a rescue convoy found me. The convoy consisted of four or five vehicles, including a fire engine and several police vehicles. There were also paramedics on the scene and I was later told that there was even a reporter from the local paper.

I assured the medical personnel that it had been a routine landing and that I was not hurt. About ten minutes after that, one of the men gave me a cell phone and said representatives of the National Transportation Safety Board (NTSB) and the FAA were on the phone. Once I had declared "MAYDAY" and it was obvious that the plane would not be landing at an airport, both the NTSB and the FAA were immediately notified; the NTSB, because they are responsible for accident investigations; and the FAA, because of their role in aviation. Technically, I could not move my aircraft until they were satisfied that the plane was not involved in a "reportable" accident. If it were a reportable accident, the plane could have been impounded to allow the NTSB to inspect the aircraft to determine the cause of the accident.

The NTSB official did the talking, asking what happened, and whether there was airplane damage or injuries. When I confirmed that there were no damages or injuries, he said the plane could be moved, that no paperwork needed to be filed, but to call a Brian Allen at the FAA office in Sacramento once the plane was relocated.

He also urged me to call Dennis James, who heads up an extremely efficient and professional small family business that relocates downed aircraft. He indicated that there are only a handful of such specialized companies in the entire United States and I was lucky to have had this failure in the Sacramento area where Dennis was located. I was able to reach Dennis on my cell phone and he agreed to help.

All of the vehicles left the area at about 2:30 except for Sheriff Deputy Crawford who stayed with me until the plane was relocated to the Lincoln Airport. We were not alone, however. As a curiosity, we attracted the approximately fifty cows in the pasture, but we could not let them get close to the fragile plane. I say "fragile" because one of these cows could do a lot of damage just brushing alongside the fuselage. I was sitting in Deputy Crawford's air-conditioned squad car (the temperature was in the 90s) and periodically he turned on his siren to chase the cows away. They didn't seem terribly intimidated, but they did slowly turn and walk away.

Relocation of the Aircraft

Dennis James and his team showed up at about 5 p.m. They were very professional. They arrived with a crane big enough to take the roof off of any good-sized house, and a flatbed trailer. After an hour of careful work, they hoisted the plane, complete with its wings still attached, and placed it at an angle on the flatbed trailer. They did everything in very slow motion to make sure they didn't damage the plane. They took the doors off both sides so their hoist straps would not damage the aircraft. The wheel covers were removed so that the wheels themselves could be tied down securely to the flatbed.

Then came the very slow movement of the flatbed trailer, with the plane strapped securely to it, along a narrow pasture farm road to the county road. At three places, the plane had to go between electrical poles that were located across from each other along this farm road

Here the plane is being carefully lifted onto a flatbed trailer and tightly secured.

As you can see, even at an angle the wingspan is wider than the distance between the electric pole on the right and the tower on the left. It took about 20 minutes to get the plane past this obstacle. There were two other places like this one, where I didn't see how we could get by, but these professionals did.

and the clearance between the two sides was less than the width of the wings. I didn't think it could be done—but I was wrong. They used the crane to lift the flatbed at the rear, and then turned it at an angle so that they could get first one wing past a pole, and then the other wing. They never made so much as a scratch on the plane.

Once they got to the county road, another squad car joined Deputy Crawford and they blocked the two-lane road from other traffic so that the plane and trailer could stay in the middle. Fortunately there was a route to the Lincoln Airport using back roads that had little traffic. It took two hours to travel approximately five miles from where the plane was secured on the flatbed to Lincoln airport. By that time it was getting dark.

One side note: At the Lincoln Airport the security fence was locked, and no one was around. This did not faze Dennis. Even if the gate was unlocked and could be opened, it was not wide enough to admit the plane. He had a simple solution. He hoisted the plane off the flatbed trailer, up and over the fence, and lowered it onto the tarmac on the other side. Dennis and another man were similarly hoisted over the fence. Then they took off the hoist and hand-pulled the plane to a secure area where they tied it down. So much for airport security.

The following evening, May 19, my mechanic, Geoff Schussler, flew down from Seattle on Alaska Airlines to personally inspect the engine and help determine the cause of the failure.

Broken Oil Line

It was not hard to determine the cause of the engine failure. An oil line had broken and the engine had been deprived of its lifeblood—oil. But what caused the oil line to break? Was something systemically wrong with either the engine or the airplane itself? Fortunately I can report emphatically, "no."

The airplane had come with a "Hobbs hour-meter" which is an electric clock-like device intended to record flight time of the aircraft. Normally it is connected in such a way that it starts recording when

Here the plane is being lifted over the security fence at Lincoln Airport.

the engine is running, and stops when the engine stops. This provides a record of the total usage of the engine which approximates flight time.

The Hobbs meter was installed differently on my aircraft at the factory. It was connected directly to the master electrical switch so that whenever battery power was turned on, the Hobbs meter recorded the time. If you wanted to turn on the navigation radio to enter a flight plan before you started the engine, the Hobbs meter would start recording flight time even though you were on the ground without the engine running. Since you need to keep track of engine and flight time primarily for purposes of required maintenance, the time recorded by my Hobbs meter would be inflated.

My mechanic had suggested hooking the Hobbs meter up to an oil pressure switch. When the engine was running, the oil pressure would turn the Hobbs meter on. This type of switch is easy to install, and I told him to do so.

Unfortunately it had been a faulty installation. The details are not important other than to note that it was installed in the wrong place and using the wrong type of fitting—one made of brass instead of steel. Brass is a soft metal and not as strong as steel. Eventually engine vibration caused it to break, which resulted in the loss of oil and the subsequent destruction of the engine.

I believe the initial vibration just north of Redding was the start of the sequence that eventually caused the brass fitting to fail. The wire to the gauge was broken in the same area, also due to the vibration.

Engine Replacement

The engine was clearly shot. There was a crack in the engine case where a connecting rod or something tried to break through the case as the engine seized. We did salvage the twin carburetors and both the oil and water radiators.

As I noted earlier in this chapter, the Rotax engine is unique and few aircraft mechanics have had experience with it. It was obvious that we were going to have to replace the engine but I didn't want just anybody to do it. Fortunately when I called Kerry Yunck—a Rotax guru at one of the few authorized Rotax overhaulers then in the U.S.––and told him what happened, he said he would travel from South

Florida to Lincoln and replace the engine personally. He suggested that I have Geoff Schussler, my mechanic, join him to help, and in that way Geoff would also get some first-hand experience with the engine. And that is what we chose to do. It was a two-day project. Geoff flew down on the airlines and, once the engine was installed, flew N144MG back to Orcas for me.

It was a full month before the plane was back in my hangar, but it came back with a new engine and not a scratch on the airplane.

Hindsight

In hindsight, looking at a sectional map in the comfort of my home, I saw that there had been a small airport fairly close to where the engine seized that was within easy gliding distance. At that time I was aware there was an airport fairly close, but did not know the details. Based on the terrain, I assumed it was a fairly short runway, although actually, it was 3,700 feet. But at the moment of decision, with smoke coming from the engine compartment, I could not know whether the smoke would increase or not. I also had every reason to believe there was a fire in the engine. Trying to land "dead-stick" on a relatively short runway on unknown terrain, while possibly being blinded by smoke, or oil on the windshield, seemed an imprudent choice. It would be too easy to either overshoot or undershoot the runway and end up crashing into rocky terrain with disastrous results.

It is always easy to second-guess decisions made under pressure, but I believe my decision to trust my life to what turned out to be a cow pasture was the right one. Certainly the outcome is hard to fault.

Luck Was Truly On My Side

On reflection, I was extremely lucky in many respects. First, I had plenty of altitude. If this flight had been on the weekend, I would likely have been flying much lower with relatively little time to select a suitable landing site. If I had been at 2,000 feet instead of 6,500 feet, I would have landed in the foothills instead of a level field. I was also lucky that the oil line failure occurred when it did, and not an hour or two later when I would have been over the Siskiyou mountains where there would be little chance of a successful landing. An hour earlier, I had been over very rocky terrain with no pastures or suitable terrain within gliding distance.

If I had landed anywhere other than near Sacramento I would not have been able to obtain the professional services of Dennis James and his relocation company. I have since learned that the relocation of aircraft usually incurs significant damage because most people neither know how to do it nor have the right equipment. I was also lucky that on my landing roll I did not encounter rocks, gullies, or even ruts. Such obstacles could have flipped the plane on its back and possibly caused a fire by fuel spilling from the wing fuel tanks.

If Dave Rutherford had been with me, his extra weight would have caused the plane to descend faster, shortening the distance the plane could glide. I would not have been able to get to the field on which I successfully landed.

If the failure had taken place near my home on Orcas Island, the outcome might have been truly chilling. Every landing and takeoff at Orcas takes place over very cold water, and a successful ditching is a long shot. A water ditching for a fixed-gear aircraft usually results in the plane being flipped over on its back and sinking rapidly.

If an engine failure was destined to occur, I could not have picked a better time or place. Yes, I did a good, but routine, job of maintaining control and landing the airplane once the engine quit, but it was truly luck that everything else was in my favor. I must be honest in saying that this experience traumatized me and awakened me to what can happen at any time to a pilot. Intellectually I have known that engine failures happen, but my fifty-plus years of flying without an engine failure had also blinded me to the possibility that such a thing could happen to an experienced, cautious pilot like me.

PART V

REFLECTIONS
2009

36

Managing Risk—Ice

The pilot's principal job is to manage risk, recognizing that even then, there are risks that cannot be fully managed. In this and the following two chapters I reflect on my fifty plus years of flying and offer some observations about managing risks. This chapter deals with the formation of ice in flight while flying IFR. This is not a definitive discussion. Others have written about ice in far more depth, but I want to give you the benefit of my own experience.

My Experience

Over the 28 years of ownership of my Cessna T210, I had perhaps a dozen encounters with ice conditions that could have been serious. I relate two of these here.

The first took place on a flight in 1979. I had been flying in clear skies from Washington, D.C., but there was a low cloud layer at my destination, Elkhart, Indiana. The weather was above minimums and I made an instrument approach. I descended into the cloud layer at 3,000 feet and unexpectedly started picking up ice. I was in icing conditions for less than five minutes, but in that time I picked up enough ice on a transmitting antenna on the top of the fuselage to cause the twelve inch high rod antenna to vibrate, and then to break off. Fortunately I had two transmitters, each with its own antenna. When I lost communication I switched over to the other radio.

After landing I found that the whole plane had been coated with ice in only five minutes, and I had no warning. Both points are important to remember—no warning, and very rapid ice build-up can occur.

Ice Capital of the United States

In May, 1983 Inge and I flew to Orcas Island in northern Washington State where, earlier in the year, we had purchased a lot for a future retirement home. In the following years we were to make many transcontinental trips to and from Orcas Island, located just a couple of miles south of the Canadian border, and just west of the Cascade Range of mountains. The Cascade Range is a hundred-mile-wide mountain range that stretches from Mt. Lassen in northern California to Canada. Our flight route passed just south of 10,775 foot Mt. Baker, located just fifty miles from Orcas Island. The portion of the Cascades north of Mt. Rainier is considered by pilots as the ice capital of the United States.

So what is so significant about these mountains? They are not that high, and my Cessna T210 can climb to 25,000 feet. In a nutshell, ICE! Flying in clouds above these mountains will almost always result in significant ice accumulation on the plane. Why? Because the prevailing winds are from the southwest and the Pacific Ocean. Clouds forming over the Pacific are water-laden, and as they are forced upward on the western slopes of the Cascades, they become more and more saturated with moisture. Furthermore, the freezing level even in summer is often less than ten thousand feet. So flying at, say, 12,000 feet in clouds almost always results in my picking up ice.

Heavy Ice On Descent

I found this out the hard way on this flight. I was flying nonstop from Billings, Montana, to Orcas Island, a distance of a little over 700 miles. I was IFR, flying at 14,000 feet, and 2,000 feet above the solid cloud layer over these mountains. Mt. Baker was in clouds. Once I got just past Mt. Baker I was "cleared to descend to 8,000 feet." I then descended into the ice-laden clouds at about 12,000 feet. My logbook entry was succinct: "heavy ice on descent."

"Heavy" ice meant that the accumulation was taking place so fast that I had to get out of it quickly! Ice buildup on the wing destroys the airfoil shape, increasing the stall speed perhaps even to the point where I could lose control of the plane. In heavy ice you have only minutes to stop the accumulation before this can happen.

The fastest way to descend is to reduce power, slow down, and then lower the landing gear to create drag which helps to prevent the plane from picking up speed. Doing so, I could usually descend at close to 1,500 feet per minute which meant I could descend from 14,000 feet to 8,000 feet in four or five minutes. But I had to be aware of the terrain below me. While Mt. Baker itself was 50 miles from Orcas, the mountains did not stop just west of Mt. Baker, but gradually got lower and lower until by the time you were about 20 miles from Orcas the ground was close to sea level. 15 miles from Orcas, and you were just about over water, and you could almost be certain that the freezing level over the water was at least five thousand feet or higher. If you got down to this altitude the ice would stop accumulating and would start to melt.

About the lowest I could go in my descent while over the lowering mountains west of Mt. Baker was 8,000 feet until I was 20 miles west of this mountain. When I started this descent I did not know what the freezing level was, and whether at 8,000 feet I would be under the overcast or below the freezing level. There were some tense moments on my part because there was enough ice accumulating on the plane that I probably could not have flown in level flight at 8,000 feet, even with full-power, particularly if the ice was continuing to build.

In this case the freezing level was about 9,000 feet, and at 8,000 feet I was below the clouds and I could maintain this altitude until the terrain got lower. I had not expected the ice, and should never have started my descent until I was sure I could descend below the clouds and the freezing level.

Cumulative Experience

There is no question I was sufficiently scared by this experience that thereafter I treated the Cascade Mountains with great respect and recognition that it is not whether there is ice in the clouds, but how much, and this was true in both the summer and winter. Flying westbound when there was a cloud layer below me, I learned not to start my descent until I was over the waters of Puget Sound. Often a solid layer over the Cascades would be only a scattered or broken layer over Puget Sound. The weather was definitely different. These waters seemed to have a temperate effect on the freezing level. I also learned from experience that over Puget Sound the icing conditions in the clouds would be much more benign than they were over the Cascades.

I followed much the same approach on my eastbound flights. I learned to climb to my cruising altitude above the clouds over the water before turning east toward the Cascades. I could usually climb to that altitude well west of the mountains, and while I might have to climb through clouds, often there was no ice, or if there were, it would be more benign. It often was possible to get on top without picking up any ice. And if I did encounter ice, my "out" was to descend and try another day.

One final observation. The tops of the cloud cover over the Cascades were seldom higher than eighteen thousand feet, and more likely thirteen or fourteen thousand. With an optimum cruising altitude of twenty-five thousand feet I could almost always stay on top until I was over Puget Sound.

Observations

My Cessna T210 was not authorized to fly in icing conditions. Many non-pilots assume that this is because of the added weight of the ice. That is not the principal problem. The ice changes the shape of the airfoils of the wing, the horizontal and vertical stabilizers and, most important, the propeller. When ice changes the shape of these airfoils, they can no longer produce the lift they were designed to provide. The only real ice protection I had was on the blades of the propeller which had electrical heating elements on them to keep ice from adhering. This was very important because if ice distorts the airfoil of the propeller blades it destroys the ability of the propeller to convert engine power into forward speed. In addition to the heating elements on the propeller blades there was also a heating element on the pitot tube, which is used in the measurement of airspeed. Without such heat, ice would form and block the air flow, causing erratic or no air speed indications.

Induction or Carburetor Ice

In addition to ice that coats the outside of the plane, which is called "structural" ice, there is also "induction" ice which can block the airflow to the engine, causing it to stop. Induction ice, often called carburetor ice, was much less of an issue with my plane because it had a fuel-injected engine and did not have a carburetor. Instead, fuel was fed directly into each cylinder. Ice could still form in the induction air-flow to the engine but this

This picture shows the black electric heating elements on the inner half of the leading edge of the propeller blades (arrow). They are designed to keep ice from forming on that surface, but must be activated before encountering icing conditions in order to be effective.

was not likely because the incoming air first went through the turbo-charger which compresses the air. The process of compression heated the air, virtually eliminating any chance of an ice blockage of the air supply. Ice could still form on the outside of the air filter located in front of the engine where air enters the engine compartment. If that were to happen I could open an alternate air source that had no filter on it, thus bypassing the air filter. I will not comment on carburetor ice since most of my experience has been with fuel-injected engines.

Where You Find Structural Ice

Ice normally forms only when you are flying in clouds where there is also *liquid* water and the temperature is at or less than 32 degrees Fahrenheit. Both conditions are required: water in liquid form, and a temperature at or below freezing. My experience was that if the outside temperature were between 25 and 34 degrees Fahrenheit there could be ice. The colder the temperature the less likely it is that the water would still be in liquid form. If the water in a cloud is already frozen—that is, snow, sleet or hail—it would not normally stick to the surface of an airplane unless it were wet snow, that is, close to the freezing temperature.

Freezing rain is probably the worst possible icing condition. It can occur when there is a temperature inversion where there is warm air from which rain is falling into colder air below and this colder air is also below freezing. A temperature inversion most often occurs where a warm air system overruns cold air, usually at a warm frontal boundary. The temperature has to be close to 32 degrees and if you are flying in the lower, cold and freezing air, the rain from the warm air above is likely to instantly freeze on the plane. The forecast of freezing rain anywhere near my flight altitude, or at airports where I might land, always caused me to abort the flight because you have no "out" if you encounter it. Normally you can descend into warmer air where the ice would melt but not if the below-freezing air extends down to the surface.

Is Ice Predictable?

Sometimes "yes," and sometimes "no." Forecasters using powerful computers can predict temperatures and water saturation at each altitude, and predict the likelihood of ice. But ice formation is very fickle, and it is difficult, if not impossible, to know for sure if there will be icing conditions. These forecasts are made many hours ahead of time and conditions can change rapidly. Since ice can be life-threatening, a forecaster will usually warn of ice even if the likelihood is fairly low. If an icing accident occurs, he is off the hook. While I have no reliable statistics, my experience has been that I encountered ice less than 25% of the time that it had been predicted. This is not a condemnation of the forecast, but recognition that ice forecasting is not an exact science.

To-Go, or Not-to-Go

This creates a dilemma for the pilot when making the go or no-go decision. If every time ice were forecast the pilot stayed on the ground he wouldn't fly much of the time. This is not just a winter issue but a year-round one since if you fly high enough you will be in sub-freezing temperatures even when the ground temperatures are in the 90s. The standard temperature at 25,000 feet is about minus 35 degrees Fahrenheit. With the Cessna's high altitude capability I ran into the possibility of ice on virtually every IFR high altitude flight.

So, how did I decide whether to go or not? Here are some of the questions I considered in making my decision.

First and foremost, what would be my 'out' if ice were encountered? Can I safely get out of it? Unless the answer is 'yes' the rest is moot.
Is heavy icing forecast?
Is freezing rain forecast anywhere along my route?
What are the forecast temperatures at the minimum en route altitude?
What pilot reports have been filed and did they mention ice?
Are there airports along my route to divert to if needed and are their forecasts well above minimums, and are the forecasts holding up?
What are the existing and forecast cloud top reports and can I get on top without picking up ice?
How long would I be in forecast icing conditions, and how soon after takeoff?
If I had to return to my departure airport, would the weather be suitable?
Are the forecast temperatures such that I could safely descend into above-freezing temperatures?
If I picked up ice and could descend below the clouds would I still have enough fuel to limp to an airport that was above minimums?
What type of terrain would I be flying over?

Once satisfied with the answers to the above questions, and I decide to make the flight, I then made doubly sure in my pre-flight inspection that both propeller and pitot heating elements were working. These elements burn out and I would not attempt any flight into possible icing conditions unless they were both functioning.

In-Flight Watching For Ice

Once I was airborne, I turned on both the propeller and pitot heating systems and left them on for the entire period I might encounter ice. Once in clouds, I monitored the outside temperature and watched carefully for the first signs of ice, which are often subtle. In my Cessna T210 the first signs usually showed up at the bottom left corner of the windshield as a patch of very light, snow-like dusting of ice, perhaps as small as a square inch. Another place ice seemed to form early was on the outside temperature probe which was in the top center of the windshield.

Once this first sign of ice appeared, I would lean forward to look at the leading edge of the wing. The initial "dusting" of ice, however, was not visible because the wing was painted white which tends to hide the ice until it started developing in earnest. The leading edge of the radar-radome on the right wing was painted black and I could often see the ice forming on it fairly early in the process. At night there was a spotlight on the front left side of the airplane which I could turn on to look at the wing root for ice. I should add that I would never fly at night IFR if ice were forecast.

What Do You Do If You Encounter Ice?

You take immediate steps to get out of it. There are three possible actions: make a 180 degree turn and retreat into the no-ice area you were just in, climb to get above the ice, or descend to an altitude where the temperature is above freezing. What you don't do is to ignore the ice, hoping it will go away. Ice that may be minimal at the first indication can rapidly increase to the point where the airplane could be close to stalling.

180 Degree Turn

The safest immediate course of action is the 180 degree turn in order to get back into the no-ice conditions you were in. Call the controller and tell him that you are picking up ice and request a clearance to make a 180 degree turn back to no-ice conditions. Once you are back out of the ice you can then evaluate the situation and decide what to do next.

If the ice buildup is rapid, don't wait for the controller to give a clearance. Every minute's delay in making this 180 degree turn will mean you will be in these icing conditions for two minutes longer. Just start the turn and then advise Center: "Center, N5119V is making a 180 degree because of rapid ice buildup." Don't ask for his permission, just tell him what you are doing. The pilot in command is authorized to take whatever action is necessary in an emergency. If the Controller balks, all the pilot has to do is to declare an emergency. Heavy buildup of ice can be life-threatening. My experience has been that mentioning the word "ice" will get his immediate attention. It is then his job to clear the airspace of other traffic.

Often the 180 degree turn will take the pilot back into VFR conditions where he may be able to climb or descend to another altitude free of clouds, or warmer temperatures.

Climb To Get Out Of the Ice

Temperatures decrease the higher you go. The standard temperature lapse rate is 3.6 degrees Fahrenheit for every thousand feet. This means if you are flying at 8,000 feet with an outside temperature of 30 degrees Fahrenheit and you start to pick up ice, you can climb to 10,000 feet. In theory the temperature would normally be about 7 degrees colder. The ice you were picking up at 8,000 feet might not exist at 23 degrees. It takes only two to three minutes to climb 2,000 feet, and I found that many times I could stop the ice buildup by climbing quickly to get into colder temperatures. I always had to remember that the ice buildup would not melt until I got into warmer temperatures, and if by climbing the ice builds up to any significant degree the fuel efficiency of the plane would be affected.

Another related possibility is to climb above the clouds, but you need to be comfortable that you know where the tops are. Center controllers can advise you on that, and perhaps even call another, higher-flying plane and ask what their conditions are. The pilot also needs to recognize that the tops of the clouds may turn out to be considerably higher than forecast. My experience of flying above clouds is that tops of clouds are almost always higher than they look. Also remember that the rate of ice buildup could be significantly higher near the top of clouds. Pick up enough ice and the plane will lose its ability to climb at all.

My experience has been that while climbing to get out of the ice is an alternative, it is fraught with risk and is viable only when you know with certainty where the tops are, and the ice accumulation during climb is at a very low rate.

Descend to Get Into Warmer Air

The third alternative is to descend into warmer air where either the ice will melt, or at least will not continue to build-up. This assumes that you can get down to above-freezing temperatures by descending, or if you are flying high enough, get below the clouds where the ice buildup will stop. This is only viable if the freezing level is well above the IFR minimum en route altitude.

Summary

Ice is deadly. Any pilot who thinks he can fly in icing conditions for very long is badly informed. Ice is unpredictable, and forecasters tend to err on the side of forecasting ice when in doubt. That creates a dilemma: if a pilot were to cancel a proposed flight every time ice were forecast he would never fly. The key to flying when ice is predicted is to do so only when there are plenty of "outs" for getting safely on the ground, and then to act decisively at the first sign of ice. If in my pre flight planning I had any doubts, I would stay on the ground.

37

Managing Risk—Thunderstorms and Being Prepared to Survive

When you ask an experienced pilot who uses his plane for travel what risks he is mostly concerned about, he will quickly tell you "ice and thunderstorms." Both have several things in common. Both can kill you, both are weather related, both can be avoided by staying on the ground, and when tragedy occurs, "get-home-itis" is often a factor. I offered my thoughts on ice in the previous chapter.

I am happy to say I managed to avoid tangling with thunderstorms. In this chapter I relate my principal strategy for doing so—the use of radar, supplemented in the later years with a stormscope. To a large extent, the technology I was using has been replaced in the last half dozen years by satellite downloaded weather displays in the cockpit.

The second part of this chapter deals with the reality that irrespective of the pilot's experience, every flight could end in a forced landing, far from civilization, where survival depended on being prepared. The chilling thing is that a forced landing can happen to the student pilot on his first cross-country flight as easily as it can to the five-thousand-hour pilot. I offer my thoughts.

The author lived for 15 years on an island, where every landing and takeoff was over water. I have also included a section dealing with the survival aspects of flying over water because I have seen very little written about this subject. Unfortunately I also saw a number of planes that went down, and lives lost because the pilot was not prepared.

Thunderstorms

Thunderstorms are a hazard that all pilots should be afraid of. No one can tangle with the awesome power of a thunderstorm and expect to come out ahead. More likely they will come out in pieces.

My favorite contemporary aviation writer, Richard L. Collins, in a classic book, *Thunderstorms and Airplanes—The Complete Book On Flying In Thunderstorm Country,* ISBN 1-56027-426-3, discusses this subject in great depth, and I recommend it to all pilots. His book was written before the days of satellite downloaded weather displays in the cockpit, but it is still essential for the pilot to understand thunderstorms: how and when they develop, their life-cycle, and how to interpret the downloaded data. This new technology only provides data to assist the pilot.

I stopped flying under instrument flight conditions in 2003, before such satellite equipment had become fairly common. Observing other pilots since then has left me with the impression that too many pilots get the latest piece of equipment and then fail to learn how to interpret the data provided. Collins' book is still relevant.

Actually the simplistic rules for avoiding one of these monsters is straightforward—stay miles and miles away from thunderstorms and under no circumstances fly into one. It is relatively easy to avoid a thunderstorm when you are in clear skies and can see an afternoon thunderstorm building, perhaps fifty or more miles ahead of you. Stay 20 miles away from it and you probably will be safe.

This is not so easy when you are flying in clouds and have no way of seeing what is ahead of you. The use of radar is the time-honored way multi-engine aircraft avoid blundering into a thunderstorm. Thunderstorms normally have a great deal of rain in them, and it is this rain that the radar is actually detecting. Big raindrops show up as more intense than small drops.

Radar for Single-Engine Aircraft

Very few single-engine planes have radar for a simple reason. The radar antenna is just a little smaller than the size of a satellite dish for TV. In a multi-engine aircraft, this antenna is in the nose. On a single-engine aircraft, the propeller and engine occupy that space. Most of us would not trade the engine for a radar antenna.

In 1978, RCA came out with a unique radar unit that used an elliptical-shaped antenna that was small enough so that it could be put into a pod partially recessed into the leading edge of the wing. The antenna was a compromise between size and distance-detection capability. It was very effective in showing thunderstorms within about 25 miles, but beyond that distance it took a big thunderstorm to show up on the radar screen.

This radar unit was approved for installation on a Cessna T210, and I decided to have one installed for safety reasons. RCA made the radar unit itself, but the Robertson Aircraft Corporation in Seattle made the in-the-wing installation. I acted promptly in ordering this installation. Over the years I have learned that when you see an aviation product you want, you had better buy it now, rather than wait. Too many excellent new products are made by small, under-capitalized companies that do not survive very long.

I had my plane ferried out to Seattle in mid-June, 1979. There was a lot of FAA red tape because this was the first 1975 model Cessna to

The radar pod extends several inches ahead of the leading edge of the wing. The reason for the top and bottom bulge in the pod is to allow the pilot to tilt the elliptical antenna inside the pod up and down from the horizon. This was strictly weather-detection radar and not intended to either map the surface of the land or detect other aircraft. I found it could easily differentiate water from land which was useful when living on Orcas Island.

The radar screen can be seen in this in-flight picture. It is picking up some rain which is visible in the lower center of the radar screen. The aircraft is positioned at the bottom center on the screen. The screen display is in three levels of gray. If you look closely you can see several brighter areas, indicating higher precipitation rates. The display of the highest precipitation level actually flashes to get the pilot's attention.

have this wing modification. In addition, the wing had already been modified with the extended wing tip tanks which also changed the wings' flight characteristics. Eventually this was all worked out, and I picked up the plane toward the end of July.

I have no real knowledge of how many of these radar units were installed, but not very many because I don't recall seeing any advertisements for them after 1979, and I never ran across another aircraft with this installation. The radar with the installation cost about $8,000 ($23,000 in 2008 dollars). It was also a high maintenance unit, but I had no problem getting it serviced. I had to have the radar pod refurbished every four or five years. The radar was still functioning twenty-five years later when I sold the plane.

I had a great deal to learn about interpreting the radar display. Unlike larger radar units that had color displays that helped a pilot to judge the intensity of the radar return, mine was three levels of gray, with the highest intensity level of return, showing in a flashing display. I also had to learn about attenuation in which large rain cells blocked the radar energy from showing what was on the far side of the cell. It would appear as though there was only one cell when in fact there might be an even more deadly cell behind the nearest cell.

Shortly after this installation, I arranged to take a United Airlines two-day radar training course in Denver at their national training center. This was the same course that United then gave to their airline pilots as they retrofitted their fleet with weather radar. At the time there were almost no single-engine aircraft with radar. Later Cessna made available a radar unit that hung in a pod from the underside of the wing.

I am sure the radar installation added a substantial margin of safety to my flying. I never penetrated a thunderstorm in my four thousand flying hours in the plane, and I am sure I was able to make flights I would have hesitated making without this equipment.

Stormscope

Sometime in this same time frame another electronic device became available, the Stormscope. While radar detected rain, this new device detected static created by lightning strikes which are also associated with thunderstorms. The direction finding antenna was usually installed on the belly of the aircraft. Lightning creates electromagnetic static, and based on the strength of this static, a display similar to that of a radar screen showed where these lightning strikes originated.

These systems complemented each other, but radar was still considered more useful because it showed precipitation as the thunderstorm was developing, and before lightning started. Further, the Stormscope estimated the distance from the aircraft based on the strength of the electromagnetic static received by the stormscope. If this static was very intense the Stormscope assumed the lightning was close by. This was marginally accurate.By contrast, Radar determines distance by measuring the time out and back of reflected radar energy, which travels at the speed of light. This was very accurate.

About five years before selling the plane, I did install the latest stormscope equipment, and found that having both radar and a stormscope gave the pilot the best picture.

Be Leery of Scattered Thunderstorm Forecasts

A couple of observations. Big, frontal storms are easy to see and stay away from, but often I would be flying in an area of scattered, smaller, and less powerful cells. I learned to beware of forecasts which suggested there were only scattered thunderstorms with, say, twenty-five percent coverage. Twenty-five percent sounds like it would be easy to fly around because seventy-five percent of the sky would be cell-free. Sometimes that might be possible, but my experience was that you would be taking a big chance in trying.

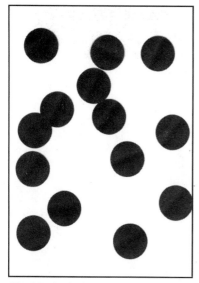

The black circles representing thunderstorms occupy 25% of the space in this illustration. A pilot would have great difficulty flying from bottom to top if all he had was radar.

Look at the illustration on the left. In this block of airspace the black circles represent thunderstorms, which occupy 25 percent of the space. It is not obvious to me how you would safely navigate through this airspace.

Eyeball Radar

Regardless of the level of sophisticated equipment, I learned there were many times when flying under an overcast VFR instead of IFR made more sense. I could only do this when there was good visibility (ten miles or more) and the terrain was reasonably flat. I also had to be sure that the ceiling was at least 3,000 feet over the route I was taking. I would then fly under visual flight rules which allowed me to use my most important detection equipment—my eyeballs. I could usually see rain and ugly looking clouds a long way ahead and then easily detour around the shower. I found that flying using my eyeballs was very effective in such situations. Often this made it possible to avoid having to climb to a high altitude to stay above the overcast, or not making the flight at all.

Being Prepared To Survive

Complacency

As student pilots we were taught to always know where we would make an off-field landing if the engine were to stop. As part of this training the instructor would unexpectedly pull the throttle back to idle, and tell us to locate an appropriate field and set up the plane to land there. In almost all training exercises the plane would be over level ground with an obvious field the student should select. The instructor never does this where there are no obvious landing sites, say, over a forest, or hilly terrain.

Once we have our private license most of us seldom go through this exercise again and we become very complacent, forgetting that it can happen at any time. As a result we blind ourselves to the risks we take when a direct-to route is selected without regard to where we could land and walk away if the engine were to suddenly stop.

Today's general aviation aircraft, when properly maintained, are very dependable, and many pilots never experience a forced landing. This leads to complacency and failure to plan for a "what if" situation. But forced landings do occur. An AOPA Safety Foundation analysis of the National Transportation Safety Board accident investigation reports for 2006 show that twenty-five percent of all accidents that year were the result of either engine failure or fuel starvation, and also involved aircraft damage, injuries, or a fatality. That was almost one-a-day. Fly long enough and there is a good chance that a pilot will experience a forced landing. It could occur in the first year, or, as was my experience, after 50 years of flying (*Chapter 35, Then There Was Silence–An Engine Failure!*).

Questions To Ask Before Every Flight

Here are the things that I think every pilot should automatically ask before a flight:

•**Terrain** What is the terrain over which I will be flying? Realistically, what are the odds of surviving a forced landing over that terrain? And if I did survive, is it likely that someone will find me in time, particularly if there were injuries? Would another route be more sensible even though it might be longer?

•**Passenger Risk** If I am carrying passengers, do I have the right to expose them to this risk. If one of my passengers is a senior citizen, or has health problems, would he or she likely survive? A healthy 25-year-old has a much better chance of survival than someone much older.

•**Clothing** Do all occupants have clothes warm enough to keep from freezing at night in the event of a forced landing? Too often pilots fly with casual, light-weight clothes, including shoes or sandals,

This Personal Locator Beacon is an ELT intended for personal use, not only for pilots but also for hunters, skiers, hikers or anyone traveling in remote areas. This unit contains a GPS receiver and when activated transmits its registered identification as well as location on 406 MHz.

without recognition that such clothing would be totally inadequate if the unthinkable happened. It is possible to take off on a hot, summer day, fly up and over a 5,000 foot mountain range, and then land on the other side in a valley with equally hot weather. What if the engine stopped while over this mountain range?

•**406 MHz ELT**   Does the aircraft have a 406 MHz ELT? Better yet, do I also have a Personal Locator Beacon (see picture) which also transmits on the 406 MHz and 121.5 MHz frequencies? Is it within easy reach in the event of a forced landing? I say within reach because there is always a possibility that the pilot will be pinned inside the aircraft in the landing and if he can't reach it, what good is it?

•**Survival Equipment**   Am I carrying survival equipment appropriate for the route I will be flying? Is there a good first aid kit in the plane? Food? What about water? Water is more important to survival than food.

•**VFR Flight Plan**   If flying under visual flight rules (VFR), have I filed a flight plan? Most pilots, including the author, become complacent and tend to forget the insurance a flight plan provides. It is easy to assume that you can always contact an FAA flight service station anytime you need help, but you may be too low, or your radio may malfunction, or you may lose your electrical system.

•**Potential Liability**   Legal liability is a factor most pilots do not think about. We are in an age of litigation, and if the unthinkable happens, you will likely be sued. If any of your passengers are hurt or killed, they or their families will likely take action against you even though you were doing them a favor in taking them with you. Do you have enough insurance to protect you and your family assets? If you are also killed, your entire estate will likely be at risk. The other side will try to prove you were negligent whether you were or not.

At one time a one million dollar single-limit policy was considered adequate. Not any more, but you may have difficulty getting higher limits, or you may find per-seat liability limits that are totally inadequate. I mentioned that I had a forced landing. Fortunately I did not have a passenger. After that experience I would not take anyone with me other than family because of this liability concern.

In-Flight Considerations

One of the most difficult things a pilot has to learn is when to throw in the towel, and get on the ground. Many pilots find it difficult to recognize that something is going wrong and they need to take immediate action. They waste valuable time in denial.

My policy has always been straightforward. If something seems to be going wrong, it probably is, and it is time to get on the ground. I don't assume that somehow the problem will go away on its own. If I am on an IFR flight plan, I declare an emergency and tell the controller I want vectors to the closest suitable airport. If VFR, I switch to the emergency frequency 121.5 mc, and tell the FAA what the problem is. If the engine has stopped I want to be very sure they know where I am so they can get to me once I am down. I have declared an emergency perhaps eight or ten times in my fifty years. It is painless, and it works, but too many pilots delay unnecessarily before uttering the words: "MAYDAY!" "MAYDAY!" "MAYDAY!"

Flying Over Water

For 15 years, our home was on Orcas Island in the San Juan Islands of Washington State. Every takeoff and landing was over open water. By "open" water I mean water that ocean-going ships used. The water is cold, and hypothermia takes over after about 15 minutes. Survival is dependent on the pilot and passengers being prepared on every flight. When the engine stops, there is almost no chance of survival if you

Here the author is wearing his two-cell life vest designed for pilots who will be wearing the vest for hours at a time. There are numerous pockets for survival equipment, including the Personal Locator Beacon shown two pages back. I would not fly over water without wearing this vest.

aren't prepared. What is the preparation?

•**Recognition** First and foremost is recognition that it can happen. As with all flying it is easy to forget that engines do stop. The difference is that over land you may have a chance at finding level ground and, once on the ground, the biggest risk is probably behind you. A water landing is different. Even if you manage to get out of the aircraft—and this is by no means a certainty––you have only a few minutes to get out of the water before hypothermia takes over. Once that happens, death quickly follows.

•**Life Vest** Each person on the plane must be wearing a life vest. An engine failure is most likely to happen on takeoff when the engine is producing 100 percent power to get into the air. The failure may happen just a few hundred feet in the air, so it may be less than a minute before impacting the water. That is no time to be looking for life vests, or attempting to put one on. Even if you are at several thousand feet you won't have much time, and as pilot you need to be flying the airplane, looking for a boat, and calling for help. Being distracted by passengers desperately looking for their life vests is the last thing you need.

•**Life Raft** You need to have in the plane where you can get to it, a life raft with a boarding ladder attached to the raft. It is worthless if it is in the baggage compartment. I emphasize a boarding ladder because it is difficult to pull yourself up and into a raft which is bobbing in the waves, particularly in cold water and after the shock of the landing. Just as important, this raft has to be located where you can reach it after the abrupt stop from the water impact. Everything will be thrown around the cabin. If the life raft is not secured it will be thrown out of reach, perhaps back into the tail of the airplane at impact. I usually secured my raft on a seat with a safety belt.

Without a life raft, and the ability to get into it, the pilot or passenger has little chance of survival in cold water. The webbing hanging down in the front is a sea ladder without which a person in cold water, and probably in shock, would have great difficulty getting into the raft. This is a light weight Winslow raft of the type the author carried, and highly recommends.

•**Passenger Briefing** Your passengers need to know what to expect in the event of a water landing. If the plane has a fixed landing gear, the probability of the plane flipping onto its back is high and everyone will be hanging upside down, held in place by their safety belts. Cold water will be gushing in and everyone will likely be totally disoriented. With retractable gear, leave the gear retracted. There is more of a chance that the plane will survive right side up. It is also likely that the nose of the plane will be pitched downward, and instantly submerged. If so, the windshield will likely collapse, allowing the cabin to almost instantly fill with water.

There are many other things the passengers should know. Tell your passengers that you could be unconscious and their first priority is to get out of the plane themselves, whether you are able to or not. Show them the raft, the inflation rip cord and how to use it to inflate the raft. Your passengers need to be told not to inflate their life vests until they are out of the plane. Make sure that on takeoff their safety belts are as tight as possible. As pilot-in-command you are responsible for their safety which largely depends on your briefing.

•**Loose Objects** At impact with the water, all loose objects will become missiles, particularly those on the top of the instrument panel. Before takeoff make sure that everything is secured.

•**Unlatch the Doors** Once the plane is in the water a major problem is opening the doors to get out of the plane. There have been numerous incidents where the door would not open because the latch had gotten bent at the time of the impact. Even if this does not happen you have to push the door with great force because the outside water will resist opening until the cabin is itself filled with water. With a water-filled cabin this becomes a life or death issue. You may not have much time once it becomes apparent you are going down, so priority number one before impact is to unlatch the door, open it slightly, and then extend the latch so that it is on the outside of the fuselage and cannot easily be jammed in a closed position.

Pilot Responsibility

As the pilot in command it is your responsibility to be sure your passengers are aware of what they should do if a water landing occurs. I know some pilots are reluctant to do so, fearing their passengers may be scared and not want to fly over water. This may be true, but how could you live with yourself if something happened? They have confidence in you or they wouldn't be flying with you. In turn, you have a responsibility to brief them fully.

* * * * *

I have one other strong recommendation if you are going to regularly fly over water. You should attend a water ditching survival training program. In 2002 I attended a one-day program put on by a small company in Victoria, British Columbia. The company, *Aviation Egress Training*, teaches the pilot what to expect in a ditching, and how to successfully get out of the plane when you are upside down, under water, and in shock. The instructor indicates that "90 percent of the people who end up in the water while flying, drown needlessly." I don't know if that figure is right or not, but his program is designed to assure that you are one of the 10 percent who make it. You learn by experiencing what it feels like, and how disoriented you are when your plane is suddenly underwater. It is worth flying from anywhere in the United States or Canada to Victoria in order to attend this course.

38

Observations of an Old-Timer

This chapter is primarily for private pilots, student pilots, and future pilots in which I offer my observations on a number of aviation subjects. I am perhaps presumptuous, but I feel qualified and obligated to do so. I have survived more than half a century of flying single-engine planes, with only one taxi accident, in large measure because I benefitted from the observations and advice of other old-timers. While I don't feel like it, at age 75 I recognize that in the eyes of most readers I am now an old-timer myself.

Managing Risk

No matter how many hours you have, or how few, your airplane can kill you on your very next flight. The laws of physics and gravity never take a vacation, and every flight is a contest between you and your airplane, with the airplane playing for keeps. It doesn't matter if you are 22 years old and believe you are immortal, or a successful businessman who has a fancy new plane with all the latest bells and whistles. If you take nothing else from this chapter, remember that your next flight could be your last.

Aviation has inherent risks, and the pilot's number one job is to minimize such risks. Almost everyone can learn to fly given enough time and training, but too many pilots in their enthusiasm for flight overlook their role in managing risk. From his first training flight a pilot needs to evaluate risk dispassionately and take steps to manage it. You cannot eliminate risk entirely but you can greatly reduce it.

Throughout this chapter I will constantly make reference to reducing risk because if you don't, it is just a matter of time before you will either scare yourself, barely surviving, or you will become a statistic. You may think it can't happen to you, but it can.

Pilot Skills and Training

Trust Your Instincts

In aviation activities—either on the ground or in flight—if you sense that something is not right, it probably isn't. Trust your instincts and either identify the reason for your discomfort, or get on the ground, fast. My experience has been that when something is starting to go wrong it can only get worse with time. In flying you are playing for keeps, and denial is your worst enemy. It robs you of valuable time to take action before something worse happens.

This intuitive warning could be almost anything that doesn't seem quite right, even without your being able to pin down the reason. Perhaps it is a slightly different engine sound, weather that was not as forecast, a fuel gauge that shows more fuel than there should be, or an oil pressure gauge that is "pinging" at the top end of the scale. Or you might sense that things are starting to escalate and you are getting in over your head. Regardless, trust your instincts and get back on the ground where you can then sort out the issues. There will be lots of times when your uneasiness will turn out to be wrong, but as they say:

> *It is better to be on the ground, and wishing you were in the air,*
> *than to be in the air, and wishing you were on the ground.*

The Elusive Perfect Flight
Critically Grade Yourself

I have made very few perfect flights. I know this because for most of my 50 years I have critically graded myself on a 1 to 5 scale after each flight. On virtually every flight there was something that I could have done (or not done) that would have improved the flight or made it safer. This review process became second nature, and I am sure was one of the reasons I am still around.

Recurrent Training

The most neglected issue for private pilots is maintaining competency in the fast-changing world of aviation. Under present FAA rules, once a person receives his private or commercial license it is good for life provided he completes a biennial flight review (BFR), and has a valid medical.

I obtained my commercial license in 1956 at age 23, and my current FAA license proclaims:

> *...(I) have been found to be properly qualified to exercise the privileges of a commercial pilot... with single-engine land and instrument ratings.*

According to the FAA, the flight check ride and written tests I took more than fifty years ago still are valid today. Yet, I have never exercised the privileges of a commercial pilot, and I have never been re-tested for my commercial piloting skills.

I have been retested on my instrument skills but I would not have been required to do so if I had complied with the required minimal in-flight instrument flight maneuvers every six months. Even then, an instrument instructor—not an FAA examiner—could have given me the check ride to get me legally current.

When I got my commercial license and instrument rating, the flight check ride was in a 1946 two-seat Cessna 140. The only IFR equipment was a war surplus turn-and-bank gyro and a low-frequency radio range receiver that allowed the pilot to follow a "beam." This was a 1930s navigation system which was then obsolete in most of the country.

Why am I reciting ancient history? To emphasize that having a license to fly does not mean you are qualified to do so. It really is a license to learn. I have already emphasized that the pilot's most important responsibility is to manage risk. Recurrent training is part of risk management.

In the last ten years the cockpit of a modern small aircraft has gone from stand-alone analog flight instruments and avionics to integrated digital "glass" cockpits where virtually all information is on one or two large screens, integrated with a sophisticated autopilot and computer navigation avionics. These glass panels come with instruction manuals that are complex and hundreds of pages long. My impression is that few private pilots really learn how to use all the features of this new equipment.

In theory the biennial flight review given by an instructor is supposed to review the flying skills of the pilot using the equipment in the aircraft, but the two-hour BFR is extremely superficial. The instructor himself may not be familiar with the specific equipment in the plane being used for the flight check, and is not in a good position to evaluate the pilot's skill using it.

Airline captains are required to go through extensive recurrent training every six months. Why isn't it prudent for a private pilot, particularly those flying in an instrument environment, to do so, too? The single most important action a pilot can take to manage risk is to establish his own recurrent standards, and then take action to achieve them.

Age and Learning to Fly

There is no maximum age limit on learning to fly, and I have known pilots who learned to fly in their sixties, after they retired. One of the reviewers of this book, Don Dick, didn't take his first lesson until after he turned 70. These "mature" older, new pilots tend to be very conservative in their flying and concerned with minimizing risk.

At the other end of the age spectrum, I know a number of teenagers who soloed on their 16th birthday (including my son). Being younger, they tend to learn motor skills quickly, but have less concern about taking risks. They believe they are immortal.

There is another category of pilots. They are middle age, type-A personalities, successful in their careers, and time-driven. Doctors are a good example. While they may start their flying in a training aircraft, once they get their license they tend to buy too sophisticated an aircraft given their experience level. Many never really learn to use all of the features of their equipment. They are busy people but sophisticated equipment is no substitute for cumulative experience. Being time-driven, they also are particularly vulnerable to one of aviation's most deadly viruses—get-home-itis.

I am reminded of a tragic accident a few years ago where the pilot lost control of his plane and was killed along with his passengers. He was flying VFR from the New York City area to Cape Cod, largely over Long Island Sound. It was a dark, high overcast night with no moon. He was a low-time pilot and had owned this aircraft for only a short time. It had an autopilot which he used on the flight, but as he neared his destination, apparently he disconnected the autopilot, and hand-flew the plane in descent. At that point, because of the dark water he was flying over, he apparently lost his horizontal reference and went into an uncontrolled spiral that terminated with the plane hitting the water, and sinking. The tragedy is that if he had not disconnected his autopilot but instead had commanded it to start descending, this would never have happened.

While it is speculation on my part, I suspect he had not mastered all of the functions of the autopilot and was not sure how to program the autopilot to descend. He probably also did not recognize the risks of flying at night over water where there were no lights to establish an horizon. Pan American World Airways had an advertising slogan: "the priceless extra of experience." That was what was missing here.

Use of An Autopilot

I have said elsewhere that flying IFR as a single pilot is very demanding. The airlines have two pilots, not just because of possible incapacity of the captain but because of the workload. When I bought my Cessna T210 in 1975, one of the most important pieces of equipment I installed was an autopilot. It was my copilot. It had the ability to hold altitude, fly either a straight line, or follow a navigation signal, even correcting for crosswinds automatically.

In the 1970s era, autopilots were looked down on as somehow being a crutch that real pilots did not use. I disagreed. The workload of flying an airplane on an instrument approach-to-minimums requires constant attention, whereas monitoring the flight being flown by the autopilot allowed me to stay on top of the big picture. If a problem developed with the autopilot I could immediately take over manually.

This greatly increased the safety factor. Today few aviation writers pan autopilots, recognizing their importance.

The pilot's objective is to lower risk. Being macho and flying under instrument conditions without a good autopilot is not wise. If my autopilot were not functioning, I would cancel my flight if the weather was, or could become, IFR. If you fly under IFR conditions and are serious about minimizing risk, your plane should also have a functioning autopilot.

406 MHz ELTs and Personal Locator Beacons

Every aircraft owner who has not done so should replace their 121.5 MHz ELT with one of the new 406 MHz ELTs. While the FAA has not mandated this replacement (as of August, 2009), the monitoring agency has stopped satellite monitoring of 121.5 MHz ELTs. The 406 MHz ELTs are several-generation improvement over the 121.5 MHz ELTs which were initially mandated by Congress in 1970. This is a no-brainer for a pilot wanting to manage risk.

The new system is more than just a frequency change. It is part of a new global satellite system used for all types of rescues, virtually anywhere in the world. Boaters, hikers, hunters, and anyone in a remote area can now purchase a hand-held Personal Locator Beacon (PLB) and use this system. I highly recommend that all pilots carry one of these PLBs on their person, in addition to the aircraft-installed ELT. It may seem redundant, but after a crash-landing the pilot may be able to get out of the plane, only to have fire consume the aircraft and the plane's 406 MHz ELT.

Failure to File VFR Flight Plans

Most pilots fail to file a VFR flight plan when traveling cross-country, and I am as guilty as the next pilot. That is a mistake which increases risk. I usually rationalize that with all the electronic equipment in the plane I can always make a radio call for help if the engine stops. But what if you lose your electrical system, or if you are flying low over the boondocks and you lose radio contact?

Filing a VFR flight plan takes time and I suppose that is the primary reason it is not done every time. For the most part, I did file a

VFR flight plan when traveling in remote areas, particularly when making long, cross-country trips. The fallacy with that approach is that there are many places within 50 miles of a major city—New York City, for example—where, if you went down you might not be found for a long time. Wooded areas swallow an airplane and only a ground search would find you. Remember that one of the limitations of the ELT signal is that it is line-of-sight, and could be blocked by obstructions such as a forest. That is why we should all file VFR flight plans.

Annual Flying Hours

A pilot who doesn't fly frequently increases his risk. While it is an arbitrary number, I believe a pilot should fly at least 50 hours a year, and in the same plane or, if he is renting, in the same model. Fewer hours suggest that the pilot probably does not have the time to keep on top of the skills and knowledge needed to minimize risk.

Study the Accident Reports

There are many lessons that you do not want to learn from personal experience. Reading the accident report summaries, or even the National Transportation Safety Board's complete reports, is an excellent way to learn from others.

In studying these reports, note the number of accidents involving experienced pilots who had thousands of hours and years of experience. If they can get into trouble, so can you. As I said at the beginning of this chapter, your airplane can kill you on your very next flight.

Airplane Observations

Airplane Utility

Most new pilots have exaggerated expectations of the utility a personal airplane provides. They dream of using an airplane to go places on weekends with airline dependability. Typically, a new pilot living, say, in Morristown, New Jersey, might think that he could commute to a summer home in New Hampshire on weekends. Unfortunately there is no certainty that the weather will cooperate, even in summer.

There is also the very real risk that the pilot in that circumstance will push his luck, flying in marginal weather to get home. He may be under pressure to do so because of an important meeting the next day. This is called "scud running" or "get-home-itis," and it can be fatal. He may get away with scud running initially, but sooner or later he will push his luck once too often.

If the pilot gets his instrument rating, this will increase his ability to fly in marginal weather. But it must be remembered that an instrument rating is only the first step in getting experience that will allow you to fly in weather. A lot of pilots get instrument ratings, but many never use the rating, or stay current. I would guess that half or more of those who get an instrument rating will not be legally current two years later. The demands of instrument flying require much more training and continuing practice than most new pilots realize.

Eventually this pilot will realize that his dream of being able to fly with airline dependability is exactly that—a dream. Unless by that time he is hooked on the thrill of flying for its own sake, he will likely sell the plane and drop out of aviation.

Buyers Beware

Nowhere is this more true than when buying a used airplane. One of the biggest mistakes an inexperienced buyer can make is to allow emotion to enter into the decision to buy a particular airplane. New paint jobs, interiors, or clean engines, may suggest a well-cared-for airplane but they can also cover up years of deferred maintenance which can end up costing the buyer thousands or even tens of thousands of dollars after purchase.

The best way to avoid getting a surprise after purchase is to get your mechanic to make a pre-purchase inspection. You don't want to rely on the seller's mechanic because he has a conflict of interest. If there are maintenance deficiencies it is a reflection on his work. He is not interested in protecting you, but rather in satisfying his customer, the seller.

A good inspection and review of the log books could take the better part of a day, and more, if travel is involved. Figure on spending upwards of $1,000, plus travel costs. If the $1,000 scares you, then you really are inexperienced, and probably should not be buying that plane.

Another observation. Don't buy an airplane in average condition if there is one in top condition even if it costs substantially more. A seller never gets his money back when he upgrades an aircraft with new avionics, a new paint job, a new interior, or major overhaul of the engine.

I have seen pilots buying a plane in average condition with the thought that they would then bring the plane up to their, higher standards. Almost without exception they end up spending far more than the difference in purchase price of a top-maintained plane.

An example. I spent $90,000 on my Mooney Mite, a plane made of plywood and fabric. It was built in 1955 and the linen fabric covering over the plywood had never been removed from the fuselage. I felt it was time to be sure it was structurally sound. The engine had never had a good overhaul either. The plane needed to be totally restored. I sold it a few years later for $32,000 which was top dollar in 2006. The buyer recognized that the plane was probably better than new.

New Airplane Purchase

Some pilots purchase a new airplane with the expectation that by buying a new one they can avoid a lot of maintenance issues. That may or may not be true. On my Cessna T210, which I bought new, and without avionics, it took me close to 18 months before I got all the bugs out of it. Cessna was good in terms of reimbursing me, but I had the frustration of having to identify the discrepancies and getting them repaired. That was in 1975 but I have heard of similar experiences with some of today's new airplanes.

Buying More Airplane
Than You Can Afford

One of the major reasons why airplane owners drop out of flying is a financial one. They find their costs are much higher than budgeted, and most often it is higher maintenance cost. Insurance, fuel, annual inspections, and financing costs are relatively easy to budget. What is hard to budget is maintenance. Most new owners are not prepared for unexpected major repairs or overhaul costs.

When I started flying I was told by an old-timer that I should budget my maintenance costs at five percent of what a new plane would cost that year with the same equipment and performance. For example, assume that a new Cessna 172 today costs $200,000. If a pilot bought a used 172 for $50,000 he should expect to spend about $10,000 (five percent of $200,000) on plane maintenance, not $2,500 (five percent of $50,000). In the following year, he should expect to spend five percent of that year's new cost. Each year would increase based on the then new price.

What often happens is a new prospective owner will decide to buy as big, or as fast, a used plane as his monthly budget can afford. Obviously the older the plane is, either in years or flying hours, the lower the selling price will be. Maintenance, however, will be much higher. Be particularly leery of the representations on the condition of the engine. A freshly overhauled engine, to me, is a red flag unless the overhaul was performed by a recognized engine shop. (see below).

My advice? Even if you have unlimited funds, start out with an unsophisticated airplane, probably only two-seats, with 150 horsepower, or less, engine. Your objective should be to get several hundred hours flying experience before buying a more sophisticated or faster one.

Chapter 39–Cost of Flying Over Fifty Years show the actual costs I incurred, both in actual dollars spent, and also in 2008 inflated dollars for each of my aircraft. It perhaps will provide some insight into costs.

Engine Overhauls

A major engine overhaul is probably the largest expense an owner will incur. Like everything else, you can get a cheap overhaul that barely meets minimum standards, or, at the other extreme, you can trade in the old engine for a brand new engine, or a factory-overhauled engine that conforms to new-engine standards. Costs, and quality, run the gamut between these extremes, and usually you get what you pay for.

Many new pilots look at the "time between overhaul" (TBO) assigned to their model engine an absolute indicator of when an overhaul will be needed. They just assume they will not have any major engine costs until that number of hours has been reached. I wish I could confirm that was correct, but, there are many variables that can greatly affect engine life: Frequency of use, total number of hours flown annually, oil change interval, shock cooling, mishandling of engine power settings, cylinder-head and oil temperatures, and if the engine has had a prior overhaul, the quality of that overhaul. My experience has been that bigger horsepower engines are less likely to reach TBO than smaller engines. In part, this may be because of engine mishandling which becomes more critical on bigger engines.

Often overlooked, are the break-in procedures for a new or overhauled engine. Failure to follow these prescribed procedures can easily result in an improper break-in that will show up in increased oil consumption, lower than expected compression, and reduced engine life.

An engine does not often fail in flight, but when it does, the pilot is faced with big problems. This gets us back to the pilot's number one job—managing risk. Skimp on engine maintenance, or an overhaul, and the risk increases.

The Myth of Two Engines

First, a caveat. The comments that follow are addressed to the private pilot. They do not apply to the pilot who flies for a living and maintains professional-level skill.

Contrary to what most new pilots think, having a second engine is not an insurance policy. There are several reasons. What is important to realize is that most twin-engine aircraft have two engines for one reason: they need the aggregate power of both engines. Many, if not most, engines fail on takeoff when every bit of power of both engines is needed. In theory, if one engine fails on takeoff the plane will fly on one engine, but only if the pilot is sharp and does everything right and by the book.

All multi-engine pilots have to demonstrate their ability to handle a takeoff engine failure, both at the time they get their multi-engine rating, and at their biennial flight reviews. This demonstration is not the same as losing an engine when the pilot is not expecting it. When a failure actually occurs, the surprise and disbelief is very real, and many private pilots do not maintain the necessary skills to react quickly enough. The margins of safety are so thin that an engine failure on takeoff is often fatal. The accident statistics are clear on this.

As long as I have been flying there has been debate on whether a single-engine plane or a twin-engine plane is the safer. I come down on the side of the single-engine. Look at the risks. If you have two engines, the chance of losing an engine is twice as high as losing the only engine on a single-engine airplane.

If that failure is on takeoff, when the plane's airspeed will be close to the stall speed, the twin-engine pilot has to do everything right, and quickly—lower the nose to keep from losing speed, identify the failed-engine, pull its throttle back, feather its propeller, advance the other engine's throttle to maximum power, keep the plane from veering to-ward the failed engine, retract the landing gear—all the while flying the airplane and trying to level out or climb as appropriate. If the plane is at gross weight on takeoff, the plane, with one engine out, may have only a two-or-three-hundred foot rate of climb capability, and then only if the pilot has done everything by the book.

By contrast, if the engine on a single-engine aircraft fails, the plane becomes a glider without a tendency to veer to one side or the other. The pilot knows exactly what he needs to do: quickly lower the nose keeping the airspeed well above stalling speed, and then look for a suitable place to glide to for his landing. This should be pretty much straight ahead. As long as he keeps control, the odds are in his favor that he will walk away from the plane.

Obviously, an engine failure while at altitude favors the twin-pilot because he has time to trim up the plane without the pressure of being close to a stall, and near the ground. The subsequent airport landing with one dead engine itself requires considerable skill, however, so there is still risk.

Shut Down Both Engines?

Some recommend that in the event of a failure on takeoff of one engine on a twin-engine plane, that the private pilot pull back both throttles to idle and then land in the same way the single-engine pilot would do. Why would a pilot do that? This eliminates two things that can get the pilot into trouble. First, it eliminates the pilot having to decide which engine has failed and the risk that he will shut down the good engine by mistake. Second, it removes the veering toward the bad engine which greatly increases drag and the resultant airspeed drop, with a real chance of stalling. Once stalled, close to the ground, there will be an uncontrollable crash, and the odds of personal survival are greatly reduced.

Whether this is the right approach or not is clearly for the pilot to decide. He knows the level of his skills, and the risks involved.

Turbochargers

I have been asked by pilots whether they should buy an aircraft with a turbocharger. My answer is always qualified. Three things need to be present for me to answer "yes."

First, the pilot has to be willing to spend a lot of time learning about high altitude engine operation and human survival. Much of this training can only be experienced by flying at high altitudes. It goes without saying that an instrument ticket is a must, since all aircraft are under positive control above 18,000 feet.

Second, there is no point in having such equipment if the pilot is not going to use it at these flight-level altitudes. To make it worthwhile, he has to fly frequently on long trips where the time to climb to twenty-five thousand feet is followed by several or more hours of cruising at that altitude. The pilot based in the East or Midwest who flies mainly short trips (300-500 miles) is not a good candidate for such sophisticated equipment. Initially he may gain the knowledge, but unless he uses it, he will lose it.

Finally, the pilot needs to have the financial resources to maintain his aircraft at the highest standards. 25,000 feet is not the place to have a problem. The temperature at this altitude is often 100 degrees colder than it was when he took off, perhaps only an hour before. The oxygen system is another complexity, and involves frequent inspections, as well as knowledge and experience in using oxygen. When things go wrong, they happen quickly. The owner on a tight budget, or with limited experience, is not a good candidate.

Having qualified my answer, I never regretted having been one of the early private pilots to have an aircraft so equipped. The demands were great, but flying above the weather, often with a tailwind, gave me a sense of satisfaction that I treasure when I look back on my 28-year love affair with the Cessna T210.

Maintenance

Your Crew Chief

The most important person in your flying is your crew chief, that is the mechanic who maintains your aircraft. I deliberately use the title "crew chief" because you rely on him to keep your plane airworthy, and without him you could not fly. He is truly your partner, and your life is in his hands. He is a major factor in managing your risk.

Encourage him by letting him know that anytime he sees something that needs fixing, you want him to do so, that you value his judgement, and won't quibble about his bills. Speaking of which, some pilots try to nickel and dime their mechanic, and are slow in paying their bills. Most maintenance shops have a cash flow problem, with some customers making a practice of not paying their bills on a timely basis. I did just the opposite, and made it a practice to always pay my bill on the day I received it. I understood their cash problem, and it was a way that I could express my appreciation. As a result I always got great service.

To me, it is remarkable that we have as many dedicated people to maintain our aircraft as we do. Certainly this is not because of high wages, which tend to be less than those of auto mechanics who have none of the responsibilities that your crew chief has. I am sure it is because of their love of being part of aviation. Make sure your crew chief knows you consider him a valued partner.

Deferred Maintenance is Dangerous and Expensive

When something breaks on an airplane, it should be fixed unless it is strictly a cosmetic issue. Many owners defer maintenance until the next annual inspection. If you are going to have to fix it anyway, why would you want to fly with something broken until the next annual?

Maintenance issues tend to escalate once you start to defer maintenance. You also take a risk that if an accident happens, and the FAA gets involved, they could claim your plane was not airworthy. If so, your insurance company could decide to deny your claim, even if the broken part had nothing to do with the claim.

Avionics Maintenance

Flying IFR and having avionics equipment failing on you is not conducive to pressure-free flying. It pays to choose a good avionics shop, regardless of where it is located. For twenty years I would fly the 300 miles each way from Washington Dulles Airport to Columbus, Ohio, to get avionics installations and maintenance from ElectroSonics. Why? Because avionics maintenance was every bit as important as airframe and engine maintenance, and I found that it paid to go to a shop that had a great deal of experience. ElectroSonics had a staff of thirty or so, and they had made the initial installation on my Cessna T210. I knew that they had the knowledge, skills, and parts to keep my avionics in top shape.

I had my Cessna T210 for 28 years, and much of the avionics were replaced every five to seven years. There were several reasons. Technology, particularly in the last 20 years, has become more sophisticated, and I always wanted to keep my plane up-to-date. I also found that after about five years this equipment became more prone to failure. Flying in the demanding world of single-pilot instrument flying made failure of certain equipment a safety issue. New equipment and technology increased safety margins. Besides, there was a good used market for equipment that was only five to seven years old.

Carbon Monoxide

Carbon monoxide is a serious risk in flying. It is odorless, deadly, and dissipates from the blood stream leaving few clues. Carbon monoxide is created by the incomplete combustion of fuel in the cylinders when the engine is running with a rich fuel mixture. Most pilots assume that the only source of carbon monoxide in the cabin is from a defective muffler heat-exchange system. That is not correct.

Two of the nine planes I owned had a carbon monoxide problem where it got into the cabin through air vents, doors or canopy leaks, or though the tail cone of the plane. How? Carbon monoxide is discharged from the exhaust stacks and the plane then flies through this discharge before it dissipates. In a non-pressurized cabin, the outside flow of air around openings into the plane apparently can create a slight reduction in air pressure in the cabin from a venturi-like effect. In turn, this tends to suck in exhaust gases, including the odorless carbon monoxide.

Most pilots seem oblivious to the carbon monoxide risk. Those that recognize the risk almost always put an adhesive-backed cardboard chemical spot detector on their instrument panel. These detectors are almost totally worthless, and provide a false sense of comfort. Once installed they only have a 30 to 60 day useful life, and I know of no pilot who actually replaces them on that schedule. Just as important, these chemical spot detectors are not sensitive to low levels of carbon monoxide and probably would not register until the level reached 100 parts per million. OSHA says the limit in the work place is 35 parts per million.

While few accident reports mention carbon monoxide as a causal factor, I would submit that whenever an accident is deemed to be "pilot error" there is a possibility that carbon monoxide could have been a factor. Carbon monoxide in the blood is cumulative, that is, exposure during a single flight of 100 parts per million over a three hour period has the same effect as if the pilot had been exposed to 300 parts per million over one hour.

The pilot breathing carbon monoxide becomes hypoxic, which causes headaches, a state of confusion, dizziness, and visual disturbances, all of which can impair a pilot's performance. As the concentration of carbon monoxide in his blood increases, the pilot loses the ability to recognize what is happening. Could carbon monoxide poisoning be the real cause of some of the accidents deemed to be pilot error? While there is no way to be sure, I have to think that when an experienced pilot makes stupid mistakes that are totally contrary to his normal behavior, this is certainly a possibility.

All pilots should carry a high quality, sensitive carbon monoxide detector unit, whether they own their own plane or rent. I was shocked at the levels I found in the planes I was flying. You may be, too. There are a number of units on the market and an internet search is a good place to start. I got my unit (Quest Technologies, SafeTest 90) from Sporty's Pilot Shop. This is an industrial quality unit that was certified to be accurate.

When to Quit

A long time ago I asked an old timer when should I stop flying as I got older, recognizing that we lose some of our dexterity and skills with age. He told me not to worry about that question; that if I were honest with myself, I would know when that time had come.

He was right. In 1992 when we moved to Orcas Island I concluded it was time to stop flying at night. The airport on the island was just 3 miles from a 2,500 foot mountain, and there was no instrument approach. Further, every landing and takeoff at night was over dark water. I had read the accident statistics and concluded my night flying was over. I never again flew at night.

Then in 2003, as described in more detail in *Chapter 33, Decision Time*, I concluded that I should stop flying in bad weather. Once I reached that conclusion, I sold the Cessna. I still had my Mooney Mite, and later purchased a Tecnam Light Sport Aircraft, both of which were good-weather-only planes. I sold the Mite in June, 2006.

Then in the fall of 2008, I concluded I was not flying the Tecnam Light Sport Aircraft enough to stay current. In many ways this plane was a harder plane to fly because of its very light weight, and required more—not less—current time to be safe.

My last flight was just two months shy of the fifty-fourth anniversary of my first flight. I have known other pilots who have not listened to their inner-voice, and made one too many flights. With the hangar door now closed, I can proudly say I was a lucky pilot.

39

Costs of Flying Over
Fifty-Four Years
1955 to 2008

I am a Certified Public Accountant by profession and have kept meticulous personal records of my aviation expenditures for more than fifty years. This attention to detail has both positive and negative aspects. On the positive side, I know where I have spent my income. On the negative side, I am not sure this really has importance or meaning. How does one place a monetary value on the experience of slipping the bounds of gravity and looking down on earth from above, or soaring with the eagles?

So it is with some reservation that I share this data. I caution the reader not to be judgmental, particularly if he or she is not a member of the airmen's world.

Costs By Airplane

I have summarized my costs by aircraft on the following two pages. These are expressed in terms of historical dollars, that is, what I actually spent. At the bottom of this chart I have converted the total costs year-by-year into 2008 dollars to provide comparability to today's dollars.

471

SUMMARY OF TOTAL COSTS OF EACH AIRCRAFT OWNED
Fifty-four Years—1955 to 2008

	Cessna 140 N76527	Cessna 170A N5750C	Aeronca 7AC N836211	Luscombe 8A N71497	Cessna 172 N2549Y
Purchased	March, 1955	Sept., 1956	May, 1963	Oct., 1963	July, 1967
Purchase Cost	$1,500	$4,300	$800	$1,950	$7,861
Sold	Sept., 1956	Feb., 1959	Oct., 1963	July, 1967	March, 1969
Sales Price	$2,100	$3,789	$790	$2,500	$5,500
Hours Flown	432	474	171	428	251
Maintenance, & Other	$300	$968	$577	$1,057	$1,959
Equipment Additions	$0	$0	$0	$710	$0
Aircraft Insurance	$200	$712	$107	$501	$800
Tie Down and Hangar	$0	$246	$125	$900	$400
Estimated Fuel	$755	$1,327	$239	$633	$763
Estimated price per gallon	$0.35	$0.35	$0.35	$0.37	$0.38
Fuel Flow	5	8	4	4	8
Total Costs	$655	$3,764	$1,058	$3,251	$6,283
Per Hour	$1.52	$7.94	$6.19	$7.60	$25.03
Expressed in 2008 dollars:					
Total Costs	$5,250	$28,771	$7,456	$22,235	$38,875
Per Hour	$12.16	$60.70	$43.60	$51.95	$154.88

SUMMARY OF TOTAL COSTS OF EACH AIRCRAFT OWNED
Fifty-four Years—1955 to 2008

	Cessna 182 N3162S	Cessna T210 N210MG	Mooney M18 N4187	Tecnam Bravo N144MG	Total All Aircraft (as of 8/06)
Purchased Purchase Cost	Sept. 1972 $9,500	Sept. 1975 $80,500	Dec. 1995 $12,500	March, 2006 $101,406	$220,317
Sold Sales Price	Sept. 1975 $10,500	Oct. 2003 $145,432	June, 2006 $32,500	May, 2009 $92,625	$295,736
Hours Flown	563	3,998	530	180	$7,027
Maintenance, & Other	$8,842	$486,335	$100,570	$18,795	$619,403
Equipment Additions	$210	$141,578	$5,000		$147,498
Aircraft Insurance	$1,459	$105,906	$3,200	$9,556	$122,441
Tie Down and Hangar	$1,726	$32,909	$0	$2,734	$39,040
Estimated Fuel Estimated price per gallon Fuel Flow	$4,335 $0.55 14	$121,079 $1.51 20	$3,101 $1.46 4	$4,532 $4.75 5.3	$136,765
Total Costs	$15,572	$822,875	$91,870	$44,398	$989,728
Per Hour	$27.66	$205.80	$173.27	$246.65	
Expressed in 2008 dollars:					
Total Costs **Per Hour**	**$67,948**	**$1,682,805** **$420.86**	**$121,256** **$228.70**	**$47,375** **$263.19**	**$2,021,970**

54 Year Analysis of Costs By Category

The chart below shows the total costs incurred over this 54 year period by type of expense expressed as a percent of the total cost. It shows the relationship, for example, between fuel and maintenance costs. What is perhaps most striking about this data is that fuel costs were a relatively small portion of my total costs. As you can see, maintenance was more than four times the cost of fuel. Over the years I have often been asked how much fuel it costs to fly between two cities. The person asking the question is clearly judging from the answer how expensive it was to fly.

54 Year Cost By Category All Aircraft	
Category	Percent
Maintenance	62.6%
Equipment Additions	14.9%
Insurance	12.4%
Tie-Down/Hangar	3.9%
Fuel	13.8%
Less Gain on Sale	-7.6%
Total Net Cost	100.0%

Some readers may point out that fuel was $0.35 a gallon in the early years whereas now it is running fifteen or twenty times that amount (August, 2009). But the cost of living was much less back then. In fact, if you adjust the $0.35 fuel cost in 1955 to 2008 dollars using CPI data, that same gallon would cost $3.05.

Maintenance Cost By Aircraft

The chart on the next page shows the relationship of maintenance costs to the total cost of owning each of my nine airplanes.

The Mooney Mite expense is the exception. I had the airplane restored to new condition at a cost of $90,000. This was not routine maintenance, but I felt it needed to be done since this fifty-year-old airplane was made out of plywood and fabric. I did not want to be flying in an aircraft that I was not comfortable with as to structural integrity. When I came to sell the Mite, I could only recover a small portion of this restoration cost.

Final Observations

Every family has to make choices in how they spend their income, and we were no different. You will note that before we were married I had no automobile; instead, my priority was an airplane.

I like to tease my wife by telling her ours was a marriage of convenience. I had an airplane, and no car, and she had a car and no airplane. Once married, we, together, chose aviation.

She, too, has experienced flight as a pilot, and all of our

Maintenance Percent of Total Costs	
Plane	**Percent**
Cessna 140	45.8%
Cessna 170A	25.7%
Aeronca 7AC	54.5%
Luscombe 8A	32.5%
Cessna 172	31.1%
Cessna 182	56.8%
Cessna T210	59.1%
Mooney Mite M-18	109.4%
Tecnam Bravo	42.3%
All Planes	62.6%

family vacations involved flying and seeing places we could never have seen without an airplane. Others chose boating or golf or some other hobby on which to spend their money.

Over the fifty plus years we spent about a million dollars (two million in 2008 dollars). Was this a good investment? Do we have any regrets about allocating such a large percentage of our income in this direction? Clearly the answer is "no."

Aviation has been a life-long avocation. We have lived in a world that few people on this planet have been privileged to enjoy. We have seen the earth as only an eagle could see it, and we have experienced the adventure and excitement of "climbing new mountains."

> ## How can one put a price tag on being part of this airmen's world?

40

Old Pilots, Bold Pilots and Lucky Pilots

I used to believe the old adage that there were old pilots, and bold pilots, but no old, bold pilots. I now believe there is a third category–lucky pilots. The only old pilots are those who have also been lucky pilots.

I qualify as an old pilot, not because I am now in my mid-seventies and flew for more than fifty years, but because I was lucky. Yes, I did a reasonably good job of managing risk, but if I had not also been lucky, I would not be here today.

I believe many other private pilots have reached this same conclusion, consciously or subconsciously. Many stopped flying because of a bad experience and recognition that it was only luck that saved them. Others who were equally skilled, or even more skilled pilots, are no longer with us because they were not so lucky.

"Luck" Defined

Let me define "luck" from my aviation vantage point. Luck, to me, is surviving a situation or an event in which I had a greater than even chance of being killed or seriously injured, and survived for reasons largely beyond my control. In many instances I survived because of timing; I happened to be in the right place when the event occurred. Fifteen minutes earlier or fifteen minutes later, the outcome would have been different.

By this definition it does not matter whether the dangerous situation was caused by me—either through carelessness or pilot error—or by circumstances beyond my control. I was at risk, and if I had been killed, it would not have mattered (to me, at least) whether it was my fault or not.

Nine Lives

This chapter reviews nine events where I believe I was lucky to have survived. You'll see why I believe each of these events qualifies as having had a lucky outcome.

For the reader's ease, I have not only identified the event or situation but tried to summarize the pertinent factors, all of which are described in more detail in earlier chapters. I apologize to the reader who needs no such help.

#1— April 9, 1955, 8:30 P.M.
First Flight Home (Chapter 3)

I had had my private license for just a few days and had flown only forty-four total hours when I undertook to fly 550 miles from Presque Isle, Maine, to Rochester, New York, over some of the most desolate country in the Northeast. I was delayed in leaving Presque Isle and found myself flying for the first time after dark, and against 50 mph headwinds, in an airplane that flew only 105 miles per hour. When I arrived over the Rochester Airport in gusty, bumpy conditions, the engine started sputtering for lack of fuel. Between the two wing tanks I probably had a total of three gallons left when I landed.

I had not realized how strong the headwinds were, and in those days there was no navigation or radio equipment to tell you. I probably would not have made it if the Rochester Airport had been another ten or fifteen miles further away or the headwinds slightly higher. It was a dark, stormy night, and if the engine had run out of fuel I would have landed blindly somewhere, unable to see the terrain until the last moment. It would have been my first and probably last night landing.

#2—June 4, 1955, 10 P.M.
Sixty Seconds I Will Never Forget (Chapter 4)

Probably the most common way pilots kill themselves is to fly into clouds or fog where they cannot tell whether the plane is flying straight and level or is turning, or even if the plane is halfway upside-down. In clouds or fog, one sees nothing through the window and cannot fly straight and level without some outside reference or reference to instruments. Darkness compounds this difficulty.

I was at eight hundred feet above the ground on a dark night just a couple of miles from Presque Isle Air Force Base when I unexpectedly entered a fog bank extending upward from the ground. Within the first 30 seconds in the fog bank I lost three hundred of my paltry eight hundred feet while the plane veered off to the right. I was in the start of what is referred to as the "graveyard" spiral.

A few seconds later I broke out of the cloud bank, and fortunately found myself at the edge of the airport. The runway lights were visible and I landed without difficulty. A crash would have been inevitable if I had not flown out of that fog bank when I did.

#3—September 9, 1955, 11 P.M.
A Few Seconds of Stark Terror (Chapter 5)

I was flying on a stormy night with heavy headwinds, again en route to Rochester from Presque Isle. I had refueled in Burlington, Vermont, and then flown directly south to circumnavigate the Adirondack Mountains. I turned westward at Albany on the direct route to Utica, Syracuse, and finally Rochester using the low-frequency radio range stations to keep on the airway. The ceiling was about thirty-five hundred feet and I was flying at twenty-five hundred feet. Visibility was three to five miles.

Suddenly the oil pressure gauge started dropping towards "zero" and without oil the remaining engine life was probably no more than ten minutes. I had to get on the ground fast.

Luck was again with me. Almost at the same time the oil pressure started dropping, I saw a lighted airport beacon about 45 degrees to my right. The beacon had a split white beam—a beam that appears to be two, almost instantaneous, beams. Such beams are located only at military airports for identification purposes. Only one military airport lay anywhere close to my route, and I instantly knew I was just four or five miles from Griffiss AFB in Rome, NY.

The airport was still open and fortunately the military tower was monitoring our only transmitting frequency. A sleepy airman responded to our MAYDAY call, and we made it to Griffiss and landed with the engine still running. I was very lucky. I could not have made it to Syracuse, the next landing site, which was some 35 miles away.

#4—August 19, 1978, 10 A.M.
Thirty-Two Thousand Feet (Chapter 18)

On this occasion, I established an unplanned "altitude-in-level-flight" world record of 32,420 feet with my Cessna T210. In order to get as high as the plane would go I was flying at an airspeed only a mile or two per hour above the plane's stall speed. At the time I did not appreciate the risks that I was taking at that altitude.

I had an official observer on board. We were wearing oxygen masks using a built-in oxygen system, but this system was not intended to be used above 25,000 feet. One cannot live without adequate oxygen in the blood. The atmospheric pressure at 32,420 feet is just 24% of sea level pressure. This means that only a fraction of the oxygen we were breathing was being absorbed into our blood. We were at this altitude for only a few minutes, but clearly we were being oxygen-starved. It is surprising that neither of us lost consciousness. We were probability impaired but did not realize it.

Flying at 32,420 feet also created another hazard. As I said, the plane was flying only a mile an hour, or two, above its stalling speed, and we could not know how the plane would respond if it stalled. We could easily enter a spin at that altitude and have difficulty getting out of it. From all I subsequently learned it is quite possible that the plane would not have responded in the same way as it would at a much lower altitude. We were lucky we didn't need to find out. I am not a test pilot, and 32,000 feet is no place to pretend that I was one.

#5—March 11, 1993, 9:00 P.M.
Mayday at Flight Level 250 (Chapter 23)

I was at 25,000 feet en route from Orcas Island, Washington, to Memphis, Tennessee. I had made a single refueling stop in Rapid City, South Dakota, and was over Missouri on the second leg, less than two hours from Memphis. It was night when the red warning light came on. The electrical system had failed and the alternator was not producing any electrical power. Suddenly, all of the plane's navigation, communication, and light systems were running off of the plane's battery, which would last only five or ten minutes.

The electrical failure itself was not a crisis that put the flight in jeopardy, because I had a hand-held portable transmitter and receiver and could have received navigation vectors from Air Traffic Control and continued on to Memphis. But FAA rules, as well as common sense, require that whenever there is a failure of this magnitude the pilot needs to land at the closest suitable airport. Springfield, Missouri, was about 40 miles ahead, so that became my destination. I immediately reduced power to 35 percent and lowered the landing gear while I still had battery power. This created drag on the plane which allowed me to descend at a faster rate to less-hostile altitudes. I informed Air Traffic Control of my intentions. The battery died about five minutes later.

Then, descending through 19,000 feet, I found that the throttle control would not move and I could neither increase nor decrease my engine power. I didn't know why. Once I got down to much lower altitudes I would need to increase engine power because 35 percent power with the landing gear extended was not enough power to level off and fly in level flight. If not resolved the plane would continue to slowly descend which would have necessitated a forced landing at night in unknown terrain. As it turned out, the throttle control started functioning properly when I was down to about 8,000 feet, and I landed at Springfield without further incident. The next day I found that moisture in the throttle cable had frozen when I reduced power at 25,000 feet. It thawed at about 9,000 feet.

I was lucky. If this incident had happened earlier in the day while I was over the high Rockies it is unlikely that I could have descended low enough to find warmer temperatures, and a forced landing in the

Rockies would have been very iffy. The only thing I would have had going for me was that it would have been daylight and I would have seen where I would crash, or perhaps found a valley between mountains where I had some chance of survival.

#6—January, 1995
Synthetic Oil and the Class Action (Chapter 24)

I hired Dr. Michael Wood, engine expert, accident investigator, and expert witness to examine my engine when it was torn down to see what damage Mobil synthetic oil had done. There was a great deal, and he told me that I was a very lucky man since I had been in imminent danger of experiencing an in-flight, catastrophic engine failure. He further indicated that this failure could have occurred anytime, but surely within the next fifty hours.

Every takeoff and landing at my home airport on Orcas Island was over very cold waters, in which I probably could not survive a forced landing. Furthermore, within the previous few months I had made a number of flights over the western mountains where an engine failure would also have threatened my life.

Luck was with me once again. Yes, I had prudently followed up my concern about the synthetic oil, but that could have been too late. If the engine had failed I would likely have become a statistic, and no one would have known why. It is hard to retrieve an airplane for examination that is in deep water, lost in high mountains, or smashed to smithereens.

#7—May 24, 2002
Turbocharger Failures (Chapter 25)

The turbocharger failure on the morning of May 24, 2002, was a catastrophic failure in which turbo blades breached the turbocharger housing, allowing engine oil to be pumped overboard. Within a few minutes all of the oil would have been lost, and the engine would have frozen.

I was lucky. I was over the Bellingham airport when this failure occurred and was able to land within two or three minutes. If the failure had taken place ten minutes earlier I would have been flying over open water from Orcas to Bellingham. The plane would have sunk and no one would have known why the engine stopped.

Even more chilling is that there is evidence that the failure sequence started the day before. Inge and I had been flying nonstop from Oakland, California, to Orcas, directly across the high Siskiyou Mountains of northern California. We were on an instrument flight plan above a storm at 19,000 feet. If the final failure had occurred during that flight our engine would have stopped and we would have descended into clouds and likely hit a mountain without ever seeing it. The Siskiyous are high, rugged mountains and we'd have had no chance of surviving a crash. Neither we nor the plane would likely ever have been found.

#8—July 21, 2003, 1:00 P.M.
Mooney Mite Fuel Leak (Chapter 30)

An in-flight fuel leak from the sole fuel tank located immediately behind my head occurred just after I had flown over the mountains of Glacier National Park, many of which were close to 10,000 feet high. There was no way to stop the leak. It occurred because a plastic fuel line, that served as a fuel gauge, was starting to pull off of a fuel fitting on the fuel tank. I described it as "spurting a fine mist of fuel."

I could not reach this fuel line or the fuel fitting on the tank. It was lucky that I could not, because I probably would have caused the tube to come completely off the fitting, in which event the fuel would have come out in a solid gusher. I would have been drenched in fuel and in a few minutes the engine would have stopped because the fuel was soaking me, rather than feeding the engine.

I was also lucky that I was on the east side of these high mountains where I could have landed belly-up in the desert below me. That probably would have destroyed the plane but at least I would have had a chance of survival. If the engine had stopped while I was over the mountains, I would have been in a very bad position.

I advised the FAA of this emergency and was able to make it to the Cut Bank Airport where the local fire department had been notified of my emergency. The fine mist of fuel continued until after I landed. Once on the ground, when I was first able to reach this plastic fuel line, it slipped off the fitting. I had to stop the fuel from gushing out by pressing my thumb on the fitting until the fire department arrived.

#9—May 18, 2006, 1:30 P.M.
Then There Was Silence—An Engine Failure! (Chapter 35)

I described having an engine failure while flying over the foothills of the Sierra Nevada Mountains. Timing was everything!

I was flying high enough (6,500 feet) so that I had seven or eight minutes of gliding time. That was enough to get me away from the foothills of the Sierra Nevada Mountains. I could not have made a successful landing in those rocky foothills.

The field I was able to glide to turned out to be a pasture on which about fifty cows were standing, fortunately, all under a grove of trees. More importantly, the ground itself was without ruts or rocks where I landed. If there had been either, the plane would likely have flipped over on its back, rupturing the fuel tanks and increasing the danger of fire. As it was, the airplane was not damaged at all, although the engine was junk and I needed a new one.

The reader will recall from the details in chapter 35 that this failure sequence started the previous day while I was over high mountains near Mt. Shasta. If the final failure of the oil line had occurred then, or even 15 minutes earlier than it did, the outcome would have been far different.

Finally, this forced landing was in a part of the country where there was a family business that relocated crashed aircraft. There are only half a dozen such specialized companies in the United States. I reached the owner by cell phone from the field I landed in. He and his team came and were able to lift the plane onto a flatbed truck and then, with help from the local police, move it to a nearby airport. Most airplane damage occurs during relocation because there are so few people who know how to do it properly, as well as who have the right equipment. In my case, there was no damage.

Other Lucky Events

I have deliberately described only nine "lucky" incidents, but another four or five would also qualify. For example:

Chapter 8 (My Short Career in Off-Field Landings), in which I took off with no right wheel brake on a narrow, short farm road that had a high, severe embankment drop-off at the 90 degree turn in the road, by which time I had to be airborne.

Chapter 10 (Romance in the Air), in which a tornado devastated a good portion of the Billings, Montana Airport, just after we had landed on our honeymoon flying trip around the United States. The tornado alert came just minutes after landing. I was able to get my Cessna 170, between two rows of T-hangars, but was not tied down. Several rows away the tornado destroyed a row of T-hangars and the planes in them. If I had been in that row I would likely have been badly hurt, if not killed.

Chapter 21 (Atlantic Adventure), in which I did not recognize the compass failure until almost too late.

Chapter 22 (Freedom to Fly), in which a fuel injector fitting into one of the cylinders had not been tightened correctly, and allowed raw fuel to spray continuously over the engine cylinder while I was in flight. I was probably "saved" by the extremely cold temperatures (five degrees Fahrenheit) and the decision to make an emergency landing at Wichita.

Chapter 25 (Turbocharger Failures), in which the first failure was not a crisis only because it happened close to an airport.

Chapter 32 (Emergency Landing at Madison), in which I sensed that something was wrong and made a precautionary landing at Madison.

I leave it to the reader to decide whether these, and perhaps other incidents, should have been included.

Other Old Pilots Have Also Been Lucky Pilots

My close calls have not been unique. If you talk with other "old" pilots you will find that they, too, have been lucky, although the details are different in each case. In fact, almost all pilots, whether they have flown for 200 hours or thousands, have had experiences which, if looked at critically, can be seen to have contained a large measure of luck. Younger pilots often ignore the part that luck played, feeling that they are invincible. Certainly I did, in my early years.

I have also seen some less experienced pilots who became scared by situations they had encountered, recognizing that luck had played a decisive role in the outcome. Many times such pilots end up leaving aviation entirely.

Other pilots may think that it was not luck but their superior piloting skills that played the decisive role. To be sure, skill and experience do play a major part in overcoming unexpected events. What becomes sobering to these "hot-shot" pilots is losing a friend or mentor who was far more experienced than they were.

In my case, I only need to think about my good friend, test pilot Scott Crossfield—the first man to fly at twice the speed of sound, and then at three times the speed of sound, and survive. He helped design the X–15 Rocket Ship and was the test pilot before it was turned over to the Air Force. He also had a Cessna 210, and we had shared that interest since the mid-1970s. His luck ran out in 2006.

Fate Is The Hunter

Ernest K. Gann, 1910-1991, was one of the best known aviation writers of his time. He dedicated his 1961 classic, *Fate Is The Hunter*, with these words:

To these old comrades with wings...forever folded.

He then listed 400 names, mostly those of airline pilots, on the following eight pages. At the end of this list, he simply said:

Their fortune was not so good as mine.

Ernie Gann then related a number of personal experiences in a 400-page book, events in which he, too, had been lucky. If you have not read this book, I recommend it to you.

The End

This brings me to the end of the adventures of this "lucky" pilot who for almost fifty-four years enjoyed being part of the Airmen's World. I have now taken my own advice and closed the hangar door for the last time before my luck ran out. I am still a citizen of this other world and will continue to encourage others, much as other old-timers did with me.

If I were 22 again and had a chance to start my flying all over again would I do so knowing the part luck plays? The answer, without hesitation, is "yes."

Ernie Gann, in his first book, *Island In The Sky,* stated in his Foreword:

Flying is hypnotic and all pilots are willing victims to the spell. Their world is like a magic island in which the factors of life and death assume their proper values. Thinking becomes clear because there are no earthly foibles or embellishments to confuse it. Professional pilots are, of necessity, uncomplicated simple men. Their thinking must remain straightforward, or they die—violently.

I have been under that spell since my first flight on June 24, 1940 when at age six I left my parents on the ground and flew United Airlines flight number five from Chicago Midway to Portland, Oregon, to spend the summer with my grandparents. I was thrilled then and I am still thrilled today.